ISSUES
IN
INDIAN ECONOMY

ISSUES IN INDIAN ECONOMY

VOLUME I

Edited by
K.R. GUPTA
M.A., Ph.D.

ATLANTIC PUBLISHERS AND DISTRIBUTORS

Published by
ATLANTIC PUBLISHERS AND DISTRIBUTORS
B-2, Vishal Enclave, New Delhi-110 027
Phones : 541 3460, 542 9987

Sales Office
4215/1, Ansari Road, Darya Ganj, New Delhi-110 002
Phones : 327 3880, 328 5873, 328 0451
Fax : 91-11-328 5873
e-mail : info@atlanticbooks.com
web : www.atlanticbooks.com

ISBN 81-7156-571-9 (Vol. I)
ISBN 81-7156-572-7 (Vol. II)
ISBN 81-7156-931-5 (Vol. III)
ISBN 81-7156-573-5 (Set)

Typeset at
APD Computer Graphics, Delhi

Printed in India at
Mehra Offset Press, Delhi

PREFACE

In recent years phenomenal changes have taken place in the world economy. The economies of developing countries have undergone a particularly fast process of change from protectionism to globalisation, from nationalisation to privatisation, and from restrictions and controls to delicensing and liberalisation. The New GATT Accord and the setting up of WTO is an important milestone in the direction of freeing world trade.

The process of change accelerated in Indian with the introduction of New Economic Policy in 1991. During the last four years Indian economy has undergone changes which were inconceivable even a decade ago. The process still is far from complete yet and it is not easy to hazard any guess about its future course or its ultimate outcome

Licensing and controls are being dismantled. Nationalisation is giving place to privatisation. Import of capital and technology is being liberalised. Terms and conditions for the import of capital and technology are being eased. Attractive terms are being offered to multinationals to induce them to set up production units in India. Fast progress is being made in the direction of making the Rupee completely convertible. Imports have been liberalised; import duties have been drastically reduced; more and more items have been added to the OGL list. Bank interest rates have been freed.

In order to make a critical analysis of the changes that are taking place in various fields of the Indian economy, we have planned to bring out five Volumes covering different fields and including different shades of opinions. The present is the first Volume of the planned five Volumes. The contributors of this Volume are leading experts in their respective fields.

It is hoped that the book would be found useful by the researchers and students of Economics, businessmen, government executives concerned with the formulation and execution of economic policies, parliamentarians and legislators, and the general readers interested in knowing the changes that are taking place in our economy.

I express my deep gratitude to all contributors who have worked hard to write their papers.

New Delhi **K.R. GUPTA**

CONTENTS

	Preface	*iii*
1.	Political Economy of Development Paradigms in LDCs With Reference to India *— Raj Kumar Sen*	1
2.	Real Issues and the Policy of Free Marketism *— Kumar Das*	15
3.	Growth and Structural Changes in the Indian Economy —V. *Lakshmana Rao and K. Neelaveni*	30
4.	Structure of Indian Economy	49
5.	Structural Adjustment Reform and Economic Development in Thrid World Countries : An Analysis *— G. Nancharaiah*	73
6.	Structural Adjustment and Fiscal Management in Indian Economy : Rationale and Options *— M.R. Aggarwal*	84
7.	Indian Agriculture and the New World Economic Order *— A. Atchi Reddy*	99
8.	Need and Importance of Considering Ecologically Sustainable Economic Development in Indian Economy *— (Mrs.) N. Manonmoney*	166
9.	Public Distribution System in India : Why to Revamp It? *— (Ms.) S.D. Sawant*	176
10.	India's Foreign Trade *— N. Parthasarathy*	193
11.	Economic Environment of Rural Communities Linkages Through Rural Development Programmes *— L.N. Gupta*	213

12. Parents' Child-Sex Preference Behaviour in India : An Empirical Investigation 221

— *B.K. Vashist*

13. Process of Urbanisation in India : A Regional Dimension 236

— *P.G. Marvania*

14. Industrial Development in India 252

15. Recent Developments in Indian Industry 288

16. Village and Small Industries and Food Processing Industries 311

1

POLITICAL ECONOMY OF DEVELOPMENT PARADIGMS IN LDCs WITH REFERENCE TO INDIA

DR. RAJ KUMAR SEN
Rabindra Bharati University

The paradigms of development economics keep on changing since the development of development economics as a separate discipline after Keynesian revolution. Its origin can be traced to the political eagerness of the market economies to provide a viable planning as followed in the USSR. In this attempt economies like that of India which achieved development in the true sense in ancient periods but declined due to foreign subjugations are all relegated to the Rostovian traditional society in the new development economics which considered income growth and industrialisation as synonymous with development relied chiefly on unbalanced growth, foreign aid dependent and export-led growth and regarded inflation as contributing positively to the expansion of effective demand. India tried to combine both socialist and the alternative paradigms to derive the mixed economy framework to maintain her political neutrality but adopted centralised planning in this context. Political beneficiaries of this brand of development economics neglected the alternative paradigms consisting of balanced growth, employment generation, provision of mass consumption goods, humanistic rather than materialistic approach, wider connotation of development in the form of human resource development even when it became clear that the trickle-down theory of traditional development economics failed to benefit those for whom the strategies are said to be adopted and several types of crisis and bottlenecks became evident within a decade of application of such strategies. In India income inequality, price instability, black money, stagnant per capita availability of mass consumption goods, consumption dualism and corruption and large share of population living under poverty line compelled the policy makers for political considerations to adopt measures for poverty alleviation etc., as an appendage to the basic planning strategy without correcting the structural factors responsible for such maladies. What is more serious, even such inadequate measures gave rise to political controversies. The future lies in people's awareness in mounting political pressure on policy makers to free development economics from politicisation, to shift the focus to human resource development, to consumption planning along Gandhian lines and to decentralise properly for the realisation of development in the true sense of the term. Development should be a part of our natural process of life, it will not be so if it is attempted to thrust upon from outside. All these expectations may appear unrealistic in the present context of revival of 'income only' strategies under the current craze of economic reforms in a large number of countries in the world including India. But the basic unsustainable character of such policies is bound to lead to new paradigms of development economics in near future specially for large densely populated countries like India with continental features and magnitudes.

I. The Problem

> "Our muddling intellect
> Mishaps the beauteous forms of things we
> murder to dissect."

What Wordsworth told us long ago about the negative side of human inquisitiveness in general, we can unfortunately agree with him also about the paradigms (used in the dictionary[1] meaning of pattern, example etc.) of development economics as observed in the LDCs and in India in particular when we have entered in the last decade of the present century. While many have identified a number of factors for the current decline of the applicability and appropriateness of the "development economics considering the experiences of the LDCs during 1950—80, we have made an attempt to follow the political economy approach as a major explanation of the present state of the developing economies with illustrations drawn mainly from the Indian Planning experience.

While it is argued that the typical problems of the present day underdeveloped countries arise because they have been 'opened up' to outside forces in the form of foreign trade, investment and colonial rule[2], and the present population problem of high population density countries like India is primarily due to their successful development as agricultural countries in the past,[3] it is conveniently forgotten that it was not India but the major European countries were 'opened up' through foreign trade with India from ancient days as these countries were suffering from scarcity of goods like spices, bullion, fine cotton cloths etc. Instead of being predominantly agricultural, Indian economy at that age achieved substantial progress in industrial fields like construction, ship-building, textiles, ornaments etc. Her interaction with various parts of the world was due to her achievement of excellence in various fields. In particular India's level of development was not at all low by any standard during 2nd century B.C. (Ashoke the Maurya), 3rd century A.D. (golden era of Gupta period), 10th century A.D. (Cholas in South India propagating Indian culture to the East Indies) and similar other times. It was the search of the trade route to India that led the European sailors to discover America and the development of a new continent of the future. But in the Rostovian analysis of stages of growth, Indian development in the earlier periods and the achievements of other prosperous ancient civilisations like Greek, Roman, Inka, Maya, Aztek etc. are all relegated to the so-called "traditional society" after which they were expected to reach the state of 'preconditions to growth'. It amounts to consider the western type of growth after the industrial revolution in England in 1776 as the only form of growth conceivable. The political impetus of development economics is too evident in the total effacement of the incidents of earlier uplifts of the ancient lands in the standard of living, culture, literature, religion, seats of learning, trade and commerce, statecraft, and what not. Poverty was there but where it is not present including even the most materially advanced countries of the present day world?. The concern about poverty alleviation is as old as the society itself. What is new, is the integration of such programmes with the development economics aimed at the benefit of the so-called poor countries with an eye on the interest of the materially richer ones. 'Accumulation', the key word in Marxian theory of capitalist growth, has been also the guiding force in the initiation of the colonialism by the European countries.

II. The Perspective

While economic historians should have given more thoughts for analysing the causes of the fall of the developed economies of the past, a new branch of economics called 'development economics' but 'economics of growth' in reality instead emerged. Of course, there were a number of economic reasons for this growth of 'growth economics' but primarily the political eagerness of the non-socialist countries to provide a viable alternative path to material progress comparable with that claimed to be achieved (now known to be over-estimated and only at a cost of great sufferings of humanity) by the erstwhile USSR. The level of industrial advancement attained through centuries was found to be gained through economic planning within decades. This unique short cut of the growth process by socialist techniques had no answer from the market economies. Naturally, there was the apprehension that poor and backward countries would fall an easy prey to socialist enhancement and ultimately the whole system of market economy will be at stake. The clue of public investment to solve this problem was already provided by Keynesian theory. With Harrod-Domar model came the emphasis on accumulation of savings through curtailment of present consumption. The World War II led to the grave necessity of reconstruction of war devastated economies. Processes of foreign aid-led recovery originated through the Marshal Plan. At the same time the decolonisation process started with the independence of the erstwhile colonies, like India (1947). The theories of Big Push and Critical Minimum Effort preached the basic requirement of huge quantity of investment and this requirement made the dependance on foreign aid and grant inevitable. Whatever gap was left to compete with politically the Soviet type of economic planning, that was filled by the propagation of unbalanced growth theory emphasising the concentration of investment in the core sectors of the economy. The newly independent countries readily adopted this prescription of policy mix for the initiation of their economic growth.

While during fifties such growth strategies apparently provided a popular package for the underdeveloped economies, they served implicitly three significant political objectives of the rich countries. The first objective of providing a viable alternative of the Soviet policies for the developing economies was however quite evident when Rostow called his theory as an 'anti-communist manifesto'. The second objective of retaining an economic control on the newly independent countries while the political control was lost was manifested through the policy of sanctioning condition-tied aids implemented directly and through partially controlled international financing agencies. The third objective was however to capture the huge markets of such overpopulated countries like India. To achieve such objectives the developing countries are always told about their huge difference in the per capita income from that of richer countries. It has been always preached that it is only the development paradigms of the developed countries that the countries willing to develop must follow. But the underestimation of the per capita income in the Asian countries due to the existence of extensive non-monetised sectors (though declining), numerous transactions outside the market mechanism and the characteristics of substantial share of the labour force (particularly the women) remaining excluded from the social accounting system as they are not paid wages, is never highlighted. Nor it is mentioned that the newly independent nations participating in the Bretton Woods Conference[4] failed to clinch their proposals for stable raw material prices for their exports and as a result of unfavourable conversion factor, their national income is further underestimated.

It is this difference in the per capita income between the rich and poor countries that was held to be the sole culprit in this politics of economic growth and an increase in its level and ultimate income equalisation between the two groups in the distant long run was considered to be the panacea of all evils. In the Marxist prediction of slowing down of growth rates of rich countries and growing problems of unemployment, such prospect was not considered to be an utopia even by the developing countries themselves. All theories of economic growth adopted maximisation of national income as the virtually single objective function under one situation or another and the trickle down theory of benefits of growth to the lowest level of the masses gained so much currency in these countries that considerations of increasing income inequality, growing unemployment and price instability and such other crucial problems are either neglected or conveniently bypassed. Being assured of a continuous market for their industrial products in the aid-receiving countries, the rich countries also could carry on technological advances in all sectors of their economy as the obsolete machineries and many other rejected products (even in the field of life saving drugs and nuclear wastes) could safely and easily find their way in such countries. Following the paradigm of export-led growth, the rich countries were further assured of a stable supply of agricultural or mineral products as in order to earn more and more foreign exchange, the developing countries are compelled to export increasing share of their domestic agricultural or mineral products even when their own people are left underfed or even starving. And all these are done in the name of economic growth and growth only.

III. The Neglect

Of course, the so-called development economics did not contain only such growth theories emphasising income maximisation through unbalanced growth and investment plans financed by export earnings, foreign aid and inflation. In the conventional stream of thinking on development economics specially applicable to the developing economies, we come across with the contributions of Lewis and Nurkse who emphasised on the dualities and disguised unemployment existing in such economies and opted for a balanced growth strategy for them. In particular Nurkse preferred an improvement of market mechanism in the growing economies as opposed to overall economic planning. Schultz drew our attention to the importance of 'human capital' and not space, energy, cropland or other physical properties of the earth, and this resource is decisive in improving the welfare of poor people throughout the world[5]. In fact we have nearly forgotten in the discussions of growth strategy that economics is concerned with the study of 'mankind' in his ordinary business of life and not with the study of simply increase in the stock of material goods and services. Hle Myint[6] very correctly and timely warned by pointing out that 'in practice there is a real danger of macromodels of economic development running on their own steam without any reference to the fundamental human problems of backwardness on the subjective side.'

However, we must mention Gunner Myrdal who clearly pointed

out the inadequacies of the growth theories inherited from the Western economies for their fruitful application in the developing countries. He objected to the definition of development in terms of growth only and naturally questioned the utility of empirical research on the basis of unrealistic and unreliable data in backward economies. In countries with people suffering from acute poverty and ugly income inequality, he preferred the implementation of income equalisation measures to a just quantitative increase in the GDP. The institutionalist approach of Myrdal was advocated much earlier by M.K. Gandhi in a different manner through his conception of self-reliant village economy. His concept of economic development was not identified with growth only in materialistic terms but contained the objective of upliftment of the 'man' himself and increasing the human potential. Considering the unique features of the individual countries, he relied on the policy of decentralisation and prescribed to help those who need it most in his notion of antyodaya (rise of one who lies at the bottom). Very recently this approach to enhance human potential has been echoed in the writings of A.K. Sen where economic development may be conceived as the process of expanding the capabilities of the people which ultimately leads to the expansion of entitlement. The Gandhian idea of consumption planning and humanistic approach to economic growth has been considered as vital for such economies also by Schumacher.[7]

Recently Gandhi's plans have been revisited in the Human Development Report which advocated that the prosperity of nation lies in people-friendly forms of decentralised governance.[8] During the formation of the Five Year Plans in India the wage goods model was prescribed as a more appropriate alternative than the Mahalanabis model for the supply of mass consumption goods to the Indian economy.

However, in spite of all round cautions and warnings against the blind invitation of conventional growth strategies, the policy makers in the developing economies preferred to turn almost a deaf ear to all such concerns. The rich countries engaged in the provision of aid to the developing countries to finance their investment plans also continued to encourage the same type of planning strategies even when the World Bank emphasised clearly to tilt the preference of such economies to the development of human resources. Of course, such neglect of prescriptions for shifting to the new paradigm of development economics by the policy makers of both developed and developing economies may be considered as only natural considering the political motivation of the beneficiaries of such growth strategies. Such beneficiaries are usually a small but very influential section of the population and they will resist in all possible ways to change the conventional development paradigm, which resulted in the growth of only their welfare. This may be considered as an inevitable consequence of unbalanced growth in general and manifested in all sectors of the economy including the various groups of the population. The example of differential rates of development experienced by northern and southern parts of Italy during the thirties shows clearly how the initially developed regions of a country generate vested interests in not allowing the development process to expand into the then underdeveloped areas of same country.[9] There is no reason why the same type of inter-group interactions will not take place between the beneficiaries of growth and the remaining population. The performance of the Indian economy and the inertia of a constant development paradigm in her planning strategies are not exceptions of this type of socio-economic process.

IV. The Crisis and the Concern

However, in the decade of eighties, it was no longer possible even for the policy makers of various developing economies including India to turn a deaf ear to the prescriptions of the development economics urging them to change their emphasis from 'material' to 'man'. This was made possible when such economies not only failed to achieve the desired results from their growth efforts but also reached a situation where they faced serious crisis in a number of areas like environmental and ecological balance, development of human resource and their optimum utilisation, inflation and balance of payments situation, income and wealth inequality, moral and ethical value judgements, generation of black money etc. It has been shown[10] on the basis of the conventional criterion of the growth of per capita income at constant prices that between 1980 and 1986 the low income economies as a group has not only been unable to uplift themselves into the next higher income group of economies but also the scenario has been deteriorated further as a number of members (six) of the middle income economies have now been considered as members of the lower group. This disquietening feature has taken place in spite of an accelerated growth efforts on the part of these countries adopted along traditional lines. As per the findings of the latest World Development Report (1993), the situation has not changed significantly even in 1991.

The last two decades of development efforts have no doubt resulted in substantial amount of industrial development, agricultural breakthrough, marvels of medical facilities, revolution in communication and software technology. But at the same time they have also witnessed rapid population growth in the LDCs leading to a stagnant or declining per capita food intake, serious deteriotation of agricultural soils due to deforestation, soil erosion, desertification, water logging etc., energy crisis and environment pollution of all kinds, imbalance in the ecological features, widespread growth of black money, decline of moral values and widening gap of in the country and inter-country living standards with the existence of poverty particularly in rural areas and similar other maladies which may be said to be due to wrong and faulty choice of and total reliance on income growth techniques. The various projections about the future could not draw a more or less favourable scenario for the LDC in particular. Even the socialist countries following centralised target oriented planning could not solve the problem of adequate supply of food items, housing and many items of modern livelihood and are now compelled to liberalise and privatise to some extent their economic policies in the form of so-called glasnost and perestroika which landed most of them into chaos, misery and ultimately to disintegration of the country itself.

The Indian planning experience is also no exception either. While her golden age started to decline since the 13th century after her subjugation under the foreign invasion and barbarous onslaught on her age-old culture and religion, the decline became nearly complete under the British rule when her outlook towards development was thoroughly upturned with the spread of western education and technology in the Indian life during the second half of the nineteenth century. She became to be known as a predominantly agricultural country to the outside world being robbed off whatever industrialisation of the traditional type was left to her. Being influenced by the centralised scientific socialist planning ideology on the one hand and the political pressure to protect the interests of the private owners of the capital invested in the economy on the other, the policy makers of India neglected the traditional wisdom of Indian economic thought and existing characteristics of the economy and prescribed a combination of centralised planning relying on unbalanced growth with a vast unorganised market economy. While such combination was labelled as a unique economic system called mixed economy, the results also became mixed and this became evident even from the first decade of planning. Thus the serious price instability associated with industrial growth led the Indian planning to discard the concept of the positive role of inflation for raising the effective demand and to adopt the paradigm of 'growth with stability from the Fourth Plan onwards.[12] The political concern about the failure of the trickling down theory of growth benefits ultimately led to the functional use of the concept of 'poverty line' and adoption of various packages of poverty alleviation programmes[13] since the Fifth Plan. But this did not result into any fundamental change in the growth strategy of Indian planning. The role of such programmes as appendages to the basic structure shows on the one hand the implicit official recognition of the failure of centralised planning in a market economy to alleviate poverty and on the other the natural doubt expressed about the efficacy of such programmes in the long run. At the same time new emphasis has been placed on decentralisation of planning in various economic spheres[14] and also in political arena like panchayats and municipalities but it is not clear whether such decentralisation can be harmonised with the present plan structure. Moreover, this step has sparked new debates in the centre-state relationship. Under the influence of the international concern about environmental and ecological degradation due to industrial growth, a separate department on environmental development has been established in the current decade in both Central and State governments of India. But such steps had no significant effect on environmental protection as officially a number of massive projects (*e.g.* Narmada Sagar Dam etc.) are adopted which have been universally criticised as the cause of potential permanent and irreparable damages to the basic geographical characteristics of the Indian economy. The political necessity of military progress has not hesitated to sacrifice most fertile arable lands even in a democratic set-up when all the inhabitants are against such steps (e.g. Baliapal Missile Testing Range Project). The claim of self-sufficiency in food production has been made at a time when more than one-third of the population are under poverty line (during the Seventh Plan) and are not able to fulfil their demand for two square meals per day. Such economic claims with political motivations are nothing but natural consequences[15] of pursuing the conventional development paradigm without any fundamental change in them nacessitated by the resulting consequences. It is true that the export-led foreign aid dependant growth strategies have not yet led India to the debt-trap unlike the Latin American countries but the experts have smelt danger in the near future for the Indian economy if some concrete steps are not adopted to change the scenario.[16] The role of land reform in enhancing land productivity has also been unfortunately politicised and resulted in unnecessary and unnutural centre-state dispute on farm size and productivity[17] in the context of public distribution system of foodgrains. The official statistics even are not above the doubt of political manipulation as found commonly in totalitarian states. The generation of black money to an alarming level due to the adverse demonstrative effects of consumption dualism has led to massive spread of corruption at every level in the absence of any effective form of consumption planning in the Five Year Plans.[18] The associated decline of moral values resulted from focus on material gains only during the growth process and the political neglect of the role of moral values in the production process are also significantly responsible for such critical situation of the economy.

V. The next phase

It is now clear that political forces resulted from both economic and political vested interests which are trying their best to forestall the necessary changes that should take place in the paradigms of development economics in the Indian set-up in particular and generally for all the LDCs in the perspective of performances of the countries engaged in development efforts. Apart from the Hayekian serfdom resulting from totalitarian centralised economic planning, the inefficiency of this system to deliver the goods to the masses has been amply demonstrated by the recent experiences of USSR, Hungary,

Poland, Romania etc. and their followers in different continents. In overpopulated and vast heterogenous economies like India where freedom of opinion is still not completely thwarted, public opinion must compel the policy makers to follow the development efforts in the true sense of the term. The basic premise of 'limited resources but unlimited wants' must be substituted by a new premise of 'limited resources and limited wants' for the real development of the currently low income economies.[19] This requires to impart Gandhian humanism to the development strategies which must follow the alternative approach of Human Resource Development as in this approach only paradigms of development economics can attain their true meaning and purpose. People must be aware about the true way to remove their sufferings and once they are able to do so, the political myth about false paradigms of development are bound to go. The development efforts when become part of life, are bound to succeed. But when they divorce the people from their focus, the sufferings continue and aggravate. Truly,

> "He who binds to himself a joy
> Doth the winged life destroy;
> But he who kisses the joy as it flies
> Lives in eternity's sunrise"
>
> (William Blake in *Gospels*)

Of course, at the current juncture of rapidly changing events, the present wave in favour of market dominated strategies, have moved the hands of the clock of the development paradigms backward. The failures of the statist model as the guide to development has resulted in an altogether diminution of the role of state instead of putting it into the correct path. This so-called free market wave has captured now most of the low and middle income countries and propagated *laissez faire* as the only solution to the ills of the world. India, unaware of her own economic strength and potential, has also subscribed to this view, after experimenting with a mixed economy framework for four decades. The unipolar world, resulted after the breakdown of the Soviet Union and power of the international financial institutions like the IMF and World Bank to impose economic reforms on debt-dependent economies seeking conditional loans, have nurtured the current development paradigm. But at the same time it is also felt that this is creating serious problems in the countries which have embraced it in a simplistic manner and like its predecessor, this paradigm also is unsustainable. After three years to economic reforms, India for instance, has experienced a reduction in her per capita GNP in dollar terms and the so-called economic benefits from reforms have been largely illusory. On the other hand, the adverse effects on inequality, unemployment, poverty and pollution are appearing to be quite significant. This is to be considered in the context of the fact that India houses the largest number of the poor in the world and the unemployment problem is one of her most crucial problems for a long time. In fact from the experiences observed throughout the world, it may be said there are appearing indications that the free-market wave is on its way out.[20] The bankruptcy of the development paradigm preached by the high income North being gradually exposed, the low income South requires to find out its own appropriate alternative with roots in its age-old tradition and "based[21] on an austere life that avoids over-exploitation of high energy resources and overburdening of the environment". And even though political pressures appear today as unsurmountable, we must have faith in people's wisdom and power. Following Tagore, 'we must be firm in faith, and the dawn will surely come.'

REFERENCES

1. The Concise Oxford Dictionary of Current English.
2. Myint, H. — *The Economies of the Developing Countries*, B.I. Publicationfas, New Delhi, 1977, P. 18.
3. *Ibid.*, p. 24.
4. Meir, G.M. — The Formative Period in Meier & Seers (ed). *Pioneers in Development*, World Bank, 1984.
5. Schultz, T.W. — *Investing in People.*, Hindustan Publishing Corpn. Delhi 1981.
6. Myint, H. — *An Interpretation ofEconomic Backwardness*, Oxford Economic Papers, June 1964.
7. Schumacher, E.F. —*Roots ofEconomic Growth*, Gandhian Institute ofStudies, Varanasi, 1962.
8. UNDP — Human Development Report, 1993.
9. Saraceno, P. — The Process of Industrialisation of an Overpopulated Agricultural Area : The Italian Experience in Bhagawati, J. and Eckaus, R.S. (ed.) *Development and Planning*.
10. Sen, R.K. and Dasgupta, M.K. — The Development Scenario of the Low Income

Economies in the Eighties : An Empirical Evaluation (Paper presented in the Indian Econometric Conference, Bangalore, 1989.)

11. US International Communication Agency — The Global 2000 Report to the President, 1980.

12. Sen, R.K. — Problems of Growth with Stability and a note on the Destablising Role of our Income Tax Structure. Occasional Papers 1980, Rabindra Bharati University, Calcutta.

13. —— Poverty Measurement and Indian Planning (Invited Lecture with Alak Ghosh) at Stockholm, Sweden 1987, *Society and Change*, June 1988, New Delhi.

14. —— and Roy, K.C. — *Decentralised Planning and Primary Health Care in L.D.Cs.*", with reference to India, Indian Economic Conference Volume, 1988, Jadavpur.

15. Sen, R.K. — "Application of Centralised Planning in India : An Appraisal", *Artha Shastra*, V. 5, No. 1, 1986.

16. Roy, K.C. and Sen, R.K. — LDC's Borrowing, Debt Trap and Development, *Journal of Developing Societies*, V. 5, No. 3-4, 1989, Leiden, Netherlands.

17. Sen, R.K. — "The Resurgence of the Economy of West Bengal," *Artha Shastra*, V. 8, No. 2. 1989.

18. —— The Unsanctioned Economy and Consumption Dualism in Monga, G.S. and Sanctis, V.J. (ed.) : *The Unsanctioned Economy*, Himalaya Publishing House, Bombay, 1983.

19. Roy, K.C. — The Development Profile of the Low Income Countries with Reference to Human Resource Development, XXIV International Summer Seminar Proceedings, Berlin, GDR. 1987.

20. Bracho, F. — *Health, Environment and Economics*, Better Living publications, Caracas, 1992.

21. Gurumurthy, S. — *Article in The Illustrated Weekly of India*, March 28 — April 3, 1992, Bombay.

2

REAL ISSUES AND THE POLICY OF FREE MARKETISM

PROF. KUMAR DAS
Deptt. of Economics
Utkal University

In the face of present economic crises, which has manifested in widespread stagnation, unemployment, poverty, backwardness, corruption, depletion of foreign exchange reserves and escalation of debt-service ratio, which is largely attributable to the past profligacy and long term fiscal improvidence and the process of liberalisation of early seventies, the present Government has preferred to dismantle the old planned economic system and follow the new path of Structural Adjustment Programme (SAP). In the process of this transition India has accepted all the stringent conditionalities of IMF and World Bank under the garb of "high-tech" and pragmatism of "efficiency". At least India is required to globalise, liberalise and marketise its economy.

Erroneous Premises

The Structural Adjustment Programmes (SAP) is a market-oriented multifaceted, multi-objective, multi-instrument programme. It relates essentially to the industrial sector of the India Economy. The subsequent announcement of New Industrial Policy (NIP) of India is quite compatible and consistent with SAP. It is very difficult to assert that the transition to market economy is completely relevant for Indian economy. It is because the diagnosis of the economic malaise of Indian economy is based on three erroneous premises :

(a) Public sector is inefficient and unproductive.

(b) There is no competition in the public sector.

(c) Controls and regulations breeds corruptions and stagnation.

It is very ridiculous to have these wrong notions. It is unfortunate that profit making is considered as the index of efficiency for the public sector of India, when it is given the charge of running the public utilities on a non-profit basis. So a non-profit making public utility should not be judged as inefficient for not making profit.[1] It is wrong and inconclusive to assert that public sector is inefficient and its performance is unsatisfactory. The performance of the public sector in the aspects of employment is much better than that of the private sector over the period. The achievement of public sector in the aspects of capital formation is better than that of the private sector. There is no theoretical base or empirical evidence to show any correlation between ownership and efficiency.[2] Performance of an industry depends on various factors which have nothing to do with ownership. Secondly it is assumed that enterprises cannot possibly engage in competition if they happen to be publicly owned. Many eminent economists like Lange and others have shown that pattern of ownership does not impede the competitive character of the industry. Thirdly it is true that controls and regulations breed rapacious rent seeking and political corruptions. But unfortunately it is also true that there exist corruptions on the scale of billion dollars even in G-7 countries, which indicate that free market economies are by no means free from corruption. Hence liberalisation is not the way to curb corruption.

It is a fact that the understanding of the issues is at stake. Hence the diagnosis and consequent prescription seems to be wrong and irrelevant. It is true that the Indian economy is passing through an abnormal financial crisis which has never been visualised. It has occurred not because of economic factors but for the irresponsible Governments. The successive Governments have preferred to abdicate their responsibility to the nation for the sake of short term partisan political gains, unbriddled populism in trying to achieve everything and please every one. It is the result of sheer political system and political cynicism.

The major thrust of SAP is marketisation. It envisages privatisation of PSEs, withdrawal of subsidies, liberalisation of credit facilities, withdrawal of all sorts of restrictions on private sector investment activities and restriction on investments in the public sector. Thus the main objectives of New Economic Policy are :

(1) *modernisation* of the industrial sector in order to achieve international competitiveness,

(2) *marketisation* in order to ensure efficient resource allocation, and

(3) *globalisation* of the economy in order to achieve international integration and specialisation.

It is interesting to note that there is convergence of views of North and South. SAP now holds the centre-stage in the attention of both groups of economists of the advanced industrial countries and developing countries. Marketism has been proclaimed as the benign means of relieving the West from 'recession' and third world from 'stagnation'. Ardent Votaries of SAP advocates for blind pursuit, which may have disastrous effects (Hossain 1993).

SAP may be a necessary condition but not sufficient condition for resumption and reignition of growth. Growth may be an assured product but its sustainability is not guaranteed. It is tantamount to put the cart before the horse. It is a gross mistake on the part of the Indian policy-makers to believe that globalisation shall boost up the development process. In fact it is the development that generates and reinforces the need for globalisation. Development after a point necessitates the dovetailing of the domestic economy with the global engine. Without development of domestic economy, globalisation is likely to lead to ossification of the structure of underdevelopment.

Inherent Contradictions

It is admitted that SAP is needed — there is not dispute about it. But the SAP that India has accepted is inherently conflictual. Even the long term objectives of SAP are not realisable. It is because the adjustment policies are conceived on wrong presumptions. It is embeded with contradictory objectives. Firstly, liberalisation of interest rate will reduce private investment instead of promoting privatisation. Secondly, elimination of subsidies (on food/fertiliser) shall lead to the rise in prices, which ultimately shall bring down the real income of the poorer sections. So the income distribution will become worse than that in the pre-SAP period. Thirdly, liberalisation of trade through the rise in import bill and fall in Government revenue shall aggravate the balance of payment deficit instead of reducing BOP deficit. Fourthly, with devaluation, import of capital goods on large scale shall escalate the import bills and capital cost, which shall reduce production. Fifthly, free market forces, through intensification of the free use of environmental resources shall cause ever increasing deterioration of environmental standard. Better environmental standard is never expected from free demand and supply forces. Thus in order to extricate the economy from those contradictions, and distortions, all the problems have to be tackled at its root through a genuine SAP with an alternative set of economic reforms, which should address the real issues.

It is true that India has failed on all the three fronts namely, self-reliance, full employment and irradication of poverty, through its planned effort of over 45 years. It is true that the planning has resulted in a huge and unproductive primary sector, slender and stagnant secondary sector and a bloated tertiary sector. It has created a dysfunctional and regressive urbanisation. The growth impulses generated and the benefits accrued therefrom through market mechanism at some nodes get impounded mostly within the urban limits instead of being diffused to the neighbourhood. It has created both "dole-subsidy culture" and "star-culture" in the alibi of rural development.[4] There is imperfection, backwardness, inefficiency, dualism, defeatism, fatalism and corruption afflicting all sections of society and pervading all sectors of the economy.[5]

The remedy, whatever may be the reason of the present stagnation and inefficiency, does not lie in the type of SAP being pursued. SAP is just another instalment of the liberal doctrine and liberal utopia.[6] It is merely an experimental path, with different institutional framework and operational rules. It is based on myopic premises and still hooked on to the theory of 'trickle down effect'. Higher rate of economic growth is believed to automatically solve all other critical issues like unemployment, inequality, poverty and rural development. It is purportedly ordained with the ideology of '*laissez faire*', where even Adam Smith did not contend an undiluted free marketism. Even Smith was advocating for invisible hand (marketisation) subject to the laws of the state and moral codes of the society. Thus SAP in India may fail because it is based on naive illusion and ignores the fundamental factor of unequal development.

Competitiveness, which is the main thrust of internationalisation has an attractive but deceptive appearance. The "high-tech" concept, which is never defined, is based on naive illusions. There are many complex facets, and hypocrisy and the failure to comprehend it may result in wrong kind of internationalisation. The policy of globalisation for India is premature and misconceived rather than wrong. The standard prescriptions of new economic policy are largely meant for an overheated industrial economy in order to :

(i) reduce investment demand at home,

(ii) make exports competitive, and

(iii) attract foreign fund to ease BOP situation.

The identical policy of devaluation and monetary tightness, for instance, is applied indiscriminately, which may be appropriate to some countries and may be harmful for some others. Therefore, current world-wide movement towards market induced strategies, dismantling the state structures and ideologies cannot be understood by clubbing all these countries together. One needs to distinguish among four groups of countries :

(1) industrially advanced capitalist countries,

(2) erstwhile centrally planned command economies,

(3) newly industrialised countries and

(4) developing countries of the South.

Thus with unfrittered openness scrambling to embrace the market is common for all but the driving forces are different for each.

Real Issues

In the context of Indian economy, the following three issues may be raised :

(a) can marketisation reduce the incidence of rural poverty?

(b) can marketisatioin improve the employment scenario?

(c) can marketisation ensure a genuine competitiveness?

(a) *Rural Poverty*

The New Economic Policy, which has been designed in the tune of SAP, overlooks various social objectives such as eradication of poverty, greater emphasis on public sector, faster expansion of basic and key goods, prevention of concentration of economic power in private hands, regional balance and promotion of small industries and khadi and village industries etc. It rather runs counter to all these objectives. Instead of interdependence it is likely to create only a lethal dependence.

At this stage of industrial development in India at least one cannot afford to :

(i) forget that there are many supply side bottlenecks, and

(ii) regard distribution merely as an offshoot of the development process.

All strategies for economic development and policies for combating backwardness, poverty, unemployment, stagnation etc. are constantly being perverted by the new political and bureaucratic practice. It is a kind of trial and error method having no theoretical foundation nor empirical evidence. It is very difficult to achieve rapid industrial development with existing supply side constraints, which have to be removed by long-term deliberate planning. The existing resources can not be readily converted into foreign exchange simply by fiscal restraints and sound exchange rate policy. One cannot throw the baby with the bath water with the excitement about the new economic thinking. On the contrary, a society as divided and unequal as India's simply cannot afford to regard distribution merely as an offshoot of development process. The development process has to have a very clear accent on raising the productivity of all classes and particularly of the weaker and poorer sections of the society.

SAP seeks ostensibly for creating more space for private enterprises. But attractive market incentives for capital formation is only a necessary but not sufficient condition for resumption of private investment and industrial development. All efforts are misguided to promote the growth of 'finance capital' at the cost of industrial capital and at the cost of investment in agriculture and infrastructure. Promotion of 'finance capital' is likely to shore up speculative activities rather than sustained industrialisation.[7] Therefore, SAP is unlikely to bring either allocative efficiency or 'productive efficiency.' There is no theoretical support or empirical evidence as to the effect of liberalisation on economic growth. At the most, Indian market may remain as a captive market for the recession-ridden countries. Market forces may fail to unleash forces for growth and at the most they tend to generate low-income activities horizontally.[8]

Simultaneous attempts towards stabilisation and economic liberalisation may lead neither to macro economic stability nor to the restoration of growth sustainability. 'Trickle down effect' of SAP shall be more than neutralised by corruption, bureaucratisation, unemployment, industrial unrest and low productivity. These problems cannot be handled by 'safety nets'. Draconic and abrupt removal of protection is likely to spell disaster for many large scale and small scale industries. The industrial sector of the economy is likely to drift into stagflation with low industrial growth and high inflation, which will further aggravate the poverty profile of the economy. Unsuccessful fiscal compression has created 'double squeeze' and failed to yield the expected reduction in Government's fiscal deficit. It has produced (i) an industrial recession and joblessness, and (ii) price rise of essential goods. Therefore SAP is likely to lead to continued stagnation rather than a meaningful structural adjustment. It will fail to bring the majority of rural poor into the vortex of economic development.

(b) *Unemployment Problem*

As an answer to the second question raised above it can be said here that the large scale centralised approach with its heavy emphasis on capital-intensive industrialisation shall take most of the investible capital. This approach has never raised the volume employment and has never served the poor. The type of industrialisation that the (NEP) contemplates is not going to be of any benefit to the rural poor. Industrial growth and employment are not related to each other. During 1983-88 Planning Commission of India itself admits that the highest growth rate is associated with lowest growth of employment. SAP is emphasising on modernisation, automation and computerisation. SAP and NEP are not attuned to increasing employment in the small scale sector. At the most, it may generate a few job opportunities for highly skilled people. Industries shall require labour which cannot be supplied by the village poor. It produces the goods which they do not consume. Hence the industrial activity is mostly labour-displacing. All types of anciliary industries are likely to be pre-empt and a type of vicious process of deindustrialisation is likely to set in.

The unbridded entry of MNCs now enjoy complete administrative, bureaucratic and political patronage in India. It is a deadly alliance which tends to drag India into a neo-colonial dependency. Acceptance of globalisation slogan is pushing the economy headlong into a set of policies which is in a way irreversible. By giving primary importance to the role of MNCs in the bid to attract foreign investment all considerations of investment for the economy in terms of satisfaction of mass needs and self reliant growth have been extinguished. This fits perfectly well with an investment pattern and production structure to subserve a social milieu and life style which has no relevance for the broad mass of the people and at the same time impedes the progress towards economic self-reliance. Globalisation without adequate preparedness would be tantamount to opening up the Indian economy to unfair competition. The adjustment programme is likely to be counter-productive. There is no dearth of examples of countries which following the path of structural readjustment have all suffered substantial deterioration in the terms of trade. The outcome of SAP has ranged from moderately successful to disastrous condition. Newly industrial countries are the most indebted countries of the third world (Amin, 1990). They are the real peripheries of enclave market of the developed world. So one should not feel excited with the examples of 'Eastern tigers'. One should observe the deadly consequences of SAP with Argentina, Bolivia, Peru, Morrocco, Syria, Venezuela, Brazil, Mexico and many other African and Latin American countries.

For the village poor, we need to create permanent and productive jobs. It is imperative to search and adopt village scale and family-suited technologies, sophisticated in their conception and simple in their application. Thus ignoring the realities, efforts are directed primarily towards an imitative industrialisation.[10] This path seems to be undesirable, counter-productive, unaffordable and ecologically unsound. The implications for employment are literally incalculable.

(c) *Competitiveness*

As an answer to the third question, it can be said here that the type of competitiveness, SAP is contemplating for the third world is very fragile. A country passes through three stages in acquiring long-term competitiveness. First stage of competitiveness is factor-based, which delimits the standard of living. It is very temporary and fleeting. Second stage of competitiveness is capital-based, where both human and non-human capital combinedly support the rise in standard of living. Third stage of competitiveness is innovation-based, which refers to the ability to produce and innovate new products and processes. It is true and lasting. New Economic Policy of marketism is likely to ensure only factor-based competitiveness but no innovation-based competitiveness. According to Professor Porter, investment in infrastructure, education, health, and other basic needs, domestic competition, large home market, national commitment to success, all together contribute to the movement from stage-I to stage-II and stage-III. But SAP unfortunately does not contemplate on these aspects. Thus globalisation for India is likely to generate a tendency to perpetuate a structure of fragile competitiveness. It entails a type of international specialisation which may thwart any dynamic process leading the economy to the third stage.[11]

Long-term competitiveness, based on innovation, leads to the rise in standard of living. It does not depend on budget deficit, exchange rate and interest rate. German and Switzerland have achieved their competitiveness with their currency appreciation. Japan, Italy and S. Korea have achieved their competitiveness with large budgetary deficit and high interest rates. Competitiveness is not even reflected in the share of export in the National Income. There are many examples, where standard of living has improved as a result of competitiveness, while their share of export in National Income has declined or remained unaltered. India with SAP, is heading towards a kind of restructuring its export basket, which will consist of large proportion of high productivity goods, which may raise its export share in National Income. But it may adversely affect the standard of living of its people. It is always desirable to restructure the export basket, which will consist of large proportion of high productivity goods. It may cause a temporary fall in the share of export in National Income, but its benefit percolates to all and it ensures a sustained improvement in the standard of living for all.

Thus answers to above three questions are consistently negative. Therefore, the transition for the economy as backward as Indian economy, which suffers from rigidity of many types on various fronts, macroeconomic instability and imbalances, non-accountability, bureaucratism and corruption at all levels, is likely to only foster the interest of modern capitalism. It merely tends to increase :

(a) the role of MNCs;
(b) the capital intensity;
(c) the cost of R&D;
(d) automation and computerisation;
(e) role of advertisement;
(f) search for new markets; and
(g) consumerism with cultural onslaught.

It is really very difficult to comprehend the full range of consequences of New Economic Policy. It is certainly tending to reinforce the global oligopolistic power of MNCs in the rich industrialised countries to the detriment of all consumers of the entire world. In the long run the whole world is going to be saddled with stonewalled monopoly of MNCs instead of contemplated competition. The abrogation of MRTP Act and Indian Patent Act has made a blatant defiance and complete reversal of its social values, and constitutional values *i.e.* sovereign, socialist, secular, democratic republic enshrined in the preamble of Indian Constitution. India is gradually moving from self-reliant syndrome to a dependence satelitic paradigm.

India has prefered to accept a kind of dependence, only in the name of "greater access to high-tech" and "catching up with the rest of the world."

Thus India is marching mindlessly with the New Economic Policy which seems to be irrelevant. Instead, India requires a type of structural reforms before opening up its economy to the competitive regime which should have ensured:

(i) higher standard of living to the village people,
(ii) production for mass-consumption,
(iii) organisational and institutional reforms,
(iv) bureaucratic and political reforms,
(v) educational reforms and effective programme for skilling, and
(vi) use of labour-intensive technology.

Looking Ahead

The symptoms of the present economic crisis of India are basically attributable to structural deficiencies and rigidities of the development process that have an inherent tendency to generate macroeconomic imbalances which have jeopardised the growth process. It is also true that plethora of direct controls over investment, production, prices, imports, foreign capital and even exports have played havoc with the industrial efficiency and, therefore, with the process of economic development. Rigidity and regulation breeds corruption, which is the biggest, most pervasive and corrosive problem of India. It weakens the links between policy decisions and their implementation. The real problem does not lie anywere other than "economic rigidity and non-accountability". India has not yet achieved that flexibility in the domestic economic system in order to reap the benefits of the internationalisation process. Without caring for a proper diagnosis, Indian economy is carelessly marching on a knife-edge balance with great risk and uncertainity. Hence at this juncture India instead of following the new path of marketisation must ensure following four things :

(i) *Macroeconomic Consolidation* : Macroeconomic imbalances will be more accentuated with the globalisation process. Hence one needs to take a critical overview of the performance of the four decades of planning. One needs to pinpoint the structural and strategic deficiencies. Indian economy requires positive and more effective fiscal policies in order to direct investment and production in tune with its national priorities and potentials. But the New Economic Policy has attuned fiscal policy to make Indian economy more vulnerable externally and less egalitarian internally. Even Japan helped the consolidation of its industrial sector through protective measures for a considerable period before globalising its economy. Thus a set of sustainable policies is needed which are much more desirable for promoting private investment than an attempt at liberalisation which may be reversed because of lack of solid macroeconomic foundation and weak political support.

(ii) *Efficient Public Sector* : Inefficiency will prevail as before with privatisation and internationalisation. The management and work culture in both private sector and public sector suffer from same kind of inefficiencies, ccrruption and inflexibility. Hence, Indian economy needs an efficient and sizeable public sector with multi-objective and multi-year planning.[14] It needs to invigorate, revitalise the public sector and promote its efficiency. It needs reorientation, regrouping and a radical resurrection but not a wholesale retreat. The role of the public sector nas to be duly emphasised with the belief that the state is more knowledgeable and objective and the market, controlled by private hands, is rigged, imperfect and shortsighted. Market is a bad master but good servant.

(iii) *Economic Flexibility and Accountability* : Root of India's economic malaise lies in political and institutional factors. Economic rigidity and irresponsibility will not go with globalisation and privatisation. Hence India needs to have economic flexibility in the domestic economic system and accountability in the bureaucratic, political and administrative system. The politicians, bureaucrats and businessmen are in fact not accountable to any forum. The bureaucracy have in fact an effective command over not only the administration but also on economic policy-making of the country. They are going to benefit more out of the excitement about the NEP and SAP. It needs debureaucratisation, flexibility and accountability. The major problem is rigidity. It is the challange which has to be met by all political leaders, trade unions, journalists, Economists and Planners all over the country. There has to be a consensus and national debate on the required degree of domestic autonomy, flexibility and decentralisation.

(iv) *Decentralisation* : The root cause of poverty and backwardness lies in the neglect of the countryside and that is where the remedies must begin (Myrdal '68). Despite the slogans of decentralisation the enertia of the past still carries the day.[15] 'People Participation' has been distorted both in spirit and purpose. Participation of people's representatives in the name of 'peoples participation' has created a dole-culture and perpetuated the existing brutal socio-economic structure. It has remained rhetorical, wishful and nauseatingly hypocritical.[16] Thus it needs genuine democratic decentralisation, through which the basic physical, institutional, economic and administrative parameters of rural development can be geared. It needs a 'participative model' instead of a patriachal model (Das 1990). India needs to have 'peoples programme' with government's participation and not government's programme with the peoples participation. Decentralisation can overcome all economic, political, technical, socio-cultural and institutional constraints. It can ensure a functional people's participation, effective delivery system to neutralise the vested interest, horizontal and vertical integration and a dynamic relationship between planning and implementation. Decentralisation can only guarantee spatial, sectoral and operational balance through micro-spatial planning. It can ensure entitlement from below and not endowment from above, autonomy by right and not entrustment by discretion and majority rule with minority fights, and not minority rule with majority despair.

NOTES

1. This point is elaborated by Rudra, A. (1991) "Privatisation and Deregulation", *Economic and Political Weekly*, 21st Dec. p. 2934.
2. The argument is developed by many economists including Nagraj, R. (1991), "Public Sector Performance in Eighties", *Economic and Political Weekly*, 4th Dec. p. 2881.
3. Import liberalisation undermines the health of BOP without necessarily improving the export performance.
4. Large majority of Indians got imbibed in a culture where they are refused to think and act collectively on their own even if the group is homogeneous. It implies a dependence paradigm *par excellence*, see Prasad (1994).
5. Economic performance over the plan-decades is less than satisfactory whether one takes the capitalist index of growth of income or socialist indices of eradication of poverty and reduction of income inequality. The benefits of all welfare measures have pitiably remained confined to the upper crust of the weaker section and has not percolated to the 'real poor'. The social, economic, and political sub-systems are so strongly interlocked that the real poor remain outside the enclosure. The institutions and power arrangements howsoever democratic these may be have turned out to be oilgopolistic in nature, consequently biased in favour of the urban and/or elite class (Das 1990 : 1-35).
6. Amin (1990) holds the strong view that structural adjustment is a real recolonisation; sweetened by charity. He is not optimistic about the "Eastern tigers". NICs are not semi-peripheries on 'the way to catching up' but in every sense the real peripheries of tommorrow – a type of perpetual polarisation. The choice before the third world is therefore adjustment or delinking. Delinking has become a cul-de-sac. The most pernicious problem with delinking posture is that it is a posture of retreat.
7. This point is dealt by Sau, R. (1994), "Foreign Direct Investment, Portfolio Investment and Macroeconomic Stability", *Economic and Political Weekly*, 12th Feb., p. 386.

8. According to Hassain (1993) blind pursuit of SAP, disregarding the peculiarities of a given underdeveloped economy can be disastrous for it. The State has to play a leading role to induce private enterprise to look beyond the country's frontiers to establish a viable base for industreis.

9. It is very unfortunate that there is very little quantitative discussion on employment problems. All discussions on it tends to be rhetorical or ideological rather than operational. See Alagh (1994 : 30).

10. Globalisation does not logically entail an end to the agenda for economic nationalism *per se*. Success stories of growth in the context of internationalisation of capital have occurred in those East Asian countries of the third world which have pursued their relentless policy of economic nationalism. On the contrary economic retrogression has been witnessed in Latin America, due to their pursuit of liberal policy. This logical point is convincingly derived by Patnaik (1994).

11. Long term competitiveness depends only on productivity hence on scientific innovations and technological progress and nothing else. see Porter (1992).

12. In Marx's good society people do not compete with each other, they cooperate. They regard competition a law of jungle. Capitalism is barbaric in the words of Oscar Wilde. A capitalist is one who knows the price of everything but the value of none. Commodification is the rule, what is consumerism today was named by Mark "commodity fetishism" and condemned as a vice typical of capitalism.

13. Basu (1994) argues that unfortunately in India we have chosen points of monitoring corruption without any heed to its side effects of generating a larger bureaucracy and meddlesomeness with general economic functioning. This is one of the reasons for the economy's sluggishness.

14. Patnaik (1994) argues that the earlier 'dirigisme' despite an overarching state presence, suffered from the fact that no purposive action was contemplated either internally in the sphere of land relations or externally in the sphere of manufacturing export. Interestingly the new marketism, which he terms as "*transcendental marketism*" has exactly the same characteristics. Thus Indian economy needs state intervention and planning but of East Asian variety.

15. Poverty became only an alibi for Government intervention which were actually undertaken to protect and promote the interest of the Indian Proprietory class. Ironically but not surprisingly it was in the basic needs area that India's failure have been most glaring. Highest priorities have been followed by greatest failures. Bardhan (1981).

16. We have to have a pattern of development which would focus on the people; and it implies local area development which in term calls for a fundamental decentralisation of political and economic authority, which amy resolve the manifold social, ethnic, religious, linguistic problems (Ghosh 1992).

REFERENCES

1. A.Y.K. (1994) "Liberalisation and Planning", *Mainstream*, Feb.
2. Amin Samir (1990), *Delinking : "Towards a Polycentric World"*, Ze Books, London.
3. Bardhan, P. (1984), *The Political Economy of Development in India*, Basil Blackwell and Oxford University Press.
4. Basu, Kaushik (1993), "Structural Reforms in India", *Economic and Political Weekly*, 27th Nov.

5. Das, Kumar (1990), *Rural Development Through Decentralisation,* Discovery Publishing House, New Delhi.

6. ——,(1992), ''Paradox of Poverty and Planning in India'', *Economic Quarterly,* Berlin.

7. Ghosh, A. (1992), ''Federalism Democracy and Decentralisation'', *Economic and Political Weekly,* 14th Nov.

8. Hassain, M. (1993), *Sustainable Medium Term Development for Bangladesh,* Centre for Economic, Social and Environmental Research, Dhaka.

9. Myrdal G. (1968), *Asian Drama,* Part-5, Panthon Press, New York.

10. Patnaik P. (1994), ''International Capital and National Economic Policy'', *Economic and Political Weekly,* 19th March.

11. Porter, Michael (1992), *The Competitive Advantage of Nations,* Macmillan, London.

12. Pradhan, H. Prasad (1994), ''Self Reliant Progress *Versus* Dependence Paradigm'', *Mainstream,* 29th Jan.

3

GROWTH AND STRUCTURAL CHANGES IN THE INDIAN ECONOMY

V. Lakshmana Rao
Professor and Head,
Department of Economics, Andhra University

and

K. Neelaveni
Research Scholar,
Department of Economics, Andhra University

In this essay we present an overview picture of the Indian growth experience with focus on both growth and structural changes that occurred in the Indian economy in the post-independence period. The period covered is generally 1950-51 to 1992-93. The interest is to map the broad contours of the Indian growth experience over a period of a little more than four decades.

Trends in Real NNP and Per Capita NNP

Table 1 gives trends in NNP and Per Capita NNP. Over the whole period under study, the NNP at factor cost at constant (1980-81) prices recorded an average annual growth rate of 3.85 per cent, while per capita NNP growth rate was only 1.68 per cent. Thus during the period 1950-51 to 1992-93, the population recorded roughly a growth rate of 2.17 per cent. The per capita NNP at constant (1980-81) prices increased from Rs. 1126.9 in 1950-51 to Rs. 2215.8 in 1992-93. Thus during the 43 year period, the per capita income approximately doubled itself. Income growth rates in four years were negative. The years were 1957-58, 1965-66, 1972-73 and 1979-80. Substantial real income growth rates (equal to or more than 5 per cent) were recorded in years 1953-54, 1956-57, 1958-59, 1960-61, 1963-64, 1964-65, 1967-68, 1969-70, 1970-71, 1975-76, 1977-78, 1978-79, 1980-81, 1981-82, 1983-84,

1988-89 and 1989-90. Thus, in a period of 43 years, 17 years were relatively good years when NNP recorded substantial growth rates. During the large number of years per capital income registered negative growth rates. In 12 out of 43 years per capita income recorded negative growth rates. Population growth has been responsible for low per capita income growth rate even during the years when national income recorded significant growth rates.

It is interesting to look at the growth rates of the NNP and per capita NNP (Table 2) during different plan periods as they will give an overview of the Indian growth experience. During the first five year plan period (1951-56) the NNP in real terms grew at an annual compound growth rate of 3.6 per cent, while per capita income grew at 1.7 per cent. The performance of the economy during second plan period significantly improved over the previous plan period. The growth rates of national income and per capita income were 3.9 per cent and 1.9 per cent respectively, higher than the first plan growth rates. The growth rates significantly fell during the third plan period. While the NNP grew at an average annual rate of 2.3 per cent, the NNP per capita grew at the rate of 0.1 per cent only. During the three annual plans, growth rates picked up significantly. They were 3.7 per cent and 1.4 per cent respectively. During the Fourth Plan the growth rates fell again. While the NNP growth rate was 3.3 per cent, the NNP per capita grew at the rate of 0.9 per cent. The growth rates were — 6.0 and — 8.2 respectively during the year 1979-80. During the Sixth Plan (1980-85) period the growth rates were significantly high. The NNP and NNP per capita grew at annual compound rates of 5.4 per cent and 3.2 per cent respectively. Growth rates slightly increased during the subsequent Seventh Plan (1985—90) period. They were 5.6 per cent and 3.6 per cent respectively.

From tables 1 and 2, one can notice significant fluctuations in income and per capita income. Several factors explain these economic fluctuations during the period 1950-51 to 1992-93. Fluctuating weather conditions (alternating droughts and floods and periodic unfavourable monsoons), unfavourable increase in capital-output ratio, balance of payments problems and the consequent foreign exchange crises, wars with China and Pakistan dislocating the development efforts, international transmission of inflation through foreign trade, particularly oil price hikes during early 1970s and later, and structural imbalances which have developed in the economy as development proceeded were some of the major factors to be noted in this connection.

It is generally accepted that one of the structural changes that occur in the course of economic development is a progressive shift of labour from agriculture and allied activities to secondary and tertiary sectors. Studies based on historical data have amply demonstrated the validity of this Fisher-Clark thesis[1]. In the case of the western developed countries (Hagen prefers the term 'more developed') it is shown that while the proportion of the active population engaged in agriculture declined from 77 per cent in 1700 to 29 per cent in 1960 the corresponding percentage for secondary and tertiary sectors increased from 11.5 and 11.5 to 38.0 and 48.0 respectively.

While the broad trend in sectorial reallocation of labour as development proceeded is thus firmly established, the interesting fact about these structural shifts in economic activity for our purpose is not so much the ultimate decline in the importance of agriculture as the rate at which it occurred. To quote Paul Bairoch, "the proportion of active persons in agriculture diminished at a rate of less than 0.4 per cent a year uptill 1860, about 0.9 per cent from 1860 to 1950, but at 4 per cent from 1950 to 1970. The changes in the redistribution of the active population in western developed countries have thus been more important in the last twenty years."[2]

We have to look at these historical trends of disparate rates of relative decline over time of employment in agriculture for a clue to understand the problems of industrialisation of less developed countries (LDCs). The two main economic forces frequently mentioned behind the above trends are differing degrees of income elasticity of demand for products of different sectors and rapid growth in productivity caused by technical progress initially in secondary activities and later with considerable time-lag in agriculture. While the former represents impact (the magnitude of which will be significant only after a country achieves a fairly high level of per capita income) of demand side changes on economic development and sectorial reallocation of resources, the latter represents the influence of a vital phenomenon on the supply-side.

The time patterns of changes in sectorial demand structure and technologies go a long way as explanatory factors of the above trends. Although it took a long time for these changes to work themselves out in the industrialized economies, international demonstration effect on consumption pattern and transferability of superior technologies may very much reduce the time necessary for the LDCs to achieve significant level of economic development. These same factors may also give rise to some peculiar difficulties as the recent experience of LDCs has brought out. While it is not necessary for our purposes to enter into these details,[3] we can draw two valid inferences from the historical experience of industrialized economies.

First, while decline of the labour force engaged in primary sector did take place, we should not lose sight of the "long continuing importance of agriculture". Second, the character and timing of innovation in the respective sectors govern the nature and speed of transfer process. But as we see in what follows, there are other factors which are playing an important role both on the release and absorption sides of transfer process.

In economic development literature, a familiar hypothesis is that as an economy develops the relative importance (as measured by the share in income and employment) of agriculture would decline and the relative importance of the secondary and tertiary sectors would increase. If we go by the employment criterion, structural change is not significant. The percentage of labour force engaged in agriculture declined from 74 per cent in 1960 to 70 per cent in 1986. The percentage of labour engaged in industry increased from 11 per cent in 1960 to 13 per cent in 1986, while in services sector it increased from 15 per cent to 17 per cent. Thus, the structural change is not significant if go by the employment criterion. But if go by the income criterion, as can be seen from Table 3, the structural change during the period 1950-51 to 1992-93 has been very significant. The share of agriculture and allied activities in Gross Domestic Product at factor cost decreased from 56.46 per cent in 1950-51 to 32.31 per cent in 1992-93. The share of industry in Gross Domestic Product at factor cost increased from 15.05 per cent in 1050-51 to 26.88 per cent in 1992-93. The share of service sector in Gross Domestic Product at factor cost increased from 28.49 per cent in 1950-51 to 40.81 per cent in 1992-93.

Table 4 gives sectoral growth rates. During the first two plan periods income originating in agriculture grew at the annual average rate of 2.88 per cent and 3.35 per cent respectively. But during the Third Plan period because of unsatisfactory monsoon conditions, among other unfavourable factors, the income originating in agricultural sector recorded negative growth rate (average annual rate of — 0.28 per cent). Given the structure of the Indian economy, the growth in the National Income has largely been determined by the trends in agricultural production. The reason is that agriculture has been single largest component of GDP and agriculture has overall impact on other sectors via input linkages, employment and incomes. The average performance of agriculture sector has shown significant improvement during the period 1966-67 to 1970-71 as can be seen from Table 4 giving sectoral growth rates. As economic development proceeded, the share of agriculture as noted before, declined from 54.91 per cent during the First Plan period to 32.31 per cent in 1992-93. Agriculture has been subject to wide year to year fluctuations due to the weather factors. Wherever irrigation and power are available on an assured basis, agriculture has performed remarkably well in terms of production and use of new technologies.

As can be seen from the table (Table 4), the performance of agriculture has shown significant improvement in 1980s as compared to the earlier decade.

Manufacturing sector will occupy a crucial position in India's future economic development. The country's ability to grow fast, be competitive and create an expanding base for direct and indirect growth of productive employment will depend upon the growth and efficiency of the manufacturing sector. This sector received the support of better technologies after a good start in the second and third plans (the average annual growth rates during the plans were 6.28 per cent and 6.62 per cent respectively), but the growth performance of manufacturing sector declined during the late 1960s and 1970s, but picked up again in 1980s (Table 4). The performance during 80s was supported by initiation of steps towards liberalisation in import and industrial policies, besides relatively better performance of the infrastructure sectors, particularly energy and transport. Due to the foreign exchange crisis and curbs on imports and general resource crunch constraining demand, the manufacturing sector experienced a recession during 1991-92. The provisional general index of industrial production in 1991-92 stood at 212.4, the index for the previous year had been 212.6. But given the efficacy of corrective steps already under implementation, the industrial growth is expected to pick up again.

A major strength of the economy has been the large base of natural resources. The strategy for self-reliance in food and basic industries was pursued through large allocation of investible resources to the development of irrigation, energy and transport sectors. With growing experience in project execution, the period of project completion (gestation lag) that is the time lag between investment and profits, could be reduced. The shortfalls in plan targets of power, railways, coal, oil etc. were sharply reduced during the 1980s. This also contributed to a reduction in ICOR.

Economic growth has brought about a structural change in the economy. This is evident in the form of a shift in the sectoral composition of production, diversification of activities and a gradual transformation of a feudal and colonial economy into a modern industrial economy. The composition of gross domestic product has changed steadily during the planning era. While the share of agricultural and allied activities fell from 54.91 per cent during the First Plan period, the share of manufacturing increased from 11.88 per cent during the First Plan period to 20 per cent during Seventh Plan period. The share of service sector increased from 28.32 per cent to 38.35 per cent. The expansion of service sector has not only been conducive for employment generation but also for better efficiency of the system and better quality of life.

In the post-independence period, India experienced uninterrupted growth and development until the early 1960s. But the economic growth process received a set-back from 1963 onwards largely because of exogenous shocks and Mother Nature's periodic unkindness. Chinese aggression in 1962, war with Pakistan in 1965, Bangladesh liberation effort in 1971, spectacular oil price hikes engineered by OPEC in 1973 and again in 1979, and alternating floods and droughts have been some of the events which were responsible for slowing down of economic growth and development process.

Now we examine various dimensions of India's growth and development experience during the last two decades. Wherever relevant, reference is made to the low-income economies (LIEs) as a group also. LIEs are those with the GNP per capita of $ 635 or less in 1991. India is one of the low income economies by this definition. With land area of 3,288 thousand sq. kms. India in mid-1991 was supporting 866.56 million population. The density of population in 1991 was 264 (population per sq. km.), significantly higher than the average for the LIEs (81). During the period 1970-80, population growth rate experienced by India was 2.3 per cent, while the average for the LIEs was 2.2 per cent. During the subsequent 1980-91 period the Indian population growth rate fell to 2.1 per cent, while in the case of the LIEs, it fell to 2 per cent. In 1991, the latest for which comparable data are available[4], the per capita GNP of India was $ 330, the average for the LIEs being $ 350. While per capita GNP growth rate during the period 1980-91 for the LIEs was 3.9 per cent, it was 3.2 per cent in the case of India (if we take a longer time period 1965—89, the growth rate of GNP per capita in India was only 1.8 per cent, significantly lower than the average for the LIEs (2.9 per cent). As for the GDP growth rate of India during the period 1970—80, it was 3.4 per cent, significantly lower than the average for the LIEs (4.5 per cent). During the subsequent 1980—91 period the growth of Indian GDP increased to 5.4 per cent, while the average for the LIEs increased to 6 per cent. Thus, although India experienced significant economic growth during the period 1970—1991, the Indian economic performance fell short of the average for the LIEs.

What was the experience of India in respect of inflation which has become a global phenomenon during the last two decades? During the period 1970—80, the inflation rate experienced by India was 8.4 per cent, which was slightly higher than the average inflation rate experienced by the LIEs (8.2 per cent). During subsequent 1980—91 period inflation rate registered a slight decline in the case of India, while it increased in the case of the LIEs (12.6 per cent). The Indian as well as the LIEs experience during the period 1970—91 demonstrates that moderate inflation rates are not inimical to economic growth. But it is to be noted here that international country cross-section statistical studies did not reveal any firm relationship between inflation rates and economic growth performance of countries.[5]

Usually low-life expectancy go with low-income levels of countries. Although in India life expectancy at birth has been increasing gradually, it is still significantly lower than the life expectancy in the case of high income countries and lower than the averages for the LIEs. In 1991 the Indian life expectancy was 60 years, while it was 62 in the case of LIEs. Another important demographic indicator of economic development is infant mortality rate (deaths per thousand live births). The infant mortality rate in India has been declining during the last 40 years. It declined from 150 in 1965 to 137 in 1970. It further declined to 90 by 1991. The average infant mortality rate for the LIEs in 1965 was 124 and it declined to 71 by 1991. Relatively low life expectancy and significant infant morality rates thus constitutes another dimension of the Indian economic and demographic experience.

The human capital approach to economic development rightly emphasises the health status of the people as a significant factor in economic development. In respect of health related indicators, India experienced significant progress. Population per physician in India decreased from 4890 in 1970 to 2460 in 1990. The corresponding figures for the LIEs were 14080 and 6760. Population per nursing person in India was 3710 in 1970 and it declined to 1700 by 1984. The corresponding figures for the LIEs were 5580 and 2180. Daily calorie supply per capita in India increased from 2021 in 1965 to 2229 in 1989. The corresponding figures for the LIEs were 1975 and 2486.

Education is a major means of accumulating human capital. It plays an important part in progressively increasing resource productivity. In India the enrolment in primary education during the period 1970—1990 increased from 73 per cent to 97 per cent of the relevant age group. The corresponding figures for the LIEs were 73 per cent and 100 per cent. Enrolment in the secondary schools increased in India from 24 per cent in 1970 to 44 per cent in 1990. The corresponding figures for the LIEs were 21 per cent and 41 per cent. The enrolment in higher education in India in 1970 was 6 per cent, while the average for the LIEs was 2 per cent. By 1988 the enrolment in higher education in India increased to 9 per cent. In India in 1988 the percentage of population of working age (15-64 years) was 58.4 per cent, while the average for the LIEs was 59.8 per cent.

In economic development literature, a familiar hypothesis is that as an economy develops the relative importance (as measured by the share of income and employment) of agriculture would decline and the relative importance of the secondary and tertiary sectors would increase. Let us examine these structural changes. The share of agriculture in GDP was 45 per cent in 1970 and it decreased to 31 per cent by 1991. The share of industry increased from 22 per cent to 29 per cent during the period 1970—1991. The share of tertiary or service sector increased from 33 per cent to 41 per cent during the same period. Similar structural changes are observable in respect of the LIEs as a group. In respect of the LIEs, the share of agriculture in GDP declined from 38 per cent to 29 per cent during the period 1970—1991. While the share of industry and service sector increased from 29 and 33 per cent in 1970 to 34 and 38 per cent respectively by 1991.

Levels and growth rates of consumption are important indicators of levels of living and improvement in economic welfare. The growth of private consumption in India during the period 1970-80 was 2.9 per cent per annum which was significantly lower than the average for the LIEs (4.1 per cent). During the subsequent 1980—91 period the consumption growth rate in India was 5.3 per cent, higher than the average for LIEs (4.8 per cent). Thus, over the whole period 1970—91, there was significant growth in private consumption both in India and the LIEs.

Given the aggregate incremental capital output ratio (ICOR) the higher the rate of investment (investment-income ratio), the higher would be the growth rate of income. The growth in investment would be indicative of growth in the capacity output. The gross domestic investment as per cent of GDP increased from 17 per cent in 1970 to 20 per cent in 1991 in India. During the same period the rate of investment in the LIEs increased from 21 per cent in 1970 to 27 per cent in 1991. The growth rate of investment in India increased from 4.5 per cent during the 1970—80 period to 5.1 per cent during the 1980—91 period. The growth rate of investment in LIEs remains constant at 7.0 per cent during the two periods. The growth rates of

GDP both in India and the LIEs were not commensurate with the levels of investment because of rising incremental capital-output ratios.

Within the manufacturing sector of the Indian economy there did take place some structural change. The share of food and other agro-based industries in the total value added by manufacturing declined from 13 per cent in 1970 to 12 per cent in 1990. If we consider textiles and clothing along with food and other agro-based industries, the share in value added by manufacturing declined from 34 per cent in 1970 to 24 per cent in 1990. The share of other industries (machinery and transport equipment, chemicals and other manufactures) increased from 66 per cent in 1970 to 77 per cent in 1990. Thus significant structural change took place in the manufacturing sector during the period 1970-90. In the case of the LIEs also the structural change in the manufacturing sector was significant. Productivity Index of manufacturing (Gross Output per employee) increased from 83 in 1970 to 169 in 1989 (1980 as base year). Both increase in capital intensity and technical progress, among other factors, explain this productivity improvement. With the 1980 as base year, earning per employee index rose to 127 by 1989.

Energy consumption per capita (measured in Kgs of oil equivalent) is an important indicator of the level of economic development of a country. The energy consumption per capita in India increased from 113 in 1970 to 337 in 1991. The corresponding figures for the LIEs were 166 and 376. The two oil shocks during the early and late 1970s (steep increase in oil prices engineered by the OPEC) made the oil importing economies, particularly their BOP situation, very vulnerable. What has happened to the oil imports of India? Energy imports as percentage of merchandise exports increase from 8 per cent in 1970 to 26 per cent in 1991. The correspondent figures for the LIEs were 6 per cent and 10 per cent. Thanks to the oil price hikes, the annual growth rates of commercial energy consumption declined in the LIEs. In the LIEs average annual growth rate of energy consumption declined from 7.0 during the 1970-80 to 5.6 per cent during 1980—91. In the Indian case, however, it increased from 6.4 per cent (1970-80) to 7.2 per cent (1980—91). Energy production in India registered an annual growth rate of 6.8 per cent during 1970—80 period and it fell to 6.6 per cent during subsequent 1980—91 period. The corresponding figures for LIEs were 7.3 per cent and 4.8 per cent.

Indian economy is an open economy. Exports as per cent of GDP in India worked out to be 8 per cent in 1991. The corresponding figures for the LIEs was 17.6 per cent. The imports as per cent of GDP in India in 1991 were 9.2 per cent. The corresponding figure for the LIEs was 18.2 per cent. Broadly speaking, India depends to a lesser extent on foreign trade than the LIEs. This does not belittle the role of and the need for dynamic foreign trade sector in the Indian economic development.

The average annual growth rate of exports during the period 1970—80 in the case of India was 4.3 per cent significantly higher than the average growth rate for the LIEs (3.50 per cent). During the subsequent 1980—89 period, the export growth rate of India increased to 7.4 per cent, while that of the LIEs increased to 6.6 per cent. Thus the exports of India registered higher growth rate during 1980—91 compared with the LIEs. As for the growth in imports, average annual growth rate of imports increased from 3.0 per cent during the period 1970—80 to 4.2 per cent during the period 1980—91, in the case of the LIEs the growth rate declined from 6.0 per cent to 2.7 per cent. Thus the Indian foreign trade performance is found to be better than that of the LIEs as a group.

As for the structure of merchandise exports the primary product exports in 1970 accounted for 48 per cent of total exports of India. This share significantly declined by 1989. The share was 27 per cent. The corresponding figures for the LIEs were 72 per cent and 43 per cent. Thus there was decline in relative importance of primary product exports both in India and the LIEs. The share of other commodities (machinery and transport equipment and other manufactures) increased from 52 per cent in 1970 to 73 per cent in 1991 in Indian exports. The corresponding figures for the LIEs were 27 per cent and 56 per cent. Thus the dependence of India on primary product exports has been significantly lower than that of the LIEs. The share of textiles and clothing as per cent of total exports was 25 per cent in 1970. In 1991 the share of textiles was stable. In the case of LIEs the share of textiles increased from 13 per cent in 1970 to 23 per cent in 1991.

As for the structure of merchandise imports, India had in its imports in 1970, 48 per cent of primary products. This share declined to 40 per cent by 1991. The corresponding figures for the LIEs were 29 per cent and 27 per cent. The share of manufacturing imports in India increased from 52 per cent in 1970 to 60 per cent in 1991. The corresponding figures for the LIEs were 71 per cent and 72 per cent. As for the destination of manufactured exports, in 1965 industrial market economies accounted for 55 per cent of India's manufactured exports and this share increased to 59 per cent by 1986. The corresponding figures for the LIEs were 56 per cent and 45 per cent. The developing economies accounted for 32 per cent of India's exports in 1965 and this share declined to 24 per cent by 1986. The corresponding figures for the LIEs were 33 per cent and 48 per cent. The other economies (other than industrial market and developing economies) accounted for 13 per cent of India's manufactured exports and this share declined to 10 per cent by 1986. The corresponding figures for the LIEs were 11 per cent and 7 per cent.

As in the case of several other developing countries, India also was running deficits in the current account of her balance of payments. In 1970 the current account deficit (before official transfers) was $ 591 millions. By 1991 the deficits stood at $ 3477 millions. The receipts under net workers' remittances increased from $ 80 millions in 1970 to $ 2540 millions by 1991. The gross international reserves of India increased from $ 1023 millions in 1970 to $ 7616 by 1991. The corresponding figures for the LIEs were $ 3907 millions and $ 86647 millions. The international reserves in 1991 expressed in months of import coverage amounted to 3.3 months in the case of India in 1991, while it was 5.1 months in the case of the LIEs. If we use the norm of reserves adequate to cover imports for three months, the reserve position of India was to be considered as just satisfactory (the deep economic crisis faced by India in the early 1990s will be considered in the concluding part of the paper). The adverse balance of payments situation of India is reflected in the continual decline in the external value of rupee. The rupee value of dollar in 1970 was 7.5 and in 1993 the rupee value of dollar was around 31.

Like several other developing countries, India had been

experiencing increasing external debt burden. Its total long term debt increased from $ 18709 millions in 1980 to $ 64315 million in 1991. As per the external debt service ratios, total long-term debt service as per cent of exports of goods and services increased from 9.3 per cent in 1980 to 30.7 per cent in 1991. The corresponding figures for the LIEs were 10.1 and 21.0.

Inequalities in income distribution in India have been getting aggravated over a period of time. In 1989-90, the lowest 20 per cent of households enjoyed only 8.8 per cent of total income, while the highest 20 per cent enjoyed 41.3 per cent of income. The highest 10 per cent of household enjoyed 26.7 per cent of income. These figures show the significant inequalities in income distribution.

The new government which assumed office in June 1991, faced a serious economic crisis. The balance of payments situation was severely adverse, with foreign exchange reserves barely enough for two weeks of imports. International confidence reached such a low point that access to commercial lending was almost closed, and NRI deposits were being withdrawn at a rapid pace. Industrial growth had turned negative because of severe import compression, and inflation was accelerating. Between 1989-90 and 1990-91 inflation rate went up from 4.4 per cent to 10.3 per cent. Behind the crisis were a few major changes witnessed during the 1980s. There was an increasing reliance on foreign capital in 1980s. The second major change occurred in the financing of public sector investment. In 1976-77 public saving financed 49 per cent of gross public investment. By 1989-90, the ratio came down to 16 per cent. The third change was in respect of inflation. In the earlier years seasonal factors were playing an important part. Inflation rate varied between good and bad agricultural years. But the general price level did not fall or even stabilise in any year throughout 1980s. This irreversibility of general price level set in a positive price expectation.[6]

Faced with the grim situation, the newly installed government at the centre in June 1991 has been going ahead with a policy package, economic liberalisation being its significant feature. We have to wait and see whether the new policy package will yield the desired results.

While one can discern several dimensions of economic progress of the Indian economy in the post-independence period the rate of economic growth had not been adequate enough to take care of the twin problems of unemployment and poverty. Added to this are the problems of growing inequalities in income distribution and in regional development. The Indian economy has all along been vulnerable to exogenous shocks. The Chinese agression, wars with Pakistan, oil price hikes in early and late 1970s and the Gulf war were some of these exogenous shocks. The time immediately ahead is full of uncertainty so far as the India's economic performance is concerned.

NOTES AND REFERENCES

1. A brief but very useful discussion is in Everett E. Hagen, *Economics of Development*, Richard D, Irwin Inc., 1968. pp. 45-48. Also Simon Kuznets in *Modern Economic Growth* (Yale University Press, 1966) devotes considerable space to discuss the structural changes associated with economic development, pp. 86-158. On page 1 of the book, he presents a very comprehensive definition of economic growth.
2. All the figures and most of the interpretation that follows are from Paul Bairoch, *The Structure of the Active Population from 1950-1970* (mimeo), p. 11 and p. 13, Table III.
3. Literature on both these aspects is very wide and no attempt is made to quote specific studies.
4. *World Development Report*, 1993.
5. A dated but thorough study of inflation and growth based on country cross-section data is one by A.P. Thirwall, *Inflation, Saving and Growth in Developing Economies*, London : Macmillan, 1974.
6. B.B. Bhattacharya, *India's Economic Crisis, Debt Burden and Stabilisation*, Delhi : B.R. Publishing Corporation, 1992.

TABLE 1

Trends in NNP and Per Capita NNP at Constant Prices (1980-81)

Year	NNP at factor cost at constant prices (1980-81) Rs. in crores	% Change	Per Capita NNP at factor cost at constant (1980-81) Rs.	% Change
1	2	3	4	5
1950-51	40454	—	1126.9	—
51-52	41443	2.4	1135.4	0.8
52-53	42613	2.8	1145.5	0.9
53-54	45292	6.3	1195.1	4.3
54-55	47111	4.0	1220.5	2.1
1955-56	48288	2.5	1228.7	0.7
56-57	50955	5.5	1270.7	3.4
57-58	50051	—1.8	1228.7	— 3.7
58-59	53869	7.6	1288.7	5.3
59-60	54775	1.7	1285.8	— 0.2
1960-61	58602	7.0	1350.3	5.0
61-62	60168	2.7	1355.1	0.4
62-63	61655	1.7	1347.2	— 0.6
63-64	64216	5.0	1384.0	2.7
64-65	68942	7.4	1454.5	5.1
1965-66	65734	— 4.7	1355.3	— 6.8
66-67	66089	0.5	1335.1	— 1.5
67-68	71519	8.2	1413.4	5.9
68-69	73285	2.5	1414.8	0.1
69-70	78177	6.7	1477.8	4.5

1970-71	82211	5.2	1579.6	2.8
71-72	82675	0.6	1492.3	— 1.8
72-73	81991	— 0.8	1446.0	— 3.1
73-74	86010	4.9	1482.9	2.6
74-75	87116	1.3	1469.1	— 0.9
1975-76	95433	9.5	1572.2	7.0
76-77	96253	0.9	1552.5	— 1.3
77-78	103670	7.7	1635.2	5.3
78-79	109466	5.6	1689.3	3.3
79-80	102937	— 6.0	1550.3	— 8.2
1980-81	110685	7.5	1630.1	5.1
81-82	117140	5.8	1692.8	3.8
82-83	119704	2.2	1690.7	— 0.1
83-84	129892	8.1	1789.7	5.9
84-85	133808	3.4	1810.7	1.2
1985-86	139025	3.9	1841.4	1.7
86-87	144242	3.8	1870.8	1.6
87-88	149787	3.8	1900.9	1.6
88-89	165751	10.7	2059.0	8.3
89-90	177552	7.1	2160.0	4.9
1990-91	185683	4.6	2213.1	2.5
91-92	185503	0.1	2167.1	— 2.1
92-93	193222	4.2	2215.8	2.2
Average Annual Growth Rate		23.85		1.68

TABLE 2

Annual Compound Growth Rates

	NNP at factor cost at 1980-81 Prices	Per Capita NNP at 1980-81 Prices
First Plan (1951-56)	3.6	1.7
Second Plan (1956-61)	3.9	1.9
Third Plan (1961-66)	2.3	0.1
Three Annual Plans (1966-69)	3.7	1.4
Fourth Plan (1969-74)	3.3	0.9
Fifth Plan (1974-79)	4.9	2.6
Annual Plan (1979-80)	— 6.0	— 8.2
Sixth Plan (1980-85)	5.4	3.2
Seventh Plan(1985-90)	5.8	3.6

TABLE 3

Sectoral Distribution of GDP

Year	Agriculture, Forestry and Logging, Fishing, Mining and Quarrying	%	**Industry** Manufacturing, Construction, Electricity, Gas and Water supply	%	**Service Sector** Transport, Communication and Trade, Banking and Insurance, Real Estate and Ownership of dwelling and business services, Public administration and Defence and Other services	%	Gross Domestic Product at Factor Cost
1	2	3	4	5	6	7	8
1950-51	24204	56.46	6451	15.05	12216	28.49	42871
1959-60	30670	52.21	10732	18.27	17243	29.35	58745
1969-70	38805	45.06	19821	23.02	27483	31.92	86109
1979-80	43005	37.55	28963	25.35	42265	37.00	114236
1989-90	67064	33.29	55597	27.60	78792	39.11	201453
1992-93*	71746	32.31	59708	26.88	90635	40.81	222089

*Quick estimates

TABLE 4

Sectoral Growth in Gross Domestic Product (Per cent Per Annum, Based on G.D.P. Series at 1980-81 Prices)

Sl. No.	Sector	1951-52 to 1955-56	1956-57 to 1960-61	1961-62 to 1965-66	1966-67 to 1970-71	1971-72 to 1975-76	1976-77 to 1980-81	1981-82 to 1985-86	1986-87 to 1989-90
1	2	3	4	5	6	7	8	9	10
1.	Agriculture	2.88	3.35	—0.28	5.36	2.33	1.33	3.16	3.59
2.	Mining & Quarrying	4.40	6.96	6.76	1.31	5.38	4.53	6.91	7.03
3.	Manufacturing	5.84	6.28	6.62	3.96	3.33	4.86	6.99	6.72
	3.1 Registered	6.18	8.24	8.34	4.67	2.39	5.28	8.56	6.30
	3.2 Unregistered	5.62	4.38	4.60	3.16	4.61	4.39	4.88	7.41
4.	Electricity, Gas and Water supply	8.68	12.08	12.84	9.54	6.83	6.91	8.41	9.60
5.	Construction	6.80	6.70	6.83	4.36	1.47	5.11	3.36	4.06
6.	Trade, Hotels & Restaurants	4.79	5.77	5.39	4.22	4.10	4.49	5.96	6.53
7.	Transport, Storage and Communications	4.38	6.99	6.27	4.72	6.54	5.78	6.81	8.04
8.	Finance and Real Estate	3.12	2.83	3.31	3.54	3.61	4.56	6.39	8.27
9.	Public Administration and Defence	3.45	6.83	8.97	6.83	4.89	5.89	6.26	8.69
10.	Others	2.79	3.32	4.24	3.61	2.95	3.00	4.56	6.12
	Total	3.61	4.27	2.84	4.66	3.08	3.24	5.06	5.81

Source : Eighth Five Year Plan.

4

STRUCTURE OF INDIAN ECONOMY

Gross Domestic Product And National Income

Gross Domestic Product (GDP) at factor cost at constant (1980-81) prices in 1992-93 has been estimated at Rs. 222089 crores as against Rs. 213590 crores in 1991-92, registering a growth of 4.0 per cent during the year as against the growth of 1.1 per cent achieved during the previous year. At current prices, GDP at factor cost in 1992-93 has been estimated at Rs. 627913 crores as against Rs. 551552 crores in 1991-92, showing an increase of 13.8 per cent during the year.

At constant (1980-81) prices, the national income (*i.e.* net national product at factor cost) in 1992-93 has been estimated at Rs. 193222 crores as against Rs. 185503 crores in 1991-92 showing a rise of 4.2 per cent during the year. At current prices, the national income in 1992-93 is estimated at Rs. 544935 crores as compared to Rs. 477868 crores in 1991-92, showing a rise of 14.0 per cent during the year.

The per capita income (per capita net national product at factor cost) in real terms has been estimated at Rs. 2216 for 1992-93 as against Rs. 2167 for 1991-92, registering an increase of 2.3 per cent during the year. The per capita income at current prices has been estimated at Rs. 6249 in 1992-93 as against Rs. 5583 for the previous year.

The overall performance of the economy during the year 1992-93 has been impressive as compared to the dismal picture in the previous year. With the exception of forestry and railways, all the sectors recorded positive growth rates at constant prices. Particularly significant has been the achievement of agriculture sector, which registered a growth rate of 5.3 per cent as compared to the decline of 2.7 per cent in the previous year. The sector electricity, gas and water supply, trade, hotels and restaurants, transport by other means, communication,

TABLE 1

GDP and National Income

Year	GDP (Rs. crores)		NNP (Rs. crores)		Per capita NNP (Rs.)	
	current prices	1980-81 prices	current prices	1980-81 prices	current prices	1980-81 prices
(1)	(2)	(3)	(4)	(5)	(6)	(7)
1989-90	408661	201453	357931	177552	4354	2160
1990-91	475604	211260	416495	185683	4964	2213
1991-92	551552	213590	477868	185503	5583	2167
1992-93	627913	222089	544935	193222	6249	2216
	Per cent growth over previous year					
1989-90	15.9	6.9	15.7	7.1	13.3	4.9
1990-91	16.4	4.9	16.4	4.6	14.0	2.5
1991-92	16.0	1.1	14.7	—0.1	12.5	—2.1
1992-93	13.8	4.0	14.0	4.2	11.9	2.3

public administration and defence and other services have recorded growth rates of over 4 per cent during the year.

The value of output in respect of agriculture after recording a fall of — 2.8 per cent in 1991-92, has shown a growth of 4.4 per cent in 1992-93 (Table 3). This is mainly due to substantial increase in the production of coarse cereals. The increase in production is also significant in pulses and oilseeds during the year. However, it may be observed that the production of coarse cereals and pulses declined during 1991-92 and in fact, the production of pulses during 1992-93 is less than the record production achieved in 1990-91. During the year, the oilseeds recorded an all time high production of 20.27 million tonnes, despite a steep decline in the production of rape-seeds and mustards by 17.0 per cent, mainly due to the increase in production of groundnuts (by 24.8 per cent) and soyabean (by 24.9 per

TABLE 2

Per cent Change Over Previous Year in GDP of Selected Sectors of the Economy

(at 1980-81 prices)

sector	1981-82	1985-86	1990-91	1991-92	1992-93
(1)	(2)	(3)	(4)	(5)	(6)
1. Agriculture	6.3	0.3	4.1	−2.7	5.3
2. Manufacturing	8.0	4.0	6.2	−3.2	2.0
3. Electricity, gas and water supply	9.4	8.2	6.9	7.5	6.5
4. Trade, hotels & restaurant	6.5	8.1	5.7	0.3	4.8
5. Railways	8.5	10.8	3.3	6.0	−1.1
6. Communication	7.5	2.7	6.4	6.9	10.3
7. Transport by other means	3.3	9.8	4.8	6.9	7.1
8. Banking & insurance	7.1	13.1	2.1	21.7	2.5
9. Public administration and defence	2.3	7.7	1.1	2.2	4.3
10. Other services	4.5	4.7	7.5	5.8	5.7
11. Total GDP	6.1	4.1	4.9	1.1	4.0

cent). Further, cotton production increased by 19.3 per cent, while jute & mesta and sugarcane showed declining trends. Another notable feature during the year was the decline in the consumption of chemical fertilisers despite a significant rise in the output of agriculture. This was in sharp contrast to the picture in 1991-92, when the consumption of chemical fertilisers increased by 6.7 per cent, when the output of agriculture sector declined by 2.8 per cent.

In the industrial sector, the general index of industrial production (Table 4) for the year 1992-93 has been placed at 216.2. This is higher by 1.7 per cent over the previous year index of 212.5. For the first time since 1980-81, the index of industrial production showed decline during

TABLE 3

Performance of Agriculture

(Unit for value data Rs. crores at 1980-81 prices and for production million tonnes)

Item	1990-91	1991-92	1992-93	Growth 1991-92	Growth 1992-93
(1)	(2)	(3)	(4)	(5)	(6)
1. Value of output	80565	79176	82527	— 1.7	4.2
1.1 Agriculture	63383	61589	64280	— 2.8	4.4
1.2 Livestock	17182	17587	18247	2.4	3.8
2. Value of selected inputs					
2.1 Chemical fertilizer	5291	5646	5506	6.7	— 2.5
2.2 Diesel oil	1042	1109	1140	6.4	2.8
2.3 Organic manure	726	726	775	0.0	6.7
2.4 Feed of livestock	8220	7984	8145	— 2.9	2.0
2.5 Seed	2091	2090	2116	0.0	1.2
3. Production of selected crops					
3.1 Paddy in terms of Rice	74.29	74.68	72.61	0.5	— 2.8
3.2 Wheat	55.14	55.69	56.76	1.0	1.9
3.3 Coarse cereals	32.70	25.99	37.04	— 20.5	42.5
3.4 Pulses	14.26	12.02	13.60	— 15.7	13.1
3.5 Foodgrains	176.39	168.38	180.01	— 4.5	6.9
3.6 Oilseeds	18.61	18.60	20.27	— 0.1	9.0
3.7 Cotton*	9.84	9.71	11.58	—1.3	19.3
3.8 Jute & Mesta**	9.23	10.29	9.00	11.5	— 12.5
3.9 Sugarcane	241.05	254.00	230.83	5.4	—9.1

* Million bales of 170 kg. ** Million bales of 180 kg.

1991-92, due to decline in production in a number of manufacturing industries. The index showed positive growth during 1992-93, although marginal. The industries, food products (3.5 per cent), cotton textiles (1.7 per cent), wood, furniture, etc. (2.9 per cent), paper and printing (0.6 per cent), leather and fur (0.3 per cent), rubber, petroleum products (3.1 per cent), chemicals (5.3 per cent), non-metallic products (1.3 per cent), basic metal industries (3.6 per cent) and transport equipments (3.9 per cent) showed positive growth rates. On the other hand, the industries beverages, tobacco etc. (— 4.5 per cent), jute textiles (— 3.8 per cent), textile products (— 21.8 per cent), metal products (— 9.6 per cent), non-electric machinery (— 4.1 per cent) and electric machinery (— 3.0 per cent) showed negative growth rates.

TABLE 4

Indices of Industrial Production at 2-Digit Level

Industry code	1990-91	1991-92	1992-93	Growth 1991-92	Growth 1992-93	Industry name
Mining	221.2	221.5	224.8	0.1	1.5	Mining
20-21	169.8	166.2	172.1	—2.1	3.5	Food Products
22	104.8	119.1	113.7	13.6	—4.5	Beverages, Tobacco etc.
23	126.6	126.2	128.4	—0.3	1.7	Cotton Textiles
25	101.6	90.4	87.0	—11.0	—3.8	Jute Textiles
26	103.2	97.2	76.0	—5.8	—21.8	Textile Products
27	197.2	185.0	190.4	—6.2	2.9	Wood, Furniture
28	198.0	209.6	210.9	5.9	0.6	Paper & Printing
29	194.3	196.6	197.2	1.2	0.3	Leather & Fur
30	174.0	172.4	177.7	—0.9	3.1	Rubber, Petroleum
31	254.1	262.8	276.7	3.4	5.3	Chemicals
32	193.1	205.2	207.9	6.3	1.3	Non-Metallic Products
33	158.8	168.5	174.6	6.1	3.6	Basic Metal Industries
34	143.1	139.9	126.4	—2.2	—9.6	Metal Products
35	186.9	184.4	176.8	—1.3	—4.1	Non-Electrical M/C
36	563.6	493.6	479.0	—12.4	—3.0	Electrical M/C
37	192.5	191.5	198.9	—0.5	3.9	Transport Equipments
38	321.8	269.8	273.6	—16.2	1.4	Other Manufacturing
Manufg	207.8	204.6	207.0	—1.5	1.2	Manufacturing
Elect.	236.8	257.0	269.8	8.5	5.0	Electricity
General	212.6	212.5	216.8	0.0	1.7	General

The infrastructure industries (Table 5), barring crude petroleum and fertilizers, registered positive growth rates during the current year.

TABLE 5

Production of Infrastructure Industries

Sector		Unit	Production 1990-91	Production 1991-92	Production 1992-93	Growth 1991-92	Growth 1992-93
1.	Power	BU	264.2	286.7	301.0	8.5	5.0
2.	Coal	Mnt	211.7	229.3	238.2	8.3	3.9
3.	Steel saleable	Mnt	9.3	9.9	11.1	6.5	12.1
4.	Rly. freight traffic	Mnt	318.4	338.0	349.6	6.1	3.4
5.	Cement	Mnt	48.8	51.7	54.3	5.9	5.0
6.	Fertilizers	Mnt	9.0	9.9	9.7	9.1	— 1.4
7.	Petroleum						
	(a) Crude	Mnt	33.02	30.3	26.9	— 8.2	— 11.1
	(b) Refinery	Mnt	51.77	51.4	53.5	— 0.8	4.1

The performance of railways is assessed with the growth in passenger and freight traffic (Table 6) which are of the order of — 4.1 and 0.5 per cent, respectively. One of the reasons for this is the sluggish growth of the industrial sector. During the year, the gross trading income has registered a growth of 4.3 per cent as compared to a decline of 0.8 per cent in the previous year, mainly due to the increase in agriculture production. Key indicators showing the performance of other tertiary sectors are also given in Table 6.

The overall impact of these changes in the gross domestic product arising in different sectors can be seen in Table 7 which gives the percentage share of gross domestic product by broad sectors. The share of primary sector has gone down from 39.6 per cent in 1980-81 to 34.0 and 32.3 per cent at current and constant prices respectively in 1992-93. This fall has given a rise in secondary as well as tertiary (services) sectors.

TABLE 6

Key Indicators for Tertiary Sector

Item	Index 1980-81=100			Growth	
	1990-91	1991-92	1992-93	1991-92	1992-93
(1)	(2)	(3)	(4)	(5)	(6)
1. Gross trading income	185.2	183.7	191.6	—0.8	4.3
2. Railways					
2.1 passenger net Kms.	141.8	150.8	143.9	6.3	—4.6
2.2 freight tonne Kms.	153.1	162.1	162.9	5.9	0.5
3. Communication					
3.1 combined index of postal article and communication activity	182.6	195.1	215.3	6.8	10.4
4. Transport by other means					
4.1 number of buses in public sector	142.1	147.1	150.3	3.5	2.2
4.2 volume of cargo handled at major ports	190.3	195.1	204.3	2.5	4.7
4.3 volume of traffic carried (in air traffic)	151.4	151.3	149.5	—	—1.2
5. Index of aggregate deposits at the end of year in real terms	260.6	275.1	287.4	5.6	4.5
6. Index of net receipts of non-banking financial institutions in real terms	804.3	1220.8	1273.3	51.8	4.3

During the year 1992-93, the growth, in implicit prices of net domestic product is 9.5 per cent. The growth in the implicit prices for

TABLE 7

Per cent Share of Gross Domestic Product by Broad Sectors

Industry	At current prices			At 1980-81 prices	
	1980-81	1985-86	1992-93	1985-86	1992-93
(1)	(2)	(3)	(4)	(5)	(6)
1. Primary	39.6	35.7	34.0	36.3	32.3
2. Secondary	24.4	25.5	25.2	26.0	26.9
3. Transport including storage comm., trade, hotels and restaurants	16.7	19.3	20.6	17.6	18.3
4. Finance and real estate	8.8	8.5	8.2	9.4	10.9
5. Community and personal services	10.5	11.0	12.0	10.7	11.5

manufacture is highest (11.5 per cent) among all the sectors. This fact has also been supported by directly available index number of wholesale prices.

Table 8

Price Indices (1980-81 = 100)

Item			Growth	
	1991-92	1992-93	1991-92	1992-93
(1)	(2)	(3)	(4)	(5)
A. Derived from National Accounts (implicit)				
1. Net domestic product	356.9	281.4	14.8	9.5
2 Private final consumption expenditure	242.3	264.7	13.6	9.2
3. Gross fixed capital formation	278.8	304.5	16.5	9.2
3.1 construction	355.1	388.7	15.8	9.4
3.2 machinery & equipment	233.0	255.9	14.9	9.8
B. Directly Available				
4. Wholesale prices * (all commodities)	228.0	251.0	13.7	10.1
5. Consumer prices *				
5.1 agricultural labourers	242.5	272.4	19.3	12.3
5.2 industrial workers	269.3	295.0	13.5	9.5
5.3 urban non-manual employees	264.0	291.4	13.6	10.4

* Indices are available with base other than 1980-81. These have been converted to base 1980-81=100 by arithmetical conversion.

Consumption Expenditure, Saving and Capital Formation

In order to derive the GDP at market prices, the GDP at factor cost is adjusted by adding indirect taxes net of subsidies. As the various components of expenditure on gross domestic product, for example, consumption expenditure and capital formation, are normally measured at market prices, the discussion in the following paragraphs is in terms of market prices only.

Private Final Consumption Expenditure

Private final consumption expenditure (PFCE) in the domestic market at current prices works out to Rs. 427682 crores in 1992-93 as against Rs. 383835 crores in 1991-92. PFCE thus formed 60.6 per cent of GDP at market prices. At constant (1980-81) prices PFCE works out to Rs. 161573 crores in 1992-93 as against Rs. 158428 crores in 1991-92. The per capita expenditure in 1992-93 works out to Rs. 4905 at current prices and Rs. 1853, at constant (1980-81) prices as against Rs. 4484 and Rs. 1851 respectively in 1991-92. The expenditure on almost all items both at current and constant prices increased in 1992-93 as compared to the previous year. The shares of the various groups have remained almost the same during 1992-93. The overall impact of these changes on the pattern of private final consumption expenditure can be seen in terms of expenditure on durables, semi-durables, non-durables and services in Table 10. During the period 1980-81 to 1992-93, the share of expenditure in durable goods and services has increased.

Domestic Savings

Gross domestic saving (GDS) at current prices in 1992-93 amounted to Rs. 157186 crores as against Rs. 142479 crores in 1991-92, constituting 22.3 per cent of GDP at market prices as against 23.1 per cent in the previous year. Though there is an increase of 10.3 per cent in the GDS, the rate of saving has undergone a marginal fall of 0.8 per cent due to relatively higher growth (14.6 per cent) in the GDP at market prices. The fall in the rate of saving is mainly on account of household sector. The rise in absolute level of saving has been contributed by all the three institutional sectors of the economy. The saving of the household sector went up by 6.2 per cent from Rs. 115524 crores in 1991-92 to Rs. 122718 crores in 1992-93 and that of the private corporate sector by 20.2 per cent from Rs. 16215 crores in 1991-92 to Rs. 19490 crores in 1992-93. The saving of the public sector showed a steep rise of 39.5 per cent from Rs. 10740 crores in 1991-92 to Rs. 14978 crores in 1992-93. The increase in saving of the household sector is mainly due to sharp rise in net deposits and provident and pension funds and saving in physical assets. The steep rise in the public sector is due to decrease in the dissaving of the government administrative department from Rs. (—) 12860 crores in 1991-92 to Rs. (—) 12072 crores in 1992-93 and increase in the saving of both departmental and non-departmental enterprises. The net domestic saving has correspondingly gone up from Rs. 80204 crores in 1991-92 to Rs. 85617 crores in 1992-93 and constitutes 13.5 per cent of net domestic product at market prices as against 14.5 per cent in the previous year. As in the case of gross saving, the net saving of the household sector has gone up by 4.9 per cent from Rs. 92958 crores in 1991-92 to Rs. 97497 crores in 1992-93 and that of the private corporate sector by 18.8 per cent from Rs. 5306 crores in 1991-92 to Rs. 6304 crores in 1992-93. The net saving of the public sector remained almost at the level of 1991-92. The substantial increase in the gross saving of public sector was offset by the increase in the consumption of fixed capital from Rs. 28800 crores in 1991-92 to Rs. 33162 crores in 1992-93.

TABLE 9

Private Final Consumption Expenditure

Year	At current prices		At 1980-81prices		Growth at 1980-81 prices	
	Total (Rs. crores)	Per capita (Rs.)	Total (Rs. crores)	Per capita (Rs.)	Total	Per capita
(1)	(2)	(3)	(4)	(5)	(6)	(7)
1989-90	290072	3529	149738	1822	4.4	2.2
1990-91	331896	3956	155641	1855	3.9	1.8
1991-92	383835	4484	158428	1851	1.8	—0.2
1992-93	427682	4905	161573	1853	2.0	0.1

Capital Formation

Gross capital formation at current prices increased from Rs. 148715 crores in 1991-92 to Rs. 172908 crores in 1992-93 whereas at constant (1980-81) prices it increased from Rs. 49723 crores in 1991-92 to Rs. 58033 crores in 1992-93. The rate of gross capital formation at current prices also increased from 24.2 per cent in 1991-92 and 24.5 per cent in 1992-93. The rates of capital formation in 1991-92 and 1992-93 are higher than the corresponding rates of saving because of the positive net capital inflow from abroad which was Rs. 6236 crores in 1991-92 and Rs. 15722 crores in 1992-93. The net capital inflow from abroad for the two years forms 1.0 and 2.2 per cent of GDP at

TABLE 10

Private Final Consumption Expenditure by Type of Goods in the Domestic Market (at current prices)

(Rs. crores)

Year	Durable	Semi-durable	Non-durable	Services	Total
(1)	(2)	(3)	(4)	(5)	(6)
1980-81	1507 (1.5)	12779 (12.9)	67378 (67.9)	17628 (17.8)	99292 (100.0)
1985-86	3826 (2.2)	24203 (13.6)	116504 (65.5)	33225 (18.7)	177758 (100.0)
1990-91	8494 (2.6)	44716 (13.5)	211229 (63.6)	67457 (20.3)	331896 (100.0)
1991-92	8642 (2.3)	46077 (12.0)	249861 (65.1)	79255 (20.6)	383835 (100.0)
1992-93	9271 (2.2)	48287 (11.3)	278797 (65.2)	91327 (21.3)	427682 (100.0)

Note : figures in parenthesis show percentage to total.

market prices. The rate of gross capital formation at constant (1980-81) prices also increased from 20.6 per cent in 1991-92 to 23.0 per cent in 1992-93. The rate of net capital formation at current prices in 1992-93 was 16.0 per cent as compared to 15.6 per cent in 1991-92 and at constant (1980-81) prices, it was 14.8 per cent in 1992-93 as compared to 12.2 per cent in 1991-92.

Within the gross capital formation at current prices the fixed capital formation amounted to Rs. 150241 crores in 1992-93 as against Rs. 135260 crores in 1991-92, thus showing an increase of 11.1 per cent over 1991-92. All the three institutional sectors contributed to this increase. The fixed capital formation of the public sector at current prices increased by 6.0 per cent from Rs. 58749 crores in 1991-92 to Rs. 62257 crores in 1992-93; private corporate sector by 22.6 per cent from Rs. 25630 crores in 1991-92 to Rs. 31420 crores in 1992-93 and hold sector by 11.2 per cent from Rs. 50881 crores in 1991-92 to Rs. 56564 crores in 1992-93.

TABLE 11

Domestic Saving

(Rs. crores)

Item	1980-81	1985-86	1991-92	1992-93
(1)	(2)	(3)	(4)	(5)
1. Gross Domestic Saving	28786	49655	142479	157186
1.1 household sector	21848	35880	115524	122718
1.2 private corporate sector	2284	5318	16215	19490
1.3 public sector	4654	8457	10740	14978
2. Net Domestic Saving	16699	23418	80204	85617
2.1 household sector	16356	24962	92958	97497
2.2 private corporate sector	584	1387	5306	6304
2.3 public sector	–241	–2931	–18060	–18184
3. Net Capital Inflow	2094	6234	6236	15722
4. Gross Domestic Product at market prices	136013	262243	615655	705566
5. Gross Rate of Saving	21.2	18.9	23.1	22.3
5.1 household sector	16.1	13.7	18.8	17.4
5.2 private corporate sector	1.7	2.0	2.6	2.8
5.3 public sector	3.4	3.2	1.7	2.1

The change in stocks of inventories at current prices measured as additions to stocks, increased from Rs. 12475 crores in 1991-92 to Rs. 26037 crores in 1992-93. The increase was shared by all the three institutional sectors. The change in stocks of the public sector showed an increase from Rs. 3015 crores in 1991-92 to Rs. 10729 crores in 1992-93, the private corporate sector and the household sector also increased from Rs. 2270 crores and Rs. 7100 crores in 1991-92 to Rs. 6253 crores and Rs. 9055 crores in 1992-93, respectively.

Gross capital formation by industry of use (unadjusted for erros and omissions) at 1980-81 prices (Table 13) indicates a rise of about 20.1 per cent which was more pronounced in the manufacturing sector (35.2 per cent) and trade sector (148.9 per cent). In case of trade sector, the rise is primarily due to substantial rise in the level of inventories.

TABLE 12

Capital Formation

(Rs. crores)

Item	At current prices		At 1980-81 prices	
	1991-92	1992-93	1991-92	1992-93
(1)	(2)	(3)	(4)	(5)
1. Gross Capital Formation	147735	176278	49372	59140
1.1 gross fixed capital formation	135260	150241	48514	49342
1.1.1. public	58749	62257	20960	19953
1.1.2. private corporate	25630	31420	10793	12070
1.1.3. household	50881	56564	16761	17319
1.2 change in stocks	12475	26037	858	9798
1.2.1 public	3015	10729	— 611	5768
1.2.2. private corporate	2270	6253	1046	2604
1.2.3. household	7190	9055	423	1426
2. Errors and Omissions	980	— 3370	351	— 1107
3. Gross Capital Formation (adjusted)				
3.1 gross	148715	172908	49723	58033
3.2 net	86440	101339	26575	33658
4. Capital Formation as Percentage of Domestic Product at Market Prices				
4.1 gross	24.2	24.5	20.6	23.0
4.2 net	15.6	16.0	12.2	14.8

PUBLIC SECTOR

In the year 1992-93, the public sector contributed about 27 per cent in the GDP, 42 per cent in gross domestic capital formation and 9 per cent in domestic saving, the major share being from the non-departmental undertakings. Comparing to share in GDP, the data show a much higher share in capital formation and a lower share in saving. The public sector comprises of administrative departments, departmental enterprises and non-departmental enterprises. A large amount of capital formation in the administrative departments is either in the form of roads and bridges, or in the form of other assets which are used to generate essential services which are made available to the population free of cost or at a highly subsidised cost. In case of departmental enterprises also, the prices of the output are generally administered prices and not the market prices. However, in case of non-departmental enterprises, although there are no such conditions yet due to high capital costs and long gestation period, the share in income and saving generation is lower than share in expenditure on capital formation. A sizeable part of capital formation is financed from resources outside the public sector.

TABLE 13

Gross Capital Formation in Selected Industries

(at 1980-81 prices)

(Rs. cores)

Industry	1991-92	1992-93	Per cent change in 1992-93
1. Agriculture	4581	4567	— 0.3
2. Mining and Quarrying	2350	2830	20.4
3. Manufacturing	10055	13595	35.2
4. Trade	2262	5629	148.9
5. Total	44187	53086	20.1

Table 15 presents growth in gross domestic product at constant (1980-81) prices arising in the public and private sector. It can be seen that the pattern of growth of public sector is not similar to that of private sector, even when the agriculture sector, which is highly seasonal, is removed. The pattern is not the same even for the non-departmental enterprises which are purely commercial in nature. This is obvious because the nature, the problems and constraints faced by the private sector are different from those in the public sector. The activities of public sector are mainly concentrated in the sectors dealing with other services (education and medical), manufacturing and storage apart from total or near total coverage in electricity, gas and water supply, railways, communication, public administration and banking and insur-

TABLE 14

Performance of Public Sector at Current Prices

(percentage share in total economy)

Item	1980-81	1985-86	1991-92	1992-93
(1)	(2)	(3)	(4)	(5)
1. Gross Domestic Product	19.7	24.9	26.9	27.2
1.1 administrative departments	7.3	8.5	9.2	9.3
1.2 departmental enterprises	3.2	4.0	4.0	4.1
1.3 non-departmental enterprises	9.2	12.4	13.7	13.8
2. Gross Domestic Capital Formation	41.4	49.3	41.8	41.4
2.1 administrative departments	10.6	10.7	8.0	
2.2 departmental enterprises	11.4	10.9	8.0	
2.3 non-departmental enterprises	19.3	27.7	25.8	
3. Gross Domestic Saving	16.2	17.0	7.5	9.5
3.1 administrative departments	8.9	— 1.0	—9.0	—7.7
3.2 departmental enterprises	0.9	2.9	3.1	3.5
3.3 non-departmental enterprises	6.4	15.1	13.5	13.7

ance sectors. Any analysis at sectoral level is not meaningful because of uneven quality of basic data and differences in approach in computation of the GDP between these two sectors.

The share of public sector in gross domestic capital formation at current prices, which was 41.4 per cent in 1980-81, rose to 49.3 per cent in 1985-86 and thereafter declined again to 41.4 per cent in 1992-93. The decrease in the share of public sector in gross domestic capital formation has been due to decrease in the corresponding share of departmental and non-departmental enterprises in recent years. The share of public sector in gross domestic saving has declined from 16.2 per cent in 1980-81 to the level of 7 to 9 per cent in recent years. This is primarily due to negative saving in the administrative departments which is the result of increase in the interest components on public debt and subsidies besides rise in government consumption expenditure. However, in the year 1992-93, there has been a decrease in the negative saving in the administrative departments.

TABLE 15

Growth in Gross Domestic Product at 1980-81 Prices

(per cent)

Year	Total GDP	GDP — Public Sector				GDP — Private Sector		
		Total	Admn.	DGU	NDCU	Total	Agrl.	Non-Agrl
1981-82	6.1	3.6	3.3	—	5.2	6.7	6.4	6.9
1982-83	3.1	10.3	10.7	5.3	11.6	1.4	—1.4	3.4
1983-84	8.2	6.5	3.7	3.5	9.6	8.6	11.8	6.4
1984-85	3.8	8.2	8.6	7.9	8.0	2.7	—0.2	4.9
1985-86	4.1	9.4	9.6	12.2	8.5	2.6	0.3	4.3
1986-87	4.3	9.6	6.6	1.2	14.4	2.8	—1.8	5.8
1987-88	4.3	7.1	10.1	8.8	4.4	3.5	0.5	5.3
1988-89	10.7	8.9	7.7	1.7	11.9	11.2	18.0	7.2
1989-90	6.9	8.8	10.4	2.4	9.4	6.3	1.1	9.7
1990-91	4.9	3.5	3.5	2.3	3.7	5.3	4.2	6.0
1991-92	1.1	9.1	1.8	7.2	14.8	—1.4	—2.8	—0.6
1992-93	4.0	4.3	5.3	3.0	3.9	3.9	5.3	3.1

Table 16 presents the purpose-wise distribution of government expenditure at current prices for the years 1980-81, 1985-86 and 1991-92. There has been a six-fold increase in the current expenditure as compared to only three-fold increase in capital expenditure during the last twelve years. Another fact which emerges is that the attention of government has been relatively more on social services like health, education and general administration than on the economic services.

LONG TERM TRENDS

A look on the long-term series since 1950-51 to 1992-93 has been summarised in the form of growth rates and other rates (*e.g.* rate of capital formation etc.) in Table 17. The per capita income at constant (1980-81) prices registered an annual average growth of 1.7 per cent per annum in the total period 1950-51 to 1992-93. The national income in the same period grew at an average rate of 3.9 per cent per annum. The highest level of growth which is of the order of 5.9 per cent has been achieved in the Seventh Plan period. Against this scenario, expenditure aggregates like private final consumption expenditure, Government final consumption expenditure and gross domestic capital

TABLE 16

Purpose Classification of Expenditure of Administrative Departments

(at current prices) (Rs. crores)

Purpose	1980-81		1985-86		1991-92	
	current exp.	capital exp.	current exp.	capital exp.	current exp.	capital exp.
(1)	(2)	(3)	(4)	(5)	(6)	(7)
1. General public services	2976	378	6472	1233	16659	2674
2. Defence	3473	16	8687	25	18931	168
3. Education	3744	115	8525	287	21416	665
3.1 administration, regulation & research	60	1	222	2	733	13
3.2 schools, universities & institutions including subsidiary services	3634	114	8303	285	20683	652
4. Health	845	98	2007	218	4505	410
4.1 administration, regulation & research	107	2	280	6	536	9
4.2 hospitals, clinics & individual health services	738	96	1727	212	3969	401
5. Social security and welfare services	599	157	1714	294	5008	430
6. Housing and other community amenities	405	840	978	2591	3178	4519
7. Cultural, recreational and religious services	160	127	313	191	728	218
8. Economic services	5378	8392	12607	14510	33086	21120
8.1 general administration, regulation & research	333	113	1040	79	1718	191
8.2 agriculture, forestry, fishing & hunting	2891	1115	5769	1385	14215	4281
8.3 mining, manufacturing & construction	578	3197	3269	5420	5841	3919
8.4 electricity, gas, steam and water	299	2285	449	4741	5638	8032
8.5 atomic energy	87	40	250	120	648	130
8.6 transport and communication	557	1420	974	2400	2392	4100
8.7 other economic services	633	222	856	365	2634	467
9. Other services	272	99	621	156	350	55
10. Total	17852	10222	41924	19505	103861	30259

Table 17 (a)

Annual Average Growth Rate

Plan Period		GNP at factor cost		NNP at factor cost		Per capita NNP at factor cost	
		at current prices	at 1980-81 prices	at current prices	at 1980-81 prices	at current prices	at 1980-81 prices
(1)		(2)	(3)	(4)	(5)	(6)	(7)
First Plan	1951-56	1.8	3.7	1.5	3.6	—0.3	1.8
Second Plan	1956-61	9.5	4.2	9.4	4.0	7.2	2.0
Third Plan	1961-66	9.6	2.7	9.5	2.4	7.1	0.2
Annual Plans	1966-69	12.2	3.9	12.2	3.7	9.8	1.5
Fourth Plan	1969-74	11.1	3.4	11.0	3.3	8.5	1.0
Fifth Plan	1974-79	10.7	5.0	10.3	5.0	7.9	2.7
Annual Plan	1979-80	9.5	—4.9	8.2	—6.0	5.6	—8.2
Sixth Plan	1980-85	15.1	5.5	15.0	5.4	12.5	3.2
Seventh Plan	1985-90	14.3	5.9	14.2	5.9	11.7	3.6
Annual Plan	1990-91	16.2	4.7	16.4	4.6	14.0	2.5
Annual Plan	1991-92	15.4	0.6	14.7	—0.1	12.5	—2.1
Annual Plan	1992-93	14.1	4.3	14.0	4.2	11.9	2.2
Average	1951-93	10.8	4.0	10.6	3.9	8.3	1.7

formation have registered growth rates of 4.6, 8.3 and 11.7 per cent respectively at 1980-81 prices in the Seventh Plan. It can be seen from the Table 17 (c) that the share of private consumption expenditure has come down from 81.5 per cent during the First Plan period to around 64 per cent in the recent years.

This reduction in the share of private consumption expenditure occurred alongwith a rise in gross domestic capital formation whose share has increased from 13.5 per cent during First Plan to about 23 per cent in 1992-93. However, Government final consumption expenditure has also doubled in the same period starting from 5.1 per cent in the First Plan period. Another striking feature of the economy in this long period is that the capital formation was always more than the domestic saving except for the Fifth Five Year Plan period, when the saving was marginally higher than the domestic capital formation.

TABLE 17 (b)

Growth Rates of Important Expenditure Aggregates

Plan Period		PFCE in domestic market		GFCE		GDCF		Gross savings
		at current prices	at 1980-81 prices	at current prices	at 1980-81 prices	at current prices	at 1980-81 prices	at current prices
First Plan	1951-56	—	3.7	5.1	1.2	12.5	9.5	9.5
Second Plan	1956-61	—	3.6	9.8	6.1	12.7	7.5	8.5
Third Plan	1961-66	8.8	2.7	16.6	13.0	11.9	6.8	13.1
Annual Plans	1966-69	11.9	3.6	10.2	2.8	5.9	—3.1	7.7
Fourth Plan	1969-74	10.6	2.5	11.0	5.8	19.1	9.7	20.4
Fifth Plan	1974-79	10.3	4.5	13.6	4.8	15.7	6.5	16.2
Annual Plan	1979-80	8.6	—2.8	14.8	6.1	4.2	—10.6	2.3
Sixth Plan	1980-85	14.8	5.5	16.9	6.5	12.6	1.9	11.4
Seventh Plan	1985-90	12.4	4.6	17.4	8.3	21.9	11.7	21.1
Annual Plan	1990-91	14.4	3.9	14.0	3.4	19.6	11.2	16.4
Annual Plan	1991-92	15.6	1.8	12.4	—0.4	2.0	—15.8	11.7
Annual Plan	1992-93	11.4	2.0	13.2	3.3	16.3	16.7	10.3
Average	1951-93	11.6*	3.6	12.8	5.9	14.1	6.2	13.5

* Relates to period 1961—93.

FACTOR INCOMES

Tables 18 (a), 18 (b) and 18 (c) present the factor incomes by broad industry groups and by organised and unorganised sectors. From table 18 (b), it is evident that the share of organised sector in the toal NVA, has been rising from 30.0 per cent in 1980-81 to 35 7 per cent in 1991-92. Consequently, the share of unorganised sector declined during this period from 70.0 per cent to 64.3 per cent. The same trend is also evident in both the factor incomes, namely, the compensation of employees and the operating surplus/mixed income. Among the broad industry groups except agriculture and allied activities, the decline in unorganised sector operating surplus/mixed income is prominent. On the other hand, in the agriculture, forestry and fishing sectors, the contribution of unorganised sector has increased since 1980-81 from 95.2 per cent to 96.6 per cent.

At the all-India level, the compensation of employees, which accounted for 36.8 per cent in the NVA in 1980-81, now account for 38.2 per cent in 1991-92. While the compensation of employees account for about 50 per cent in the secondary sector, its proportion is quite low in the primary sector.

TABLE 17 (c)

Share of Aggregates in GDP at Market Prices

Plan Period		PFCE in domestic market		GFCE		GDCF		Gross savings
		at current prices	at 1980-81 prices	at current prices	at 1980-81 prices	at current prices	at 1980-81 prices	at current prices
First Plan	1951-56	—	81.5	6.0	5.1	10.7	13.5	10.3
Second Plan	1956-61	—	77.7	6.6	5.2	14.5	17.7	11.7
Third Plan	1961-66	79.1	74.0	8.1	6.9	15.4	18.2	13.2
Annual Plans	1966-69	79.9	74.7	8.3	7.9	15.9	19.1	13.7
Fourth Plan	1969-74	75.7	71.3	8.9	8.7	16.9	19.4	16.1
Fifth Plan	1974-79	73.1	69.6	9.2	8.6	19.9	20.7	20.4
Annual Plan	1979-80	71.4	71.6	9.8	9.7	22.1	22.3	21.6
Sixth Plan	1980-85	71.1	71.1	10.0	9.8	21.1	20.6	19.6
Seventh Plan	1985-90	66.4	68.7	11.8	11.2	23.7	21.5	21.2
Annual Plan	1990-91	62.4	65.2	11.6	10.9	27.4	24.8	24.0
Annual Plan	1991-92	62.3	65.8	11.3	10.8	24.2	20.6	23.1
Annual Plan	1992-93	60.6	64.1	11.1	10.6	24.5	23.0	22.3
Average	1951-93	72.6*	72.9	8.9	8.2	18.0	19.2	16.5

* Relates to period 1961—93.

TABLE 18 (a)

Factor Incomes in Broad Industry Groups

(Rs. crores)

Industry		1980-81			1985-86			1991-92		
		orga-nised	unorga-nised	total	orga-nised	unorga-nised	total	orga-nised	unorga-nised	total
a. Agriculture, forestry and fishing	1. CE	939	8788	9727	1959	13691	15650	2901	30099	33000
	2. OS/MI	1170	33194	34364	1667	54971	56638	2812	129891	132703
	3. NDP	2109	41982	44091	3626	68662	72288	5713	159990	165703
b. Ming., manfg. ele. and constrn.	1. CE	10092	3212	13304	20694	6463	27157	45432	17120	62552
	2. OS/MI	5150	8401	13551	13691	14122	27813	31091	31407	62498
	3. NDP	15242	11613	26855	34385	20585	54970	765223	48527	125050
c. Services	1. CF	13519	4047	17566	28328	8702	37030	70616	20764	91379
	2. OS/MI	2203	19624	21827	6037	37237	43274	21987	85158	107145
	3. NDP	15722	23671	39393	34365	45939	80304	92602	105922	198524
d. Total	1. CE	24550	16047	40597	50981	28856	79837	118948	67983	186931
	2. OS/MI	8523	61219	69742	21395	106330	127725	55890	246456	302348
	3. NDP	33073	77266	110339	72376	135186	207562	174838	314439	489277

TABLE 18 (b)

Share of Factor Incomes by Organised and Unorganised Sectors

Industry		1980-81			1985-86			1991-92		
		organised	unorganised	total	organised	unorganised	total	organised	unorganised	total
a. agriculture, forestry & fishing	1. CE	9.7	90.3	100.0	12.5	87.5	100.0	8.8	91.2	100.0
	2. OS/MI	3.4	96.6	100.0	2.9	97.1	100.0	2.1	97.9	100.0
	3. NDP	4.8	95.2	100.0	5.0	95.0	100.0	3.4	96.6	100.0
b. ming, manfg. elec. and constrn.	1. CE	75.8	24.1	100.0	76.2	23.8	100.0	72.6	27.4	100.0
	2. OS/MI	38.1	62.0	100.0	49.2	50.8	100.0	49.7	50.3	100.0
	3. NDP	56.8	43.2	100.0	62.6	37.4	100.0	61.2	38.8	100.0
c. services	1. CE	77.1	23.0	100.0	76.5	23.5	100.0	77.3	22.7	100.0
	2. OS/MI	10.1	89.9	100.0	14.0	86.0	100.0	20.5	79.5	100.0
	3. NDP	39.9	60.1	100.0	42.8	57.2	100.0	46.6	53.4	100.0
d. total	1. CE	60.5	39.5	100.0	63.9	36.1	100.0	63.6	36.4	100.0
	2. OS/MI	12.2	87.8	100.0	16.8	83.2	100.0	18.5	81.5	100.0
	3. NDP	30.0	70.0	100.0	34.9	65.1	100.0	35.7	64.3	100.0

TABLE 18 (c)

Distribution of Factors Incomes by Broad Industry Groups in Organised and Unorganised Sectors

Industry		1980-81			1985-86			1991-92		
		organised	unorganised	total	organised	unorganised	total	organised	unorganised	total
a. Agriculture, forestry and fishing	1. CE	2.8	11.4	8.8	2.7	10.1	7.5	1.7	9.6	6.7
	2. OS/MI	3.5	43.0	31.1	2.3	40.7	27.3	1.6	41.3	27.1
	3. NDP	6.4	54.3	40.0	5.0	50.8	34.8	3.3	50.9	33.9
b. Ming., manfg. elec. and constrn.	1. CE	30.5	4.2	12.1	28.6	4.8	13.1	26.0	5.4	12.8
	2. OS/MI	15.6	10.9	12.3	18.9	10.4	13.4	17.8	10.0	12.8
	3. NDP	46.1	15.0	24.3	47.5	15.2	26.5	43.8	15.4	25.6
c. Services	1. CE	40.9	5.2	15.8	39.1	6.4	17.8	40.4	6.6	18.7
	2. OS/MI	6.7	25.4	19.8	8.3	27.5	20.8	12.6	27.1	21.9
	3. NDP	47.5	30.6	35.7	47.5	34.0	38.7	53.0	33.7	40.6
d. Total	1. CE	74.2	20.8	36.8	70.4	21.3	38.5	68.0	21.6	38.2
	2. OS/MI	25.8	79.2	63.2	29.6	78.7	61.5	32.0	78.4	61.8
	3. NDP	100.0	100.0	100.0	100.0	100.0	100.0	100.0	100.0	100.0

TABLE 18 (d)

Share of Factor Incomes Within Each Broad Industry Group

Industry		1980-81			1985-86			1991-92		
		organised	unorganised	total	organised	unorganised	total	organised	unorganised	total
a. Agriculture, forestry and fishing	1. CE	44.5	20.9	22.1	54.0	19.9	21.6	50.8	18.8	19.9
	2. OS/MI	55.5	79.1	77.9	46.0	80.1	78.4	49.2	81.2	80.1
	3. NDP	100.0	100.0	100.0	100.0	100.0	100.0	100.0	100.0	100.0
b. Mining., manfg. electricity and constrn.	1. CE	66.2	27.7	49.6	60.2	31.4	49.4	59.4	35.3	50.0
	2. OS/MI	33.8	72.3	50.4	39.8	68.6	50.6	40.6	64.7	50.0
	3. NDP	100.0	100.0	100.0	100.0	100.0	100.0	100.0	100.0	100.0
c. Sevices	1. CE	86.0	17.1	44.5	82.4	18.9	46.1	76.3	19.6	46.0
	2. OS/MI	14.0	82.9	55.5	17.6	81.1	53.9	23.7	80.4	54.0
	3. NDP	100.0	100.0	100.0	100.0	100.0	100.0	100.0	100.0	100.0
d. Total	1. CE	74.2	20.8	36.8	70.4	21.3	38.5	68.0	21.6	38.2
	2. OS/MI	25.8	79.2	63.2	29.6	78.7	61.5	32.0	78.4	61.8
	3. NDP	100.0	100.0	100.0	100.0	100.0	100.0	100.0	100.0	100.0

5

STRUCTURAL ADJUSTMENT REFORM AND ECONOMIC DEVELOPMENT IN THIRD WORLD COUNTRIES : AN ANALYSIS

PROF. G. NANCHARAIAH
University of Hyderabad

Introduction

The 1973 oil shock and the fall of gold-exchange standard put a tremendous burden on the balance of payments position of third world countries. And industrial nations also suffered from prolonged recession, on account of 1973 oil shock, leading to a decline in the supply of capital in the international market. As a result the interest rates had risen in the international market which in turn raised the cost of borrowing to the underdeveloped countries. Since exchange rates were floating, there was continuous currency depreciation in underdeveloped countries since 1973 onwards and it caused increased burden of debt and debt servicing to them. There was another oil shock in 1979. This accentuated the problem of balance of payments and the burden of debt and debt servicing although the rise in oil prices in 1979 was less compared to that of 1973. Loan default was the case with many developing countries in early eighties while economic growth was crippled in industrial nations due to demand constraint.[1] Under these circumstances the Brettonwood Institutions — International Monetary Fund (IMF) and World Bank (IBRD) — initiated a strategy of development which was popularly known as structural adjustment reform as a cure to the balance of payments and growth problems of third world countries in particular and recession problems of industrial nations in general. Its major objective was to promote export-led growth in developing economies through market mechanism. Many third world countries adopted this structural adjustment reform in 1980s.[2]

The important instruments of structural adjustment reform are devaluation, import liberalisation, removal of subsidies and reducing fiscal deficit, privatisation of public enterprises and the use of market forces to guide production and allocation decisions. Thus structural adjustment reform emphasises market mechanism as strategy of development rather than the state intervention and promotes export-led growth. However, this paper confines to the analysis of structural adjustment reform with reference to devaluation and import liberalisation.

This paper attempts (1) to analyse theoretical implications of structural adjustment reform with special reference to devaluation and import liberalisation for economic development, and (2) to study the impact of economic liberalisation on Indian economy since 1966 devaluation and also to examine the pre-conditions required and the role of the State for the success of structural adjustment reform in the light of the experience of some of the East-Asian nations.

Devaluation

The standard neo-classical theory states that devaluation leads to desired structural changes in the economy and improvement in the balance of payments through its initial effect. Devaluation makes the exports relatively cheaper in terms of foreign price and thus improves the international competitiveness while imports become dearer in terms of domestic currency. Under the assumption of elastic demand for exports and imports, devaluation is expected to improve export performance and contain imports encouraging import competing industry (substitution effect) and thus leading to improvement in the balance of payments. In this process if importables and exportables are clubbed under a single category of foreign goods while others under domestic goods, since there is an increase in the price of foreign goods relative to domestic goods in the post-devaluation period, the neo-classical theory expects the re-allocation of resources from the production of domestic goods to foreign goods leading to higher rates of economic growth and improvement in the balance of payments. This is what is called structural adjustment in the terminology of I.M.F. Thus neo-classicals view devaluation, which works through relative price change, as superior to other non-price methods of different controls on imports and incentives to exports which require Government intervention, in improving the balance of payments.

However, structuralists argued that devaluation leads to redistribution of income. The devaluation leads to rise in general prices due to rise in the prices of imports which are also used as inputs in industrial production. This leads to redistribution of income in favour of entrepreneurial and business class from working class as the wages of the workers could not cope with the rising prices, particularly in unorganised sectors of the economy.[3] Structuralists also argued that when the real wages go down, real consumption also goes down. This may in turn lead to decline in the real investment. Thus devaluation could be contractionary rather than expansionary. Then devaluation cannot lead to increase in economic growth. Moreover devaluation increases debt burden and associated debt servicing burden. The effectiveness of devaluation is limited in the case of underdeveloped economies due to following reasons also. Many of the third world countries are still primary exporting countries whose foreign demand is relatively inelastic. The domestic demand for imports is also relatively inelastic. In such a case devaluation cannot improve the balance of payments. Moreover if demand for its exports is very less elastic, the terms of trade of devaluing country may so deteriorate that the increase in the export revenue due to increased sales of exports will be more than offset by the loss of revenue due to decline in the unit price of the exports.

Most of the underdeveloped economies are competing with each other in the international market for certain products. As a result there is a problem of competitive devaluation. Moreover industrial nations' markets are increasingly becoming protective markets and as a result, underdeveloped countries access to these markets is limited.[4] Above all, in case of countries like India, where domestic market is very large, the producers may find it more profitable to sell their commodities in the domestic market, when domestic prices rise due to devaluation, rather than exporting.

Import Liberalisation

Import liberalisation has been justified on the following theoretical grounds. "Easy access to imports is necessary both to improve access of exporters to imported inputs and to reduce the unduly high profitability of domestic production in sectors protected by import licensing, which draws resources away from export activity.[5] It is also argued that since the beginning of first Five Year Plan in the name of import substitution lot of protection has been given to the domestic producers at the cost of consumers in India. But domestic capitalists could not improve their efficiency to the level of international standards. Hence there is a need of exposing these domestic producers to external competition. In this regard, it is to be noted that although there is a need of liberalising essential imports required for achieving targeted GNP growth rate, the liberalisation of all kinds of consumer goods will have some harmful effects. It may widen the trade gap. Another negative effect would be on the domestic industry. In the process of high degree of competition, domestic industry suffers and shrinks. As a result employment opportunities would be drastically reduced. In course of time domestic productive forces may be ruined and for everything we have to depend on external sources. Therefore there is an immediate need to contain non-essential imports.

At global level about 76 countries mostly third world countries including some former socialist countries exposed to structural adjustment reforms and received 258 loans, valued at $ 41 billion during 1980—91 subject to the conditionalities of carrying out market-oriented reform in their respective economies. The 1992 World Development Report* indicated that out of 78 middle and low income countries only 12 countries improved GDP growth in the 1980s compared to 1965—1980, 65 countries registered decline in their growth rates in 1965—1991. When we take 19 countries which exposed to structural adjustment intensively, only 5 out of 19 countries registered higher growth and also registered increase in domestic investment while 11 countries registered negative growth rate on investment. Export growth improved only in 7 countries out of 19 countries compared to 1965—1990.[6] Thus the economic growth of a few countries improved while the many other countries experienced deterioration in their economic growth after the structural adjustment reform.

Economic Liberalisation and Indian Economy

India initiated economic liberalisation from mid-sixties and

**World Development Report*, 1992, pp. 218-252.

increased it to some extent in 80s and intensified further since 1991 onwards. On June 6, 1966 Indian rupee was devalued by 57.5 per cent in terms of U.S. dollar.[7] In 1966-67 there was 11 per cent improvement in the balance of payments which was mostly due to decline in imports. The inflation rate was 12 per cent in 1965-66 and rose to 15 per cent in 1967-68. As a matter of fact, total exports declined due to fall in agricultural exports, while there was some improvement in the manufacturing exports. Of course this fall in agricultural exports was attributed to drought conditions prevailing in the country. However, the improvement in the balance of payments was attributed to devaluation due to its effect on imports by Jagdish Bhagawati and T.N. Srinivasan.[8] Afterwards imports were rising continuoulsy at higher rate than exports. The trade balance which stood at — 475.2 crore in 1960-61 fell to — 421.6 crore in 1970-71 and rose to — 5967.2 crores in 1980-81 and further rose in 1989-90 to — 12413.4 crores.[9] The value of the rupee was depreciating continuously during 1980—91 except in the years 1981 and 1983. This is evident from trends in nominal exchange rates, nominal effective exchange rates and real effective exchange rates during 1980—91 (Table 1, p. 82). Despite this depreciation, trade gap remains to be about 3 per cent on average in terms of GDP during this period although there was some increase in exports during 1987—90.

In July 1991 Indian rupee was devalued again by about 18 per cent in terms of U.S. dollar and pound sterling. If we look at balance of payments after July 1991, we find a decline in trade gap from Rs. 10,640 crores in 1990-91 to Rs. 3,835 crores in 1991-92.[10] This improvement in balance of payments was mostly due to compression of imports during 1991-92. But it again rose to about Rs. 10,000 crores in 1992-93, mostly due to liberalisation of imports.[11] During 1992-93 imports have been liberalised to a great extent. Import duties have been reduced in stages with the maximum duty lowered to 150 per cent in July 1991, 110 per cent in February 1992 and 85 per cent in February 1993. Duties on capital goods have been reduced to levels ranging between 25 per cent and 35 per cent for many categories.[12] Inflation rate has risen to the level of 17 per cent in August 1991. However, it fell down to 7 per cent by the end of 1992-93. GNP declined to 1.2 per cent in 1991-92 and recovered to 4 per cent in 1992-93.[13]

During 1959-60 to 1985-86 there is a strong rising trend in capital intensity, weaker rising trend in labour productivity and a secular decline in capital productivity. The rate of growth of labour productivity in manufacturing was 2.2 per cent per annum while capital per unit of labour increased at the rate of 4.9 per cent and capital productivity declined at the rate of 2.5 per cent per annum.[14] At the same time there was an increase in the labour productivity and total productivity in manufacturing sector. But for manufacturing sector as a whole employment registered growth rate of — 0.7 per cent per annum in the first half of the eighties. Of course real wages increased.[15] It is also to be noted that the liberalisation process was intensified from later part of 1970s. This clearly indicates that the method of production in industrial sector has become capital-intensive during the period of liberalisation of external sector and if it becomes more and more capital -intensive, its employment potential drastically declines which is detrimental to the economic growth. The employment potential would also be adversely affected due to privatisation of public sector units.

The share of public sector in total GDP (1989-90) was less than 30 per cent. This means that Indian economy is predominantly private. The share of public sector in total investment hovers around 45 per cent which means that the public sector is critical for growth.[16] The gross capital formation in the republic sector has increased from 2.8 per cent in 1950-51 to 11.5 per cent in 1984-85. In the Seventh Plan the average rate of capital formation in the public sector fluctuated around this level.[17]

The share of public sector in employment is very significant. In 1991, 18.97 (Mn) were employed in public sector while 7.85 (Mn) were employed in private sector. That is, the share of public sector in employment was 70.7 per cent while private sector's share was 29.3 per cent.[18] Public sector plays an important role in achieving import substitution in major sectors since the First Five Year Plan. In physical terms import substitution was achieved in good measure. It should also be noted that in many developing countries like Burma, Venezuela and Zambia the public sector share in total investment is more than 50 per cent of the total. Given the stage and socio-economic structure of Indian economy, the importance of public sector should not be undermined. Private sector may not accept the responsibility of the employment requirement.

State intervention and regulation of markets

In this part an attempt is made to analyse the preconditions necessary for the economic liberalisation and a case is made that, given the socio-economic structure in India, higher degree of state intervention is essential while opening the economy to market forces to some degree. As a supporting evidence, I present the role played by the state to attain higher growth rates in some of the East Asian countries – South Korea and Taiwan (Province of China).

In South Korea after liberation there were two important institutional changes in agriculture and industry which had significant long term implications for the country's economic development.[19] Land reform was initiated in 1948. It set a limit of 3 hectares on the ownership and virtually abolished tenancy. The landlord's land was virtually confiscated and redistributed. This reform had reduced the social and political tensions in the countryside. This also lead to increase in agricultural production and more even distribution of income and wealth. Educational reform laid emphasis on improving primary, secondary and technical education. In 1980 the rate of literacy of the labour force was 100 per cent. Educational reform laid foundations for the creation of an educated and skilled labour force essential for the success of any industrial policy.

Korea also adopted import substitution policy during 1950—60. It also used all kinds of restrictive measures to give protection to its industry during this period. From 1960 onwards it shifted to outward-looking strategy with labour intensive technology. From 1961 onwards Korea followed a strategy of development with the objective of rapid growth through planned industrialisation. Strong and stable government during 1963—1979 was highly responsible to implement plan projects and to achieve the targeted results. Regarding the management of labour, the government exercised tight-control over their activities, although labour organisations were allowed to exist, particularly in export promotion industries. But heritage of confucian culture contributed more to the discipline of labour. Government controlled agricultural and many industrial prices.

During 1960 and 1978 Won was devalued on several occasions and imports were regulated through non-price methods also.[19] GNP rose from less than 10 per cent in 1961 to 17 per cent in 1978. The share of manufacturers in employment rose from 8 per cent in 1959-60 to 22 per cent in 1977-78. It may be noted that both public sector and private sector contributed to the increased investment during the phase of high growth.

As far as income distribution is concerned, Korea continues to enjoy greater equality of income and of land ownership in agriculture than that found in most non-socialist developing countries.

Thus the success of South Korea with outward looking strategy is due to state intervention which could bring necessary internal reform and regulate markets and also due to confucian culture. This is also true in the case of Taiwan (Province of China). Land reform also had a very positive impact on employment in Taiwan. After reform the number of people involved in agriculture increased rapidly from 400,000 to about two million between 1952 and 1968. There was substantial increase in output too. In addition to redistributing assets simultaneously investment was made in health, education and skills of their people. Labour productivity has been increasing at an annual rate of 10 per cent or more and half of this has been attributed to investment in education and technical skills.[20]

Now let us look at India's Socio-economic Structure

The percentage of people below the poverty line was estimated by the Planning Commission at 29.9 per cent at all India level in 1987-88. About 65 per cent of the workforce depends on agriculture and its allied sectors and more than 70 per cent of the total population live in rural areas. As per 1980-81 agricultural census about 75 per cent of the operational holdings are marginal and small accounting for about only 26 per cent of the total area under cultivation while top 11 per cent of the total holdings account for more than 52 per cent of total area under cultivation. The distribution of land remains to be skewed despite land reforms. This is mostly responsible for social tensions in rural India.[21] In addition to economic inequalities Indian society is characterised by social inequalities, which exists in the rural areas to some extent due to caste.[22] This also crippled the development of working forces. Moreover 48 per cent of the total population is illiterate as per 1991 census.

Under these circumstances, in the light of the experience of South Korea and Taiwan also it becomes obvious that state has to play a crucial role and industrial strategy of development must be labour-intensive one in case of India. Land reform and educational reform are the preconditions even for the success of economic liberalisation.

Conclusions

The following conclusions can be drawn from the above analysis. The liberalisation of external sector started with 1966 devaluation and it was further liberalised from late 1970s onwards. During this period of liberalisation there was no significant improvement in exports while imports were raising. Trade gap was about 3 per cent in terms of GDP on average during this period. Further liberalisation of imports in 1992 led to worsening of balance of payments. Devaluation cannot be a permanent solution to external problems, although it could improve temporarily balance of payments by containing the imports, as it leads to rising prices and redistribution of income in favour of rich. During the period of liberalisation industrial output became more capital-intensive and lead to decline in the rate of employment. Hence industrial strategy should be labour-intensive. The importance of public sector should not be undermined in the process of economic development. In case of South Korea, and Taiwan which adopted outward looking strategy of development, state played a strategic role in establishing egalitarian society and in regulating market forces. In India also, given the stage and structure of the economy, state has to play crucial role in bringing necessary institutional reform and regulating market forces.

The available empirical evidence at global level also indicates that structural adjustment reform cannot be a unique strategy of development for all the third world countries. The strategy of development has to be altered according to existing socio-economic and political conditions of a particular country.

TABLE 1

Nominal and Real Exchange Rate of Rupee

	Nominal Exchange Rate		Nominal Effective Exchange Rate Index*		Real Effective Exchange Rate Index*	
	Exchange Rate (Rs./$)	Depreciation (%)	Index	Depreciation	Index	Depreciation
1980	7.86		100.00	—2.6	100.00	
1981	8.66	—9.19	97.37	—2.6	100.90	0.9
1982	9.46	—8.42	95.80	—1.6	97.82	—3.1
1983	10.10	—6.38	92.87	—3.1	101.00	3.3
1984	11.36	—11.12	86.46	—6.9	99.48	—1.5
1985	12.37	—8.13	81.20	—6.1	97.96	—1.5
1986	12.61	—1.92	69.46	—14.5	90.94	—7.2
1987	12.96	—2.71	62.29	—10.3	85.54	—5.9
1988	13.92	—6.86	55.86	—10.3	81.36	—4.9
1989	16.23	—14.23	49.62	—11.2	74.69	—8.2
1990	17.50	—7.28	43.83	—11.7		
1991	22.74	—23.05				

* This index has been compiled by IFMR in a study sponsored by Exim Bank. The nominal effective exchange rates are export weighted geometric averages of the exchange rates of the rupee against 18 principal exports partners of India, with 1980 = 100. The weights are the shares of each country in the total exports of India to the 18 countries during the five years 1982-83 to 1986-87. The real effective exchange rates are the nominal effective exchange rates deflated by the ratio of wholesale prices in 18 major trade partners. The weights used in calculating the nominal indices are the ones used in calculating the weighted prices. Since exchange rates are expressed as foreign currency units per Rs. 100, a rise (fall) in the index indicates appreciation (depreciation) of the rupee.

(This table is reproduced from working paper of Export-Import Bank, "India : Promotion of international competitiveness and exports of manufactured goods", May 1992, Bombay).

REFERENCES

1. Krishna Kumar, T., "Fund-Bank Policies of Stabilisation and Structural Adjustment : A Global and Historical Perspective", *Economic and Political Weekly*, Vol. XXVIII, No. 17, April 24, 1993, p. 818.
2. Rehman, Sobhan, "Rethinking the Market Reform Paradigm", *Economic and Political Weekly*, Vol. XXVII, No. 30, July 25, 1992, p. E-66.
3. Alexander, S.S., "Effects of Devaluation on a Trade Balance", *IMF Saff Papers* 11, April 1952, p. 273.
4. Sarkar, P., "Rupee Depreciation and India's External Trade and Payments Since 1971", *Economic and Political Weekly*, Vol. XXVII, Nos. 24 and 25 July 13—20, 1992, p. 1265.
5. Government of India, Discussion Paper "Economic Reforms – Two Years After and Task Ahead", *Southern Economist*, August 1, 1993, p. 28.
6. Rehman, Sobhan, *op. cit.*, pp. PE-66-72.
7. Sen, Pronab, "The 1966 Devaluation in India : A Reappraisal", *Economic and Political Weekly*, Vol. XXI, No. 30, July 26, 1986, p. 1322.
8. Bhagwati, J.N. and Srinivasan, T.N., *Foreign Trade Regimes and Economic Development*, National Bureau of Economic Research, New York, 1975, p. 127.
9. Govt. of India, *Economic Survey* 1992-93, p. s-76.
10. "Statistics", *Economic and Political Weekly*, Vol. XXVIII, Nos. 1 and 2, January 2-9, 1993, p. 10.
11. *Ibid.*, *Economics and Political Weekly*, Vol. XXVIII, Nos. 29 and 30, July 17-24, 1993, p. 1486.
12. Govt. of India, Discussion Paper, *op. cit.*, p. 23.
13. *Ibid.*, p. 21.
14. Ahluwalia, I.J., *Productivity and Growth in Indian Manufacturing*, Oxford University Press, Delhi, 1991, pp. 50-51.
15. *Ibid.*, p. 193.
16. Raipuria, Kalyan, Rajesh Mehta, "Role of Public and Private Sectors in India's Development", *EPW*, Vol. XXVI, Nos. 31 and 32, August 3-10, 1991., p. 1973.
17. Ahluwalia I.J., *op. cit.*, p. 15.
18. Tata Service Limited, Department of Economics and Statistics, *Statistical Outline of India, 1992-93*, p. 133.
19. The information relating to South Korea has been taken from Eprime Eshang, "Successful Manipulation of Market Forces : Case of South Korea, 1961—78.", *EPW*, Vol. XXVI, Nos. 11 and 12, Annual Number 1991, pp. 629-643.
20. United Nations Development Programme, *Human Development Report, 1993*, Oxford University Press, Delhi, p. 38.
21. Parthasarathy, G., "Roots of Naxalism : The Land Question and Law and Order", *Front Line*, February 14, 1991, p. 110.
22. Nancharaiah, G., *Land and Caste*, Himalaya Publishing House, Bombay, 1988, pp. 102-107.

6

STRUCTURAL ADJUSTMENT AND FISCAL MANAGEMENT IN INDIAN ECONOMY : RATIONALE AND OPTIONS

DR. M.R. AGGARWAL
Department of Economics,
Panjab University

India adopted the path of planning to accelerate the process of economic development, to achieve an optimum allocation of resources from the point of view of the society's welfare, and to reduce the gulf in income and wealth and tackle the fundamental problems of poverty due to gradual realization that the market forces or signals won't operate efficiently and could not be relied in the long run for achieving these aims. Numerous measures, both fiscal and monetary, based on the assumption that there does exist a strong trade off between growth and equity and the distribution of the gains of growth would not automatically "trickle" down to the weak and lower strata of the society, were initiated. However, there is a considerable difference of the opinion among the intellectuals whether there really exists a trade off or complementarity between the two. The strategy followed up to 1970, was mainly based on Nehru-Mahalnobis model of planned development or "Trickle Down Paradigm" optimism.

There was however a marked decrease in the "Trickle down" optimism after 1970 and the problems of poverty, employment generation and income distribution were adopted explicitly by the planners as major goals. Whereas during 1950s and 1960s, these goals were more or less implicit, but were made explicit through the introduction of various anti-poverty programmes. In other words, the emphasis was shifted from quantitative dimension of growth to qualitative dimension of growth. In the early 80s India started facing huge fiscal and trade deficits together, and selective import liberalization programmes coupled with the policies of decontrol/deregulation in the various sectors of the economy under the leadership of Smt. Indira Gandhi and Rajiv Gandhi, though on a small scale, were being injected to solve these problems. It was realised that the management of aggregate demand policies or total "absorption" are more important as compared to aggregate supply management for solving the basic problems faced by the Indian economy. These policies however were being reversed, may be due to political compulsions.

The new government immediately assuming office at the centre announced new policy measures, to be implemented quickly in the various sectors of the economy, *viz.*, two bouts of devaluation of the rupee (July 1-July 3, 1991), the suspension of cash compensation support for exports, enlargement of the volume of REP licenses for imports thus linking imports with exports, trimming and rationalizing the structure of mounting subsidies, particularly to fertilizers, sugar and exports and deregulation, decontrol and delicensing of the industrial sector in order to revitalize the economy by releasing the powerful brakes on the production, productivity and efficiency.

Before we should examine the major elements and rationale of the New Economic Policy, it is quite important and essential to know the various instruments used by the state in order to achieve these goals of growth with equity and social justice.

(i) Massive investment in the public sector, during the successive plans, to tackle deep rooted structural problems. The private sector was regulated and carefully monitored, in a way as to play a supporting role to state enterprises.

(ii) Use of industrial licensing to promote growth in some of the basic industries and hence to balance aggregate support and demand.

(iii) The licensing was assumed to shut out domestic competition, and with imports being licensed in relation to capacity, excess capacity was encouraged.

(iv) In addition to entry barriers, the Government often introduced strict exit barriers to protect workers from unemployment, and underemployment.

(v) Constraints were introduced considerably to assess transfer of financial restructuring and bankruptcy.

(vi) In the agricultural sector, public policies in the form of price support, procurement, input subsidies and provision of concessional credit provided the necessary incentives to farmers for adopting modern agricultural practices.

(vii) There was practical export pessimism. Hence overvalued exchange rates, multiple exchange rate systems, import controls, high tariffs and quantitative trade restrictions were recommended and used to support "import substitution" strategies for industrialization, and long run growth.

Lastly, a highly complex and bureaucratic import licensing system was followed by an equally complex system of export incentives, *viz.*, import entitlement for exporters in the form of import licenses, which provided a huge subsidy to exporters. But all these controls did create distortions both in export, import and domestic sectors. This actually means that India should produce whatever it can and export whatever it produces.

Successes and failures

India's economic growth measured in terms of rates of growth of total and per capita real gross domestic product during the period 1980—89 has not only been successful but also surpassed the rates achieved by the industrial and EE countries and other developing countries except East Asia and China. (i) GDP has grown at 5.6% as compared to 3.0 and 4.3% of industrial and developing countries (Table 1). Industrial sector registered a rate of growth of 7.6% during the same period. India is expected as per the forecast to achieve 5.2 and 3.5% growth rates in total and per capita (i) GDP during the coming decade which are highly impressive. (ii) The ratio of savings to GDP due to expanding financial system and various incentives, displayed a sharp increase, from 10% in 1951 to 15% in 1965 and to 21% in 1989, particularly due to high rate of growth of GDP though the "resource gap" between (S and I), as percentage of GDP, has increased from 2% to 2.9% during the period 1965—88. (iii) The incremental capital-output ratio which indicates the efficiency of investment, which increased from 6.6. to 7.3 during the period 1961—69 to 1970—89 declined thereafter and was 5.7 which is still on the high side. (iv) The percentage share of machinery and transport equipments, and manufacturing exports to total exports increased from 49% to 73% during the period 1965—88. (v) There has been significant improvement in most of the ratios — indicating a qualitative change in structure of development relating to literacy, health and education during this period.

TABLE 1

Growth Rate of Real GDP and Per Capita GDP (1965—2000)

Group and Region	Real GDP growth rates			Real FDP per capita growth with rates		
	Trend 1965—1980	Recent experience 1980—89	Forecast 1989—2000	Trend 1965—1980	Recent experience 1980—89	Forecast 1989—2000
Industrial countries	3..7	3.0	3.0	2.8	2.5	2.6
Developing countries	5.9	4.3	5.1	3.4	2.3	3.2
South Asia	3.6	5.5	5.1	1.2	3.2	3.2
India	3.6	5.6	5.2	1.2	3.5	3.4
Other	3.9	5.0	4.8	1.2	2.2	2.4
Sub-Saharan Africa	5.2	1.0	3.7	2.0	—2.2	0.5
East Asia	7.3	8.4	6.6	4.8	6.7	5.1
China	6.4	10.1	6.8	4.1	8.7	5.4
Other	8.1	6.4	6.3	5.5	4.2	4.6
Eastern Europe Middle East	5.3a	1.4a	1.9	4.5a	0.8a	1.5
North Africa and other Europe	6.3	2.9	4.3	3.9	0.8	2.1
Latin America, and the Caribbean	6.0	1.6	4.2	3.4	—0.6	2.3

a. Estimates. *World Development Report-1990* (World Development Indicators).

Failures (Economic and Social)

(i) Various studies, employing different statistical techniques on the income and consumption data clearly reveal that the proportion of the people below the poverty line stood at around 55% in 1970s but did decline sharply in the late 1970s and mid-1980s as its ratio was around 40% (Table 2). Nevertheless the number of people who live over "knife-edge" between hunger and starvation have remained quite substantial. 200-300 million people still live below the poverty line. In 1985, India had 41% of the poor of the total poor of all the developing countries. On the basis of head count index, according to latest World Development Report (1990), the poverty is the highest among all the regions of developing countries, in India.

TABLE 2

Percentage of Population Living Below the Poverty Line — Expert Group Estimates

Areas	1973-74	1977-78	1983-84	1987-88
Rural	56.4	53.1	45.6	39.1
Urban	49.2	47.4	42.2	40.1
Combined	54.9	51.8	44.8	39.3

Source : Govt. of India — *Economic Survey, 1993-94.*

(ii) The public sector both at the Centre and State level which was developed to reach the commanding heights of the economy and to generate surplus has not only absorbed large amounts of scarce resources without giving much return, but has shown huge losses continuously. In fact, in a sense, it has "crippled" the economy with "inefficiencies", due to the technological stagnation, high cost to consumers and unproductive employment.

(iii) The fiscal deficit, primarily due to increasing Government expenditure as compared to its revenue, which stands now more than 8% of the GDP as compared to 6% at the beginning of 1980s and 4% in the mid-seventies is very precarious. It has forced the Government to borrow both internally and externally to finance not only public investment but also its current expenditure.

(iv) The balance of payments situation despite high rate of growth of GDP has become equally alarming partly due to commercial borrowing at market rates by the Govt. in 1980s. The current account deficit which was about 1.9% of the GDP in the past several years is estimated to be now more than 2.5% of the GDP. The external debt servicing burden consequently has increased and stands at present at 21% of the current account receipts and 26% of the exports of goods and services, despite high rate of exports as compared to imports in the 1980s.

(v) The economy was facing a double digit rate of inflation, which is hurting the most to the poor and weaker sections of the society. The rate of inflation is about 12% per annum now and is likely to accelerate further due to hike in administered and procurement prices and rupee devaluation.

New Economic Policies : A Review

It should be mentioned at the very outset that all these measures need to be examined as a package and not in isolation as unemployment, fiscal deficits and huge trade deficits are inter-related and influence each other in more than one ways. And any attempt to examine them in isolation would frustrate the very purpose of the "package", keeping in view our long run development priorities.

Devaluation of the Rupee

In order to analyze in depth the impact of devaluation on the economy, one must know first of all, the degree of "openness" of an economy. Greater this degree of openness higher will be in general the repercussions and *vice-versa*. In India, the size of the degree of "openness" is relatively very small and is in fact the lowest in the whole of Asia. The export and import sectors constitute roughly at present 6.5% and 9.5% of GDP, which means, the trade sector constitutes about 16% of GDP. Even in China roughly 20% of GDP *i.e.* 11.5% and 8.5% of exports and imports, come from the external sector. Secondly, India's share in the total exports of the world remained less than 1% and stood at 0.5% (1991) only.

The rate of growth of exports, though increased during the period 1960—80 from 3% to 4.6% due to various incentives, is still very very low as compared to that of China and South Korea (Table 3).

TABLE 3

Rate of Growth of Exports, 1960—80

	1960—70	1970—80
India	3.0	4.6
China	25.6	26.0
South Korea	34.1	25.7

Source : *World Development Report*, 1990.

However, the rate of growth of exports and imports increased very remarkably particularly after 1985, as is clear from the Table 4.

TABLE 4

Annual Rate of Growth of India's Exports and Imports (1985—90)

	1985	1986	1987	1988	1989	1990
Exports	7.1	8.3	16.0	15.4	15.1	15.0
Imports	6.1	4.0	12.6	15.0	12.3	14.0

Source : *Asian Development Outlook — 1991 (ADB).*

As per the traditional elasticity approach, the trade balance of any country is a function of relative income and prices. It is not possible for any country to influence the income level of the trading partners but it can certainly influence the relative prices through the changes in rates of exchange, *i.e.* by devaluation or revaluation. Devaluation, by lowering down the value of a currency in terms of other currency, increases the competitiveness of traded goods. It, in a way, affects all the traded goods and all the trading partners. It is, therefore, an "Average Concept". Under normal circumstances, given the satisfactory working of the Marshall-Learner conditions, it must increase exports and reduce imports and hence will improve the balance of payments position of an economy, resorting to devaluation.

The Table 5 clearly shows that there has been, since 1960, continuous depreciation of the exchange rate of the rupee, but it has depreciated significantly after 1988 against the major currencies of the world. Also our exports have picked up remarkably after 1986. We

TABLE 5

Exchange Rate of the Indian Rupee (1960-91)

	Per US $	Per DM	Per Pound Sterling	Per 100 Yen	Per SDR
1960	4.76	1.13	13.33	1.32	4.73
1970	7.50	2.05	18.00	2.10	7.51
1980	7.93	4.05	18.88	3.91	10.11
1986	13.12	6.76	19.29	8.25	16.05
1990-91	17.94	11.43	33.19	12.80	24.80

Source : RBI, *Reserve Bank of India Bulletin* (Various Issues).

find a very significant correlation (0.67) between the depreciation of the rupee and the rate of growth of exports after 1980s. In other words, it means that the Indian rupee was already kept overvalued which has discouraged in a big way our exports in the international markets. There is no doubt that the devaluation of the currency is a clear sign of the weak management of the economy, but on the other hand, it is equally true that to keep the value of the currency at a artificial higher level is also bad in the long run as it retards the export potential of the country and hence income and employment level. After the final collapse of the Bretton-Woods system in 1973, the managed floating exchange rate system appeared on the international scene. India in the initial stages adopted a "wait and see" attitude but finally adopted a managed floating. The Indian rupee was linked with a basket of 5 currencies with the major goal to adjust exchange rate in such a way as to promote the competitiveness of Indian exports in the global market. In such a situation, any disturbance in the current account of the balance of payments is automatically passed on the exchange rate of the currency. And after 1980 onwards, the exchange rate of the Indian currency, due to mounting deficit in the balance of payments, started depreciating but it was not, in reality, allowed to fall due to intervention by the Government. Hence the devaluation of the Indian rupee, at present, was a clear cut necessity and the Finance Minister was highly justified in legalizing the depreciation of the Indian currency. There is no doubt that a part of our exports which are under bilateral agreements would remain unaffected, but roughly 60% of our exports are competitive and hence will be greatly influenced. But devaluation is certainly a double-edged weapon, whereas the rate of growth of exports is increased, the imports become certainly costlier and the 57% of our total imports are clearly inelastic; thereby pushing the level of prices. Also the burden of debt service is increased.

TABLE 6

Commodity Composition of India's Imports 1965—88 (%)

	Food	Fuel	Other primary goods	Machinery and Transport	Other manufactures
1965	22	5	14	37	22
1988	5	13	9	20	53

Source : *World Bank Report* (1990).

Further, it is argued in the academic quarters that an increase in the rate of inflation (due to devaluation) will nullify the price advantages gained by the domestic exporters. Some of the studies *viz.* those of Cooper, Conolly and Taylor, Blejer and Haveili, based on multiple regression, indicate clearly one thing that though devaluation is certainly inflationary but does not support the general fear that the resultant price increases nullify the effects of devaluation. This is more or less true in the case of India as the resultant impact of inflation depends upon the "degree of openness or trade linkages" which is of course very small in India. Whereas various studies have shown that the rate of growth of supply of money in the past and inflationary expectations have exerted considerable influence on the level of prices in India. As we have already noted that India could not have a desired rate of growth of exports, the planners in order to meet the planned target of GDP took the help of external resources to fill up the gap between revenue and expenditure of the Govt. External resources constituted around 24% of the plan outlay of Second Plan, 28% of the Third Plan outlay and on an average 15-20% of Fourth, Fifth and Sixth and Seventh Plans. In fact external capital inflows, on the basic assumption that there does exist a positive relation between growth and capital inflows, were resorted in order to overcome the dominant constraints (foreign exchange in the initial stages and savings in the later stages of development) and "poverty trap" instead of placing reliance on the better export performance which should not be confused with an adoption of "export-led growth" strategy.

Admittedly, in the sixties and seventies, this strategy worked very well. But the scenario changed in 80s due to the drastic structural change in the capital inflows, second oil shock and deterioration of the terms of trade, both commodity and income.

TABLE 7

Structure of Foreign Capital Inflows in India 1970—87 (%)

	1970—80	1981—87
ODA	99.7	80.4
Direct investment	3.3	3.0
Portfolio investment	— 1.4	7.3
Export credit	— 1.5	9.4

UN, *International Financial Statistics,* and *Balance of Payments Year Book* (Various Issues).

Table 7 clearly shows that the concessional aid which was around 99.7% of the total inflows fell to 80.4% during the period 1970—80 to 1980—87, forcing India to rely on commercial borrowing, export credit and NRI inflows. Consequently, the debt-service ratio which was relatively low *i.e.* 8.1% in 1981 increased to 26.4% of GDP in 1990. India in fact has become the net exporter of capital; what is the remedy? It is very obvious that India will have to increase her exports where there is considerable scope and cut down "inessential" luxurious items' imports in order to free the economy from the clutches of payments imbalances.

It should be noted here that there is nothing wrong for going for commercial borrowing provided these inflows are utilized, productively and efficiently, which is of course not so in the case of India. China has been borrowing commercially to the tune of 50% of her total inflows, and is free from these problems (Table 8).

TABLE 8

Distribution of Foreign Capital Inflows in China (1989)

Private flows	50%
Out of which direct investment	12%
Commercial borrowing	33%
Export credit	5%
Public flows	50%

UN, *International Financial Statistics,* and *Balance of Payments Year Book*, 1991.

Privatization of Public Sector Units

The performance of the public sector, in terms of rate of return on capital invested and generation of savings, as a percentage of GDP is highly dismal. The public sector is simply contributing savings 2.1% of GDP which declined as compared to 1970-71 (Table 9). This sector instead of acting as a dynamic growth agent, accumulating and generating additional resources and seizing the ''commanding heights'' of the economy, has been converted into growing unproductive employment agencies and is showing clear signs of mismanagement and inefficiencies, as is quite evident from the high capital-output ratio.

TABLE 9

India's Gross Domestic Savings as a % of GDP (1950—90)

	Household	Private Sector	Public Sector	Total
1950-51	7.7	1.0	1.8	10.4
1960-61	8.4	1.7	2.6	12.7
1970-71	11.3	1.5	2.9	15.7
1992-93	17.4	2.8	2.1	22.3

RBI — *Annual Survey* (Various Issues).

While current socio-economic conditions do not justify privatization of core public enterprises in industry and infrastructure, it is worth examining privatization of loss making public sector units particularly which largely cater to the needs of rich, middle classes *viz.* five star hotels, tourist complexes etc. and of sick units producing low priority consumer goods. The sick "state" units may be given to the workers or private sector or NRI and an "unemployment insurance scheme" could be introduced in case there is an unemployment, which will be financed jointly by the state and industrial sector. Some steps have already been taken in this regard but much remains to be done. Besides this, there is an urgent need of introducing internal reforms *i.e.* promoting new management practices, technological transformation attention of qualify control and marketing, and financial planning in the core public sector, to improve their performance.

The direct taxes, indirect taxes and savings of public sector are the major sources of the total revenue of the Government. At present, there does not seem to be much scope for increasing the indirect taxes as the indirect taxes-GDP ratio is already very high, around 15% and any increase in this ratio will be inflationary under the present circumstances as bulk of the indirect taxes are levied on capital goods and intermediate goods. On the other hand, the direct tax-GDP ratio has remained more or less the same during the last decade, due to reduction in basic rates, increase in allowances and exemptions and widespread evasion. The tax revenue is bound to go up with the simplication of the present complex tax laws, widening the tax base, and tightening the tax machinery. On the other hand, a gradual cut in various subsidies, defence expenditure, and grants to states and UTs which constitute the major items in the Government expenditure (50% of the total in 1989-90) (as has been done in Indonesia in 1989) is a need of the hour. However, the Government must ensure that the impact of the cuts of subsidies particularly of food and fertilizers should not fall on the urban poor, weaker and poor strata of the society by improving the public distribution system, and effectively implementing the major poverty elimination and employment generation programmes. This is due to the fact that doing away with these subsidies will substantially increase the prices of these items. Secondly, a cut in the fiscal deficit will also make the "exchange rate" stable, because the variations in the exchange rates cannot be viewed in isolation as these depend upon internal policies which reinforce one another in a consistent manner. Lastly, rapid growth of the productive employment, on a continuing basis, is one of the surest way to reduce the absolute and relative levels of the incidence of poverty both in the rural and urban sectors. In fact, this will have to be our main priority. Admittedly, one of the major responsibilities of the state is to create favourable conditions for providing gainful employment at the existing wage rate to its growing labour force, but the Government in the final analysis, can't be taken as the main provider of employment, because in India a very small percentage of people to the total working labour force is employed in the organised sector, which works directly or indirectly for the Government and a large section of the population is being absorbed by the agricultural and related sectors, and unorganised sectors of the economy. One can't hope to increase productive employment in the organised sector, until there is a corresponding increase in the total real output which is functionally related to increase in real income, and employment. In the agricultural sector, the employment in general is linked, besides the successful introduction of institutional reforms, to the growth of capital stock or productivity and the expanding quantum of investment. It however, must be noted here that it is not enough to employ people, but they must be employed efficiently so that productive assets are created on a continuing basis for generating further employment. In other words, to achieve these aims, in the near future, it becomes essential to change the rate of investment and drastically change the traditional "labour-management" relations in a way to protect the workers from exploitation, by introducing simultaneously unemployment insurance schemes and income stabilization arrangements and to increase production and productivity of the agricultural sector through institutional reforms. These are some of the measures which must be taken and should become an integral part of the future sound development policy alongwith the macro-stabilization measures. The state, in other words, will have to intervene systematically and through multiple channels in the different sectors and sub-sectors of the economy, to foster the agents of development *i.e.* policies to bolster savings and investment as percentage of GDP and maintain realistic exchange and interest rates, and subsidize credit to poor and weaker sections of the society.

It is heartening to note that a broad consensus seems to have emerged on the national scene regarding a strong need and relevance of the "domestic liberalization" reforms in the various sectors and it is felt that it is not possible to have a high rate of industrial and agricultural growth if price and factor distortions in commodity and factor markets, and "bureaucratic intervention" continue to operate both at the centre and state levels. These "interventions" now in fact have become counter-productive and have outlived their utility. However, opinions differ markedly regarding the timing, sequence and the need of the external sector liberalization, without having successful domestic liberalization. Manipulation of the real exchange and interest rates and the invitation to global firms by way of foreign investment are the two major pillars of the "external sector" liberalization. We have already discussed the relative merits and demerits of having right type of real exchange rates and interest rates in the present economic scenario. The only comment which I should like to make here is that there is no harm in inviting them in the hi-tech areas, with clear-cut policies regarding their equity, repatriation of profits and capital, technology transfer and suitable negotiations with regard to TRIPs and TRIMs, but as far as possible be discouraged in the light manufactures and small sectors, where India has acquired remarkable expertise by way of exports over the years and the area which happens to provide maximum employment to the maximum number of people.

Further, better export performance, and push through an increase in productivity competition and efficiency and the efforts to become "global" cannot be achieved unless the external trade and investment climate is reasonably "free" and "fair". However, during the last two decades in particular, international economic environment has become quite unfavourable and even hostile as far as the South is concerned due to what "Friedman" calls the increased use of protectionism, "managed trade", advent of regionalism and bilateralism, and slower rate of growth of USA. In order to minimize the effects of the depressed international environment, the South including India, on the one hand, has to identify new markets among themselves by forming an effective regional group for realizing the virtues of free trade, and on the other, the North will have to make all-out efforts to foster "freer", "fairer" and non-discriminatory open "multilateral trading system" by dismantling various tariffs and non-tariff barriers on the exports of third world countries, and by strictly adhering to the various rules and regulations of GATT. The net impact of recent GATT Treaty ratified by 125 countries including India on April 13, 1994, is yet to be seen, particularly in terms of increasing India's exports and dismantling of tariffs and non-tariff barriers at the global level in the near future. The phasing out of MFA is a clear-cut gain for the South.

To conclude, there is no denying the fact that the foreign exchange reserves have gone up significantly, the rate of growth of exports has tremendously increased, the rupee is steady, and the rate of inflation has come down, after the introduction of reforms, but it is (i) not enough to curb the rate of inflation, but to maintain it, at a lower level, to achieve macroeconomic stability, *i.e.*, around 5 to 7 per cent, (ii) essential to improve productivity and efficiency of resources, both in the public and private sectors through better financial management and planning and altering the traditional approach to labour-management relations; (iii) very urgent to de-regulate the capital market and reform the financial sector by making RBI independent and to take an integrated view of the whole economy, (iv) imperative to have better export performance by rationalizing the structure and quantum of subsidies, keeping realistic interest and exchange rates with a lower overall fiscal deficit as a percentage of GDP and finally to bridge the gap between revenue account and expenditure account by increasing tax base and reducing Government's current expenditure, instead of capital expenditure which is more or less a ''soft option''. Finally, it should be noted that these measures will have to be supplemented by administrative measures which directly and indirectly affect the production and productivity in the agricultural and related primary and traditional sectors having a sizeable number of people living under conditions of severe poverty and deprivation to solve the chronic problems of unemployment, poverty and disparities in the absolute and relative levels of income and wealth in the near future.

7

INDIAN AGRICULTURE AND THE NEW WORLD ECONOMIC ORDER

A. ATCHI REDDY

Professor

Department of Economics

University of Hyderabad

ABSTRACT

The chief object of this paper is to analyse the effects of the New Economic Policy on Indian agriculture starting with 1991. The new economic policy of India has often been attacked for its pro-Western bias in view of the recent debate on New GATT Accord. The doom's day prophesies of the pessimists do not stand for any logical test. The Indian farmers are an entrepreneurial lot and the new policies of globalisation and privatisation help them to come out from their shackles of subsistence farming to commercialised production. They do not clamour for subsidies but search for markets in the world at large to export their surpluses, especially the cash crops. This can go a long way in boosting Indian agriculture which would create enough employment opportunities in rural India.

I. INTRODUCTION

The new economic policy of India has often been attacked for its

*My primary debt is to the farmers of a number of villages who reacted and responded to my queries beyond my expectations in my recent rural in itenieraries. I am grateful to Shri Anil Agrawal and his working group for posing a number of issues and problems discussed in this paper, and to all the academicians that raised questions and encouraged me to revise the paper, and to Dr. K. R. Gupta who wished to publish it. Responsibility is fully mine for all the interpretations and ideas expressed here including the gaps and mistakes in explanations. Mr. Madduri Lakshmi Narayana has been helpful in typing it into a neat draft.

pro-western bias. It is labelled as 'a mirage of development' and a 'democratic deceit' imposed on the masses of India. Its representative agents are supposed to be the 'tax-evading neo-rich' led by a vast army of 'the liberal minded middle class young professionals' who lack sufficient ground in the economic history of India. Having been involved deeply into the recent internal crises of India — the Punjab, the Kashmir and all sorts of extremism and the regional, communal and caste politics — the Indian intellectuals are unable to devote sufficient thought to a threadbare analysis of the implications of the new economic policies to the Indian economy. The scope and nature of a number of concepts of the new economic policy — privatisation, globalisation, marketisation, reforms, restructuring, structural adjustments and the new world order — remain to be sufficiently explored, analysed and discussed. This is a testing ground for the predictive faculties of the economic science; and it is unavoidable for the policy makers to decide one way or other if timely advice is not available. Then, there will be little use of blaming the Indian economics as Manmohanomics.

Is not the Indian budgeting inspired by the Dunkel spirit? Are not its provisions imported from abroad? Is not Indian agriculture neglected in the successive budgets under the new economic policy? Is the Indian democracy likely to be crushed into a gattocracy? Is not India likely to be trapped into a Gattastrophe? Is not India going to be at the receiving end of the Western surrogate capitalist policy? Is not the process of rural development in India decelerated? Do we not understand the perceptions, interests and ultimate goals of the global players the U.S.A., the I.M.F., the MNCs, the EC and other regional economic unions? Do they not have some similarities in the colonial economic history? These are a few of the questions asked by the serious and highly sensitive social scientists of India after 1991. The newly reformed economic policy has been ushered in India since 1991; but at what cost? What happened to the goals of equity and social justice? Is the common man forgotten? Is the avowed principle of self-reliance disappeared over-night? Does it hamper our agricultural growth? These are the doubts expressed about the cost of the new economic policy regarding its path of diversion from the old socialist economic policy followed in India during the pre-1991 period. It is feared that the common man of India has been marginalised and rich sections are favoured; agriculture is neglected and industry is favoured; domestic problems are neglected and international pulls are answered. Where does the Indian economy go from here? Most of these issues are so serious that we cannot brush them aside as journalistic rhetoric or populist propaganda.

At the outset, it should be noted that the new economic policy was adopted in 1991 and since then it has come to stay with us. Also, the GATT agreement (Uruguay Round) including the Dunkel Draft were already signed by the Government of India; and there is not much use for the farmers of India to argue against these policies, nor what they would have been without the new economic policies. Therefore my submission is that the present and the immediate issues before the policy makers and the Indian farmers are that how to mould these policies and exploit them to bring about prosperity to the farming community.[1] What should be the priorities? What should be the proper mix, and the dosages to be administered? How to choose and adopt the opportunities to the Indian conditions and climate? How to minimize and avoid their negative aspects and losses?[2]

The chief object of this paper is to analyse the effects of the new economic policies on the Indian agriculture. It is not a single and precise analytical theme that the study of which lends to the formulation of some definite generalisations. On the other hand, it forms a descriptive analysis comprising a cross-section of the gene ideas and views generated in the recent economic literature in this area. Most of the basic information has been from my talks and interactions with the friendly academicians; and most of them in Delhi where I attended to a couple of seminars of this type.[3] It is very difficult to follow a specific theoretical frame or methodology in a descriptive paper like this.[4] A large part of it forms the area of current discussions at various forae, and most of them may be only the starting points, and not the speak anything of concluding finalities. However, the relevant sources and their authorities are duly acknowledged in all possible places. Reference to the standard and basic economic literature is omitted.

Keeping the object in view, this paper is composed into eight unequal but analytically convenient sections. The new economic policies and the chief issues involved are mentioned in the Section I, the

Introduction. A critical assessment of the old economic policies concerning the Indian agriculture is attempted in the Section II. The new economic policies are analysed briefly in the Section III. The GATT and its Dunkel Draft, so far as they are related to Indian agriculture, are noted in the Section IV. The possibilities of future development and suggestions are pressed into the Section VII while the conclusions are compressed into the last one, the Section VIII. In theory, there are two distinct parts in this paper — the new economic policies of India and the relevance of the GATT and its annexures to our policies.[5] They are combined here for mere brevity of analysis. The sectionalisation is only for the convenience of analysis and they are not watertight compartments. It should be noted that few of the points and issues are substantiated either in theory or by empirical evidence as most of them flow from the current literature.[6] Of course, the interested academicians can concentrate their further research on these lines. The passage of time will sort out, to a large extent, the degree of relevance of the new measures to the Indian agriculture.

A number of socio-economic changes can be attributed to the latest developments in the field of technology. We can ignore them only at our peril. A successful nation is one that can make use of the scientific innovations to extend its technological frontiers aimed at promoting the socio-economic interests of the nation. It is a known fact that the modern world is shrinking fast due to the unprecedented developments in the technology. A phenomenal increase in the volume and speed of the recent (since 1945) international trade is one of the indices.

The traditional 'international economy' is being replaced by the new 'global economy'. The economy that functioned amongst the nations since the First World War till the early 1980s can be called the 'improved international economy', while the one that began to function in the world since the late 1980s can be termed as the 'global economy' (C.T. Kurien : *The New Economic Policies,* 1993). 'The international economy' was the agglomeration of the national economic units whose individual decisions shaped it and helped to run it. Goods and services moved across the national borders according to the rules and regulations imposed by the national states. But the new global economy is a single unit of its own kind that started in the late 1980s. Markets have become global especially the financial markets; a global capital market has already began to emerge. The Multinational or the Transnational Corporations began to play a vital and decisive role in the economic affairs of the world.[7] The different national units are being fast integrated into a closely-knit global economy where the different national units have to play their respective roles in each market. In other words, the markets function globally and accounted only on the global scale.

It has become difficult to the national states to keep out of the global systems and they have to enter them at some point of time or other; India is not an exception to this general rule.[8] Some of the issues at stake in the context of the adoption of the new economic policies in the Indian agriculture are equity, food security and employment creation by public agencies, beside a plethora of socio-political questions like the unity and sovereignty of the Indian state, its autonomy of decision-making, or its subservient nature to the world bodies and the survival of its indigenous socio-economic fabric. In short, the survival of the Indian economy is at stake. But here we limit our present discussion only to the Indian agriculture. We note mostly the direct effects; the indirect or the secondary and the tertiary or the far related effects are either ignored or are noted only in the context of explanations. We also do not enter into the far flung economic or pure political issues like the unity and sovereignty of India. We only try to disseminate the information and show the farmers the ways and means available in the new economic policy for their economic betterment, and leaving the rest; the actual field to be sown, grown and harvested by them is included.[9]

The cultivating communities of India have got a vital stake in the new economic policies that most of them are in a confused state of mind whether they would force them into pauperisation; or would they show them the new and novel ways and means to enter into the global markets as the competitive and prosperous participants. The time has come that they should use their faculties of common sense so as to leave out the obsolete theories of their virtual dependency on the mercy of the public agencies for doles and subsidies. They should open their eyes and minds to the conditions obtaining in the world as a whole; they should participate in the world markets as the proud sellers of their quality produce and not as beggars for loans and concessions.[10] They should prove themselves as second to none in the world of farm producers. The entrepreneurial Gujerati farmers settled in the far off California are as much Indians as their close brothers along with tIndira Gandhi canal in Rajasthan. But the infrastructural differences are vast.

II. A CRITICAL REVIEW OF THE OLD POLICIES

A critical review of the past economic policies and achievements is helpful that it brings out the extent of the successes and points out to the pitfalls and failures. It can help us as a guide in formulating the future policies.[11] The agricultural policies followed in India since the Independence are subject to some critical attacks in some of the evaluations, reviews and judgements in recent times. Their suitability to this country, their achievements during the last 4½ decades and their relevance to the present and to the immediate future are questioned. The analysts have brought out that a number of them are either unnecessary for this country or have turned obsolete, disadvantageous and unsuitable for a healthy growth of its agricultural sector.[12] This kind of review is still continuing and it is difficult to pass on any final judgements; but it is worth to note some of these points before we enter into the new economic policies.

The old economic policies in the Indian agriculture are those that have been followed before 1990 and generally after 1947. The origin of the present new economic policies since June 1991 can be traced back to the frustrating experience of the old and the pre-1990 economic policies. Incidentally they reached their climax in the period of 1989-91 in the form of the crisis in the balance of payments in May-June 1991 even though the symptoms of this crisis had been there for a quite long time.[13] There had been discussions and doubts expressed about the efficacy of the economic policies followed in India since 1947 and especially with respect to their suitability for the development of the vital sectors of the economy; and agriculture as a dynamic, vibrant and self-sustaining unit. To start with, huge sums were spent on the creation of the necessary basic infrastructure like the irrigation water, power and fertilizer plants. Being faced with the acute shortages of foodgrains, the criteria of their economic efficiency had been steadily watered down in favour of the goal of increased *total output* of foodgrains.[14] After reaching a tolerable level of total output and *self-sufficiency* and nearing stagnation, again we started to think about the structural deficiencies that are often inhibiting the development of agriculture on modern lines.

Most of the critique is levelled against the insignificant achievements of the agrarian reforms in general and the land reforms in particular.[15] The entire critique of the economic policies followed in India between 1947 and 1990 can be grouped under two heads. The first school of thought is a radical and wholesale attack on the entire gamut of the policies that were followed during the entire pre-1990 period as retrogressive. They advance the view that these economic policies proved to be self-defeating in the long-run. The main policy objectives had been only transparent and short-run and they neglected the long-term and secular interests of the country. They were not always self-sustaining but needed props of support from abroad. They were not self-generating but used the productive resources generated elsewhere to oil their engines.[16]

The second school emphasizes the failures of the economic policies followed after 1978 and particularly in the decade of the 1980s.[17] They provide empirical evidence that these policies led to the BOP crisis at the end of this decade. They showed especially that the heavy international borrowings, liberalisation of the imports etc. as the immediate causes of the crisis, but do not deny the inherent weakness of our old policies.

A comparison of their arguments about agricultural policies show that both these schools of thought have got much in common. In fact, the first school claimed that the BOP crisis is the result of the non-production-oriented policies followed since the 1950s, and the decade of the 1980s saw the climax of the working of these defective policies; and the BOP crisis is only one of the invariable manifestations. The growing levels of unemployment, the bulging streams of rural-urban migration, and the degradation of the environment are some of the effects of the economically wrong, may be popular, policies followed by the Government of India and those in the States and Provinces. The direct and indirect costs of these policies, including the opportunities foregone, are so colossal that their achievements are insignificant.[18] For example, did they increase the productivity per man-hour? Did they remove the rural unemployment? Did they increase the hourly rate of agricultural wages? Did they bring prosperity and peace to the Indian farmers? Did our agricultural sector boost our industries sector by providing raw-materials, labour force and vibrant demand for its products? The central theme of these questions is the poverty of our agrarian policies.

Huge sums of funds are spent but little is actually achieved. The decade of the 1980s had been a period of economic mismanagement in India. It is often termed as 'a decade of profligacy'. India borrowed from the international agencies like the IMF/World Bank on a massive scale and spent a large part of it on unproductive activities.[19] The non-plan expenditure had increased by leaps and bounds. Almost all the public sector enterprises except a few like the ONGC had been running on net losses.[20] A major chunk of the tax revenue had been diverted to meet their losses. These frivolous policies led to a number of malpractices that had badly checked the growth of productive forces in the economy by diverting the vital and productive resources into less productive and often unproductive channels. This type of scathing criticism found increased volume of empirical evidence in the form of the generation of black-money, black-marketeering of the essential commodities, smuggling activities along the coasts, corruption and red-tapism among the bureaucracy leading to 'bank scandals' and 'scams', spending in the elections and the 'swiss accounts' and Bofors, and spending on projects that never materialised.[21]

Failures in the agricultural sector are more transparent than elsewhere.[22] The critics point out that Indian agriculture is a relative failure though not absolutely. The increased foodgrain production from 50 to 180 million tons is not at all significant when compared with the rates of growth achieved by other nations. What it lacked or lost during this period of the last 4½ decades is its competitiveness in the world markets, its self-sustained path of growth and its potential capacity for exporting a large part of its surplus produce. The productivity per man-hour did not increase.[23] The cost of providing additional employment has increased considerably, but the level of agricultural wages did not increase so as to compensate the increased cost of its provisions.[24] The Indian farmers, a major part of it, have grown so poor that the land tax has been abolished by many of the provincial Governments.[25] Our agro-based industries are forced to import a part of their raw-materials as evidenced by oil-seeds, or the latest import of cotton and edible oils. The wrong agrarian reforms are pushing out the large streams of rural residents to the urban areas.[26]

The very first shot of the critics fell on the land reforms. Some of the arguments against the land reforms are old wine in new bottles. The new emphasis is that the land reforms, especially after 1947, could not increase the productivity of our lands, their small size of holdings came in the way of modernisation and mechanisation of the Indian agriculture and they reduced the cultivation to the level of subsistence production.[27] We have missed the advantages of large scale farming, and the policies lead to the impoverishment of a large section of the Indian farming community. They argue that 'why should there be ceilings on land holdings when there are no ceilings on the industrial or the urban properties?' Not only the land ceilings but the tenancy laws are also subject to almost the same type of critique in the latest trend of liberalisation as carried on mainly by those academicians who championed the cause of free enterprise as the best way of economic development for a country like India which had been an adjunct of the British capitalism for almost two centuries, and having a strong institutional infrastructure well suited for the economic development on capitalistic lines and with the advantage of the English language, the conversing medium of international business.[28]

Land ceiling laws turned out to be irrelevant in terms of the new economic policy that is being pursued in India since June 1991. Land ceilings and tenancy laws have no rationale in the logic of economic policy. When the industrial licensing has been relaxed and totally abandoned with respect to many items, correspondingly the agricultural entrepreneurs expect that there should be a similar relaxation in the laws of land reforms including the ceilings and tenancy; or they should be completely lifted so as to allow the entrepreneurs to improve the efficiency of agricultural land use and enhancing its productivity. Some of the arguments of G. Thimmaiah ran on these lines (*Economic*

Times, 28-10-1993). He showed in his analysis a number of advantages and the possible disappearance of an equal number of dismal consequences and disadvantages by lifting the ceiling and tenancy laws. The entrepreneurial farmers and the private companies could lease in the land from the small farmers and other capital-starved sections of the land owners who may get higher net incomes from land rents than what they got from their own cultivation. The economic logic says that production organisation is the best which brings out the largest net returns; and this is applicable to Indian agriculture as well.[29]

The second argument is about the declining investments in the Indian agriculture. The rate of investment in agriculture, both public and private, has declined considerably over the last 5 to 7 years according to the data available recently. If the Government brings down the fiscal deficit, say to zero level, then they have to cut down their investment in the agricultural sector. The last four budgets of the Government of India are cited as evidence.[30] The so-called increased budgetary provision for rural development by about 40% in the latest budget proposals for 1994-95 is not directed towards the creation of infrastructural facilities or productive assets in agriculture. It is earmarked for the employment programmes known after the Prime Ministers, say the Jawahar Rojzar and the P.V. Narasimha Rao Yojana. This sort of popular public spending will only divert the productive efficiency or frequently no production at all. These policies are not directed towards the improvement of agriculture, rather to divert its surplus towards uneconomic channels.[31]

The economics of efficiency of subsidies has been subject to scattered attacks and more so from the international and aid giving agencies and donors like the I.M.F. and the World Bank. It is argued that a major part of the development funds had been frequently diverted to subsidies since the late 1970s. The public investment in agriculture had consequently decelerated from 1979 onwards. Gross investment in the Indian agriculture in real terms at the prices of 1980-81 declined from Rs. 4636 crores in 1980-81 to Rs. 4580 crores in 1991-92. It is not the absolute decline that matters; it should have been more than doubled during this period but for the subsidies. The share of agriculture in the gross domestic capital formation in 1980-81 was about 18% while it came down to around 11% in 1991-92 (*Economic Survey 1993-94*). The affected areas were the irrigation, power generation and the primary facilities of marketing and transport. Creation of the new sources and the maintenance of the existing sources of water and power of a given level of efficiency were largely affected due to the diversion of the funds for the subsidies in this decade or so. Being unable to compete with the subsidized prices of the 'public inputs', there has been a sharp decline of the private investments in these vital sectors.[32]

The apparent benefits of subsidies were only short-lived and often lead to real losses in the long-run damaging the interests of Indian agriculture. The pre-1991 policies were self-destructive with an in-built mechanism to destroy the development in the long-run. The subsidies in the agricultural sector, especially those on power, water and fertilizers, are often calculated to lead to a trend of secular-poverty by allowing the agricultural sector to operate far below the optimum level of economic efficiency. It is noted in the *Economic Survey of 1993-94:*

> "If charges for water and electricity are not raised to appropriate levels, then delivery of these critical inputs is likely to worsen over time and undermine agricultural development."

The economic logic of subsidizing a massive sector of the economy like the Indian agriculture could not draw the attention of the tax-payer to the fact that he has to pay increased prices for his foodgrains. Perhaps, the extra amount he has to incur may work out less burdensome than the corresponding tax he is paying towards these subsidies.[33]

Secondly, the subsidies rendered the Indian agriculture stupid and unfit for competition. It has developed a psychology of depending on regular subsidies. Its productivity has not improved along the international standards. The average productivity of foodgrains in the Indian agriculture during 1992-93 is only 1893 kilograms per hectare. India is producing about 180 million tonnes on a net sown area of about 103 million hectares under foodgrains. The total foodgrains production in the rest of the world is about 1775 million tonnes on a net sown area of about 600 million hectares with an average of about 2958 kgs. per hectare. In other words, our average productivity lags behind the international average by about 1065 kgs. per hectare. If we can reach the present average world level of about 3000 kgs. per hectare even by 2000 A.D., we can produce more than 300 million tonnes and we shall be in a position to export more than 50 million tonnes annually.[34] The defenders of the new economic policy argue that this much improvement is easily possible especially when we see the levels in our Asian neighbours (see Table 1).

TABLE 1

Productivity of Rice in some of the Asian Countries : 1990-91

Country	Productivity Kgs./hectare
Afghanistan	2290
China	5537
Indonesia	4228
South Korea	7191
India	1688

Source: U.N.O. Reports.

Subsidies on fertilisers have been subject to a lot of criticism in recent times. Analysts have concluded that they are helping the uneconomic and obsolete fertilizer firms, and not the farmers. The subsidies on fertilizers which were Rs. 1924 crores in the financial year 1985-86 increased to Rs. 6140 crores in 1922-93, they are not less than Rs. 5000 crores last year, *i.e.*, 1993-94 and about Rs. 4000 crores in the budget of 1994-95. Almost same is the trend in the subsidies allowed on water especially under the major projects and on power supplied by the Electricity Boards but their amounts were larger.[35] Serious doubts have been expressed whether all these subsidies had actually helped the farmers. Have they really prospered? If so, they should have actively participated in the economic development of the nation; but actually the picture is not rosy. Two types of explanations are offered against the subsidies and their disservice to the farmers and to the economy as a whole in the long term. For example, the cost of the imported nitrogenous fertilizers, net of the import duties, work out to be Rs. 4000 to Rs. 4600 per tonne in India while the factory cost of the same fertilizer ranges between Rs. 7000 to Rs. 8200 when manufactured in India. This shows clearly the shifting of the cost of inefficiency of the industry to agriculture in India under the guise of subsidies to agricultural sector.[36]

The indirect subsidies through low level of administered prices of the inputs are found to lead to wastage of productive resources. Wastage of irrigation water has become a notorious phenomenon, and it has drawn the attention of the agricultural economists in many recent seminars.[37] A number of recent instances are quoted where the watermen switched on their pumpsets and attended to other works or went to bed in the nights. Power is either free or fixed per horse power and also whether he/she consumed more or less does not matter to the SEB. Not only the acquifers are depleted, but the owners of other borewells in the neighbourhood are frequently faced with water scarcity; the power shedding and low voltage problems have become common.[38] The demand for power has far exceeded its supply due mainly to the subsidies and low rates.[39] This has led to a new development of 'water tenancy' in many districts of Southern India. Water is either purchased or a due share of the produce is paid as rent for the water supplied by the neighbour with a lucky borewell of rich yields of water. Otherwise, the water scarcity lands are leased out to the owners of the water-abundant wells.[40] Thus, the element of power subsidy has formed an unearned income and also led to unequitous in its effects.

Economic theory in general is not always sympathetic to permanent subsidies. There is economic argument against subsidies in general and specifically against subsidies to a nearly perfectly competitive sector like the Indian agriculture.[41] Subsidy granted on inputs leads to the misallocation of inputs. In other words, larger quantities of these inputs will be used at lower prices. Supply being the same, there will be an artificial scarcity for these inputs.[42] If the amount of subsidy is paid to the suppliers of these inputs by the Government, it results ultimately in the diversion of funds from some other and more productive activities, thus reducing the over-all efficiency of the economy.[43] If the suppliers of these subsidized inputs, say the P.W.D., are not paid by the Government, the consequences in the long-run are worse. They are denied their expected returns and starved of any funds for expansion or further development. This theory of neo-classical economics is applicable to the present case of subsidized power, water and fertilizers in the Indian agriculture and especially to power and water in Andhra Pradesh.[44]

Price policies and price controls of the Government of India are often attacked as anti-farmer. In cases of abundant crop yields and excess production of certain foodgrains like rice and wheat, or commercial crops like cotton and tobacco, the Government fails to export them, thereby the farmers cannot reap the profits of their favourable crops. On the other hand, the Government tries to import the foodgrains and other agricultural products when their prices are likely to increase in the country; again the farmers are losing their chance of getting high returns for their products.[45] This kind of anti-farmer policies are depressing the entrepreneurial spirit of the farmers by the subdued and unattractive markets as proved recently in the case of cotton. In spite of plenty of cotton in the Indian markets, the Government of India has decided to import about 30,000 tonnes of cotton from other countries resulting in the fall of the cotton prices in India at the time that most of the cotton growers, in Warangal and in Guntur districts, are entering into the market to sell their produce.[46]

The falling size of the net returns in agriculture are not covered by the price policies and the supporting prices fixed by the Government. The first explanation is the changing price structure against the interests of the farmers. The proportion of the total market cost of the agricultural inputs in general to the total market cost of the agricultural output has increased overtime between 1950-51 and 1992-93. This means that the net profit margin accruing to the farming cultivators has declined.[47] Of course, there are a number of limitations to this statement. It may not be applicable to some specific instances of crops or ryots. Or, the land revenue as a cost might have disappeared completely on the records. The prices in the black market might have been very high for a few products. All these are minor and exceptional cases. The major indices are two. First, the price of foodgrains in terms of industrial goods in India is cheap. Secondly, most of our foodgrains are produced with labour intensive and old techniques and under low or no mechanisation.

In other words, a given amount of labour and capital spent in agriculture yields less net gains than in industry or service sector.[48]

The compulsory levy of foodgrains is forcing the ryots to lose a large part of their potential profits on rice, wheat and sugar. What is the total administrative cost of the public distribution system in India? More than Rs. 5,000 crores is incurred annually in terms of transport, storage and distribution. The figure increases if the losses in transport and storage are added. If the same amount is diverted to the creation of productive assets like irrigation, the returns will be attractive. The vast private trading networks of the country can cater to the needs of distribution.[49] Further, who is being benefited through the public distribution system? What is the extent of black marketing? Are the benefits reaching the target groups? How much time is wasted in the collection of rations by the poor people? What is the opportunity cost of such time? A man-power researcher recently told me that the market cost of this labour time at the prevailing wage rates (Minimum Wages Act) is about double to the subsidy allowed to them on rice, wheat or sugar purchased by them.[50] The time wasted is known only *ex post*.

The minimum support prices fixed by the Government of India in actual practice turns out to be a negative subsidy in the sense that the international prices are far higher than these prices.[51] If we take into account the rice and wheat procured by the Government agencies like the Food Corporation of India, the ryots are losing at least Rs. 17,000 crores per year.[52] Accounts about the wastage and corruption involved in the F.C.I. and its subsidiaries is well pictured by the owners of the rice mills and floor mills of both trading and non-trading categories.[53] Frequently, the evaders of the levy are the gainers. Cases are found that harmful pesticides are spread over the part of the crop that is intended for the levy; they are made from aldrin, chlordane, heptachlor, dibromochloropropane, pentachloron, taxaphene, methyle parathion, nitrogen, nitrobenzene, paraquat, nicoline sulphate, dimethyle sulphate, telradifon and others that leave a residue of the poisonous element in the foodgrains, fruits or vegetables.[54]

A large part of the present rural poverty, in the Indian villages, it is argued, is due to the obstacles thrown in the way of the raising rural entrepreneurs especially after 1947 mainly with the introduction of the non-progressive measures of agrarian reforms like the land ceilings and the land tenancy restriction laws. Ali Mohammed Khusro, the former member of the Planning Commission, chided that land ceiling and illegitimization of tenancy as moth-eaten ideas and recommended that they should be discarded immediately (*Indian Express* 18-11-1993). [55] Land ceiling, a rationing measure, has become in recent times anachronistic and irrelevant for development on modern lines involving the economics of scale even in agricultural production. It did not help the poor farmers who got a few acres each, an uneconomically small holding to cultivate effectively.[56] They were tied to their meagre holdings and could not move either to avenues of higher productivity or to the industrialized urban centres.[57] A lot of tax money is wasted on extending loans to these vulnerable sections who consumed or spent them mostly on unproductive activities.[58] The unproductive consequences are frequently multiplied.[59]

The critique of the old economic policies followed in India since 1947 has centred round the rural poverty. Agricultural backwardness that resulted in poverty, had been reinforced by the land reforms which in turn created the need for subsidized inputs. All these wrong policies in effect created a large pool of surplus man-power manifested in the form of massive unemployment, the socio-economic results of which contributed to the devil's workshop of violence, extremism, drugs, militancy and crimes. It is not fair to attribute all these maladies to the wrong policies, but alternative explanations are not economically convincing.[60]

III. THE NEW ECONOMIC POLICY

The new economic policy is the result of changes in a large number of political and economic forces which can be classified under two analytical heads — the internal or domestic and the external or international.[61] The chief internal economic forces are related to the slow rate of growth of the economy sometimes faced by recession and stagnation, the high rates of annual inflation and population growth and the unemployment; the pressures for economic decentralisation, the poor results of the past seven development plans and a mounting domestic public debt became serious.[62] The external economic forces include the colossal size of the international debt and its servicing cost, the increasing gap in the balance of current payments against the country, the pressures for devaluation, the economic problems involved in reducing the imports, the necessity for upgrading our technologies and an acute problem of defence equipment being faced soon after the dissolution of the former Soviet Union.[63] The economic effects of other international happenings particularly those of Gulf should be reckoned with seriously as our foreign exchange reserves were affected during the recent Kuwaiti problem.

Indian economy in 1991 got only limited option; to open its economy to global forces and survive, and alternatively to shut it to the international forces and let it collapse and crash under the weight of the debts.[64] Taking into account the changed realities in the world after the end of 'Cold war', India cannot shut its doors to the new winds; the only precaution is that it should not allow the gale of change to wash it out. Following the middle path, the Indian policy makers chose to open the economy to the global economic forces slowly, carefully, steadily and on selective basis. The reforms may appear to be sweeping when we consider the last four budgets at a time, but they are slow when we look at them one by one.[65] The rationalisation of the tax structure, the gradual reduction in the import and excise duties, the full convertibility of rupee, de-licensing of a number of small units, the slow phasing out of the subsidies, the reduction in the budget deficits, the reduction in the rates of inflation and money supply (M3) and interest rates, the de-investment of the public undertakings and a number of measures intended for the promotion of exports are some of them. Attracting the foreign investments to a number of our industries is a leading policy measure.[66]

Most of the measures involved in the new policy are not new to the economic theory but to our country. The new economic policy was introduced in India in July 1991. Apparently, it consisted of the policy measures intended to meet the worst ever faced crisis of the balance of payments. The real nature of these measures became clear afterwards that they consisted largely of the structural adjustments taken from the theories of the text books; the suspicion among an equal number of academicians was that they were chiefly dictated by the I.M.F.-World Bank authorities as they did in some similar instances in the African and the Latin American countries.[67]

The basic features of the new economic policy are liberalistion, marketisation, privatisation and globalisation. The structural adjustment with these guidelines in the Indian economy included a thorough readjustment of the fiscal and monetary policies, trade policies, industrial licensing policies and policies towards agricultural and service sectors.[68] The crisis of the balance of payments was over; but there came the GATT with the Dunkel Draft towards the close of the year 1993. However, we are interested only in analysing the effects of the new economic policies on agriculture.[69]

The effects of the new economic policies are felt in every economic activity of India. Production of different commodities and their distribution among the different economic classes have been affected differently. The new economic policies followed in India in their nature, spirit and trend are not much different from those followed in some of the developing countries of the world. But we do not enter into the controversy that whether they are dictated or imposed on us by the outside agencies like the I.M.F./World Bank dominated by the U.S.A. or the G-7 economies.[70] As economists, our chief and immediate direct concern is their suitability to India and to our circumstances. Neither we are concerned with the politics of the GATT/Dunkel Draft, nor with the unipolar world after the collapse of the Soviet Union.[71] It is our concern to show all the available alternatives in economic theory to our farming brethren to make use of these new policies to their best advantage; and at the same time we warn them not to fall into the traps of the developed countires and to be careful about the pitfalls, and to be vigilant of the obstacles in the green avenues of agricultural progress.[72] They should try to take advantage of these new vistas to their prosperity.

A number of these benefits and losses may not be new, but their nature, extent and repercussions may vary in the regions of India. The development of the vast tracts of waste lands in India is possible under the free enterprise-capitalism in Indian agriculture. It is advocated by not less an authority on the Indian agriculture than Shri Bhanu Pratap Singh, the former minister of agriculture at the centre. He advocated that the reclamation and scientific development of waste lands and the vast tracts of the degraded forest lands should be entrusted to the corporate sector and that 50% of such developed lands should be left with the companies for their further use and development. This suggestion resembles the old land reclamation companies of Bengal around 1800 encouraged by the colonial English government.[73] A number of such companies, though started by the Europeans, were largely manned and maintained by the Indians, and the actual reclaimers were the Indian cultivators only.[74] The increased land revenue was the chief consideration in those old times. The interest may shift to the plantation crops and commercial agriculture at present; the environmentalists are supporting this idea hoping that it would add to the greenery of the surroundings.[75]

The Indian agricultural sector is not blessed with any sizeable new funds; only shifting of funds is involved in the new economic policy. A shift in the public investment in agriculture, according to the new economic policy, is from the subsidies to the creation of infrastructure. It is noted in the *Economic Survey, 1993-94* that the rate of public investment in agriculture has stagnated in the recent period especially from the 1970s; and in many areas the existing public capital assets are deteriorating for want of adequate funds for repairs and maintenance. Reversal of this degenerating trend would require a major shift in the balance of public expenditure in the agricultural sector from the large input subsidies to the creation, expansion, repairs and maintenance of the useful public economic infrastructure. Large public investment in irrigation, rural communications, schemes for controlling the degradation of the soils and water resources, should be given prominence. The survey added that funds needed for these productive purposes cannot be had *de novo* but should be diverted from the present subsidies on water, power, fertilizer and the public distribution of the foodgrains.[77] This line of argument sounds well at least in theory.

The share of agriculture in the GDP has been decreasing over the last three decades, and it is often reckoned as a desirable trend of economic development. The GDP added by the agricultural sector, Rs. 1,96,000 crores, to the national GDP, Rs. 628000 crores, is only 31% (see Table 2). But the agricultural population to the total Indian population in 1991 is not less than 65% implying a possibility of a further depression of the average per capita income in the agricultural sector.[76] It need not be stressed that the wage earners and marginal farmers are the real sufferers. But there is no evidence about their changed position during the last four years under the new policy.[78]

TABLE 2

Key Indicators of the Indian Economy 1993-94

1.	Gross national product (Rs. '000 crores at current prices)	617
2.	Gross domestic product (Rs. '000 crores at current prices)	628
3.	Agricultural production (Rs. '000 crores at current prices)	196
4.	Industrial production (Rs. '000 crores at current prices)	216
	Foodgrain production in million tonnes	180
	Money supply M3 (Rs. '000 crores)	363
	Imports at current prices (Rs. '000 crores)	63375
	Exports at current prices (Rs. '000 crores)	53688
	Inflation 1993-94*	8%

* The real rate is estimated to be around 12% by unofficial circles.

Source: *Economic Survey, 1993-94.*

It is not the gross output but the net value added that is often taken as the profit index in commercial agriculture. It is noted by the agricultural economists that there has been a slight decline in the agricultural output this year, *i.e.*, from the 182 million tonnes of 1992-93 to 180 million tonnes of the present year of 1993-94. But the value added this year is more than that of the last year. It is due to the fact that the use of potassic and phosphatic fertilizers has declined considerably owing to the rise in their prices.[79] It is also found that a number of farmers are turning towards the 'organic farming' where no chemical fertilizers are applied.[80] With increased prices of the chemical fertilizers the organic manures, especially those of dung and compost, are applied. Using dung cakes as domestic fuel is declining with the availability of cheaper substitutes like the L.P. Gas, the kerosene, the husk-bran of paddy, the cotton stalks and other types of farm waste having fuel value.[81] Thanks to the active environmentalists, reports are available that the villagers have taken to social forestry and other types of growing green plants that provide domestic fuel besides their shade, leaves, flowers and fruits.[82]

There is an argument that the small and marginal farmers who constitute the bulk of subsistence producers are not affected immediately by the new economic policy. The reasons adduced are that they directly purchase only a small part of their inputs in the market; they depend mostly on their traditional inputs.[83] Another weak though large economic group, the agricultural labourers also are not affected much so far as they are paid in grain, and they do not purchase their food requirements from the market.[84] On the other hand, these groups have got a lot to gain from the new economic policies in the long run. The increased area of crop land, the increased productivity of crop per land unit, the increasing returns to a man-hour — all combined will add to their benefits.[85] The existing agricultural workers can produce more and the farm sector can export the surplus; the food requirements of our population can be met by engaging a far reduced number of workers in agriculture. All these possible developments can be had from the experiences of the developed economies; do they apply to India in the same way? Or do we need a different theory?[86]

Following the new economic policy, the Indian Central Government has reduced the subsidies on fertilizers and food, decontrolled the potassic and phosphatic fertilizers and directed the States in India to hike the power tariff including that for agricultural uses so as to avoid the losses to the State Electricity Boards; considerations are going on to increase the water rates so as to get a reasonable returns on the capital invested; and to increase the rates of interest charged on the credit granted to the rural sector and agricultural purposes so as to eliminate the element of subsidies. Agro-processing and food-processing industries are declared as the new thrust areas. The restrictions on the movement of foodgrains are being lifted so as to make the whole country a single zone. It means that a farmer can sell his produce in any part of the country.[87] Of course, the Government of Andhra Pradesh is still thinking on this measure of free movement of foodgrains through its borders. Exports of the agricultural products on a significant scale are encouraged, and there are expectations that a large part of our surpluses would be competitively sold abroad.[88] With all these adjustments, there is no let-up in the size of the fiscal deficit which increased from Rs. 36,325 crores in 1991-92 to about 58,551 crores in 1993-94 (see Table 3).

TABLE 3

Budgetary Receipts and Expenditure 1991-92 to 1994-95

(Rupees crores)

Items	1991-92 Actuals	1992-93 Actuals	1993-94 Revised Estimate	1994-95 Budget Estimate
Revenue expenditure ..	82308	92702	110224	118811
Revenue receipts ..	66047	74128	76166	86084
Revenue deficit ..	16261	18574	34058	32727
Capital receipts ..	38528	36178	58646	59615
Capital expenditure ..	29122	29916	33648	32888
Capital surplus ..	9406	6262	24988	26727
Budgetary deficit ..	6855	12312	9060	6000
Fiscal deficit ..	36325	40173	58551	54915

Notes: Budgetary deficit is the excess of expenditure over the revenue receipts and capital receipts. When the borrowings and other liabilities are added we get the fiscal deficit.

Following the new economic policy a large part of the land reforms are rendered obsolete and non-significant, making it the most sensitive issue of the political economy. The possibility of the reversal of the land reforms for which we the Indians have been fighting for the most part of this century needs discussion. Reports state that the Government of Maharashtra State has introduced exemptions into the Land Ceiling Act to the trusts, cooperatives and large companies for horticultural purposes; and the States of Punjab and Haryana are likely to follow. Land Ceiling Laws are interpreted as obstacles for progress by a handful of academicians and politicians (G. Thimmaiah, *Economic Times* 28-10-93 and Ali Mohammad Khusro, *Indian Express*, 18-11-93). The basic logic of land reforms is questioned; there are numerous other ways of ushering in socio-economic equity. The land reforms are coming in the way of agribusiness where agriculture is treated equal to industry. It is argued that the land reforms have checked the development of the agro-based industries in India which are supposed to be an outgrowth of the agricultural sector.[89]

As it opens, the new economic policy seems to have more profits than losses to the Indian agriculture. Promises are mixed blessings since they assume a number of structural changes in our rural organisation, especially in the traditional organisation of agricultural production. It may not completely undo the old policies evolved during the last 4½ decades; but it may take lessons from the past experiences and gently move on a dynamic and steady path instead of rushing through the mad streets of 'free economy' as shown by the I.M.F. and other Western interests.[90]

IV. GATT AND DUNKEL

The new economic policy has been the outcome of a series of structural adjustments in view of the failures of the old domestic policy on the one side, and mainly keeping in view the changing economic realities of the international scene.[91] It is the constitutional responsibility of the Government to safeguard the health of its domestic economy by carrying on the necessary reforms so as to avoid a number of known impending economic crises. At the same time, we cannot rely on the pretended sympathies of the developed world shown towards our backwardness; they may press for the prompt repayment of their loans.[92] Therefore, the principles of classical economics have to be followed; we have to produce and survive. It is the size of our GDP, it is the quantity of per capita NNP, and it is the quality of our products that matter. Equity, social justice and other distributional aspects do not matter much in our international trade.[93]

The GATT (General Agreement on Tariffs and Trade) is an international trade agreement amongst the major trading countries of the world intended to safeguard the interests of the member countries. There is confusion among the masses and the farmers about the new economic policy and the GATT on the one hand, and the Dunkel Draft on the other.[94] These two are entirely different concepts in agricultural economics, though sometimes their effects appear to be similar.[95] The new economic policy is our domestic policy matter while the GATT is an international agreement. GATT has been there since the end of the Second World War (1948) but the new economic policy is only a recent change in our domestic economic policies. The new economic policy consists of every conceivable economic activity in India that comes under the public policy and budgeting while the GATT is related mainly to the international trade and the related activities. GATT imposes uniform standards over the member countries and they are often and incidentally reflected in our domestic policies whose Indian *avatara* will be the new economic policy and its trends in the next one decade or so. GATT (WTO) continues to be an option; we can come out of it if we feel so.[96]

The GATT has undergone a number of reformulations during the last 4½ decades and mainly at the behest of the developed Western countries and recently the U.S.A. is dominating.[97] The General Agreement on Tariffs and Trade, the GATT, came into being immediately after the Second World War in 1948 mainly to resolve the crises and restore the order in the international trade relations.[98] It replaced the old bilateral and the pre-war type of *ad hoc* multilateral trade agreements.[99] Its first meeting was held in 1946 in Geneva with 23 member countries. The eighth round was held in Uruguay in 1986 where about 108 member countries participated and identified 15 points for action and to be completed within a period of four years; but it had to be extended further due to a stiff resistance from France and the EC countries in general. The original 15 points were reformulated into seven broad points in their meet in February 1991[100] — trade relations in the agricultural products, trade related intellectual property rights (TRIPs), trade related investment matters (TRIMs), trade relations in the cotton fabrics, open markets, trade relations in the services sector and the institutional matters including the resolution of the trade disputes are the seven points.[101]

Doubts have begun to be cast on the bonafides of the U.S.A. regarding its economic interests, once the Soviet block has collapsed.[102] The new economic policy being followed by India since 1991 is closely influenced by the international forces including the GATT and the Dunkel Draft. To be brief, the last round of GATT negotiations started in 1986 with the main aim of improving the global trade relations and finally concluded on the 15th December, 1993. The famous Urguay Round got prominence for its new draft introduced by Mr. Arthur Dunkel of the Swiss, the then Director-General of the GATT (later succeeded by Mr. Peter Sutherland of the U.K.). There were 117 signatories in December 1993 and the general feeling among some of the developing countries is that they may be unduly exploited in future.

But what about India? It is true that we too will be unduly exploited if we continue to be backward or decline in terms of our relative economic position in the comity of nations. But we can get some advantages, and we can seize some of them from the developed countries like the G-7 provided we can play our cards carefully and provided we, the Indians, show our skills in building the assets of our nation by using its creative abilities.[103]

The speed of the GATT activities has been increased after 1990; and it is often attributed to the unipolar world dominated by the U.S.A. Not being satisfied with the Uruguay round and its slow progress, Arthur Dunkel, the Director of the GATT, issued a new version of the GATT draft in December 1991 and asked the member countries to convey their individual reaction to the new draft within a period of three weeks and the agreement to be signed within the next three weeks; it was to be enforced from the beginning of 1993. The wonder is that Dunkel had reformulated the GATT to favour the developed countries and particularly the U.S.A., and the reasons are obvious after the collapse of the hitherto communist bloc of economies. The Dunkel's new Draft can be put under four main heads :

The first is about the foreign investments in the industries across the globe. All the countries should open their economies for foreign investors. They should not impose any restrictions on the foreign investments and treat them at par with their domestic investors. The foreign investors should be free to invest in any industry they like. They should be free to use the locally available raw materials and labour or to import them if they want. The import duties on all these items should be the minimum or zero. They should be freely allowed to export as much as they want. All the regulations that check the working of the aforesaid free markets should be removed within two years of the signing of the final GATT.[104] These developments are suspected to lead to an unfettered entry of the MNCs which may pose a serious threat to the economic sovereignty of the country.

It should be noted that these investment policies are not directed against India or for that matter against any country in the world. It has promised a potential boom in the quality and quantity of international trade which is expected to increase by more than $ 210 billions during the next decade or so.[105] In fact, the developing countries, and India in particular, are showing interest to attract the foreign investors so as to meet the crisis of its BOP and debt servicing in the short-run. And the economy is expected to zoom to new heights in future.[106]

The second and the most controversial area of the Dunkel Draft is the patent rights or the Trade Related Intellectual Property Rights, the TRIPs. Accordingly, the patents are valid upto a period of 20 years; and patents can be declared not only on the methods of processing of the commodities but on the products outright. The second part of this point has thrown the Indian medical industry in problems.[107] The TRIPs will be internationally protected by the TRIMs or the Trade Related Investment Matters. Most of these conditions are in variance to those contained in the Indian Patents Act 1970.[108] It says that the period of patents ranges upto 5 and 7 years at the most, the patents are limited to the processes and not granted to the products and the genetic fields of both plants and animals are out of the Indian Patents Act of 1970. Being faced with the BOP crisis, we had no option but to shelve our own Patents Act and adopt the GATT as modified by Arthur Dunkel in 1991. Of course, we have got time and freedom to modify our rules and adjust our economy to the changed realities of the globe.[109]

All the patent laws for seeds are taken care of only by the country concerned. For example, if a new variety of G4 or G5 chillies are to be patented it is the Government of India that looks after this affair. Patent laws of the seeds are only national in their jurisdiction. There will be no international obligation from any other country to enforce the G4 chilly seeds patent in India.[110]

The TRIPs and TRIMs are supposed to be followed by the necessary national legislations of the *sui generis* system. The traditionally raised plants and animals are excluded from the TRIPs or the Trade Related Intellectual Property Rights. Only the micro-organisms and the micro-biological processes would be patented.[111] The plant varieties which add to the bio-diversity would be protected by other arrangements namely the *sui generis* system or a system which reproduces on its own. Patents will be resorted to only in the case of the endangered species and in this respect each country is free to choose and select the varieties it thinks fit to be brought under these systems.[112] There are some problems regarding the definition of the micro-organisms and the micro-biological processes. The micro-organisms consist mainly the algae, fungii, bacteria and viruses; the genes are sometimes included.[113] However, the pesticides involve agriculture in this chain, but here again we leave it to the bio-scientists, that deal with the bio-fertilizers and the bio-pesticides.

The obligatory part of the TRIPs is that we have to enact a system for the protection of the plant varieties, say the Rights of the Plant Breeders (RPB) by the year 2000 A.D. In this system of RPB, a new variety should satisfy four criteria before it is patented. They are novelty, uniformity, distinctness and stability (NUDS).[114] This RPB patent system comes into force in India only after 2000 A.D.[115] All the varieties of plants and animals pre-existing by 2000 A.D. will be excluded from the RPB system. Even after 2000 A.D. the farmers will have their rights to rotate their own seeds once they grow the RPB varieties on their farms.[116] Only thing is that they cannot sell on a large commercial scale which may endanger the rights of the researcher to enjoy the fruits of his inventions.[117] Of course, the researchers are free to use the patented varieties to produce new and improved varieties on their own account.

The third category deals with the export quotas and subsidies on exports. The New GATT Accord says that the export quotas are to be abolished and the subsidies in the member countries should not be more than 10% of the value of the produce.[118] Also the export duties should not exceed 10% of their value and there should not be any restrictions on exports. The fourth and the last category deals with the domestic economic policies of the member countries, about their internal economic regulations, subsidies and concessions. This last category of measures seem to interfere directly in the domestic policies of the member countries, though the other three categories also imply some degree of direct and indirect interferences in the economics affairs of the member countries. However, there is no guarantee that there would be no such interference into the economies of the non-member countries. Sometimes, their plight may be worse that they do not have the right to demand for provisions in case of crises.[119]

A soft corner available in the GATT for developing countries like India is that we are under no obligation to reduce the export subsidies on the agricultural products.[120] Moreover India can extend the subsidies to reduce the costs of marketing of the agricultural products, their transport charges, and other incidentals. These subsidies are not applicable to the developed countries. Of course, once India reaches the stage of a developed economy it may not need all these props; and it can compete in the global markets with self-confidence about its competitiveness and economic base.

V. ATTACKS ON THE NEW ECONOMIC POLICY

The new economic policy has been subject to an unprecedented scale and variety of criticism since 1991; and we find that all-round attacks are made against the official softness towards the GATT and the Dunkel Draft.[121] All the criticism can be grouped under two main heads: those that attack the entire gamut of the new economic policy; and those that find fault with only some selected aspects of the new policies.[122] Ideological strains and considerations beyond the limits of economic science are involved in the first group of criticism;[123] the second category are selective and often economic logic is cited to prove their unsuitability to the Indian conditions. Possibilities of the repetition of colonialism, exploitation of our bio-diversity, increased unemployment, criminalisation, health grounds and extinction of Indian culture are the chief headings of the first category. The economics of subsidies, possibilities of gluts, economics of equity, capital formation and agricultural development in India are some of the issue-based attacks of the second type of criticism; these are closely related to agriculture. The first category of criticism is too general and vague that we cannot find immediate answers in our agricultural economics while a large part of the second category of criticism can be clarified by using the knowledge of our science, the agricultural economics of India.[124] A number of issues involved here, in the second category, are subject to a periodical revision. The main difference between their revisions internally and externally is that India may need the support of some other similarly placed nations to press for a suitable change in the international agreements. In fact, the New GATT Accord too provides for the suitable changes to be discussed among the member countries and arrive at solutions for all the future problems.[125]

The GATT is frequently portrayed as a'rich man's club'. The whole gamut of New GATT Accord for the world agriculture is seen in India as a preconceived plot against the developing economies, and chiefly against the poorer sections of their farming communities. The international news media, both the print and electronic devices, the newspapers and the radio and television, pour in a variety of the dismal designs of the New GATT Accord. They are from Korea, China, Egypt, Indonesia, Malaysia, Iran, and the African countries. A part of the complaints are heard from the developed economies like Japan, France and Portugal. For example, the Korean and Japanese farmers are agitating against the imports of rice. They are also organising movements to oppose the New GATT Accord. It gathers an impression that the rich are trying to exploit the poor both nationally and also internationally; it may be industry *versus* agriculture, capitalists *versus* labourers, urbanites *versus* ruralites or the developed countries *versus* the poor nations of the world.[126] It is feared that the global trade links would bring high cost economy to India causing hardships to the poor people.

General Attacks

It is alleged by the academicians and the elite sections of Indians that India is opened up foolishly and suitably for exploitation by the multinationals. Globalisation will work against the interests of the Indian farming community, especially the poor, the illiterate, the ignorant and the small and the marginal farmers. Export-oriented agro-processing industries may favour the multinationals and a few large farmers in India. The reduction and removal of subsidies will starve the poor farmers. A more formidable argument is about the patent rights of the agricultural seeds and other genetic materials. It is alleged in a number of local dailies, especially in Telugu and Kannada languages, that the poor farmers would invariably be impoverished. They may lose their right of resowing their own seeds; they have to purchase from the patent-holding multinational companies at a very high rate.[127] The recent happenings in Mexico where the Amerindian farming community rose in revolt is sighted to corroborate Indian findings; and the seed stores of some multinational companies where damaged recently in Bangalore by the activists of the Kannada Rythu Sangha.[128]

The rich countries of the North and their multinational corporations try to get most of the agricultural products raised in the tropical South to meet their needs. Not only it is costly to raise these crops and fruits in their countries but also their cold climate is not suitable to grow them; but at the same time there is heavy demand for such crops in their markets, mostly for their daily wear and food items.[129]

This aspect is a colonial heritage. The white races who ruled most of the present day developing countries of Asia, Africa and Latin America lost their colonies in the middle and second half of the present century; and thereafterwards their access to these markets became limited subject to the needs of the local population; and also they were sometimes forced to pay high prices for the tropical products.[130] The colonial rulers who were accustomed to almost free supplies of these products during the last 2-2½ centuries do not relish the idea of the equal terms of trade.[131] They have found out subtle ways of exploitation through TRIPs, TRIMs and other such measures.

There is a crucial health ground in the proposed trade relations. The Westerners have become conscious of the risks of the heavy human consumption of beef and potatoes. The animal fats when excessively consumed are causing obesity, heart attacks and cancer. Vegetarian foods with vegetable oils are supposed to be light and help to avoid obeseness and keep bodies slim with long life. On the other hand, the vast populations of the developing economies like India are supposed to consume less than the necessary quantity of proteins and fats. By exchanging the tropical agricultural products, they argue, with the Western animal products, the requirements of both the worlds are met; the economic welfare of the globe increases largely by this kind of trade between these two sets of countries.[132] Some of the products like salt, sugar, tea, coffee, cocoa, spices and condiments are not grown in the Western world; but the Westerners are accustomed to consume them especially since the colonial days. For example, there is attractive market for the Indian tea abroad. The spices grown in Kerala are exported to a number of countries. The health of the Western countries depend largely on the tropical farm products.

Most of the global bio-diversity, both florae and faunae is found in the Asian, African and the Latin American countries. Their access to the Westerners became difficult once they lost their colonies.[133] They are making all efforts to regain the access and for their unrestricted use. After years of thinking they have evolved clever, subtle and modern ways of getting these products for their uses. The New GATT Accord, the patent rights or the TRIPs and TRIMs are these subtle ways. Countries like India which are neck-deep in their international debts had no other go but to sign the GATT on the 25th December 1993. Unfortunately, most of our academicians started serious discussions only at the end of November, and the time was not enough to spread the analytical message far and wide in this vast country. It is not clear why the Government of India kept almost silent till the last minute and signed it. Is India simply trapped into the beginning of modern version of colonialism? Or, are there any advantages of trade which it can harvest in the years to come? The possible answers go beyond the limits of agricultural economics. Agricultural plants, animals and crops had never been under the patents and the consequences of the New GATT Accord on them have to be carefully estimated and examined, listed and weighed from the point of view of Indian agriculturists *vis-a-vis* the world as a whole.

The critics of the New GATT Accord argued that the agricultural crops and their genetic materials are not invented by the Western scientists in the modern age. They have been there since times immemorial; the growers and the cultivators had chosen a few crop varieties from the virgin nature to cater to their food needs. Most of the global variety of crops and plants are found in the tropical countries and in their rain forests. The developed European countries and the U.S.A. had taken away a number of plants and animals that could survive in their climates from these countries. And they are now extending their false claims to the wild varieties that are native of the developing parts of Asia and Africa. It is a new disguise of their historical exploitation of these countries through their materialist and mechanical civilizations.[134]

The formulation of the patents on the plants and animals of the globe by a few rich companies and countries is questioned. Patents are awarded only to the inventions and they are not common to the ordinary 'discoveries'; plants, animals or the crops are natural and are not the result of somebody's inventions. Such natural wealth should always belong to the countries of their origin, or may be gifted to other countries in need. But some of the countries with developed technologies, say the U.S.A., are trying to use them through their MNCs for their own advantage. They are trying to sell these genetic materials to their own native countries and make profit, a blatant exploitation.

Not many forests and natural habitats of the species of plants and animals are left in Europe. They are forced to depend for their survival on the other naturally rich, but economically poor countries of the globe.[135] Most of their bio-diversity is likely to be monopolised by patents of the companies based in the rich countries in a few decades to come. The growing scientific personnel of the developing countries may be forced to purchase the genetic materials of their own lands from the foreigners.[136]

The bio-diversity of the Indian subcontinent is estimated to be one of the richest in the present world.[137] India is a vast country of about 330 million hectares of geographical area with soils of varied textures and fertilities, varied climatic conditions ranging from the daily rains in Assam to almost scarce rains in Rajasthan desert. Each climatic region in India has preserved its distinction through its unique varieties of plants and animals since the vedic times. Of late, the Indian scientists are involved in breeding new and high yielding varieties by using the available genetic materials. They are not paying any royalties to the cultivators that raised these plants, nor is there any provision of these crops being patented by the Indian scientists. If we agree to the New GATT Accord, the agrarian picture would change completely. The Indian scientists have to pay royalties to the foreign companies that patent the Indian varieties. In addition, the Indian farmers have to pay a high price for their requirements of new seeds patented by the foreign companies.[138]

It is suspected that the advanced countries may use the patents as political weapons against the poor countries. It is supposed that the foreign MNCs may not be foolish to quote too high prices for their seeds when sold to the poor Indian farmers. The rich companies may even subsidize them if needed. But could they be relied upon in all ups and downs? Suppose there may arise political differences, as in the case of our Kashmir or Punjab problems. In such situations, the powerful countries such as the U.S.A. may use it as political weapon to beat the poor countries into their traps. Similar incident took place in Brazil; and there is no guarantee that India will not face some such critical situation if it goes into the hands of the rich MNCs.[139] Dependency on the foreign based companies for common needs of the farmers like the seeds may turn into a complicated procedure in the country. The gullible farmer has to face a bureaucratic procedure; he may be cheated and deceived. Corruption and red-tapism are often associated with such procedures.[140]

The new economic policy, according to Prabhat Patnaik, may lead to dire consequences :

> "Unemployment and economic hardships, compounded by the removal of relief and subsidy expenditures, result in large-scale "criminalisation" in the society, a tendency towards authoritarian forms of Government and an atmosphere of civil strife which further discourages the much-hoped for inflow of the direct foreign investment for meeting global markets." (*New Economic Policy*, 1993).

The country is likely to get into a vicious circle of economic and social retrogression which may prove worse than the colonial period and it may be called the "neo-mercantilism". Highly mechanised agriculture with capital-intensive technologies may replace the labourers. Market may help the exploiters against the exploited; the surplus may be cornered by the rich farmer-*cum*-trader. A large section of the agricultural workers will be thrown out to the urban areas and the industrial sector which cannot employ these untrained and crude rural masses may throw them into the urban slums.[141]

Attacks by Specific Issues

A number of interesting arguments and counter-arguments, sometimes supported by explanations, appeared in the media, the daily newspapers, the electronic media and some periodicals. A few talks, seminars and discussions all over India were organised for this purpose.

Some of the arguments and suspicions are interesting, though a few of them are exaggerated statements and some of them are baseless polemics.[142]

A large number of small farmers and their well wishers from our academicians put forward the argument that the reduction and removal of subsidies and the increasing cost of inputs like power and water would lead to increased cost of production of the agricultural products, and the normal economic consequences would hard hit the farmers as well as the poor consumer especially the urban poor who have to pay an increased proportion of their income to purchase their food requirements.[143] If the prices of their output do not rise in proportion to the increased costs of inputs, then the marginal and small farmers would be soon thrown out of the process of production line.[144]

Subsidies in the third world countries are different in their purpose, nature and extent from those given in the developed Western countries. Subsidies on agricultural inputs in normal time are duly defended by the critics in many ways both within and beyond economics. The majority of farmers are so poor that they cannot pay high prices equally with the rich farmers. Agriculture being a subsistence sector and a traditional way of life, it is wrong to expect it to compete with industry or the service sector. A large number of infrastructural facilities are so old that they should not be expected to yield market rates of return on their capital invested. For example, the water tanks, old irrigation projects and roads in the rural areas should be charged nominal rates intended for maintenance.[145]

Subsidies in the developed countries are basically given to dump their surpluses in the poor food starved countries; but subsidies in India are given to improve rural employment. They satisfy the principles of economic equity and social justice as we do not have social security schemes and unemployment benefits in India.

The vital role of the agricultural sector in India is not recognized by the New GATT Accord. Poor agricultural sector with about 1/3 of the GDP provides 2/3 of the employment in India. Its role is far less in the developed countries; and this distinction is not realised by the New GATT Accord.[146]

Developed countries may cheat us. They may reduce subsidies on selected products; they may continue to subsidise others which are likely to be imported from the developing countries. For example, the subsidy on sugar, cotton, tobaco and chillies may not be reduced and Indian exporters of these products may not find markets abroad.[147]

A large portion of the agrarian reforms — the land ceilings, the tenancy reforms and re-distribution of ownership rights — have lost their importance. Reversal of the land reforms is an unpopular measure. it is widely feared that the outright removal of the land ceilings and tenancy restrictions may lead to unwanted consequences.[148] The large holders may purchase the lands of the poor farmers leading to large scale rural unemployment. As feared by Shri. Y.V. Krishna Rao of the Andhra Pradesh Ryothu Sangham the corporate sector comprising the agro-processing and the food processing companies would set up large captive farms by purchasing agricultural lands from the small and marginal farmers (*New Economic Policies, 1993*, p. 8). The multinational companies may enter into agriculture and follow the old type of exploitative agrarian relations a feature of the interlinked markets of the semi-feudalistic landlords. It may be immediately followed in the case of the commercial crops like tobacco, groundnut, oil seeds and vegetables in the forward states like Andhra Pradesh or Gujarat. This may lead to a type of contract farming where the benefits of increased productivity go to the large companies and entrepreneurs while the large mass of farmers may turn into labourers and petty rent-receivers.[149]

It is alleged that the agricultural reforms in India are intended to solve the problems faced by the Western economies. The developed economies of the North are suffering from gluts of dairy products, wheat and potatoes.[150] Sometimes, as we read in the news, they throw a part of their surplus into the sea so as to protect their price levels. Instead, it is better to dump them in the third world economies irrespective of their prices and terms. The European Economic Community countries are facing the gluts in the dairy products while wheat from Canada, the U.S.A. and Australia is sold cheap. A country like Pakistan does not import its wheat needs from the neighbouring Indian Punjab, but from the far away Canada.[151] There are cases when large amounts of butter, cheese and milk powder from the West are dumped into the Indian markets, sometimes as free gift. Frequently, these items are so spoiled that they are not consumption-worthy. Whatever they get by selling these surpluses in the poor countries is a net gain to them.[152] At the same time they can improve their goodwill in these countries by diverting a portion of these funds for purposes of their national interests including religious conversions.

The surplus generated in the agricultural sector will have problems and shy to be invested in the unimportant sector. The expected growth in the exports of agricultural products may not benefit this sector. It does not flow back into the agricultural sector, nor does it help our economy to grow. It would be swallowed up into the debt-servicing obligations which have been growing on for a last few decades. The total debt which is about $ 90.2 billions involves about $ 8.2 billions of interest and other charges per annum. Total debt as a % of GDP is about 40% and debt servicing as a ratio of current receipts is about 31% (*Economic Survey, 1993-94*). Food crises like those of Bengal in the early 1940s are feared once the agricultural sector is dominated by the exporters and foreign interests.[153] It is suspected that the development will become more unequitous marked by the monopolistic elements with concentration of the ownership of land and other means of production. Rural pauperisation will grow fast and poses problems for the maintenance of law and order. Socio-economic chaos may become usual.[154] The costs of all these consequences will be unbearably high and we may have to lose our 'freedom'once again.

The issue of 'seed patents' is one that attracted the attention of every Indian farmer that resowed his own seeds year after year. Fears are expressed about the expected problems of seeds to be faced by the Indian farmers. It is frequently written in the media that our ryots will lose their rights to grow their own seeds; they cannot put apart the first grade grains of a crop as seeds of the next crop. They are forced to purchase their seeds from the foreign countries and companies at a very high cost, say one hundred times to that of their produce. The operators of all the 72 million landholdings in India have to depend on others. Imagine the plight of the poorer sections of these cultivators. The result will be that a number of them will be either largely indebted, or go out of the cultivation and live as paupers.[155] Disastrous consequences are expected even in the written media. The patent rights on seeds are questioned by the intelligentsia, the scientists and the masses alike. No logic can defend a policy measure which robs the traditional rights of the farmers. The seeds are solely theirs, and they safeguarded them for generations together.[156]

There is a cartoon story on a booklet, *Dunkel Proposals : The Realities* (in Telugu, by the Bharatiya Kisan Sangh, Hyderabad, June 1993). A poor farmer purchased a patented brand of cow which gave birth to a calf. After some time, the patent company officer goes to the owner of the cow, the farmer, and claims the ownership of the calf by virtue of his patent rights. This picture may be an exaggeration but the concept is not unrealistic. Following New GATT Accord, the poor farmer cannot sell his calf on a 'commercial basis'; he is entitled to use it for his own domestic requirements. This distinction if extended logically is very subtle, and the poor farmers cannot go to the legal experts to prove their routine actions.[157] The basic genetic material is taken from the wild forests and the crops protected by the farmers and the new breeds evolved from them are sold back to the same farmers at a high cost; and there is no original addition or contribution by the patenting companies. Therefore, let them charge only for their services at one point of time only so that there need not be any seeds patented.[158] The *sui generis* system of patents poses some serious contradictions. The responsibility of safeguarding the patent rights are entrusted to the Government which have to penalize their own farmers. The *sui generis* system is so complicated a concept that most of the member countries including India are forced to sign it before they could fully realise its potential and concealed meaning and effects in the long-run. There is every possibility, for these countries to become the future victims. This has been recently explained in the media by Suman Sahai, the Convenor of Gene Campaign and her journalistic followers

The *sui generis* system is a part of the TRIPs according to which the member states have the opportunity (duty) to offer protection for their plants and seeds by patents or an effective *sui generis* system. It is feared that the *sui generis* helps the MNCs not only for cornering the agricultural surplus but to invest it in the same place so as to earn further profits. Thus the TRIPs and TRIMs are bound together by the *sui generis*.[159]

Treatment of genetic resources differently from other natural resources like the minerals and metals is questioned. Genetic resources have been declared to be the 'common heritage of mankind' in the GATT. This declaration has led to the blatantly unfair practice where the use of these resources has never been paid for. This unfair practice has been questioned by Suman Sahai and others saying that while Canada and Germany were able to earn by exporting their copper and coal, the developing countries are denied the opportunity to earn from their biological wealth of diversity.[160] If the copper and coal found in Canada and Germany constitute their property, then by the same principle the genetic resources found in the developing countries should be considered as their property. This is just the application of the principle of location for claiming them as the properties of the respective countries. The genetic resources have got some more and superior qualifications to make them the property of their native lands and their traditional inhabitants.[161]

The hard labour of innumerable generations of farmers is concealed in the genetic resources found in the modern world. The genetic resources have acquired their recognizable and economic importance because of the labour and ingenuity of the traditional and indigenous people, and specifically the farming communities. Most of the food and cash crops cultivated in the modern times had been carefully selected from the tropical forests and preserved and developed to their present status by the successive generations of farmers of the developing countries. A number of these crops, especially those that suited to the cold climatic regions, found their way into the present developed countries of the world. As evidence, a slightly variant varieties of a large number of these crops are found growing wild in the tropical forests of Asia and Africa. The 'indentured labour' of India was used largely on the commercial plantations owned and managed by the colonial powers, the English and the French. The West Indies, the African countries, the Mauritius, the Malacca Straits, and the Fiji group of islands are some of the examples.[162]

Private ownership of the genetic resources and their common heritage and common property are contradictory. If genetic resources are a common heritage, they cannot be privatised; they should be declared as the property of the tropical countries and paid for like any other resource of these countries. The economic sovereignty of the countries over the bio-diversity found in their countries has been recognised by the recent bio-diversity convention at the Earth Summit in Reo-di-Genero in June 1992. The corporate interests based in the developed economies argued that large amount of money and effort were necessary to protect the existing bio-diversity; and to secure proper returns on their investments patents were required. This point was well taken by the critics from the tropical countries who demanded due payment from the corporations towards the genetic raw materials required by them. But conventionally, the developed countries never paid this price. Most of the germplasm of the rice strains in the U.S.A. was taken from India and the South East Asian countries. The U.S. is earning huge profits by exporting its rice surpluses but ironed the owners of the rice germplasm. There are a number of such instances where the disease resistant genes of crops were taken from India and other tropical countries.[163]

The scientific definition of the micro-organism is intentionally changed and widened to suit the patent interests. The definition of what constitutes the micro-organisms is under controversy. Scientists say that the tradition and convention show the micro-organisms to consist of the bacteria, fungii, algae and viruses. But the genes and the cell lines also are included under the patentable micro-organisms in the New GATT Accord with an evil aim of patenting the new and future 'transgenic' plants and animals.[164] Even if we leave out their scientific mutilation, their commercial aims and objectives in this case are likely to pose dangerous problems for the future research and development of biology, and especially in the tropical countries. Gene, the unit of heredity, is now being used to rectify the genetic defects in the new breeds of plants and animals. Once patented, they are not available freely for research or medical uses, but at a high price. Again the same happen, *i.e.*, we have to pay high price to use our own genetic materials.[165]

The patents will lead to an awkward situation where India has to pay royalties for using the genes native of India. Fears are largely expressed by the institutions of agricultural research in India. Most of the crop research in India is undertaken by the public bodies like the Indian Council of Agricultural Research (ICAR) and the agricultural universities besides a few autonomous crop research stations. Seeds are processed and distributed again mostly by the public agencies like the National Seed Corporation, the State Seed Corporation(s), beside a few privately managed seed corporations. The budgetary allotment to the entire agricultural research in India does not exceed Rs. 500-600 crores, and certainly not more than Rs. 50-60 crores is earmarked for the seeds. This amount is nothing before the huge sums that are spent on this purpose by the MNCs. I came to know that a particular MNC based in the U.S.A. proposed to spend more than Rs. 7,000 crores for the purpose of developing hybrid seeds; the agitators of the Ryota Sangha under the leadership of Sri Nanjunda Swamy has quoted many such costly and impending dangers in their recent agitations in Bangalore.[166]

A number of undesirable consequences of the GATT in the guise of the new economic policies are hinted at by the academicians in India. One possibility is a drastic change in the cropping pattern in most of the third world countries including India to satisfy the demands in the Western markets. Vast tracts of Indian crop lands under rice, wheat, bajra, ragi and other cereals and millets may be shifted to the production of commercial crops and cash crops. It is feared that exotic varieties may replace the native traditional varieties of oil seeds, fruits and other products (Utsa Patnaik, *New Economic Policy*, *1993*, p.7). The Western consumers with large per capita incomes and purchasing power may exploit the poor Indian farmers of their bare necessities of food and clothing.[167]

The same analogy applies to our domestic economy too. The new policies are likely to lead to a large scale transfer of the rural capital and agricultural surpluses to the urban areas. This transfer may starve the agriculture of new investments. Further the commodity transfers may be followed by rural-urban movement of trained personnel. In other words, the rural catchment areas are likely to be drained and the urban storage may create problems of environment and pollution.

A large number of changes in the Indian economy during the last four budgets are attributed to the outside impositions in the guise of new economic policy. There is a general impression in India that the industrial development is given more importance than the poor agriculture in the measures of the new economic policy since 1991. The evidence is that the foreign investments, most of the foreign loans and the trade relations, are intended for the development of industry. The reduction in the excise and customs duties are mainly to help the industrial sector and not for agriculture.[168]

At the same time, it is seen that the agricultural sector is the victim of the new economic policy. Its subsidies are cut, the loans are reduced, the prices of its products are not sufficiently increased, and it is opened to the international forces like the patented seeds and the MNCs for their direct exploitation. Moreover, the signing of the New GATT Accord will badly affect the agricultural sector which is already starved of public investments. The Indian 'agribusiness' is still on the paper, but the foreign agribusiness may be imposed on it soon.[169] It is difficult to rely on the West if the Russian experience is any guide; Russia could not get even a part of its expected aid from the West.

At the most, a 'jobless economic growth' in India along with its reforms is feared by most of the critics. Most of the criticism of the new economic policy is based either on the bad experiences of the past or on the intuitive and imaginary happenings of the future. They give an impression that most of these policies add to the advantages of the rich sections within India and the developed countries abroad. They are against the poor sections in India including the rural poor — the agricultural labourers and small and marginal farmers. Also these policies are feared to work against the interests of the backward and developing economies world over. But what this long critique lacks is the possible and feasible alternatives and the necessary precautions to be taken by the people and the Government so as to avoid and minimise the negative and undesirable effects of the new economic policies.[170]

VI. CLARIFICATIONS OF SOME ISSUES AND FEARS

A number of issues raised by the critics are thrown out only as suspicions and unnecessary fears arising out of irrational thoughts and illogical inferences few of which can stand for a scientific verification. Some serious issues are there, but there are appropriate solutions too. India is not second to any other country in its rich endowments of human capital, the source of all other types of productive capital. It has the advantage of English language, the world's business medium. It has got a developed institutional system that can absorb the latest technologies as proved recently by the introduction of computers in India.[171] With all these advantages at hand, the defenders see that India is poised to become an economic giant of the globe provided it can exploit the new economic policies.[172]

The most horrified part of the New GATT Accord is about the patent rights of seeds used by our farmers.[173] At the outset, it should be clarified that the international patent rights of seeds is applicable to only those seeds which will be sold in the markets. The patent rights are not applicable to those that are raised and resown by our farmers on their own fields.[174] The solution is not so simple in practice. First, what is the line of separation between the own use and selling seeds on commercial lines? In India where a large part of the rural exchange continues to be barter, can we turn the exchange of seeds for some other commodities among the farmers of a village or the cultivators of neighbouring fields into a commercial act? What about the seed loans and grain loans when converted into seeds? A considerable part of agricultural wages are paid in produce, and they may be used as seeds for the next season. Is it possible to enforce the rules and regulations in each village and in the case of each farmer and field? Many such unclarified issues are there raised by both the farmers and the journalists and others.

An issue raised in connection with the RPB (Rights of the Plant Breeders) seeds system in rural India is regarding the hard labours of our traditional farming communities in protecting the plants and animals which are being used for the patents at present. This will not pose any problems when both the researchers and the RPB firms come from the same communities, or else, all of those involved will be Indians, and we will work for our motherland. Further, India has got opportunities to get royalties for its own patents.[175] In view of its second largest reservoir of trained scientific personnel and rich genetic pool, nothing can prevent it from developing a number of new genetic varieties and get them patented. We can export our patents and get royalties even from the presently developed Western countries most of which are not naturally endowed with rich bio-diversity.[176] Only necessary things are a strong will to develop ourselves, and the required national unity a pre-requisite for orderly progress and economic development.

Monoculture is one of the widely discussed issues in India. The fear of monoculture unleashed by some vested interests or private companies is often mentioned by some scholars as a clear possibility in India. Such anti-social and hated practices can be checked by the strong ethical codes informally followed in the rural India; or else, public agencies or the Government can check such malpractices whenever and wherever occupied.[177] It is accepted that the international markets for a number of products differ so widely that they may lead to increased diversity of crop production to cater to the needs of a variety of consumers world over. A country like India where the agro-climatic regions are suitable for a wide variety of crops, there will be no possibility of a monoculture. Moreover, the free markets may encourage the growers to go for new and exotic varieties that increase the bio-diversity.[178] In the recent times, the West Germany thrived on its diverse crops while the East Germany could not grow enough food at the time of their re-unification. The lesson is that free market and global trade relations can help the bio-diversity of India.

A related point is that the large scale exports of foodgrains may reduce their availability within India; and also the exporters may prefer to export the quality produce leaving only the inferior grades of rice and wheat for our own consumption. This possibility arises only when we see from Indian point of view. India is not only an exporter but an importer too. It can import those products where it has got higher cost of production and the same logic of quality applies here too. Therefore, we have to consider the net effects of the trade that includes both exports and imports.[179] The net trade advantages are determined by a number of variables which are determined by a number of sub-variables which cannot be predicted in advance. But theoretically speaking, any two or more parties or countries are left with more satisfaction after the trade than what they had before the trade. In fact, this is the principle of any simple exchange of commodities.[180] India may grow rich after some time and when its purchasing power improves it can order for quality products. On the other hand, in the initial stages, we can have the advantage of exchanging our quality products against large quantity of inferior products intended to feed our vast millions with cheap grain, cheap cloth, cheap shelter and so on for which we are craving at present.[181]

Inequality in the terms of trade is an issue raised by a number of economists backed by some findings. There is a complex that the developing countries enter the world market as unequal partners and leave with unequal rewards (*Human Development Report 1992*, Delhi). Keeping away may not be the alternative in the mind of these critics, but they could not find out any useful solutions. The defenders say that expecting such inequalities itself is unfounded. For example, India had enjoyed monopoly in the past in many markets in the world. The jute, the mica, the tea and the cotton fabrics enjoyed favourable terms of trade in the world. Our terms of trade can definitely improve once we reach a stage of economic prosperity. And there is no guarantee that we shall have favourable terms of trade if we wait outside the GATT for a period. We have to enter the global markets at one time or other.[182] We have to have our share of the global markets if we want to enjoy the advantages of international trade. Therefore, the earlier we enter it the better will be our terms of trade.

Subsidies is an issue that found the supporters from the ranks of the poor peasants and also some bureaucrats and industrialists. There are two types of subsidies involved in the GATT. The first are the ordinary and general or the non-product specific subsidies allowed to the farmers of all types without specifying the crops. These are the subsidies on pesticides, fertilizers, seeds, power, water and credit. The developing countries like India can provide subsidies, according to the GATT, upto 10% of their respective output costs. The present estimates in India are that all these (1992-93) subsidies would not exceed 5% of the agricultural output and therefore, we face no problem for the present. Further, the new subsidies given to the 'small and marginal farmers' are completely excluded from the GATT. Since more than 40% of the Indian cultivators fall under these two categories, the Government will be under no obligation to reduce the existing subsidies. Of course, the ceiling on subsidies to these categories of farmers is not mentioned anywhere in the GATT, nor is there any clear-cut definition of the poor and marginal farmers, or under which conditions further subsidies can be allowed or withdrawn.[183] However, a ceiling of 5% of the cost of output is imposed on the advanced countries.

The second type of subsidies are the product-specific subsidies. They are allowed in the form of support prices for the 20 selected crops.[184] Some of them in India are negative subsidies in the sense that the farmers would always get higher prices in the market; they are losing by the levies. It is calculated that the farmers are losing between 30% to 50% by selling at the support prices. Therefore, this is no ground for any criticism against the free play of market forces for inputs and outputs.

The value of the total agricultural production of India during 1993-94 is about Rs. 2,15,000 crores; the value of foodgrains alone is about Rs. 1,96,000 crores (*Economic Survey 1993-94*), 10% of it works out to 21,500 crores. But our total subsidies on agriculture in India during 1993-94 did not exceed Rs.6,000 crores; about Rs. 4,000 crores are allowed on each of food and fertilizers, totalling to Rs. 8,000 crores in the present budget of 1994-95. It is stated that our economy can never afford more than 10% as subsidies.[185]

India is not a loser in the issue of subsidies. The total subsidies on agricultural products in Japan are 65% to 70%, in South Korea they are about 50% and they work out to about 25% in the European common market countries. The GATT stipulations regarding these developed countries are that the subsidies on their domestic agricultural output should not exceed 5%. In this sense, the comparative advantage is in favour of the developing countries and the developed countries with strong agricultural base have to suffer more.[186] The subsidies in India are far below 10%, a ceiling allowed for the developing countries. Moreover xeroing the subsidies can help to reduce the fiscal deficits of our budgets in the short-run; and in the long-run it would improve the efficiency of our agricultural sector to the international levels. The agricultural sector can grow into a self-sustaining and vibrant and dynamic part of the economy that it will be no more a burden in need of props or other subsidized inputs.[187]

The theory of economic development takes us to a state of unnecessary subsidies. The withdrawal of subsidies automatically leads to the operation of the price theories leading to the rising prices of the inputs at least to cover the rising prices of the inputs as to cover their cost of production; and this results in the increased prices of foodgrains. In one sense this is true, but may be desirable also. Subsidisation of inputs is not a permanent solution to the production and promotion of any sector of the economy. Subsidy is a strictly temporary and short-run help only.[188] Often its intention is to smoothen the structural adjustments. This sort of problems are not unique to the Indian economy, they are found world over. In fact, the actual advantages of international trade are obvious in these areas. We can stop their costly production at home, or at least wind up the uneconomic units; and can import these goods from those parts of the globe where they are produced at a sustainably reasonable cost. The internal resources so released can be re-deployed into the production of other and advantageous channels of production. Thus a lot of wastage can be avoided.[189]

Fears are expressed in many developing countries including India about a GATT provision that at least 3% of our domestic markets should be opened to the international markets.[190] But this provision is not applicable to those developing countries which are in the crisis of balance of payments. Suppose, wc will cross over this crisis and the exemption will be lifted. Cannot we open at least 3% of our domestic market for normal imports in our domestic agricultural markets? We can do on two simple grounds. For a long time to come our general price of agricultural commodities continue to rule lower than those of many developed countries.[191] Secondly, since the same facility is available to us in other countries, we can export our products to a larger extent and trun the advantage to our favour. India is blessed with a large stock of cheap labour and this would continue at least right into the entire 21st century.

Dumping is feared by a number of academicians and producers of specific commodities. Fears are expressed in India that the country would be dumped with imported agricultural products and our farmers have to face unemployment.[192] Most of these fears are unfounded when we look from the global angle. The average agricultural prices in India when considered in dollar units are far less than in many developed countries. Only sugar, oil-seeds and some pulses are priced slightly higher than the international markets. Also another alternative is to estimate their prices net of all subsidies in the respective countries. In such an event these three items also are cheaper in India than in many of their leading producers in the world. India has been already placed advantageously in the global markets in the case of vegetables, fruits, rice and wheat. In fact, the deltas of India which are near the sea ports are placed most advantageously to export their surplus produce to the international markets. Also there is nothing that prevents India from imposing countervailing duties against any kind of dumping.

One possibility is that the Indian agriculture and the Indian economy as a whole may revert back to the colonial type in the name of "free trade". There is a possibility in these arguments that ultimately India may be colonized by some economically powerful foreign country. The votaries of the type of argument are Profs. Prabhat and Utsa Patnaik, Arun Ghosh and their followers (*EPW*, 29:12, 19-3-94, 683-89). The new economic policy, according to Prabhat Patnaik, is nothing more than a reversion to the policy stance that had characterised pre-independence India. This reversion is sought to be camoflaged by caveats of various kinds. There are fundamental similarities between the policy predilections of the colonial period and those at present. Some of the major features of the current new economic policy, according to Prabhat Patnaik, show this trend. They are the ceiling on fiscal deficit as a % of the GDP, the regime of liberal imports, the free market in foodgrains, the progressive elimination of food subsidies, the selective public investment with emphasis on their rate of return, the open invitation to the MNCs, the financial liberalisation and reduction in the subsidised credit to the priority sector.

But the defenders of the new economic policy answer that the real income of the Indian farmers will increase, and they turn themselves into largely commercial farmers with a market consciousness, and there will be no exploiters and exploited; but trade will be on equal terms only. The picture portrayed is quite different from that of the colonial terms of trade and this point needs further analysis.[193]

The 'new drain theory' is a criticism from the point of view of the colonial economic history of India. The new economic policy is feared to lead to some unwanted consequences among which the 'new drain theory' is one. The old drain theory was enunciated by Dadabhai Naoroji in the 1870s. India earned surplus in its merchandise trade but faced deficit in the invisibles, as in the case of interest payments, charges of banking and insurance, net profit and dividends, travel payments and other service charges. The visible surplus disappeared into the 'invisible deficits'.[194] These points have been logically and rationally derived by Prof. P.R. Brahmananda from the new economic policy.[195] All these invisibles are likely to appear in a new guise and result in draining the wealth of India to other countries that are allowed to invest in India. This way provide them sufficient time and opportunities to interfere in the internal political matters — the squabbles among the political parties[196] — and this may lead to the repetition of the colonial history though not the Islamic type of conversions.[197]

The 'new drain theory' is set aside by the defenders by using the counterbalancing logic of economic history. In the present circumstances, the net advantages of the invisibles need not always be favourable to the Westerners. At least after a few years, we the Indians too can turn into exporters of these services. For example, we have got an edge of advantage in the matters relating to computer software. The present economic policy allows the foreign capital under some strict stipulations; they have to employ Indians, they should export their wares; and their licenses can be cancelled if they turn into a threat to our national interests. Moreover, the Indians can start a number of MNCs and can spread them throughout the globe, after gaining the necessary and sufficient experience in the starting years. No such type of Islamic taxation and *inams* and the colonial type of drain would be allowed.[198]

After the necessary clarifications, the economic advantages to India from the liberal economic policies outweigh the problems. Not only a number of issues are directly clarified by the defenders, but the new economic policies can turn into a bonanza for India when used cautiously; they can increase the economic space available to India and would help to release the creative energies of the country. Patents are to our advantage and we can have a lion's share of the royalties. The monoculture is imaginary and the bio-diversity will be increased. Subsidies will be scaled down, and it is for our economic advantage only. Dumping can be checked by enacting the appropriate legislation. Revival of colonialism is only imaginery; in fact, we may become a colonial power with our immense power of human capital and scientific knowledge. The new economic policy is portrayed as a panacea for a number of our present economic problems; and India's economic future lies in its sincere and increasing participation in the global trade. India has got so much to offer to the world through trade that it can get enriched soon and help the poor countries to overcome hunger and poverty.

VII. SOME SUGGESTIONS

Should the Indian agriculture be exposed unchecked to the MNCs and other international agencies? The present state of development of Indian agriculture is not advanced enough as to face the unchecked play of the market forces at the international level. Nor such an exposure is to be imposed by any agency. Most of the expectations and suggestions are for a firm, viable, steady and sustained pace of development towards the goal of an efficient and vibrant agricultural sector. In this direction, a number of policy measures are necessary. The Indian patents should be suitably reformulated, so as to protect the interests of our farmers, and at the same time to safeguard our bio-diversity.[199] Also, the imports of poisonous chemicals into the country should be regulated and their uses banned if necessary.[200] The State should involve the farmers in all these activities.

Exposing the Indian farmers to the multinational seed companies may play havoc on their day-to-day life. The natural privileges of the farmers should be protected with regard to their seeds. After paying the initial royalty on the patented seeds, the farmers should be free of any further charges when they produce seeds for themselves or to their co-village farmers. They should be free to sell their seeds at least within India, and also to modify them so as to suit their climatic and seasonal conditions. Whatever our farmers do within our national borders, even if it is selling seeds on commercial basis, the MNCs should not have any powers to interfere in their routine activities; nor could they police their activities. The seed companies should be allowed to deal only with organised bodies manned by trained persons and without imposing any restrictions on the peasants. And farmer in any corner of India should be free to go to any Indian seed agency and get his requirements of seed subject to the overall Indian legal system. It is also necessary to organise some institutions to impart training to the farmers about the methods of sowing the new seeds and culture of crops.

Necessary legislation should be introduced regarding the rights and privileges of the farmers and the scientists. The Indian patents rights system should be so reformulated as to protect the richness of the Indian bio-diversity ensuring sufficient protection to the rights and interests of our farmers and the scientists. Our *sui generis* system should state in unambiguous terms, the rights of the farmers and the scientific community, and at the same time safeguarding our national interests. It should also state that reward for breeding companies through any form of plant breeding rights will be granted only when the labour and the innovative faculties of our Indian farming community are sufficiently rewarded. The Indian *sui generis* system should include some major conditions in their necessary details to protect our agricultural interests and to enable to follow a healthy path of growth and development. Then only we can expect that our farmers are legally protected from the profit-motivated activities of the MNCs and other multinational business interests. The indigenous practices should be retained so far as they do not come in the way of agricultural modernisation.

It is desirable to have short period of patents which can relieve the farmers from the burden of maintaining accounts of seed. The period of patent ranging upto 5 to 7 years as enshrined in the Indian Patent Act of 1970 should be retained. It should not be hastely increased to 20 years as required by the New GATT Accord. This will induce the seed companies to speed up their activities of seed production and breeding of new varieties and increases the choice of the farmers to choose among the new seeds. This provision can speed up the research in the new seeds. This provision will also help to increase the genetic heterogeneity which again can check the negative effect of the narrowing of the genetic base of a crop. The effects of shortening the period of patents will be that it may increase the size of yearly royalties. It depends again on the period of the 'use-life' of the seeds. Therefore, the farmers' organisations should educate the cultivators about the potential yields and expected period of 'use-life' of the seeds. Problems may arise due to famines, pestilence or crop pests; in such periods the farmers should be left free to continue their old brand or to switch on to new and more resistant varieties.

Free flow of scientific knowledge should be ensured both through written media and also through electronic media. The right of the breeder to use the protected genetic material to breed new varieties should be made distinct and separated from the 'research exemption' which allows research on protected genes but not their commercial application as stated in the New GATT Accord. The free exchange of scientific and experimental material and data must be ensured to the researchers so that their work and research would contribute to an unhindered progress of agricultural science. Scientific knowledge should not be patented or privatised but should be allowed to flow freely.

One possible solution to protect the peasants from the possible abuses of seed patents is that the State should take over the responsibility of 'a common pool' of seeds. This pool, an administrative unit at a district level or state level, should purchase the patent rights direct from the seed companies, or hire such rights for a specified period on behalf of the peasants; and sell out the seeds at a premium at one point of time. Depending on the size of yield, profits and the demand for a certain brand of seeds the prices of each variety of seed can be worked out. In such a system, the farmer is not directly related to the MNC, and he is free to purchase a new seed from his neighbouring farmer, or the latest seed from the "State Seed Centre" or to sow his own seed, or to purchase from any other unit in India. The only possible problems are from the 'bad bureaucracy' which can be checked by forming a type of seed cooperatives of the farmers with aid and regulation from the Government.[201]

The current practices and level of using agro-chemicals in India and abroad is not fully sustainable. The urgent need is to search for more sustainable and naturally reproducible substitutes at affordable costs. The alternatives are largely the bio-substitutes both as fertilizers and pesticides. They are based largely on the micro-organisms.[202] It is hoped in India that we can replace the costly and imported plant protection chemicals by the cheap and indigeneously produced bio-pesticides. This can be achieved before we enter into the next century provided our scientists are committed to this task of developing our indigeneous technologies.[203]

The plants and animals of India present one of the largest bio-diversity concentrations of the world. It is followed by an abundant supply of a large range of micro-organisms such as algae, fungii, bacteria and viruses. Given the enormous strength of its bio-diversity and its advantageous position in the globe, India can emerge as a global leader in the development of bio-technology and genetic engineering provided that it can use the available opportunities of trade and technology of the modern world.

Let there not be any land ceilings or compulsory levies; nor any subsidies are required in such a situation. A Guntur ryot who is advantageously placed in raising rice, chillies, cotton and groundnut can export his products to any markets in any corner of the globe.

What should be the role of the Government for the development of Indian agricultural after following the measures of the new economic policy? Let the Government reduce its unnecessary interference into the routine socio-economic affairs of the villages; the villagers as a community can solve their own socio-economic problems. It is enough if the Government can maintain strict law and order through its genuine machinery. Let the free market forces take care of the distribution and ownership of the productive assets. Let the Government be highly selective in its taxation measures aimed at encouraging the economic development. India should be careful that it should not yield to the pressure tactics of the U.S. by way of adding 'social clauses' and labour clauses to the already value loaded GATT (WTO) in favour of the U.S.

The positive economic role of the Government after following the new economic policy will change its image substantially. Regarding the agriculture, it is enough if the Government takes care of the creation, repairs and efficient maintenance of the infrastructural facilities such as the major and medium irrigation works, marketing and transport facilities. Here again the Government can be selective in the sense that the prosperous farming communities can create for themselves a large number of infrastructural facilities which are being spent on by the Government at present.

Speaking in general, the economic position of the Indian farmer *vis-a-vis* his counterparts in other countries will improve considerably in view of the following advantages enjoyed by the Indian farming community more so the commercial farmers and others in the rich river valleys of India. Sunshine is so abundant in most parts of India that the farmer can grow three rice crops provided irrigation is available continuous. India is also blessed with abundant irrigable lands and water that 60% to 85% of its net sown area can be easily irrigated. Second advantage is that the Indian agriculture can be energised mostly through the solar implements with the least cost principles of energy. Thirdly, the farming community of India, nearly 60 crores, is the largest in the world. The least estimates show that this community working on about 200 million hectares of the cultivable lands of India can easily produce 500 to 600 million tonnes of foodgrains a large part of which can be exported to the Western countries.

VIII. CONCLUSIONS

The old economic policies followed in India during the period of 1947—1990 could not yield satisfactory results. The change has been on cards in the 1980s and was introduced in the crisis year of 1991. The failure of the old policy is evident in the agricultural sector which has been highly subsidized but which could not improve to the international levels. The new economic policy is not, by any measure, an unmixed blessing for the Indian agriculture, especially in view of the seed patents, cut in subsidies and unregulated export markets as proposed in the New GATT Accord. As we have already entered into this new era, it is desirable that we reformulate our policies suitably so as to avail all the new opportunities of the open international markets; but at the same time, we should be careful to protect the interests of our farmers, the Indian economy, the Indian nation and its unfettered sovereignty.

There are some calculated prophesies about the shape of our agriculture during the new and next generation, let us say around 2025 A.D. The proportion of population engaged directly in agriculture may fall down from the present 70% to around 30% or even to 20%. The average size of the operational holdings will increase to suit the technical kits or the economic units, from the present 2.2 hectares to about 10 to 12 hectares. The resulting variation in the number of operators and the area operated will be explained by the structural changes in the organisation of production. In spite of the vast potential investments in land improvements, the scarcity for land increases and so the land prices and the rents. Indian agriculture becomes such an active industry that the productivity levels will be raised to the international levels as a result of the globalisation. As the markets will be international, we can expect the Indian system only as a part of the global economy which will be a closely inter-meshed and united global economic system.

NOTES

1. At best, my aim is to inform the farmers about the positive aspects, and at the same time, to caution them about the negative and harmful consequences.
2. What type of legislative and protective measures can be adopted by the Government of India and its provinces is not dealt with here.
3. Many of these points are found and often repeated in the news media and specific reference to them is not possible. An interesting part of this paper is the result of my discussions with a wide cross-section of the agriculturists, and the latest trip being to the village of Kolanupaka in Nalgonda district.
4. Descriptive positive economic analysis itself is a method of modern research; and a few normative aspects are adduced. Being an explorative survey of ideas, this paper may not conform to any rigid framework.
5. It is said that India's new economic policies are watched and evaluated by the international agencies from the point of view of the GATT. My approach is from the other and the Indian view; how far the GATT is relevant to India and fits into our new economic policies?
6. All branches of economics and walks of life are affected by the changes in the economic policies of the country. But we shall discuss only the chief and basic themes leaving the rest to be followed, and this is limited to the interests of the Indian agriculture.
7. The world is 'compressed' into a uni-polar single unit with the collapse of the Soviet block; the meaning of a number of terms used in international economics has changed under this disposition. The traditional theories of international trade are under stress; the number of GATT countries has risen to 117 in the latest round concluded in Geneva, and likely to increase further.
8. Keeping out of the GATT may not be possible for a huge economy like India and it is ruled out both by the economists and the politicians of India.
9. There are a number of Ryot Sanghas and other farmers' organisations in India which have already started serious discussions and the necessary actions; the agitational part is excluded here.
10. I do not mean that there should not be loans and subsidized inputs. What I earnestly wish is that they should not be induced to laziness and poverty, but should be in a

sound economic position to support the other sectors of the economy. They should be exposed to the outside realities of the world that they can internalise a large part of the externalities.

11. The premise is that past experience and knowledge can guide us into a better future.
12. It is often possible that one and the same policy measure affects agriculture and other sectors differently; but we do not go into these inter-sectorial variations in their effects. For example, high prices of food may be disadvantageous to industrial sector.
13. It is not to say that the BOP is the only crisis; it is the most important and immediate concern to India; the internal problems and crises like unemployment, poverty, militancy and regional chaonism are as well serious.
14. Increasing the total physical output of our agricultural sector had been the central core of our agricultural policy at least of the two decades of 1960-1980 until we achieved self-sufficiency.
15. Land reforms is a part of the agrarians reforms. Insignificance refers to the huge unrealised potential.
16. This sort of general critique is applicable to a number of other developing economies and a few of the developed ones like that of France as far as their agricultural sector is concerned.
17. We ignore the political motivations and vested interests (if any) involved in this critique.
18. The empirical exercises showing the extent of the failures are not relevant here. Not much work is there about the quantitative aspects of the 'potentiâl'.
19. Here the relevance of productivity is only to the extent that whether the specific project undertaken by the help of the loaning agency could generate enough net income to meet the repayments within the stipulated period.
20. Loss and profit accounts refer to purely commercial accounting of the firms concerned.
21. There are arguments that all may not be well even with agricultural development of farmers' prosperity, as seen in the case of Punjab. Here we do not link such extraneous variables as militancy or extremism to our peaceful and harmonious models of agricultural development of India.
22. The chief reason is that it is the occupation of the majority of people in India; large chunk of the poor are easily affected by poor harvests and low incomes.
23. The chief index is the low level of its wages and poverty of the majority of cultivators.
24. Major component is the increased prices of land; 'the real cost of labour hour' has increased along with the generally rising index of the 'cost of subsistence'.
25. The political considerations are ignored; or they are based on the economic ground of 'inability to pay'.
26. It is felt that a large part of the rural-urban migration is mainly due to push forces, the result of 'rural stagflation'.
27. This is only a relative picture after comparing with the agricultural economics in other countries. The fear is that there are many farmers in India who are unable to produce their 'own subsistence'.
28. Some of these points are not new but found in the Bombay Plan of 1948.

29. An evaluation of the critique is not relevant here, nor are we concerned with the virtues and vices of capitalism.

30. The fiscal deficit is not zero in any of these budgets, and the deficit of about Rs. 58,000 crores in the last budget of 1993-94 is expected to be upto 7.3% of the GDP at current prices, while the budgeted estimate in the current year of 1994-95 is about Rs. 55,000 crores.

31. The effects of these lines of spending will not increase the production, nor add to the value of productive assets, but creates demand and in turn leads to demand pull inflation.

32. It is frequently alleged that the agricultural surpluses are diverted to unproductive activities like cinemas, residential buildings and for fighting elections. They wait for the public investments in the infrastructural facilities.

33. The administrative costs and the bureaucratic leakages of subsidies are not taken into account.

34. The structural rigidities are ignored in these calculations.

35. Unofficial estimates show that the annual amount of subsidies on water work out to be more than 50,000 crores in India, while that on power consumed for agricultural purposes the annual amount of subsidies at current market cost amounted to more than Rs.20,000 crores. Of course, there are differences of opinion about the methods employed in their calculations and estimations.

36. Industrialists may retort that the imported rice and wheat are cheaper than those produced in India. Therefore, we do not enter into the comparisons of economics of efficiency of agriculture *versus* industry.

37. Over-irrigation of lands located close to the field canals are reported under the major projects of Andhra Pradesh, the Sriramasagar, Nagarjunasagar and the Godavari delta. Some recent surveys have shown that the crop yield per unit of water has largely increased in the Cauvery delta of Tamilnadu after the water supply became scarce during the last few years. If some of these reports are to be believed, the gross average annual crop yield per hectare also increased in the Tanjore delta.

38. It is often argued that the total productivity of agriculture in South India can be increased if the water is judiciously distributed and scientifically managed. It can be achieved through largely increased area under irrigation and improved yields by reducing water-logging and soil erosion. It also meets the goal of equity in the supply of irrigation waters.

39. The power sector is unable to collect the cost of production from the rural areas. Our main concern here is that the State Electricity Boards in India are frequently found in red and in arrears to the NTPC. In spite of thousands of crores of rupees sunk into the power plants — hydel, thermal or nuclear — the State Boards are unable to collect amounts sufficient to meet their maintenance and salaries, and not to talk of returns on the capital. They are depending on the external sources of capital funding for any further expansion. Apart from the subsidies to the farm sector, there may be quite a good number of other reasons for this horrible state of the SEBs. The cost of generation quoted by some foreign MNCs is Rs. 2 while the SEBs are finding it hard to collect even Re.1 per unit in a number of states. Example is the recent agitation in Gujarat State.

40. This practice of 'water tenancy' is common under the bore-wells and even on lands irrigated partly by tanks in South Indian villages, and most of it is 'concealed tenancy'.

41. Some of the basic conditions of the perfect markets like the large number of buyers and sellers and free entry etc. are satisfied in the case of agricultural production and foodgrain markets in India.

42. There would be the substitution effect which detracts the resources from other sectors into agriculture.

43. If it is met by deficit financing, then the principles of monetary-macro-theory have to be applied; the first effect is the rising levels of inflation.

44. We stop short of entering into the economics of subsidised official credit and its political role in the recent elections in India.

45. The Government might have pursued the policies of price stabilization in order to help the poor consumers and the agro-industries, but these actions result in losses to the farmers that expected gains from the free play of market forces. Is not such a price policy justified by the subsidies granted?

46. Some of the cotton growers argued that they are denied this rare opportunity to sell their cotton dear in the markets this year; they suffered heavily during the bad seasons and low prices when the Government could not save them from indebtedness and even horrible suicides in Prakasam and Guntur districts.

47. There is an argument that most of the Indian farmers, the small, the marginal and the medium, are able to survive mainly because of the subsidies. If the subsidies are completely removed, either most of them have to leave out agriculture after incurring losses; or else the prices of foodgrains will be increased enormously if the cost of production of the marginal farmers has to be fully covered. In such an event, the rich and entrepreneurial farmers will be left with high amounts of profit. Whether agricultural income taxes should be imposed, or subsidies should be granted on food directly to the poor consumers is not our concern here.

48. It is found that an average farmer in the U.S.A. can purchase a car or two from his annual net income from the farm sector. An Australian capitalist may get higher returns by investing in the wheat fields rather than producing bicycles with his capital. An average Indian farmer cultivating an operational holding strictly under the ceiling laws cannot dream of a car throughout his life, and not to speak of his annual profits.

49. It is always left to the Government to form the necessary rules and regulations for an efficient and effective functioning of the private markets by taxing which the Government can raise revenue.

50. The Yotopoulasian type of backward bending supply curve of labour are exceptional cases. The leisure preference schedule of the labourers is supposed to remain constant; labour supply increases along with the wages.

51. It is not clear whether the parity is established by using the exchange rates (market? or official?) or through other methods like the labour equivalency.

52. This is when compared to the average prices in the free markets for these commodities. Unofficial estimates in Andhra Pradesh show that the variation ranges from 30% to 50% depending upon the grade, sort and variety of rice in the case of paddy.

53. My observations are mostly from the States of Andhra Pradesh, Tamilnadu and

Karnataka where from some stories of corruption are horrible to hear. The methods of collection and amounts in each case is not known.

54. Most of these are recently banned by the Government of India; the list will increase if we name them by their brands and concentrations. The concentration and spread of each is not known.

55. The idea is not however supported by any sound economic logic or empirical findings.

56. Efforts to introduce cooperative farming failed in India.

57. Migration of workers to the industrialised urban centres is desirable so far their productivity in the urban sector far exceeds the costs of their migration. But in India such migration has frequently added to the urban slums either in Calcutta or in Bombay. Therefore, this aspect needs further analysis.

58. The cost of subsidized loans and the amounts of the written off loans in different parts of India is too well known that it needs scarcely any analysis here.

59. Not only a part of the subsidized loan is spent on toddy and alcohol, a large part of the productive resources are diverted to their production and distribution.

60. Sometimes evidence goes against this argument. For example, the agriculturally developed state of Punjab is not free from massive unemployment especially among the youth.

61. Its chief aims are to solve the internal problems of poverty and unemployment and redemption of the external debt by making use of the new vistas of the global markets.

62. The order of seriousness of these problems, and their priority on our national agenda changes often that a solution of a few may be more effective since most of them are inter-related. Thus ordering their priorities is a serious issue to economists.

63. It is a public secret that more than 75% of our defence equipment was of Soviet made. We are forced to spend a considerable part of the budget, about Rs. 23,000 crores for 1994-95, on our defence, a largely unproductive but unavoidable expenditure at present.

64. The amount of debts is about $ 88 billion and the annual servicing charges are around $ 8 billion. About 33% to 37% of our earnings through foreign trade ($ 20 to 25 billion) goes into this account. None of us prefer a Soviet type of crash.

65. India with its 'Hindu rate of growth' cannot absorb sweeping changes. The effectiveness of the slow and steady measures also are sometimes diluted due to the internal contradictions. 'Hindu rate of growth' indicates only a slow and steady path and is not related to the 'Hindu economics' advocated by some political parties of India.

66. The long-term consequences of the presence of a sizable amount of foreign capital in the country is not given any serious thought. A few economic historians like Amit Bhaduri are crying the hoarse of colonialism while a number of optimists take it as an opportunity to enrich themselves adding to the prosperity of the country. However, the foreign investors suspect the sincerity of the reformers and the effectiveness of free enterprise in India. In fact, a large amount is flowing in the form of foreign portfolio investment into India.

67. There is no hard and fast rule in the theories of economic development that the same measures should produce identical economic effects in all these countries whose economic base and socio-cultural mix varies widely. Not the liberalism and globalism, but the dictations from abroad are opposed in India.

68. The immediate and direct indices of the policy changes are the Central and State budgets, and the de-investment of the public undertakings besides the reduction of subsidies.

69. Agriculture is affected by changes in other sectors through its linkages to industries, trade and service sectors; they are referred to only contextually.

70. It is argued by some of the economists of the developed countries that a number of burdens are imposed on them by the backwardness of many new countries; their major burden is the aid programmes.

71. It may be true that the political superstructure depends upon the economic infrastructure in the long run but it needs a separate type of analysis.

72. This is where the involvement of the local and farmers' organisations is needed. They can bring about the necessary awareness among the farmers about the opportunities as well as the risks that are involved in the new policy measures.

73. The structure of the companies, the technologies used in reclamation, the motivations and the consequences to the Indian economy may differ widely in the present period after two centuries.

74. The Presidency of Madras had its own organisations to reclaim its waste lands. They had been there in South India in some form or other even before the British advent.

75. The environmentalists also are connected to their international networks as seen in the Earth Summit of 1992; therefore, the Indian farmers are advised not to be misled by their excessive pourings.

76. The trend in the present policy plans is to make the agricultural sector not only physically sustainable but it should generate enough funds to be invested in its development and preferably with surplus funds to support the other sectors in the long run.

77. Substantiation of this state needs enormous data about the costs and benefits in the agricultural production which can be gathered only by a new series of farm management studies.

78. There are indications of disappointments and distress felt in the labour circles of the industrial sector, especially when they are closed and lock outs are declared. It may take some time for agriculture to realise the effects of the new policies; a number of academicians are optimistic about the positive trends, especially towards a self-sustainable path of growth.

79. The general belief is that response to price changes of agricultural inputs takes fairly a long time for obvious reasons; unofficial reports show evidence of falling trends in the gross production of foodgrains in States like Andhra Pradesh, West Bengal and Kerala.

80. Products of this brand intended mainly for exports have already entered into the markets. It is also a practice in India that a number of farmers use only organic manures as far as the production of foodgrains for their domestic requirements are concerned.

81. Cost effectiveness of the substitutes frequently depends upon the methods of cooking and heating, the type of ovens or *choolahs* used and so on. Subsidies cannot provide a permanent solution.

82. Reports of increasing green coverge started to trickle in, but not much improvements and extension of any major green patches are shown in the satellite pictures taken over India. The rate of degradation of forests seems to have been slowed down.

83. This argument may apply mostly to the dry crops. Water, power and fertilizers are largely common on wet lands irrespective of the scale of production organisation.

84. It is doubtful whether the wage rates are not affected adversely when the cost of other inputs are increased. Also the economisation by the hitherto employers of wage labourers may favour the substitution of their family labour.

85. There is a possibility that growing commercialisation and consequent mechanisation of agriculture may require less number of unskilled workers.

86. No readymade answers are available to these queries. But it is the belief of the official circles that there is a clear possibility of realising a large untapped agricultural production, especially in the case of commercial crops.

87. The list of 'reforms' and structural adjustments is not complete.

88. Results are awaited; we hope to have the fifth consecutively favourable agricultural season during the 1994-95 during which a large number of these new policies find their effects manifested.

89. Opinions differ about the entrepreneurial capabilities of the Indian farmers after the debacle of Punjab, and the entrance into India of a number of Italian and other European food processing firms in the recent times.

90. The budgets of 1994-95, both Central and States', show that hasty and extreme measures are largely avoided in favour of a middle path and steady change. The A.P. budget has allotted Rs. 71 crores for subsidy on fertilizers in 1994-95.

91. The emphasis differs from definition to definition.

92. The suspicions of this sort led to the degradation of the prestige of India in 1991 when the credit worthiness of this country touched the lowest nadir and the country was forced to mortgage its gold.

93. The latest trend is to hire the lobbies to strengthen our socio-political arguments in the international forae. The recent Indian hiring of a lobbying firm in the U.S.A. is an example. It supports the argument that quite a few international favours can be directly purchased.

94. Their simultaneity is the chief cause of confusion.

95. Our discussion is limited to agricultural economics only.

96. Many others, but minor differences can be listed, but they are not relevant here.

97. The domination of the GATT by the U.S.A. may or may not be directly detrimental to the economic interests of India. It may depend mostly on the tactics and strategies of our policy makers to use the international forae to our advantage.

98. Another aim implied in its charter was the restoration of the war-torn economies of the Europe.

99. Most of the agreements were *ad hoc* and temporary and there was no international law regulating their enforcement.

100. The nature and extent of the GATT was completely changed in this 1991 version that the loosely related international economic federation was replaced by the closely knitted structure of a global economics which is supposed to be 'an organically unified global economy'.

101. These points can be re-organised in other ways depending on their priorities to the member nations.

102. It is frequently alleged that the disintegration of the Soviet Union was helped by the U.S.A. in the form of food exports followed by the spread of the 'free market ideology' into the 'iron-curtained' Soviet Union and its Eastern European allies. It all started with Poland. In recent times, the U.S.A. has taken the role of the 'international police' as shown by its role in the Gulf; and also India is very much drawn into the fray of the 'human rights' problems. The U.S.A. plays its role of 'big brother' over the other 52 members of the Human Rights Commission.

103. Most of these are possibilities in view of the rich human capital endowments of India. It has got the second largest trained labour force in the world which cannot be created overnight by any economically powerful country on the globe.

104. This amounts to a blatant interference into the economic sovereignty of a country; but the counter-argument is that it applies to the developed countries as well. In such a case, the role of the American Super 301 is not clear.

105. India's share in this boom works out to be about $ 4 billion this year.

106. It seems the developing countries like India are satisfied with the short-run gains and ease in their balance of payments; but the developed countries, on the other hand, are too happy to help them from a long term point of view during which they can transform their economic capital into political overlordship. Of course, this is too early to conclude on such crucial matters. India's share through increased export trade is expected to be around $ 4.6 annually.

107. It is not clear why should the period of patents be as long as 20 years in the modern world of fast changing technology. Many patented products may cease far before completing this period.

108. The possibility is that most of the patents will be owned by the MNCs which can get a large part of their funds for investment from patents; one can imagine the fate of national economic sovereignty.

109. This leaway again depends on the relative economic strength of our economy.

110. There is every possibility that the national governments can be pressurised through indirect channels by the MNCs and the other governments that control these giants.

111. Mirco-biological processes is a broad term and it can be extended to a number of products depending on its interpretations.

112. Heated discussion is going on in the news media in India by Suman Sahai and others about the possible economic and ecological effects of the *sui generis* and it is too early to conclude anything.

113. I discussed these aspects with some life scientists, but no concensus emerged; and we leave this part to the scientists since this is more relevant to the drugs and pharmaceuticals than to our agriculture.

114. No elaborate and workable concepts and definitions are provided for these four criteria.

115. The system and its legislation has to be prepared before 2000 A.D. by identifying the plants and animals that need protection.

116. This particular provision is ambiguous in the New GATT Accord.

117. 'Selling on commercial scale' when applied to the rural economic activities in India poses a number of problems of the barter, gifts and other traditional exchanges and loans of seeds.

118. Taking the past experience into account, such subsidies may often lead to retaliatory measures by the affected countries; and it may lead to losses in the case of agricultural products which cannot be stored for more than a season.

119. By all counts, small countries are likely to suffer more whenever pressed by the giants in trade for undue concessions to be granted to their friends and lobbies.

120. The reasons are two: already the Indian subsidies are less than the minimum allowed, *i.e.*, 5% of the value, and there are possibilities that the developing countries are allowed to cross this limit in exceptional circumstances.

121. We treat that the internal and external aspects are the two sides of the same coin of the new economic policy followed in India since 1991. In the latest parliamentary debate of 29-30 March 1994, a number of leaders expressed their fears, worries and indignation about the New GATT Accord.

122. This grouping is made only for analytical convenience. In fact, we are interested only in those aspects that are a direct concern to agriculture.

123. Most of them are related to economics through a broad concept of 'political economy'; we only note the issues and leave out their detailed analysis. For example, the Government of India is attacked for the 'object surrender' of its economic freedom to the world bodies and pressures from the U.S.A.

124. Clarifications are provided in the next section.

125. It is said that flexibility is the virtue of the New GATT Accord.

126. This is the basic feature based on which Karl Marx attacked the capitalism.

127. A number of these suspicions arise out of the nature of the New GATT Accord which did not take into consideration the actual socio-economic conditions of Indian agriculture. For example, it is very difficult to know whether the farmers are selling the seeds to their neighbours or helping them, or exchanging and so on.

128. We do no deny the involvement of political interests here.

129. A large portion of the food basket of some of the Western countries like the Britain, sometimes upto 50%, constitutes the imported grain and other products from the tropical countries.

130. Present prices are higher than what they used to pay for the same before the Second World War.

131. Terms of trade favour the rich countries for a variety of reasons; their development itself is an advantage.

132. This may not be suitable for a largely vegetarian country like India which is exporting a part of her meat products to the Gulf. A large slaughter house is established to the west of Hyderabad at Rudraram for this purpose (Al-Kabir).

133. The popular thesis is that the Westerners came to the East after being faced with scarcity of food and apparel in their own countries during the period of 16-19 centuries.

134. It is believed that Westerners became civilized but not advanced culturally as the East had; and culture is Oriental in its origin.

135. Large part of the Western Europe is classified 'naturally poor'.

136. It is assumed that there would be no change in the *status quo* regarding the national borders and migration.

137. Extinct species are excluded.

138. The size of our population needs increased quantities of food supplies at least for the next 1/2 century or so.

139. Global dependency can be relied upon when there are global safeguards enforced by a powerful agency; the present set up of the U.N. is proved either useless or biased.

140. There are instances in the villages of Andhra Pradesh where the farmers got the seeds and fertilizers supplied by the Government agencies often late or after the season is over. A number of such negative consequences can be listed, but they lack proper substantiation.

141. A number of such negative consequences can be listed, but they lack proper substantiation.

142. A number of arguments put forward by the rural folk, the actual cultivators, sometimes look like polemics, but they form the basis of the theoretical arguments when we polish them into economics. a number of points in this paper were drawn directly from the farmers.

143. Such statements assume 'center is paribus' conditions. Structural changes are left out. Suppose, if the income levels of the poor people increase due to the reforms of the new economic policies, then this argument loses the ground.

144. The idealistic models of economic growth such as the Jewisian and the Nurksian models are not useful here in the short-run since a number of persons replaced in agricultural sector are not suitable to be employed in the industrial and service sectors as they lack the necessary training. Nor is such a massive re-absorption is possible in India at present.

145. The justification of subsidized power for irrigation purposes by an experienced farmer of a Nalgonda village went far beyond pure economics. He says that his forefathers of the past centuries got almost free water from the three village tanks; they costed the village only the maintenance charges of these tanks. In the second stage, when open wells were dug in the later part of the last century, they began to bale out the water from the open wells by the help of animal draught power; the falling levels of water in the tanks were thus supplemented. In the third and final stage, the cultivators began to dig a number of bore-wells mainly with public funds and loans, and their depth went beyond 200 feet in recent times. Draught power became useless, and they are forced to go for the electrically energised pumpsets. All the three tanks are dry for 11 months of the year and open wells too remain dry for a major part of the year. Now who should bear the cost of energy? His argument simply put is that the modern development in agriculture is highly energy-oriented and therefore, the Government should bear the cost as it is encouraging this new but wrong path of development.

146. It is often a wonder for many foreign economists that why should a country try to retain them in their dismal poverty state of agriculture. Similarly, Dunkel too might advise them to enter into the global markets aimed at the betterment of their future.

147. This is not a new but the old colonial method of drain noted by Dadabhai Naoroji and other nationalist economists of India.

148. The immediate political consequences seem to be more serious than their economic effects.

149. There are a number of other possibilities; it all depends upon the permutations and combinations of varied measures and changes. But it is generally feared that the present form of peasant farming may be largely replaced by large scale commercial farming which will improve both production and productivity levels in agriculture, but without ensuring a measure of equity in their distribution.

150. The term North is used here to denote the developed countries of the Western Europe, U.S.A., Australia and Japan following the *North-South Dialogue*, by Willy Brandt, London 1980.

151. The economists from Pakistan argued that the wheat from India was costlier than that from Canada or Australia.

152. It is alleged that these products are supplied to the hostels and institutions run by the 'minorities' and when sold the proceeds are funded for religious purposes in India. Data are not freely available in such cases. Recent instances showed nuclear contamination of these consignments as found in Sri Lanka.

153. In spite of the surpluses, a number of weaker sections may lack sufficient purchasing power. How to empower them is a different question.

154. All these dismal expectations are sometimes unfounded in theory of agricultural development. For example, a country like Japan or South Korea encouraged agricultural development in modern times and did not face all these problems.

155. No supporters of seed patents were found from farmers in the villages I visited during the last three months in Andhra Pradesh. Supporters are found from the bureaucrats and businessmen who expect some advantages from these patents. But they too agreed that there would be a lot of administrative problems involved.

156. I also inquired about the nature of safeguards the farmers wanted. One useful suggestion is that let the Government pay the costs of patent and disburse these seeds to the farmers once in the starting and then no restrictions should be placed on them.

157. Delineating an activity as 'commercial' or 'non-commercial' is a delicate process. The barter economy presents problems, and administrative problems arise when a large number of farmers spread over the six lakhs of Indian villages are to be dealt with.

158. Such measures are applicable to the centrally sponsored agencies like the Government.

159. It is in turn related to the protection of the bio-diversity whose positive role is often suspected because of this tie-up with the exploitative terms of TRIPs and TRIMs.

160. Suman Sahai: 'Patenting Micro Organisms', *The Hindu*, 5.3.1994, p.12.

161. In this sense the genetic materials of the American continent belong to its traditional inhabitants the Amerindians, and those in Australia belong to the Austrindians.

162. Along with the Indians, the immigrant workers included a number of other nationals.

163. The continued survival of the wild plants of some families and species in Indian forests is the best evidence of their origin in this country; and later they were imported into other countries. Most of the desirable and economically viable methods of cultivation and the breeding of the appropriate genetic traits into the cultivated plants has been the credit of the farmers of the tropical countries of the world. The first disease resistant potatoes were bred by the farmers of Bolivia. Some of the first insect resistant varieties

of bean were bred by the farmers of West Africa. High yielding and disease resistant varieties of rice and wheat were developed by the agricultural scientists of Asia and mainly India (see Suman Sahai : Patenting Micro Organisms, *The Hindu*, 5-3-1994, p.12).

164. The genes from the micro-organisms can be shifted to higher orders of plants and animals in order to produce superior varieties. The latest advances in the field of genetic engineering has found techniques to store the genes of the higher forms of life for research and future use.

165. A neem-based biopesticide has been patented by W.R. Grace and Company, and U.S.-based multinational company pre-empting Indian researches. India has used biopesticides for times immemorial, but now it has to pay the license fees to use its own products and large sums towards royalties towards the patents.

166. Their chief argument is that the Indian politicians and bureaucrats are not licensed to sell away the birth right of the Indian peasants to grow their own seeds and crops and animals.

167. A number of consequential changes in the environment, technology and institutions may follow; and ultimately these changes may pose danger to the bio-diversity of the globe after the examples of the planned landscapes as found in the Western Europe.

168. It is alleged that these concessions may go ultimately against the expansion of domestic industrial sector, but favour the foreign units at the cost of the domestic units.

169. An agribusiness consortium was planned in 1992 aimed at improving the productivity levels of Indian agriculture. But not much follow up action is seen afterwards.

170. Politicians of some parties wanted the Government to follow only some impossibles. One of them is not to sign the Uruguay Round which may lead to an hardening of our economic crises. Increasing plan expenditure and xeroing the fiscal deficit also are contradictory. The 'videshi' economic policy to be replaced by a 'swadeshi' economic policy as recently advocated by the BJP is yet unclear.

171. Computer technology was encouraged by the former Prime Minister late Rajiv Gandhi as the technology of the 21st century, and India is said to be a leading country in matters of software technology.

172. China and Japan are our Asian competitors.

173. Patents or TRIPs is a broader concept comprising pharmaceuticals, but we limit our discussion to seeds only.

174. I raise certain crops in my fields under the Nagarjunasagar canals, or around Mangalagiri or Tanali, say high yielding cotton, rice, sugar or groundnut, I can freely resow my own seed, or I can sell out a part of them in the market. I have to pay high prices only for the new breeded seeds when purchased in the market. Once I raise them on my own farm, I get the right automatically to use my own seeds. It is a common knowledge, the Guntur ryots know well, that the seeds need not be changed each year, nor new varieties are available so frequently as to need changes once in less than ten to fifteen years in the case of rice or chillies.

175. Bio-diversity, in this sense, constitutes only national wealth. Of course, they can be purchased by any agency, national or international, at a reasonable price, from a country.

176. Problems of enforcement of the patents and the related administrative problems can be solved by concluding some mutual agreements amongst the countries that use specific seeds. For example, the world can be divided into broadly, the rice growing blocs, wheat growers, mango plantations and so on.

177. Since mono-culture leads to soil degradation and other losses, it is avoided by the knowledgeable farmers.

178. There are fears that the exotic varieties may lead to exotic problems. But some of the exotic varieties may be acclimatized to their new surroundings, or they can be evolved suitably as it is possible now by using the technique of genetic transformations.

179. In fact the essence of the WTO (World Trade Organisation) as the GATT is renamed, is that the whole world constitutes a single trading unit.

180. Let A and B produce a and b commodities of equal value. Their net satisfaction or utility increases when they exchange a against b, say food and clothing, since their use value has increased even though their exchange value remains the same.

181. We can exchange our quality products for quantities. It all depends broadly on the pattern of consumption. Suppose a vegetarian country can exchange its animal meat for foodgrains or oil; or superior grades of coking coal can be exchanged for large quantities of low grade coal or lignite.

182. China is a recent example. India has advantages that it entered GATT in 1948 in the earlier stages. But China is trying to enter now. But India should be clever enough to use its past experience and leverage of old membership to get a few favourable terms.

183. It seems that all such details can be worked out internally, in India, or by each State Government since agriculture is a State subject. No hard and fast rules are necessary in these administrative matters.

184. The complete list of these crops is not available to me.

185. Subsidies in the budgets are linked to the size of the fiscal deficits that lead again to inflation. A large part of the subsidies are eaten into the inflation to mitigate which they are allowed. The administrative leakages and the psychological losses are other additions. It is a known fact that the subsidy is tantamount to 'free service' and many people may not care to use it productively.

186. Most of the subsidies given to agricultural sector in the developed countries are from industry and services. Even after the direct subsidies are reduced, there are other ways of protecting their agriculturists. Suppose their tax structure may be adjusted to favour the agriculturists and so on.

187. Such development may not be a linear model of growth but a number of structural changes may be necessary.

188. Subsidies have become chronic in the agricultural sectors of many countries after the Second World War and in India after 1970.

189. Such kind of classical theories of trade assume a world free of wars and blockades. With its experiences of historical losses in wars, and recent memories of the World Wars and the possible effects of the nuclear wars, almost all nations, at least majority are thriving for peace. The globe is shrinking fast into a type of *vasudaikakutumbam* paying the way to realise the benefits that were not even imagined in the last century.

190. A country should not object the imports till it reaches 3.33% of its total annual needs.

The intention is not only to boost the world trade but to ensure that each country participates at the lowest level possible. It is estimated that the new GATT proposal can boost up the world trade by about $ 213 billions by the end of this century, and India's share is expected to be around $ 5 (4.6) billions. Of course, it is obvious that our share is too low when compared to our population or geographical size or the bio-diversity endowments of India.

191. Labour, the chief input in Indian agriculture, is likely to continue to be cheap for a couple of decades.

192. Dumping is unethical economics and sometimes resorted to for some political purposes. Independent India is not so weak as to tolerate such unethical acts. Moreover, the size of Indian market for any agricultural product is so large that it is not possible for any small company to resort to dumping on any large scale as to subvert the indigenous production.

193. Much dust against colonialism has already settled down and the advantages of colonialism including the economic development of India on modern lines, migration of Indians abroad and the inheritance (imposition) of a civilized democratic government are often noted by some defenders of the new economic policy.

194. Dadabhai Naoroji: *The Poverty and British Rule in India.*

195. Brahmananda, P.R. went a step further in linking the drain theory with the axioms developed by the late Prof. P.N. Mathur in his works. However, nothing can be directly read from Mathur's works about the drain theory of colonial India.

196. The Western Europeans came to India in the 16th and 17th centuries only as traders; next they began to construct factories in India; they raised armies to protect them; they lent to the Indian rulers; they claimed territories in return and so on. In other words, they transformed their economic capital into religious and political capital that ensured their continued rule over India till the middle of this century.

197. The Muslim rulers taxed the non-Muslims and granted *inams* to the Muslims, and this economic advantage in their territories attracted a number of converts into Islam in India.

198. For that matter, the position of India *versus* the global powers at present is entirely difficult that we are not at the receiving end of ideas, but can export a large spectrum of goods and services.

199. A training centre has been mooted by the Government of India in order to impart the necessary knowledge about the patents, the TRIPs, and other matters to their practice in India (*Hindu* 3.4.1994).

200. The import and use of about ten poisonous chemicals in Indian agriculture has been recently banned.

201. The membership and ownership by the farmers often reduces the evils of bureaucracy as proved in Israel.

202. Bio-fertilizers are preparations containing a mix of cell lines providing the major nutrients like nitrogen, phosphate, sulphate and urea.

203. Bio-pesticides involve various formulations of the micro-organisms to control the insects and pests that are harmful to plant growth. The capabilities of various fungii, algae, bacteria and viruses are being tested and studied in the scientific laboratories of India.

8

NEED AND IMPORTANCE OF CONSIDERING ECOLOGICALLY SUSTAINABLE ECONOMIC DEVELOPMENT IN INDIAN ECONOMY

DR. (Mrs.) N. MANONMONEY
Reader, School of Economics,
Madurai Kamraj University

Setting

Ecology means necessary and feasible harmony between "man" and "environment", whereas economic development means disharmony with environment. Before the age of glass and plastic, man used natural products that soon returned their component materials to the soil through the decay by micro-organisms. Today, many of our waste materials, especially synthetics are not biodegradable, that is, micro-organisms do not have the special enzymes necessary to decay such substances. The depletion and use of natural resources and generation of emissions and pollution are considered as global problems because the nature and magnitude of environmental degradation increases and the absorption capacity of the ecosystem decreases. The emerging ecological crisis has led to the conclusion of giving attention for attaining ecological ideal in many countries. Ecological ideal means the maintenance of healthy life-enhancing interaction between 'man' and the 'environment'.

In 1814, George Perkins Marsh, said to be the father of American ecology, warned that "the earth was fast becoming an unfit home for the noblest inhabitant and that unless men changed their ways it would be reduced to such a condition of impoverished productiveness, of shattered surface and perhaps even extinction of species".[1] In 1864 no one was listening to Marsh. In 1948, the situation was wholly changed. In 1960s there was a sudden concern towards ecological resources. The devastation of environment and the threat of over-population became too obvious to be ignored. Confronting with serious environmental degradation, conventional economic policy found to be challenging. There is need for changing and reshaping conventional economic policies in order to bring harmony between "economy" and "ecology" so as to attain ecologically sustainable economic development.

Nature of Economic Problems

The need for faster growth is indispensable in Third World countries like India where per capita income is very low. The problems of poverty and unemployment are still limiting the economic development of our country. Though population growth rate began to decline around 1960 and it is also expected to continue in 1990s, but attention is needed to focus on the increasing rate of population in urban areas. The main objective of Indian economic policies for the last forty years has been growth with stability, social justice and self reliance, that is development focused for the benefit of all and particularly for the poor. Attention has been given for the rate of growth of investment but the efficiency of investment has not been improved. The composition of central government expenditure is mainly on two items namely expenditure on human development (education and health) and defence. But the real public expenditure on education or health per capita has been often either stagnated or declined. Severe poverty still remains a formidable problem.[2] Our country has completed seven five year plans and now the eighth five year plan is under progress. Today, Indian economy is underlying with most serious problems such as large fiscal deficit, huge foreign debt, low levels of efficiency in various sectors, and a recessionary situation in the industrial sector, stagnant agricultural production, high rate of inflation, serious foreign exchange crunch and balance of payment crisis.

Economic Reforms of 1990s

Particularly in 1991, there was pressing need to make changes in the economic policies in India. Thus the beginning of 1990s has marked an era of economic reforms in the form of globalisation and a market-friendly approach.[3] The new economic policy of 1991 has suggested many changes relating to the structure of industry such as privatisation, entry of multinational corporations, liberalisation and technological upgradation. Internal price stability is also planned to be achieved by appropriate structural adjustment policies.[4] The World Bank Annual

Report of 1992 also has encouraged Indian economy for achieving growth through openness of economy and private sector development. Swift and decisive macroeconomic stabilisation measures along with reforms in trade and investment policy are also framed. Thus Indian economic policies are mainly concentrating on short to medium term issues. But it is inevitable to pay attention to environmental priorities. It has been argued that India has the largest pool of poor people in the world and protection of environmental quality requires 'long-run' or 'lumpy' investments which could not be taken by poor countries like India. Therefore "environmental concerns" are not substantial in the economic policies and developmental programmes in India. Today, the countries all over the world are beginning to rethink their economic strategies because environmental concerns are gaining attention in many countries.

Nature of Environmental Problems in India

Today, pollution and natural resource degradation are seen as serious impediments for development. The main reason for environmental problems in our country is the result of depletion of both renewable and non-renewable resources at a faster rate. Our government has given very little attention for the preservation or conservation of resources while designing various planning programmes. For instance, government attempts to increase food supply through increase in the productivity of land since 1970s were made partly by adopting agricultural practices particularly use of overdose of chemical facilities that led to excessive soil erosion and drainage of the productivity of land.[5] The strain on global environment threatens the survival and development opportunities of future generation.

The economic development programmes in India are mainly aiming at raising short-term productivity and the prevailing methods of resource utilisation have resulted in ecological degradation — such as desertification, deforestation, soil erosion etc. It is true that awareness of environmental problems has gained popularity only since 1980 in India. The number of environmental protection methods particularly legal methods have increased in number both at state as well as national level since 1970; but their influence has not increased much. Government programmes are mainly aiming at solving the problem of population, poverty and unemployment rather than environmental problems.

Depletion of natural resources is a physical process; but it has many economic consequences affecting the productivity and growth of economy, income distribution and finally it affects all people in the country. The seriousness and intensity of environmental problems are such as necessitate a broader look into the future economic development of our economy. The environmental problems are going to be serious in the future as the pressure on natural resources from an increasing population of 870 million in 1991 and from 1000 million by 2000 A.D. With the available 266 million hectares productive lands, nearly about 175 million hecatres are degraded in different degrees. Shortage of fuelwood and fodder has led to the depletion of forest. Air, water and coastal pollution and degradation of urban environment have resulted in ecological damages. All over India the chain of ecological damages is going on. Contamination of surface as well as ground water, uncontrolled dumping of hazardous solid waste, sinking water table and reduced fishing in polluted rivers show the extent of environment problems in India.

The rapid depletion of natural resources today will affect the future productivity in agriculture and industrial sectors. In LDCs like India, once the ecological degradation has attained a stage of "crisis", it is very difficult to control degradation because there is lack of knowledge and know-how and also lack of economically feasible alternatives to conserve and protect environmental quality. Therefore it is now the proper time to accept the concept of sustainable development – that is, an approach to harmonise both economic development and environmental protection. Thus alternative patterns of development which can ensure ecological conservation are needed. Impressive progress and concrete steps to be taken in attaining the various components of a sustainable development strategy include stabilising population, reducing dependence on non-renewable resources, developing alternative energy resources, conserving soil, adopting recycling methods etc.

Importance of Sustainable Development

Sustainable development facilitates strategies that will permit continuing improvements in the present quality of life at a lower intensity of resource use. Substantial development involves the pursuit of economic efficiency, social equity and environmental protection.[6] It is true that our country has to overcome tremendous obstacles such as poor infrastructure, weak administrative capacity, and inadequate financial resources along with adverse environmental quality. It is a striking feature that nearly one-third of population in our country lives on sub-standard income, illiteracy, bad housing, lack of medical care and malnutrition. There is not only poverty and low per capita income, there is also uneven distribution of income among people.[7]

Science and environment are possibly the two greatest ideas of the 20th century. Science has brought immense power to create unprecedented wealth; whereas environmental degradation has made the human beings realise that the economic development or wealth creation has led to the destruction of human welfare. Therefore it is necessary to reconcile environment with development. In the process of economic development, there is human intervention in the natural system. Until recently, the magnitude of intervention and its impacts were not felt much. Today these interventions are more adverse in scale and it affects drastically the life-support system throughout the world.

Sustainable development is a development that meets the needs of the present without comprising the ability of future generation to meet their own needs. A sustainable society is one that is prepared to monitor the impacts of its activities carefully, openly and democratically, analyse them and use its wisdom and knowledge to solve problems. According to Donald Huisingh, "sustainability is the capacity of the earth's biophysical life, support system to continuously sustain and nourish plant and animal life."[8] David Pearce has defined sustainable development as follows: "It involves maximising the net benefits and economic development subject to maintaining the services and quality of natural resources over time. Economic development is related not only to increase the real per capita income but also other elements in social welfare."[9] In essence, sustainable development is a process of change in which exploitation of resources, the direction of investments, the orientation of technological development, and institutional changes are all in harmony and enhance both current and future potential to meet human needs and aspirations. But this process is not easy or straightforward. Painful scarifices have to be made by the economy.[10]

Problems in attaining sustainable development

Many developed countries, particularly Germany, have realised the impact of industrialisation on the environmental quality, that is, natural resources are being overexploited and the natural ecosystems are overloaded by non-digestable pollutants. Therefore, Germany has realised that it is the right time to change the industrial society to attain sustainable development. This country has adopted comprehensive industrial restructuring or "ecological modernisation" — a concept focusing on prevention — innovation and structural change towards ecologically sound industrial development and relying on clean technology, recycling and renewable resources.[11] To bring better harmony between natural environment and industrial society, German government is adopting mainly three strategies namely (1) ecological structural change of the economy, (2) preventive environmental policy, and (3) ecological orientation of economic policy.

Even in developed countries like Germany, U.S.A. and others, implementation of pollution control legislation is not very much effective to control pollution. In legal methods, pollutants are merely transferred from one source to another, that is, from the air to the water and to the land where once again the substances cause additional problems that are costly to "clean up". Therefore at present emphasis has been shifting from pollution control to pollution prevention or waste reduction. In U.S.A., emphasis is laid on waste minimisation or pollution prevention. In many European countries, emphasis is placed on low and non-waste technologies, clean technologoies or environmental technologies.[12] All these approaches to maintain "environmental quality" result in huge government expenditure and heavy investment on environmental protection. But it seems difficult for countries like India to invest on attaining ecologically sustainable development. The question arises as to whether it is possible for less developed countries like India to incur environmental protection cost. Even when a certain percentage of gross national product of our economy is diverted towards environment protection, the question again is how to develop cost-efficient methods to protect environment. Moreover, many economists have argued that there is inverse relationship between alleviating poverty and protecting the environment. Therefore the question arises whether it is possible for the Indian government to deal with both the problems namely removing poverty and protection of environment simultaneously. The notion that there is a trade-off between environmental quality and economic development at present is disproved and in many countries and in research studies it has been proved that there is an interdependence between ecology and economy.

In India, as in the past, people have been keen about natural resources and the basic philosophy has been of harmony with "nature". But today, there are people who believe that there is the possibility of getting more money by destroying environmental resources than by conserving them. Tomorrow is not their concern. It is observed that the possibilities of increasing "natural resources" are less. It may be argued that it is possible to grow more trees and thereby restore the natural resources. But in many cases once environmental damages have occurred, they could not be corrected immediately and easily as the environmental losses are irreversible in nature. If the environmental damages are not arrested, the future generations cannot secure the access to the resources because they have been made extinct.

At present, a number of analytical issues have been raised and discussed by many economists which have engaged them in the task of framing new theories and concepts in the field of developmental economics. Today, the concept of sustainable development attracts the attention of both DCs and LDCs. Sustainable development can be pursued by controlling population growth; that is demographic features are to be kept in harmony with our ecological system.[13]

Programmes under Sustainable Development

It is very difficult to frame tools and analysis that demonstrate whether any particular natural economy is consistent with the natural environment or not. But it is accepted that for sustaining an economy it becomes important to establish some conditions for the compatibility of economic development and environment. In our country the pressure of increased population that has led to the situation of overexploitation of land, water and other natural resources. People are blamed for the sorry state of many sacred groves in our country. Pressure of development, people's growing needs, the decline in religious faith, and the breakdown of community following greater industrialisation and urban penetration in rural areas have been major factors for the decline of natural resources in many rural areas.[14] Whatever the steps taken to achieve adequate development, there are two basic considerations : (i) development needs to be undertaken in relation to the qualities and limitations of environment if environmental potential is to be realised and its deterioriaion avoided, and (ii) technological developments must be adopted with minimum environmental hazards. Enormous efforts in the form of physical, fiscal, legal, ethical, moral, political and social methods are needed by the government for the appropriate management of both human and environmental resources.

Thus there is an urgent need to limit peoples' quest for economic development and to make people realise the fact of resource limitation and the carrying capacity of ecosystems and to impress on them to take into account of the needs of future generation. Therefore, in India, efforts are needed for the proper use of living resources. Today, the building up of a sustainable future depends on effective ''environmental management''. To overcome environmental degradation, our government is adopting various measures such as fiscal measures, legal measures, environmental planning, environmental status evolution, environmental impact assessment and framing environmental policies etc. Minimising environmental degradation through the role of government in environmental management may not be attained very easily and economically especially in less developed countries like India. No government can attain proper environmental management without the co-operation of people. Therefore along with economic methods the non-economic methods such as peoples' participation in environmental management programmes, environmental education and role of voluntary agencies are considered important. These non-economic methods are not only less costlier but their effects in minimising environmental degradation are also very impressive.

Our government has mainly failed to deliver conservation-based development particularly in rural areas. The lack of support for conservation is due to lack of awareness of the benefits of conservation.

Enlightened understanding by a human being of his or her environment is needed to make success of government environmental programmes. Country-wide awareness campaigns have to be launched to cover people at state, district, block and village levels.

Environmental education is also important for making people understand the implication of their activities on "environment". One of the recent approaches to environmental education is "value stratification". The fundamental goal of environmental education is to equip people to think in terms of the future. There is need to switch over to an 'Economy of the Enough" — that is arresting economic growth and paying attention towards betterment of quality and durability of products[15].

Conclusion

Thus it is right time for our government to take into account environmental concerns in all the developmental planning programmes. The ecological consequences of development have therefore to be considered. Sustainable development demands huge sacrifices in the form of reduction in production or gross national product. Critics may argue that how it is possible to pay attention for preservation or conservation of natural resources when even today vast majority people do not have the basic necessities of human life. The pressure of population and unemployment is so great that the question arises as to whether it is feasible or possible for Indian economy to give importance to attaining ecologically sustainable economic development in its restructuring programmes. Today, the ecological degradation has reached the state of "crisis" in DCs as well as in LDCs. Therefore it is imperative for our economy to give top priority for ecological quality.

The report called, "North-South : A Programme for Survival" (1980) has pointed out that, "Few threats to peace and the survival of human community are greater than those posed by the prospects of cumulative and irreversible degradation of the biosphere on which human life depends ..... It can no longer be argued that protection of environment is an obstacle to development. On the contrary, the case of the natural environment is an essential aspect of development."

REFERENCES

1. Anthony Vann & Paul Rogers, ed. *Human Ecology and World Development*, 1974.
2. Udo Ernst-Simonis : *Towards a New International Development Strategy : Economic, Social and Environmental Concerns* (Research paper), Research Professorship Environmental Policy, Science Center, Berlin.
3. B.B. Bhattacharya, "Fiscal Management: Issues and Policy Options", *Fiscal Management of the Indian Economy*. Edited by V.R. Panchamurkhi, 1992.
4. B. Gopalakrishna Kumar, "Economic Reforms in an uncertain world". *Economic and Political Weekly*, March 21, 1992.
5. Lester, R. Brown et al., "State of the World", 1988.
6. Mohan Meenasinghe et al., "Are Economic Policies good for environment", *Finance and Development*, Vol. 30, No. 3, Sept., 1993.
7. Jagdish Bhagwati, *The Economics of Underdeveloped Countries*, 1987.
8. Donald Huisingh, *Good Environmental Practices, Good Business Practices* (Research paper), Research Professorship. Environmental Policy – Science Center, Berlin.
9. Pearce W. David & Turner Kerry, *Economics of Natural Resources and the Environment*, 1990.
10. ——, *A Common Future*, the World Commission on Environment and Development, 1989.
11. Udo E. Simonis, *Industrial Restructuring for Sustainable Development : Three Points of Departure* (Research paper), Professorship Environmental Policy, Science Center, Berlin.
12. Christian Lerpert and Udo E, Simonis, *Environmental Damage, Environmental Protection — The Case of Federal Republic Germany*.
13. Udo E. Simonis, "Developing Countries in Environmental Crisis", *Inter-Economics* Sept.-Oct., 1984.
14. Various issues of *Down to Earth* (1993), Centre for Science and Environment, New Delhi.
15. Francis, K. Thibodean & Hermann, H. Field, *Sustaining Tomorrow*, 1984.

9

PUBLIC DISTRIBUTION SYSTEM IN INDIA : WHY TO REVAMP IT?

DR. (MS.) S.D. SAWANT
Professor of Agriculture Economics
University of Bombay

The Public Distribution System (PDS) in India represents a direct intervention by the government in food market. It involves subsidised distribution of limited quantities of essential goods such as cereals, sugar, edible oil etc. Among them, distribution of cereals assumes crucial importance as it is supposed to provide food security to the poor.

Of late, however, PDS has come under severe criticism for its urban bias, its ineffectiveness in reaching the poor and its inefficiency with reference to cost of distribution. It is against this background that we would like to review genesis of the PDS and its performance in 1970s and 1980s particularly with reference to distribution of cereals. In addition, an attempt will be made to comment on implications of revamping of the PDS if it has to reach all the chronically poor households in India.

I. Genesis and Operational Mechanism of PDS

To trace the history of PDS we must go back to the Second World War period. The system of fair price shops (FPS system) was first introduced in Bombay when the war broke out in 1939. This was especially to keep check on speculative activity of the trade. The FPS system was later transformed into the rationing system in 1942 to ensure an equitable distribution of available food supplies within the country. By 1947 nearly 54 million people in urban areas were covered by statutory rationing and another 19 million in the non-statutory rationing areas of the country. The system of FPS was revoked in 1953 due to easy price situation and continued thereafter. Finally, it was around 1967-68 the name of the FPS scheme was changed to call it the public distribution system[1] (Tyagi D.S., *Managing India's Food Economy*, 1990, page 23, 24 and 38). Thus, the early history of PDS reveals that it started mainly as the urban focused scheme.

The requirement of foodgrains for public distribution was met then partly through imports and partly through levy arrangements and/or domestic procurement though dependence on imports used to be quite heavy in 1950s and 1960s, particularly in the scarcity years. Food Corporation of India (FCI) was, therefore, established in 1965 for managing public sector trading in foodgrains. Subsequently, due to comfortable domestic food situation, procurement picked up since early 1970s and provided strong support to the PDS.

Under the present system, it is the joint responsibility of the Central and State governments to ensure smooth flow of grains and other commodities to consumers. The FCI on behalf of the Central Government procures, transports and stocks the grains in the central godowns (owned or hired). Imports by the Central Government, if any, are also added to the central stocks which conceptually represent the 'central pool' of foodgrains. The state agencies lift the allotted quota of the central pool from the godowns and distribute the grains to consumers through a network of fair price shops. The states are also free to procure additional quantities of foodgrains independently and add to the allotted quota of grains for distribution, though very few states have done so. The FCI alongwith the state agencies hold and maintain the reserve ratio buffer stocks of foodgrains in addition to the operational stocks used for distribution.

The quantities of foodgrains allotted to states for distribution by the Central Government are available at all the depots of the FCI at prices, fixed by the government *i.e.* 'issue prices' which are uniform for specified varieties or qualities of grains all over India. The issue prices are usually lower than the economic costs of the procured grain where economic cost includes procurement price, procurement incidentals and distribution incidentals. Thus, by making available foodgrains, mainly rice and wheat to consumers, at prices much below their economic cost, the Central Government incurs substantial 'consumer subsidy' on distribution of grains.

Both the total quantities of public distribution and their economic costs have increased greatly over the years and consequently the total burden of food subsidy on the Central Government. The aggregate annual quantum of public distribution for all the purposes was about 10 million tonnes during the 1970s. It crossed the level of 18 million tonnes after the mid-1980s, and with that the total subsidy on food distribution, *i.e.* an aggregate of consumer subsidy and cost of holding buffer stock, exceeded the staggering figure of Rs. 2000 crores per annum. The major contribution to increased subsidy was however from faster rise in distribution costs rather than that in the procurement incidentals.[2]

Indeed, this undesirable trend in food subsidy continued beyond 1980s with the actual amount of subsidy reaching Rs. 2800 crores in 1992-93 and its expected level being Rs. 6000 crores for 1993-94. Thus, there is a strong case for containing the food subsidy by increasing its distribution efficiency and progressively reducing coverage of the non-poor.

II. Is PDS Pro-urban?

As majority of the poor population resides in rural India there is a strong justification for PDS to be more widespread in rural areas than in the urban areas. There are other reasons why PDS should support the poor in rural areas. A large number of the rural poor, mainly the agricultural labourers and other labourers including the tribals reliant on forest employment and the marginal farmers in the dry farming areas, depend almost totally on the market for purchase of food. It is they who are most vulnerable to fluctuations in incomes due to uncertain and deficient employment, seasonal variations and occasional high inflation in food prices and therefore subjected to severe risk of undernutrition.[3] Market, too, is unlikely to be non-exploitative for them.[4] In contrast, poor from the urban areas face relatively better market environment. Besides, quiet a few of them being in the organised sector of employment have their incomes indexed. Therefore, the issue of rural-urban coverage of the PDS needs verification.

It is true that since its inception the network of PDS was concentrated mainly in the urban areas and its major beneficiaries were the urban consumers at least upto the late 1970s. This is evident from the assessment of the PDS made by the Dagli Committee.[5] Indeed, the statistics of distribution of cereals through fair price shops in rural and urban areas of the country for the year 1977 provided in the Dagli Committee Report revealed that the share of urban areas in total quantity distributed was 73 per cent *vis-a-vis* the rural share of 27 per cent only.[6] The Committee, therefore, recommended that systematic attempts should be made to reach only the deserving sections of the population. We believe that the Committee's recommendations must have had definite impact on subsequent expansion of the PDS as the rural coverage did improve significantly between 1979 and 1987, though not in all the states. This is evident from the results of the special survey on utilisation of PDS by households carried out by the National Sample Survey Organisation (NSSO, 1990) during 1986-87.[7]

The analysis of the NSSO data indicates that at the all India level though the overall coverage of PDS (*i.e.* % of PDS users to all persons) remained relatively lower *i.e.* 25 per cent in rural areas as against 35% in urban areas. The rural sector's share in total cereal quantity purchased under PDS was 69.6 per cent in 1986-87 (Column 6, Table 2). Though this was lower than the rural population's share in total population (*i.e.* 78 per cent). This represents a remarkable contrast to the situation in 1977 when the rural sector's share in cereals distributed under PDS as mentioned earlier, was meagre 27 per cent. Similarly, in respect of sugar, too, the urban bias of the PDS disappeared almost totally with the rural sector's share being as high as 78.8 per cent in total PDS purchases in 1986-87 (column 7, Table 2). Cereals and sugar being the two most important food commodities distributed under PDS, it can safely be concluded that the aggregate NSS level data do not support the criticism of pro-urban bias of the PDS.

We investigated, further, the issue of pro-urban bias at the state level. For this purpose we selected 13 major states which accounted for 72 per cent share in total central pool allocations for PDS in 1987-88 and omitted the rest with less than 2 per cent share each and the union territories (column 2, Table 1). The selected states were further classified into three categories on the basis of general coverage of the PDS *i.e.* proportion of persons purchasing cereals from PDS in total population (column 5, Table 1). The category I of high PDS coverage (*i.e.* 41 to

91%) consisted of six states *viz.* Kerala, Karnataka, Andhra Pradesh, Tamil Nadu, Maharashtra and Gujarat. Category II included two medium coverage states *viz.* West Bengal (34.7%) and Assam (22.9%) and in category III there were five low coverage states *viz.* Madhya Pradesh (10%), Rajasthan (8.2%), Uttar Pradesh and Orissa (3% each) and Bihar (2.4%).

It is pertinent to note that all the high coverage states are from the western and southern region of India and have low per capita foodgrain production with an exception of Andhra Pradesh (column 4, Table 1). But medium and low coverage states belong to the central, eastern and north-eastern region of India with per capita foodgrain production being either at low or medium level. Finally, the four left out states with negligible shares in central pool allocations *viz.* Jammu and Kashmir, Himachal Pradesh, Haryana and Punjab belong to the north-western region of India and have relatively better food availability with medium or high level of per capita foodgrain production.

From the comparative analysis of the rural-urban coverage of the PDS for the above mentioned 13 states (Table 2) emerged the following conclusions :

(i) The PDS was found to be almost free from urban-bias in all the states from high coverage category with reference to rural sector's share in (a) all PDS users, and (b) in total cereal quantity distributed under PDS (columns 5 & 6 in Table 2)

(ii) Contrary to the above conclusion in 6 out of 7 states from the other two, *i.e.* medium and low coverage categories, PDS network was found to suffer from the urban bias. In all of them rural sector's share both in all PDS users and the total quantity of cereals remained below the proportion of its (rural sector's) share in total population (columns 4, 5, and 6 in Table 2). Only Rajasthan represented a remarkable exception with nearly 90 per cent share of rural areas in PDS benefits, despite its overall narrow coverage. In contrast, PDS was highly urban biased in West Bengal.

III. Is PDS Pro-poor?

Having investigated the issue of urban bias we may now examine two questions :

(i) Does the PDS benefit more to those regions where India's poor population is concentrated?

(ii) Is the PDS, wherever it operates, targeted towards the poor?

To evaluate performance of PDS in the context of the first question we need to compare shares of different states in the central pool allocations with their shares in all India population below poverty line. Ideally the two should be equal. Reality is, however, far different from what is expected. The states like Uttar Pradesh and Bihar which account for 18.9 per cent and 14.2 per cent of India's poor population received just 3.2 per cent and 4.9 per cent share of the central pool of grains (columns 2 & 3 in Table 1). Indeed, nearly 50 per cent of India's poor population was concentrated in four major states in the central and eastern regions *viz.* Uttar Pradesh, Madhya Pradesh, Bihar and Orissa in 1987-88, but they together had only 15 per cent in the central pool allocations in 1988. In other words central pool allocations were not consistent with the states shares in all India population below poverty line.

The second issue is whether the PDS provides preferential access to the poor so that majority of them are covered by it whether in rural or urban areas.

As such the present system of public distribution in India provides an access to subsidised purchases of essential goods to every ration card holder irrespective of his/her income level. This has been so because there was no explicit directive in the past from the central government to direct the PDS mainly to the poor, while allotting foodgrains from the central pool. Thus, targeting was neither obligatory for the states nor the states had put in deliberate efforts on their own to do so barring some appreciable attempts made in the states such as Gujarat, Tamil Nadu and Andhra Pradesh.

It is true that the common variety of rice and average quality wheat are being mainly sold through PDS, expecting thereby that the PDS would self-select the poor and the non-poor users preferring a better quality from the open market would remain minimal. But this is not applicable to sugar and kerosene in which case the PDS quality is unlikely to be different from the open market quality of these goods. Whether in reality such implicit targeting of PDS in respect of cereals has helped in directing the PDS more to the poor than others is worth probing. For this purpose, we analysed again the latest NSSO data for 1986-87, which provided the statistics of average PDS purchases for different fractile groups of households, arranged in ascending order of per capita total consumption expenditure.[8]

In our analysis we treated the population (*i.e.* persons) from the bottom 20 per cent households as 'poor' and the rest as 'non-poor'. The poor so defined are in fact, the 'ultra poor' who need the support of the PDS most. The estimated number of hard core poor and non-poor persons in India, as per the procedure adopted turned out to be 175.5 million (*i.e.* 24.5 per cent) and 557.1 million (*i.e.* 75.5 per cent) for the year 1986-87.[9]

If the provision of food security to the vulnerable sections of population is treated as the legitimate objective of the PDS, then on the one hand coverage of the poor, *i.e.* percentage of poor using PDS (*i.e.* purchasing cereals under PDS) to all the poor should be close to 100 per cent while proportion of the non-poor among all the PDS users *i.e.* misdirection of the PDS should be close to zero per cent. With reference to both the criteria we examined performance of the PDS at the all India level as also for the selected twelve states out of thirteen. Kerala was excluded as it represented a special case with almost universal coverage of consumers (*i.e.* above 90 per cent) both in rural and urban areas. Following broad conclusions emerged from the scrutiny of statistics provided in Table 3 :

(i) At the all India level proportion of the poor benefiting from the PDS was just 31 per cent *vis-a-vis* a desirable coverage of 100 per cent. Coverage of the non-poor was 26.33 per cent *i.e.* though relatively lower, not significantly different from that of the poor. In fact, among the total users non-poor users of PDS were 72.5 per cent *i.e.* close to their share of 76 per cent in total population. In other words, PDS benefits were shared by the poor and non-poor almost as per their respective proportion in the population, indicating neutrality of PDS towards the poor. Thus grossly inadequate coverage of the most eligible *i.e.* hard core poor was associated with substantial diversion of its benefits to the non-eligible *i.e.* non-poor. Per person per month purchases of the poor were a meagre quantity of 3.31 kg.

(column 7, Table 3) *vis-a-vis* a minimum critical requirement of at least 13 kg., a clear indication of absence of significant support to even those poor who were covered by the PDS. Thus, the poor had to depend to a large extent on the open market for their food purchases.

(ii) The state level comparison indicated that the situation was relatively better in high coverage category states particularly in Gujarat, Andhra Pradesh and Tamil Nadu, where coverage of the poor was significantly above the coverage of the non-poor (columns 2 and 3 in Table 3). It must be the result of some efforts made for targeting of PDS to the poor. Yet the situation was nowhere near the ideal *i.e.* 100 per cent coverage of the poor and near zero coverage of the non-poor. Indeed, the range of coverage in these five states was 50.74 per cent (Maharashtra) to 68.98 per cent (Andhra Pradesh) for the poor population and 36.73 per cent (Gujarat) to 61.35 per cent (Karnataka) for the non-poor.

In contrast, coverage of both the poor and non-poor was medium in medium category states and low in the third category. This was an indication of neutrality of the PDS towards the poor. Obviously, the proportion of the non-poor in total number of PDS users as also their share in total cereal purchases, by and large, remained dominant in all the states (columns 4 and 6 in Table 3).

(iii) Extent of support received by the poor in terms of their average cereal purchases was not only very moderate at the all India level (3.31 kg per person per month) but varied considerably over the states. It is pertinent that in high coverage category states it was lower for the poor compared to that for the non-poor and was between just 2 kg to 4.62 kg per person per month (column 7, Table 3).

The above observations demonstrate failure of even implicit targeting attempted under PDS in respect of cereals, in addition to absence of effective explicit targeting in all the states.[10]

IV. Revamping of PDS and its Implications

The preceding analysis of the NSSO data clearly pointed out that (i) leakage of benefits of PDS to the non-eligible was substantial in all the states, and (ii) even in respect of the poor covered by PDS, size of coverage and extent of support (*i.e.* per capita cereal purchases) varied considerably over the states. It is therefore most desirable to have the policy consensus at the all India level regarding effective targeting of PDS towards the poor through both intra-state and inter-state changes (if required) in foodgrains distribution and extent of support to be provided to the poor. The impact of such revamping on the size of foodgrains distribution under PDS and consequently on that of aggregate food subsidy would depend on the level of support of subsidised distribution to be provided to the poor *i.e.* per capita supplies of foodgrains and rate of subsidy per unit of foodgrain ensured to the poor. To demonstrate implication of revamping of PDS we carry out below an illustrative exercise for the year 1986-87 and 1993-94, under two alternative assumptions :

(i) Total support for consumption of foodgrains to all the poor to reach the level of 13 kg of cereals per month or 156 kg per annum per person so as to ensure bare minimum consumption to avoid undernutrition.[11]

(ii) Partial support of 40 kg of cereals per person per annum so as to bridge the gap between actual level of market purchases by the poor in absence of PDS and the desired level of 156 kg per annum.[12]

Table 4 shows alternative sizes of foodgrains distribution required to provide the above stipulated total or partial support in 1986-87 to all the poor (*i.e.* persons in the bottom 20 per cent households) who constitute 24.5 per cent of poulation and same percentage *i.e.* 24.5 per cent or 29.9 per cent of total population in 1993-94 (*i.e.* 900 million). How do the state-wise distribution requirements under total and partial support compare with the actual foodgrains distribution in 1986-87 is also demonstrated by Table 5.

Table 4 clearly demonstrates that if perfect targeting is achieved all the poor population can be provided partial support within the present aggregate size of PDS. This is because at the most about 11 million tonnes of foodgrains would be required, for providing 40 kg foodgrains per person per annum *i.e.* 3.33 kg per person per month. Incidentally, this is almost equal to the level of average purchases by the poor PDS users in 1986-87 (column 7, Table 3). But, obviously this is not so if total support (*i.e.* 156 kg per annum or 13 kg per month per person) is to be provided to all the poor in India. Size of public distribution then required (*i.e.* 42 million tonnes) would be nearly three times the present level or at least two to two and a half times the size of distribution between 1986 and 1990. That is to say, the option of total support would be certainly unsustainable, in view of (i) consequent substantial escalation in food subsidy, and (ii) actual offtake of foodgrains being observed to be persistently lower than the allocation since 1990-91.[13]

Table 5 demonstrates that under the option of partial support for majority of the states' allocations required to cover all the poor were much below the actual levels of foodgrains distribution particularly in all the high and medium coverage category states. Most significant exception however was that of Uttar Pradesh in which case, for exhaustive coverage of poor population, size of foodgrains distribution needed nearly 50 per cent expansion, even for partial support.

In contrast to partial support strategy, provision of total support to the poor would have involved substantial augmentation in the size of foodgrains distribution in all the states but Kerala, West Bengal and Assam. Expansion in PDS size needed was particularly very large for Uttar Pradesh followed by Bihar, Madhya Pradesh and Orissa. Therefore, a more pragmatic strategy would be to provide partial support to the poor and progressively increase their coverage while simultaneously reducing that of the non-poor.

It is true that extension of PDS to all the poor particularly from the hitherto uncovered remote and inaccessible rural areas in all the states would escalate distribution costs as PDS infrastructure must be almost non-existant in them. In addition, levels of income of the very poor in these areas may require both higher rate of subsidy per unit of cereals and higher level of support (*i.e.* higher ration quota) per person. Yet, in view of considerable excess of the prevailing levels of foodgrain distribution over the requirement under partial support strategy it may certainly be feasible to provide higher support to the relatively more poor while revamping the PDS. What is required is real concern for serious undernutrition among the poor reflected into the political will to revamp the PDS in favour of the poor.

FOOT NOTES

1. Tyagi D.S. (1990), *Managing India's Food Economy*, Sage Publications Inc, pp. 23, 24 and 36.
2. Tyagi, D.S., *op. cit.*, p. 124.
3. Sawanti, S.D. (1994), "Inflation and the Rural Poor", *Economic and Political Weekly*, February 26, 1994.
4. Dantwala, M.L. (1993), "Agricultural Policy : Prices and Public Distribution System — A Review", *Indian Journal of Agricultural Economics*, Vol. 48, No. 2, April-June 1993.
5. Govt. of India (1979), *Report of the Committee on Controls and Subsidies*, 1979 Main Report, p. 129.
6. Govt. of India, *op. cit.*, Annexes page 110.
7. National Sample Survey Organisation, "Utilization of Public Distribution System : NSS 42nd Round (July 1986-June 1989)", *Sarvekshana*, Vol. 13, No. 4, April-June 1990.
8. The Original data were not published in the N.S.S.O. report (*op. cit.*). Hence, they were borrowed from Parikh Kirit (1993), 'Who Gets How Much from PDS : How Effectively Does it Reach the Poor?', (mineographed).
9. The estimated percentage of poor, *i.e.* 24 per cent, is close to the all India estimate provided by the Planning Commission for the year 1987-88 *i.e.* 29.9 per cent (Source : Government of India, *Economic Survey 1993-94*, p. 148).
10. It is rather surprising why the middle and rich income households should prefer to purchase subsidised common variety of rice particularly in the Southern and Western states, *i.e.*, the high coverage category states. One possible explanation would be that rice obtained from PDS is used mainly for preparation of bread (*i.e.* roti) or snacks and not for whole cooking.
11. This norm is borrowed from K. Subbarao, *Improving Nutrition in India*, World Bank Discussion Paper No. 49, 1989, p. 72.
12. K. Subbarao, *op. cit.*
13. Government of India, *Economic Survey, 1993-94*, p. 66.

TABLE 1

State-wise Central Pool Allocations, Foodgrain Production, Population Below Poverty Line and Coverage of PDS

States	State's share in: Central pool allocations for PDS (1988)[1]	State's share in: Population below poverty line (1987-88)[2]	Per capita foodgrain production (kgs per annum) (1988-89)	Coverage of PDS: % of persons depending on PDS to all persons (1986-87)
(1)	(2)	(3)	(4)	(5)
West Bengal	10.9	7.28	181	35.7 (Medium)
Kerala	10.7	2.06	35	90.9 (High)
Maharashtra	10.6	9.00	151	46.4 (High)
Gujarat	7.2	3.07	134	40.9 (High)
Rajasthan	6.7	4.21	251	8.2 (Low)
Andhra Pradesh	5.9	8.24	208	57.8 (High)
Tamil Nadu	5.3	7.45	133	54.0 (High)
Karnataka	5.1	5.72	156	62.0 (High)
Bihar	4.9	14.18	144	2.4 (Low)
Assam	4.1	2.23	110	26.6 (Medium)
Madhya Pradesh	3.5	9.47	253	10.0 (Low)
Uttar Pradesh	3.2	18.85	269	3.0 (Low)
Orissa	3.2	5.67	228	3.0 (Low)
States excluded from detailed analysis				
Jammu and Kashmir	2.0	0.42	182	33.5
Himachal Pradesh	1.2	0.21	231	28.0
Haryana	1.0	0.76	601	4.0
Punjab	0.1	0.39	879	1.4
Others[3]	14.3	—	—	—
India	100.0	100.00	210	27.5

1. Government of India, *Bulletin on Food Statistics* (1987-90).
2. Planning Commission's estimates drawn from : C.M.I.E., *Basic Statistics*.
3. 'Others' include other minor states and union territories including Delhi.

TABLE 2

Rural-Urban Coverage of PDS (1986-87)

States	% of PDS users among all persons		% of rural population to total population	% of rural PDS users to all PDS users	% share of rural sector in toal quantity of PDS purchases			
	Rural areas	Urban areas			Cereals	Sugar	Edible oil	Kerosene
(1)	(2)	(3)	(4)	(5)	(6)	(7)	(8)	(9)
(I) High Coverage Category								
Kerala	91.94	86.94	81.1	82.0	82.3	80.9	70.3	79.9
Karnataka	61.91	62.66	69.9	69.7	57.4	47.9	33.4	45.7
Andhra Pradesh	59.68	51.38	77.0	80.0	79.3	96.2	68.3	63.4
Tamil Nadu	53.39	55.49	65.8	65.0	66.6	53.5	37.1	43.6
Maharashtra	47.68	43.82	66.5	68.3	59.4	61.5	57.4	25.9
Gujarat	44.60	31.98	70.3	76.7	76.7	68.1	68.0	49.3
(II) Moderate Coverage Category								
West Bengal	26.80	59.64	75.8	58.5	47.2	71.7	39.4	69.7
Assam	24.72	42.94	89.5	83.1	81.9	86.7	44.5	83.2
(III) Low Coverage Category								
Madhya Pradesh	8.21	17.40	80.4	65.9	66.3	70.4	77.9	68.6
Rajasthan	8.81	5.58	80.1	86.4	91.4	80.6	11.7	54.4
Uttar Pradesh	2.20	7.12	82.9	60.1	66.2	48.9	44.6	68.6
Orissa	1.69	13.85	89.4	50.6	58.0	66.6	66.0	83.5
Bihar	1.79	7.20	85.2	63.6	56.9	70.3	54.9	81.8
India	25.14	35.74	78.0	71.3	69.6	78.8	58.7	54.6

TABLE 3

PDS Purchases of Cereals by Poor (Bottom 29% Households) : 1986-87

States	% of PDS users among		% of non-poor among all the PDS users	% share in total cereals purchased under PDS of the		Cereals purchased per PDS user (kg. per capita per month)	
	Poor Population	Non-Poor Population		Poor	Non-Poor	Poor	Non-Poor
1	2	3	4	5	6	7	8
(I) High coverage category							
Kerala	93.33	90.17	73.29	25.71	74.29	4.62	4.87
Karnataka	64.60	61.35	74.91	24.62	75.38	2.04	2.09
Andhra Pradesh	68.98	53.98	69.81	25.58	74.42	3.61	4.54
Tamil Nadu	62.58	51.21	70.57	25.33	74.67	2.00	2.46
Maharashtra	50.74	45.00	73.64	27.00	73.00	2.78	2.68
Gujarat	54.40	36.73	68.95	23.48	76.52	2.18	3.20
(II) Medium coverage category							
West Bengal	32.86	35.30	77.82	24.57	75.43	4.81	4.21
Assam	30.19	25.45	79.69	25.11	74.89	2.68	3.16
(III) Low coverage category							
Madhya Pradesh	13.20	8.98	68.10	24.00	76.00	2.75	4.07
Rajasthan	13.07	6.55	60.46	24.28	75.72	6.29	12.85
Uttar Pradesh	2.58	3.18	79.14	25.03	74.97	7.03	5.55
Orissa	2.16	3.21	84.33	23.13	76.87	4.53	2.80
Bihar	2.15	2.47	79.34	23.96	76.04	4.42	3.65
India	31.00	26.33	72.53	25.46	74.54	3.31	3.67

TABLE 4

Size of PDS Foodgrain Distribution To Cover All Poor Only

Year/Per cent of Population	Number of estimated poor (persons)	Required size of distribution (Million[a] tonnes per annum)		Actual size of foodgrains distribution[b] (mill. tonnes)
		Under total support	Under partial support	
(1)	(2)	(3)	(4)	(5)
A. 1986-87				
(24.5% Population)	175.5	27.4	7.0	17.6
B. 1993-94				
(i) 24.5% Population	220.5	34.4	8.8	15.1
(ii) 29.9% Population[a]	269.1	42.0	10.8	15.1

a : Incidence of poverty (1987-88) as estimated by the Planning Commission, Economic Survey 1993-94, page 148, appllied to estimated population of 900 millions in March 1993.

b : Includes distribution through fair price shops, nutrition programme, rural employment programme and open market sales.

TABLE 5

State-wise Foodgrains Distribution Requirements To Cover All Poor Only (1986-87)

States	Number of poor persons (million)	Required size of foodgrains distribution to cover all poor (million tonnes per annum)		Actual size of distribution through PDS* (million tonnes)	Additional foodgrain supply needed to cover all poor (million tonnes)	
		With total support	With partial support		Total support	Partial Support
(1)	(2)	(3)	(4)	(5)	(6) = (3) — (5)	(7) = (4) — (5)
		(I) High Coverage Category				
Kerala	6.45	1.006	0.258	1.824	—0.818	—1.566
Karnataka	9.55	1.490	0.382	1.166	0.324	—0.784
Andhra Pradesh	14.80	2.309	0.592	1.707	0.602	—1.115
Tamil Nadu	13.15	2.051	0.526	1.727	0.324	—1.201
Maharashtra	15.41	2.404	0.616	1.773	0.631	—1.157
Gujarat	7.72	1.204	0.309	0.837	0.367	—0.528
		(II) Medium Coverage Category				
West Bengal	13.63	2.126	0.545	2.205	—0.079	—1.660
Assam	4.04	0.630	0.162	0.810	—0.180	—0.648
		(III) Low Coverage Category				
Madhya Pradesh	13.40	2.090	0.536	0.593	1.497	—0.057
Rajasthan	9.10	1.420	0.364	0.884	0.536	—0.520

(1)	(2)	(3)	(4)	(5)	(6) = (3) — (5)	(7) = (4) — (5)
Uttar Pradesh	32.15	5.015	1.286	0.822	4.193	0.464
Orissa	6.01	0.938	0.240	0.296	0.642	—0.056
Bihar	17.65	2.753	0.706	0.777	1.976	—0.071
Other States and UTs.	12.44	1.941	0.497	2.174	—0.233	—1.677
All India	175.50	27.378	7.020	17.595	9.783	—10.575

*Includes distribution through fair price shops, nutrition programmes, rural employment programmes and open market sales.

10

INDIA'S FOREIGN TRADE

N. PARTHASARATHY

Dean

Indian Institute of Foreign Trade

It can safely be said that the external sector of the economy received practically no attention from the policy makers, academic and trade and industry till about the beginning of the Third Plan period in the country. The major reason for this lack of attention may be traced to the fact that India had built up substantial foreign exchange reserves during the Second World War period and hence earning foreign exchange through a deliberately formulated programme for exports was not regarded as an integral part of the country's development effort. The first serious attempt to look at the country's foreign trade, particularly in the area of policy, may be said to have commenced with the establishment of the Import and Export Policy Committee during 1962. The Committee acknowledged that 'the country has not great export tradition : nor has one been developed so far, much less have we developed the necessary export apparatus'. The Committee also found that the Governments, both at the Centre and in the States, were not 'alive, to the primacy of export promotion' and, in fact, 'some of their policies, particularly in the fiscal field, have hindered the even flow of exports'. Only as late as 1970, Government of India formulated an Export Policy Resolution outlining the Government's policy in regard to export promotion.

Overall Trends

Since not much of attention was paid to the country's foreign trade during the First Plan period, as earlier indicated, possibly due to the comfortable foreign exchange position in the country immediately after the Second World War, no special efforts were probably considered necessary to promote or regulate the country's export-import trade. The average level of exports during the period, at current prices, was Rs. 605 crore per annum and that of imports, Rs. 735 crore per year, with a trade deficit of Rs. 130 crore per annum. The beginning of this period saw an unusually high export turnover of Rs. 716 crore during 1951-52 due to the Korean war; otherwise exports averaged around Rs. 600 crore per year.

The Second Plan period (1956—61) witnessed substantial growth in imports to meet the increasing demand for investment goods. Thus, the average level of imports during the Second Plan period jumped to Rs. 973 crore per annum. On the other hand, in the absence of any sustained strategy to promote exports, they remained almost stagnant around Rs. 606 crore per annum. Consequently, the trade deficit jumped by nearly three times, from an average of Rs. 130 crore per annum during the First Plan period to Rs. 367 crore per year during 1956—61.

As earlier indicated, the Third Plan period synchronised with the commencement of deliberate attempts on the part of Government of India to promote exports. These included, apart from the constitution of the Import and Export Policy Committee during 1962 referred to earlier, introduction of export incentives, establishment of export service institutions and attempts to improve export infrastructure. These efforts commenced bearing fruit towards the end of the period and exports grew from Rs. 660 crore in 1961-62 to Rs. 816 crore in 1964-65 although there was a marginal decline to Rs. 810 crore in 1965-66. The average annual level of exports during the period (1961—66) was Rs. 753 crore. However, the drought conditions in the country and the continuing requirements for capital goods and raw materials and components lead to a jump in imports from an average of Rs. 973 crore per annum during the Second Plan period to Rs. 1240 crore per annum during 1961-66 pushing up the trade deficit to an average of Rs. 487 crore per annum during the priod.

The most significant development that took place during the next three year annual plan period beginning April 1966 was the devaluation of the Indian rupee during mid-1966 leading to increased rupee earnings and outflow on account of exports and imports respectively. Thus, one would notice that India's exports, at current prices, jumped to Rs. 1157 crore during 1966-67 and imports, to Rs. 2078 crore during the same year. The continuing drought conditions made it difficult to bring about any large scale reduction in imports and consequently, the average level of imports during the three year period was around Rs. 2,000 crore per annum. Consequently, the trade deficit rose to an average of Rs. 760 crore per annum during the priod.

The Fourth Plan period beginning April 1969 can be referred to as the "Export of Perish" period which bore the impact of devaluation on export expansion and import contraction. This was also the period which saw the Indian Parliament pass the Export Policy Resolution in 1970. Consequent to the rate of growth in exports outstripping that in imports, the trade deficit declined drastically to an average of Rs. 163 crore per annum during the period; in fact, during 1972-73, there was, for the first time in many years, a surplus on trade account to the extent of Rs. 104 crore.

When it appeared that the country had almost turned the corner on the foreign trade front, the oil crisis of 1973 led to a sudden and substantial jump in the import bill of the country from Rs. 1867 crore in 1972-73 to Rs. 2955 crore in the very next year, though the all-round increase in prices fuelled by the increase in the price of petroleum had pushed up export earnings also from Rs. 1971 crore in 1972-73 to Rs. 2523 crore in 1973-74, there was a deficit in the trade account to the tune of Rs. 432 crore during 1973-74, as against the trade surplus of Rs. 104 crore recorded during the previous year.

The Fifth Plan period (1974—79) marked another phase in the country's foreign trade history. The philosophies of 'export or perish' and 'import substitution and export promotion' yielded place to a philosophy of 'export more and import more', a recognition of the fact that foreign trade is a two-way traffic. During this period, imports were considerably liberalised, while exports were promoted. There was also a selective policy of regulation of exports of mass consumption items like vegetables, sugar and vegetable oils and oilseeds. The period saw substantial growth both in exports and imports and, during 1976-77, there was, in fact, a marginal trade surplus of Rs. 68 crore, for the second time in a short period. However, overall, there was an increase in trade deficit during this period to an average of Rs. 810 crore per annum.

The subsequent two plan periods *i.e.* 1980—85 and 1985—90 were periods of steady growth in exports, imports and trade deficit. It is worth noting that, while the average annual level of exports between the Fifth Plan and the Seventh Plan grew by slightly more than three and half times, that in imports grew faster *i.e.* by more than four and half times leading to substantial growth in the negative trade balance from Rs. 810 crore per annum during 1974-79 to as much as Rs. 7743 crore per annum during the Seventh Plan period.

The subsequent three years witnessed historic changes in the foreign trade policy of the country, the main thrust of which was alround economic liberalisation. Basically, the steps initiated by the Government of India on the foreign trade front were directed towards dismantling of the complex system of export incentives and shifting the emphasis from Government regulation to market forces. As part of the exercise, the rupee was made convertible on the trade account. Under this environment, both exports and imports grew, though during 1991-92, there was a sluggishness in import growth leading to substantial reduction in the negative trade balance. However, during the very next year, the trade deficit increased to Rs. 9687 crore. Available provisional data* indicate that during April 1993 — March 1994, India's exports have touched Rs. 69547 crore (30% growth over 1992-93), and imports, Rs. 72806 crore (16% growth over 1992-93) and the negative trade balance has declined to Rs. 3259 crore.

Table 1 provides data on India's annual average level of imports, exports and trade balance during the Plan periods beginning with the First Plan period, and, year-wise data, beginning 1990-91.

Composition of Exports

Table 2 provides data on the composition of India's exports by major product/product groups for selected years beginning 1968-69 that accounted for 79 per cent of the country's total exports during 1992-93, in value, at current prices. Gems and jewellery have emerged, in recent years, as the single largest group in exports, followed by clothing (garments) and engineering goods, whereas during the sixties, it was jute manufactures, tea and iron ore that dominated the scene.

**The Statesman*, Delhi, 4 May, 1994.

Notwithstanding the substantial growth in the exports of traditional items, there is definite proof of diversification, in India's exports, in favour of value added products. Though there has been growth in exports in respect of most other product groups, the more dynamic growth sectors appear to be cotton piece goods, leather and manufactures, marine products, oil cakes, chemicals, handicrafts, clothing, engineering goods and gems & jewellary.

A close look would indicate that the items that dominate the Indian export scene can be broadly classified into three : (i) products in the production/manufacture and export of which India enjoys comparative advantage on account of factors such as climate, topography, resource endowment etc. This would include items such as tea, jute manufactures, tobacco, spices, coffee, iron ore, marine products, oil cakes and leather; (ii) items involving low technology and labour skill and intensity such as cotton textiles, cashew, chemicals, engineering goods, handicrafts and clothing; and (iii) items which are entirely dependent on imports and labour skill in the country. This would include gems and jewellery, particularly diamonds, on account of the centuries' old tradition and specialisation in the country in cutting and polishing small sized diamonds.

In addition to the product groups listed in Table 2, the other main items exported from the country have been processed foods, silk goods, rice, synthetic textiles and petroleum products.

Composition of Imports

Table 3 provides data, value-wise, at current prices, on India's imports of main groups of items for selected years beginning 1968-69. The major import of the country is, understandably, petroleum and products followed by machinery and transport equipment, these two accounting for slightly less than half of India's total imports during 1992-93. The other major items imported by India have been chemicals, iron and steel, manufactured fertilizers and non-ferrous metals. It is clear that India's imports have all along been confined to the unavoidable necessities *i.e.* items that are not available in the country in sufficient quantities but are needed to meet the development and export requirements. Besides the above, the country has been importing, from time to time, cereals, during periods of domestic shortages and/or for building up reasonable stocks. It will also be noticed that India's imports comprise bulk items to a substantial extent.

In addition to the product groups listed in Table 3, India has been importing a number of other items such as edible oil, newsprint, crude fertilizers, sulphur, metalliferous ores and metal scrap, rubber, pulses, coal/coke, raw wool, plastic materials, medicinal products professional and scientific equipment, metal manufactures, textile yarn, project goods and pearls and precious and semi-precious stones. Out of the above, substantial imports take place every year in respect of the last two groups of products. While import of project goods is an indication of the extent of construction and other projects undertaken in the country, that of pearls, precious and semi-precious stones is directly linked to the exports of gems and jewellery since, as earlier indicated, this group comprises mostly diamonds, which are imported in raw form and re-exported after cutting and finishing.

Export Markets

The major markets for Indian products, region-wise, have been the European Union, North America and Asia (ESCAP Region), these three regions accounting for 75 per cent share in India's total exports during 1992-93. The share of Africa, Eastern Europe and South America put together has been only 9 per cent.

The largest market is provided by the European Union countries in which Germany and UK have been major buyers. North America, mainly USA, is also a very large buyer of Indian items: in fact USA, as a country, is the single largest buyer from India; the ESCAP region is the second largest market, mainly because of the large number of countries which constitute the region; within the region, Japan, Hong Kong, Singapore and Belgium are the major buyers.

India's exports to no African country is substantial, barring Nigeria and Egypt. Similarly, exports to South America have always been limited, probably because of the long geographical distance between India and the region.

India's exports to East European countries including USSR have undergone a metamorphosis in recent times. This was the area that, consequent to the trade and payments arrangements, accounted for the maximum growth in India's exports till the beginning of the 90s: from less than Rs. 10 crore per annum during the First Plan period, India's exports to East Europe including USSR grew to more than Rs. 8514 crore during 1990-91: subsequently, on account of the economic restructuring taking place in this region and due to the discontinuance of the trade and payments arrangements between India and these countries, India's exports started declining.

Table 4 provides data on India's exports, major region-wise.

Country-wise, USA, Japan, Germany, UK and the United Arb Emirates are the five leading markets for Indian products.

Import Sources

It will be noticed from Table 5 that India's imports follow the same direction as exports : region-wise, West Europe, the ESCAP region and North America are the major suppliers to India : within North America, USA is the most important country and, in the ESCAP region, Japan accounts for the major share : imports from Africa, East Europe and South America are not substantial with South America occupying the last position. Within the European Union, Belgium has emerged as the major supplier to India entirely because of increasing imports of raw diamonds from Belgium by India to feed the export-oriented industry in the country, followed by Germany and UK; in the ESCAP region, besides Japan, Australia, Singapore, Malaysia, Iran and South Korea are main suppliers to the country : in Africa, Nigeria is the only major supplier.

Consequent to changes that have taken place within the region and in the mechanism of their trade with India, imports from East Europe including USSR have declined substantially after 1990-91.

Due to the fact that India imports substantial quantities of petroleum, countries such as Kuwait, Saudi Arabia, Iran, UAE and Bahrein are figuring prominently in India's import sources.

Country-wise, USA, Belgium, Germany, Saudi Arbia, Japan and UK are the major suppliers to India.

EXPORT POLICY AND INSTRUMENTS

Recognising the importance of export as a vehicle of growth and development, which, till 1970, was paid relatively less attention. Government of India passed an Export Policy Resolution in 1970. The Resolution is an important landmark in India's foreign trade policy framework which laid emphasis on the systematic development of different export sectors *viz.* agriculture, horticulture, sericulture, minerals, fisheries, forestry, textiles, chemicals, electronic and engineering industries thereby marking a shift away from the country's dependence on export of traditional items *viz.* tea, coffee and jute.

In an effort to fulfil the objectives set out in the Export Policy Resolution, various export promotion and regulatory measures have been initiated by Government of India from time to time for creating export surpluses through increased output; strengthening institutional framework, providing necessary marketing assistance for export promotion, and regulating export of commodities and services essential to the economy. The primary objective of the Government has, therefore, been to promote exports to the maximum extent by liberalising/streamlining the commercial policy and the regulatory Acts *viz.* Foreign Exchange Regulation Act, 1973 (FERA), Export (Control) Order, 1988 now replaced by the Foreign Trade (Development and Regulation) Act, 1992, etc.

Government of India have initiated measures since July 1991 to bring about a freer and more liberalised environment in the country. These measures, encompassing trade, industrial, fiscal and monetary sectors, include full convertibility of rupee, simplification and streamlining of export-import policy and procedures, substantial reduction in import licensing and other discretionary controls, pruning of Negative Lists of Exports and Imports, decentralisation of powers in the DGFT, reduction of peak import tariff level from 85% to 65%, specific directions to banks to increase availability of credit at lower rates of interest to the export sector, strengthening infrastructual facilities through greater involvement of State Governments, and making adequate institutional arrangements for export marketing.

Export Promotion

Export promotion measures initiated to step up exports from the country could be divided into three broad categories.

Export Production : In order to step up export production, sharpen competitive edge and bring about quality and technology upgradation, following measures have been initiated —

Liberalisation : Trade and industrial licensing policies have been reoriented towards exports.

Supply of Raw Materials : Licence free import of capital goods, raw materials, intermediates, components, consumables, spares, parts, accessories, instruments and other goods is permitted provided imports of such items are not regulated by the Negative List of Imports.

Export Promotion Capital Goods (EPCG) Scheme

The objective of EPCG Scheme is to allow import of capital goods, both new and second hand, at concessional rate of 15% customs duty. A manufacturer-exporter can import capital goods (including spares upto 10% of the CIF value of the capital goods) at a concessional rate of customs duty of 15% subject to export obligation and other provisions as stipulated in the EXIM Policy. The EPCG Scheme has also been extended to the Services Sector.

Import of Second Hand Capital Goods : Import of second-hand capital goods having a minimum residual life of five years is allowed free of licence subject to actual user condition.

Duty Exemption Scheme : The scheme facilitates duty free import of raw materials, components, intermediates, consumables, parts, accessories, packing materials, and computer software required for the purpose of export production under various schemes of Advance/Special/Imprest/Intermediate Licences and Self-Declared Pass Book Scheme as also Advance Customs Clearance Permit.

Investment in Plant and Equipment : Investment in plant and equipment beyond Rs. 75 lakhs is permitted to SSI Sector subject to provisions laid down in the EXIM Policy.

EPZ/EOU/EHTP/STP : Establishment of Export Processing Zones, Export Oriented Units, Electronic Hardware Technology Parks and Software Technology Parks to facilitate export production in the non-traditional sectors by exempting supplies of imports and machinery from customs/excise duties, and other terminal taxes.

Quality : To promote the concept of total quality management the

Central Government assists in the modernisation and upgradation of test houses and laboratories in order to bring them at par with international standards so that certification by such test houses and laboratories is recognised within the country and abroad.

Export Marketing Assistance

Full Convertibility : Full convertibility of Indian rupee is permitted whereby all foreign exchange receipts can be converted into rupees at market rate of exchange.

Retention Limit : Retention limit has been raised from 15 to 25 per cent of foreign exchange receipts in an account designated in foreign currency. In case of EOU/EPZ/EHTP and STP the retention limit is upto 50 per cent.

Lending Rate : Lending rates charged by the banks on term loans of three years and above have been reduced from 15 to 14 per cent.

Income Tax Exemption : Full exemption from income tax of export profits from merchandise trade has been granted.

Duty Drawback : Exporters are allowed to get refund/ rebate of duty chargeable on imported materials or excisable materials used in export production.

Export Finance : Finance for pre-shipment and post-shipment is made available at reasonable rates of interest from Export-Import Bank and other commercial banks in Indian rupees and in some cases of post-shipment credit, in foreign currency also.

Export Credit Risk Insurance : Export Credit Risk Insurance is available from ECGC at a low premium to protect exporters from risks, both political and commercial, involved in extending credit to overseas buyers.

Cash Compensatory Support : CCS was granted to make Indian exports competitive in the international markets. This facility has been withdrawn with effect from 1992.

International Price Reimbursement Scheme: Reimbursement of difference between the domestic and international price of iron and steel to promote exports of engineering goods. This scheme has been withdrawn from 1.4.94.

Jute Marketing Assistance : Marketing assistance under the Internal and External Market Assistance (IMA) and (EMA) Schemes cover those products which contain two or more fibres, in which jute is the dominant fibre by weight. While IMA provides market assistance @ 8 per cent on sale of specified jute products, EMA grants @ 10 per cent of FOB value realisation on export of specified diversified products. The benefit under EMA is available to both manufacturer-exporters and merchant-exporters. These schemes are valid till the end of the Eighth Plan period.

Export House/Trading House/Star Trading House and Super Star Trading House: Additional benefits are granted to exporters who have achieved the specified level of exports over a period of time as notified in the EXIM Policy. Such exporters are accorded a special status by the Government.

Import Replenishment : Grant of Import Replenishment Licence against exports *to the exporters of gem and jewellery products* listed in Appendix I of the EXIM Policy.

Deemed Exports : Supplies of goods and services to Five Specified Categories within the country which earn or save foreign exchange are treated as deemed exports. Such exports are eligible for facilities under duty exemption scheme, duty draw back, refund of terminal excise duty, and Special Import Licences @ 5% of FOR value of supplies made with effect from 1.4.94.

Institutional Framework

To strengthen infrastructural facilities required for export production and promotion, Government of India has set up a wide network of institutions/organisations in the country.

Transport : To provide support to carriage of goods by sea, air, rail and intermodal transport, Government has set up Inland Container Depots (ICDs), Container Freight Stations (CFSs) and Air Cargo Complexes (ACCs) equipped with container handling facilities at various places.

Board of Trade : To provide a forum for ensuring continuous dialogue with trade and industry in respect of major developments in the field of international trade, Board of Trade has been set up under the aegis of Ministry of Commerce.

States Cell : A States Cell has been created in the Ministry of Commerce to act as a nodal agency for interaction with State Governments/Union Territories, State Export Corporations, Associations of Industries and Commerce and Export Organisations like ITPO, FIEO and EPZs on matters concerning export from and imports into the States.

Market Development Assistance : This scheme, functioning under the Ministry of Commerce, was set up in 1963 with a view to stimulating and diversifying export trade along with the development of the marketing of Indian products and commodities abroad. Financial support is provided for : market research, commodity research, area survey and research; product promotion and commodity development; export publicity and dissemination of information; participation in trade fairs and exhibitions; trade delegations and study teams; establishment of offices and branches in overseas countries; grants-in-aid to export promotion councils and other approved organisations for the development of exports and promotion of foreign trade; and any other scheme which is calculated generally to promote the development of overseas markets for Indian products.

Export Promotion Councils/Commodity Boards/Export Development Authorities : 19 Export Promotion Councils, six Commodity Boards, two Export Development Authorities and Federation of Indian Export Organisations (FIEO) are functioning under the Ministry of Commerce to provide support to the exporting community.

Indian Institute of Packaging : IIP helps to bring about and sustain appropriate improvements in the standards or packaging, particularly for exports.

Indian Institute of Foreign Trade : IIFT has been rendering useful service, since 1964, in the area of human resource development for international business, through need-based training programmes, seminars and workshops, interfaced with and supported by, continuous research on a variety of topical subjects in the field of foreign trade and international business.

India Trade Promotion Organisation : Established under the Ministry of Commerce, ITPO projects the image of Indian goods and services by organising trade fairs and exhibitions, buyer-seller meets, and conducting market studies both within the country and abroad.

Export Inspection Council : Export Inspection Council subjects a number of items meant for exports to compulsory quality control and pre-shipment inspection under the Export (Quality Control and Inspection) Act, 1963. However, items bearing ISI Mark/Agmark and goods being exported by recognised Export Houses/Trading Houses/ Star Trading Houses/Super Star Trading Houses are exempted from the purview of compulsory pre-shipment inspection.

Indian Council of Arbitration : The role of Indian Council of Arbitration is to amicably settle commercial disputes arising from the export transaction/contract between the exporter and the importer.

Directorate General of Foreign Trade : DGFT, formerly known as CCI&E, assists and advises Government of India in formulation of EXIM Policy and in the implementation of the policy through the mechanism of licensing.

Export Control

Government of India also exercises control/restriction on exports and imports of such commodities and services considered vital to the economy or those that affect the domestic industry. Effort is, however, made to limit such regulation to minimum number of items.

Exports in India are controlled/regulated under the provisions of Export (Control) Order, 1988 as amended, issued under the Import and Export (Control) Act, 1947 which has since been replaced by Foreign Trade (Development and Regulation) Act, 1992. Besides, exports are also regulated under the Customs Act, Coffee Act, Tea Act, Marine Products Export Development Authority Act, minimum export price (MEP), quantitative ceilings, canalisation, export licensing, compulsory registration with EPCs/FIEO etc.

Some of the important measures initiated to control/restrict export of items which are essentially needed in the country are as follows :

Nagative List of Exports: The Negative List of Exports as given in the EXIM Policy 1992—97 (as revised upto March 30, 1994) is divided into three parts, *viz.* :

Prohibited Items	10
Restricted Items (subject to Export Licensing)	31
Canalised Items (Different canalising agencies have been designated for different products).	9

Negative List of Imports : The Negative List of Imports as given in the EXIM Policy 1992—97 (as revised upto March 30, 1994) is also divided into three parts *viz.* :

Prohibited Items	3
Restricted Items	72
Canalised Items	7

Quantitative Ceilings on Exports : The following items are subject to quantitative ceilings as given in the EXIM Policy :

1. Brown seaweeds and agarophytes excluding G-edulis of Tamil Nadu coast origin in processed form;
2. Cotton yarn;
3. Grain and flour, namely wheat, barley, maize, bajra, jowar (excluding hybrid jowar — feed grade) and ragi;
4. Meat of sheep and goat;
5. Peacock tail feathers including handicrafts and articles made thereof;
6. Manufactured articles and shavings of shed antlers of chital and sambhar;
7. Sunflower seeds;
8. Rape seeds and mustard seeds; and
9. Powder milk (skimmed or full cream) whole, and infant milk food.

Minimum Export Price : The following items are permitted for exports subject to minimum export price fixed from time to time :

1. Coir & coir products;
2. Grain and flour, namely wheat, barley, maize, bajra, jowar (excluding hybrid jowar – feed grade), and ragi;
3. Non-basmati rice.

Import Policy

As for import policy, the basic objective has been to ensure proper utilisation of the limited foreign exchange resources of the country by judicious allocation of the same on the basis of criteria based on priorities and non-availability of the same or similar items within the country. Other two objectives relate to granting protection to infant industries through import tariff and/or quantitative restrictions and maintenance of price stability of, in particular, essential items by allowing imports during periods of substantial increase in the unit price of sensitive items.

TABLE 1

India's Foreign Trade

Val : Rs. crores

	Imports	Exports	Balance
First Plan Average			
(1951—56)	735	605	— 130
Second Plan Average			
(1956—61)	973	606	— 367
Third Plan Average			
(1961—66)	1240	753	— 487
Average of Three Annual			
Plans (1966—69)	1998	1238	— 760
Fourth Plan Average			
(1969—74)	1973	1810	— 163
Fifth Plan Average			
(1974—79)	5538	4728	— 810
1979-80	9143	6418	— 2725
Sixth Plan Average			
(1980—85)	14683	8967	— 5716
Seventh Plan Average			
(1985—90)	25130	17387	— 7743
1990-91	43193	32565	— 10628
1991-92	47851	43976	— 3875
1992-93	62923	53351	— 9572

Source : DGCI & S, Calcutta.

TABLE 2

Composition of India's Exports

Val : Rs. crores

	1968-69	1978-79	1989-90	1992-93
Jute Mfrs.	218	165	298	355
Tea	157	341	905	977
Cotton piece goods	66	224	1480	3211
Leather & Mfrs.	73	328	1951	3700
Tobacco, unmanufactured	33	111	143	356
Spices	25	148	247	393
Coffee	18	144	343	377
Cashew	61	80	368	749
Iron ore	88	233	928	1104
Marine products	22	221	687	1743
Oil cakes	50	116	546	1545
Clothing	15	456	3224	6931
Chemicals	18	156	1955	3558
Engineering	86	717	2863	6476
Handicrafts	NA	97	403	2060
Gems & Jewellery	NA	729	5296	8897
Total	1358	5726	27681	53351

Source : DGCI & S, Calcutta.

TABLE 3

Composition of India's Imports

Val : Rs. crores

	1968-69	1978-79	1989-90	1992-93
Cereals	337	68	378	966
Petroleum & products	133	1677	6274	17142
Machinery & Transport Equipment	514	1260	6980	12700
Fertilizers, manufactured	139	371	1228	2023
Non-ferrous metals	89	246	1253	1144
Iron & steel	86	463	2305	2255
Chemicals Elements & Compounds	83	231	2135	4625
Total	1909	6811	35412	62923

Source: DGCI & S, Calcutta.

TABLE 4

Direction of India's Exports

Val : Rs. crores

	1968-69	1978-79	1989-90	1992-93
EU	111	1557	7123	15196
N. America	264	819	4738	10737
USA	234	771	4474	10183
ESCAP	344	1479	6338	14207
Japan	158	592	2727	4160
Africa	73	338	661	2124
South America	4	21	35	242
East Europe	267	609	5120	2359
USSR/CIS	148	411	4463	1756
Total	1358	5726	27681	53351

Source : DGCI & S, Calcutta.

TABLE 5

Direction of India's Exports

Val : Rs. crores

	1969-70	1978-79	1989-90	1992-93
EU	188	2084	11933	19124
N. America	564	1002	4713	7392
USA	446	762	4259	6219
ESCAP	264	1485	7302	14210
Japan	83	565	2820	4136
Africa	170	156	913	4011
South America	14	82	620	753
East Europe	226	649	2793	1606
USSR/CIS	105	471	2038	737
Others				
Kuwait	6	104	1160	2763
South Arabia	24	197	1448	433
Total	1582	6811	35412	62923

Source : DGCI & S, Calcutta.

11

ECONOMIC ENVIRONMENT OF RURAL COMMUNITIES LINKAGES THROUGH RURAL DEVELOPMENT PROGRAMMES

DR. L.N. GUPTA
Associate Professor of Economics
J.N. Vyas University

I. Agri-Rural Reciprocity

A country seeking for rural development must give priority to agriculture and its modernisation because agriculture forms a major component of rural development. Further, agricultural development is often viewed as the key to reducing poverty, especially rural poverty. It is observed that most of the global-poor live in rural areas and they get a large proportion of income through agricultural pursuits. It is roughly estimated that about one-third of the developing world and more than half of the low income countries live in absolute poverty. Further, more than three-fourth of these poor live in rural areas and nearly 40 per cent of rural poor in all developing countries live in absolute poverty. Therefore, agriculture and rural development may be regarded as two sides of one coin. Conceptually, there has been a significant departure from the old practice and it is true that earlier rural development was linked up only with farming operations. Later on other activities such as animal husbandry, fisheries were also added to this; still it presents a narrow dimension of rural development. In fact, rural development is much more than this. In a wider spectrum, it includes rural industrialisation, self-supporting developmental activities including the infrastructure network. Thus a close relationship is established between agriculture and rural development. Further, it is also true that possibly various agricultural measures for raising productivity might not affect the socio-economic welfare of rural masses directly but indirectly their impact has been experienced immensely by generating higher demand for labour and raising resource-use efficiency in the process of agro-transformation.

In India agriculture occupies a pivotal position because of its contribution to overall economic growth through supplies of food items, raw materials and exports. It serves as a source of livelihood for a majority of the population and provides a large market for non-agricultural goods and services. Thus, it is a primary engine of economic growth and a pre-requisite for industrial development which is a basic function of increased agricultural productivity. Professor W. Arthur Lewis holds that rising agricultural productivity supports industrial development : it permits agriculture to release a part of its labour force for industrial development, raises agricultural incomes and savings which may be channelised to finance the industrial development. Further, it enables agriculture to supply major wage goods of the industrial workers.

The performance of the Indian agriculture, as compared with the leading producing countries, is not satisfactory. See Table 1 below :

TABLE 1

Yield of Selected Agricultural Crops (1990)

(Yield figures are expressed in 100 Kg. per hectare)

S. No.	*Crop*	*Country*		*Yield*
1.	Rice	India	::	26.9
		Japan	::	63.3
		China	::	57.3
2.	Cotton lint	India	::	2.3
		Australia	::	13.3
3.	Wheat	India	::	21.2
		France	::	64.9
		U.K.	::	69.1
	Fertilizer consumption per hectare (Kg.)			
		India	::	68.7
		Egypt	::	404.3
		Korea Rep.	::	425.0

Source : *Statistical Outline of India, 1992-93*, Tata Services Limited, Deptt. of Economics and Statistics, pp. 205-206.

In paddy production the yield per hectare in India is estimated to be just one-third of Japan (being 26.9 and 63.3 hundred Kg. respectively), for wheat over one-third of U.K. For low productivity a number of factors are responsible.

Still the modern agro-practices are wanting. In terms of fertilizer consumption per hectare, our country had used 68.7 Kg. whereas it was 425.0 Kg. for Korea Rep. The problem is rather more of a complex nature as there exists vast regional variations in agro-products; overall cereals production in India increased at the rate of 4.3 per cent per annum; analysing it further, it was 9.6 per cent for the State of Punjab, 11.1 per cent for Haryana and in Bihar it was just 0.9 per cent. Further, it is seen that agriculture is the mainstay of rural-India. According to the Population Census of 1991, rural population constitutes 74.3 per cent of the total population of the country. The task of improvement of rural economy has been viewed so as to attain the cherished objectives laid down under the plans. In this regard, there has been continuous efforts for rural development during the plans, but it was the year 1978-79 that it set a landmark by giving a new dimension (comprehensive nature) to rural development measures.

It is evident that in India rural development has assumed a considerable importance. It is a strategy designed to improve the socio-economic life of the rural masses – poorest among the poor, known as the target group. Rural development is a part of the process of socio-economic development and cultural transformation. It provides a conscious effort in raising the standard of living of rural people. The objectives of removal of poverty and other economic evils are related to the process of rural transformation through rural development programmes. In this process mass mobilisation of resources for bettering the local environment on socio-economic front appears to be fundamental of rural development, but proper precautions should be taken at the conceptual and implemental levels. In a nutshell, improvement of agriculture is the basic requirement for rural development. Indeed, rural development enables diversification of economy and mobilisation of labour force from agricultural sector to non-agricultural sector.

In India the strategy for poverty alleviation has been through investment in agriculture and allied activities. The impact of economic growth in curbing incidence of poverty has been marked substantially. This is indicated in the following table.

TABLE 2

Percentage of Population Living Below the Poverty Line

Areas	1972/73	1977/78	1983/84	1987/88
Rural	54.1	51.2	40.4	33.4
Urban	41.2	38.2	28.1	20.1
Combined	51.5	48.3	37.4	29.9

Source : Reproduced from *Economic Survey 1993-94*, Economic Divison, Ministry of Finance, Govt. of India, p. 148.

The population with consumption standard below the poverty line came down to 29.9 per cent in 1987-88 (48.3 per cent in the year 1977-78). Analysing it further, it was 33.4 per cent and 20.1 per cent for rural and urban areas respectively. The comparative figures show that incidence of poverty was more acute on rural masses corresponding to urban population. Further, these poor in general are not in a position exploit the available resources, new technology and do not get adequate support from organised network of service. In this direction findings of my study would be quite contextual.

II. The Field Experience

The study relating to the implementation of Integrated Rural Development Programme in arid areas of the State of Rajasthan reveals that of the total cases surveyed nearly 48.0 per cent of the beneficiaries could cross the poverty line. Most of the beneficiaries experienced low productivity of assets and unsuitability of units for specific job with high cost of production which stood in the way to cross the poverty line. For instance, adequate income from milch animals could not be yielded due to higher prices of fodder; although in the command area sheep rearing and animal husbandry were held more profitable pursuits. Nearly, 45 per cent of the beneficiaries of 'high Castes' could not generate income as the trade lacked the label of 'Social repute'. Rigid sociological considerations and norms might be held responsible for this sort of affair. Besides, increased employment generation at rising levels of productivity is desirable as it provides effective domestic demand for increasing agricultural production and it is essential for participation in the process of growth. A large quantity of the unemployed labour force is available. To put it in the Harris-Todaro model, labour asks for high paid job; would it be possible in the existing framework of rural areas where pressure on agricultural land is high? The study highlights that nearly 60 per cent of the beneficiaries could get employment, out of this 75 per cent could get part-time jobs. The cases of full time jobs were witnessed more in the secondary and the tertiary sectors. The position of creating jobs for women was pessimistic. With regard to labour-flow, a sectoral change was noted; more mobility of labour force was seen towards non-agricultural sector. It was mainly on account of seasonal nature of agriculture, more pressure on land and low wages. Hence, more preference towards the tertiary sector was noticed due to job assurance with more income.

Turning to the magnitude of investment by the 'target group', though it is difficult to estimate, however, there were only 13 per cent of the beneficiaries who could make petty investment. The propensity of investments was more in the command area. Wha'ever the quantum of investment made, it was on traditional items such as purchase of milch animals, fodder cutting machines, bullock carts etc. With regard to saving magnitude, the beneficiaries were inspired due to availability of banking facilities but capacity to save was low. Only 7 per cent of the beneficiaries, could save and the amount saved was meagre due to their low income.

The effectiveness of the rural development programmes has also been questioned. The block machinery was found to be in effective for providing an appropriate and integrated delivery system. After the delivery of assets, no adequate attention was paid to follow-up and to their maintenance. In selection of the beneficiaries, the prescribed norms, rules, and regulations were violated. Of the total cases, about 14 per cent beneficiaries were selected whose income was above the poverty line. Women were not given due place as per the norms laid down in the IRD Programme. For instance, in the 'TRYEM' undue concentration for some vocations, lack of aptitude on the part of trainees, inadequate infrastructure facilities, lack of follow-up of the trained youths etc. were the problems noticed during implementation of the programme. Besides, the complicated and cumbersome procedure of banks and apathetic behaviour by a number of the bank officials made the bank-approach to the beneficiaries more difficult. Further, the respondents indicated that the amount of loan was inadequate and in fixing the instalments of loan repayment, the repayment capacity of the beneficiaries was not given adequate attention.

In a recent study conducted by Indian Planning Commission certain flaws in the implementation of the Integrated Rural Development Programme have been indicated, such as, inadequate admissive financial assistance, no provision for supply of inputs and raw materials, lack of linkage of loan repayment with marketing of produce and absence of arrangements for marketing of produce. Apart from this, the functionaries did not pay due attention to their work because of their frequent transfers, lack of adequate knowledge and proper training. Besides, some of the beneficiaries had no previous experience of maintenance of assets and they lacked proper working knowledge. It was also noticed that the 'Sarpanch' dominated and gripped the programme.

III. The Recent Policies

How the new economic policy and the GATT agreement shall shape the rural development activities, is a question of serious concern as well as a challenge to the implementing agencies. The LPG (Liberalisation, Privatization, Globalisation) strategy is bound to play an effective role in changing the rural socio-economic scenario. In the absence of relevant data it puts a constraint to visualise its impact on future growth of rural development. It is true that to boost productive efficiency, the strategy of privatisation has been the best means. In other words and to be more specific, to what extent the activities relating to rural development can be privatised? To consider privatisation as a source of exploitation and other socio-economic evils is misunderstood. Indeed, privatisation does not foster the monopolistic tendencies, rather it is viewed in a different way. It is for the benefit of the group to derive the best possible returns while ensuring and accelerating domestic resource generation and reduces dependence on the State resources. Since the policy of liberalisation of the Government provides bright opportunities to the foreign investors including the NRIs, the rural activities are bound to be affected. Recently, the Marrakesh Declaration on the 15th April, 1994 which is certainly a historic agreement to liberalise world trade, was signed.

IV. The Future Line of Action

What should be the future line of action to make the rural development programmes more viable, effective and conducive to improve socio-economic conditions of the rural masses. Looking to the past experiences almost all rural development programmes have been funded by the government grant or/and subsidised institutional finances/ loan, but it could not prove conducive towards overall self-sustained growth of rural development. A searching question is, what is wrong with the programmes relating to rural development? Numerous factors are responsible for this state of affairs. Here we are more concerned with the prescriptive aspect. Why not to beautify villages and provide basic facilities of life to the rural masses ? It would attract more people to stay in the villages and it might lead to migration of people from towns to villages. A number of activities such as animal husbandry, village, cottage and tiny industries, soil conservation, education sanitation etc. could be taken up under the cover of privatisation.

A mention about the Twenty Point Programme basically meant for uplifting the rural masses is quite contextual. It has not been successful and the resources mobilised by the Government have remained ineffective in attaining this objective. It is with this contention that encouragement of private initiatives would be an effective and catalytic exercise.

Further, it is quite imperative that the functionaries at various levels should be strengthened by way of upgrading their professional knowledge and competence by imparting frequent training and providing refresher courses for them. The rural area schemes to be based on thorough survey of local resources should be undertaken and viability of on-going schemes should be reviewed which might enhance the productivity and provide fair returns on investment. During the course of implementation of the rural schemes due emphasis must be given to forward and backward linkages. For better functioning/results, let the banks go to the doorstep of the beneficiaries with adequate and timely finance-packages. By introduction of regional languages, the banks may become more popular and easily accessible to the masses. A comprehensive insurance cover for all types of assets is quite necessary. A guarantee-price should be assured to the beneficiaries for their products. A time bound posting tagged with specification of duties should be given due consideration in deputation of officials. More participation of voluntary agencies is highly desirable. It is quite contextual to name that 'Lupin Rural Support Programme' has been doing an excellent work in the districts of Bharatpur and Alwar of Rajasthan. The results of LRSP have been attractive. Besides, the People's Action for Development India (PADI) has been able to mobilise rural masses for the programmes. Indeed, in India rural poverty alleviation programmes have to be viewed in the wider perspective of socio-economic transformation. Lastly, 'biomodalism' a thesis of Professor John Mellor appears to be quite relevant to the Indian economy. How the rural development programmes would set the economy and attain a balance pose a challenge to the functionaries in India and elsewhere in the world?

REFERENCES

Government of India (PEO, Planning Commission), *Evaluation Report on IRDP*, May 1985.

Government of India, — Ministry of Agriculture, Department of Rural Development, *Annual Report 1985-86.*

Binswanger, Hans and Quizon, Jaiume B., "What can Agriculture do for the Poorest Rural Groups?" — Indian Economic Association 8th World Economic Congress of the International Economic Association (1986).

Mellor, John W., *Rural Employment Linkages Through Agricultural Growth.*

Lewis, W. Arthur, *Theory of Economic Growth*, Allen and Unwin (1955).

Banerjee, Brojendra Nath, *Industry, Agriculture and Rural Development*, BR Publishing Corporation.

Desai, V., *A Study of Rural Economics*, Himalaya Publishing House.

Government of India (Ministry of Finance), *Economic Survey* (1993-94).

Director Census Operations, Rajasthan, *Census of India 1991, Series 21*, Rajasthan.

Ganguly, Ashok S., *Life after Liberalisation*, Forum of Free Enterprise.

Taori, Kamal, *Rural Development and Privatisation*, Forum of Free Enterprise.

Tata Services Ltd., *Statistical Outline of India (1992-93).*

Government of India (Planning Commission), *Eighth Five Year Plan (1992—97), Vol. I, II.*

Gupta, L. N., *Integrated Rural Development Programme : An Empirical Study*, Books Treasure (1994).

12

PARENTS' CHILD-SEX PREFERENCE BEHAVIOUR IN INDIA : AN EMPIRICAL INVESTIGATION

DR. B.K. VASHIST
Dept. of Economics
Kurukshetra University

Section I of this paper is devoted to an empirical investigation of male-bias of parents in Indian households and its relationship with family size or fertility and spacing of children. A methodology for constructing Index of Male-Bias of Parents (IMBP) and its theoretical frame is suggested in Section II. Conclusions and policy implications are contained in Section III. The study is based on a cross-section of 293 complete families in Haryana :

Number of Children in the Family

	2	3	4	5	6	7 or more	Total
Rural families	4	32	47	36	25	21	165
Urban families	44	38	21	13	8	4	128
All families	48	70	68	49	33	25	293

SECTION I

Male-Female Child Ratio, Family Size and Birth Interval

The Indian households are generally characterised by a male-bias. Having a son is almost an obsession with most of them. For instance, only 14 per cent of the parents in two-child families are willing to restrict family size with a 'no son' endowment. Others want at least one male child to be content with. As regards other family groups, 59 per cent of the parents in three-child families, 76 per cent in four-child families, 77 per cent in five-child families and not less than 84 per cent beyond that have at least two male children before deciding to complete the family (Table I).

TABLE 1

Proportion of Families in Each Parity Group Completing their Size after Having a Given Number of Male Children

Parity group (Family size completed)	Number of children							
	0	1	2	3	4	5	6	7
2	.14	.54	.31					
3	.07	.34	.43	.16				
4	.03	.26	.44	.16	.10			
5	Nil	.22	.28	.35	.12	.02		
6	.06	.03	.36	.24	.27	.03	nil	
7	.04	.12	.20	nil	.24	.28	.08	.04

After reaching a particular level of family size mostly such families decide to 'stop' as have achieved an average male-female child ratio (in subsequent discussion we shall refer to this as child ratio or simply as ratio unless specified otherwise) of at least one while other families decide to 'go ahead'. As these families have more children, an increasing proportion of them decide to 'stop' mostly after having a substantial increase in the child ratio. Interestingly, even though the ratio is lower in these families as compared to those who 'stop' earlier, they have, on average, a greater number of male children. It appears that expansion of family size is in fact motivated basically by parents' desire to have more male children when they already have female children in 'abundance', no matter in the process they may have still more of the latter (Table 2). Significantly, on comparison of birth intervals we find that these families tend to expand faster than others. It can be seen from Table 3 that the length of subsequent birth interval is positively related to the proportion of male children; families with greater proportion of female children tend to go in for next child after relatively shorter intervals.

TABLE 2

Child Ratios for Different Categories of Families within Each Parity Group

Parity group (Existing number of children)	Total number of families	Families restricting their size to the given number of exiting children			Families expanding their size beyond the existing number of children		
		Total number	Child ratio	Av. no. of male children	Total no.	Child ratio	Av. no. of male children
1	2	3	4	5	6	7	8
2	293 (100)	48 (16.38)	1.4	1.17	245 (83.62)	.83	.91
3	245 (100)	70 (28.57)	1.26	1.67	175 (71.43)	.77	1.31
4	175 (100)	68 (38.86)	1.04	2.04	107 (61.14)	.81	1.79
5	107 (100)	49 (45.79)	.94	2.43	58 (54.21)	.83	2.27
6	58 (100)	33 (56.89)	.83	2.73	25 (43.1)	1.11	3.16

It has been observed that where 'nature' is more generous in 'blessing' parents with a male child, generally they are able to realise the desired child composition sooner than others. This is a big factor making some parents succeed in their intentions for a small family. If we compare the probabilities of having a male child in a given 'trial' we find that the proportion of parents giving birth to a male child is mostly higher in small families than large families (Table 4). In view of the greater male-specific fertility in the relatively smaller families, it may be argued that most small families owe their size more to 'nature' than to anything else. In other words, there exists, in general, a negative relationship between family size and child ratio. Our evidence does not support the positive relationship observed by Repetto (1972) in his case studies of Bangladesh and Morocco. It can be seen from Table 2 that as we move across parity groups with declining child ratio we find them completing family with an increasing number of children. Thus parents' preference for a male child appears to be an important determinant of fertility.

TABLE 3

Length of Subsequent Birth Interval and the Proportion of Surviving Male Children

Parity group (Existing No. of children)	No. of male children	No. of families	Length of subsequent birth interval	Parity group (Existing no. of children)	No. of male children	No. of families	Length of subsequent birth interval
1	0	144	2.76	4	0	15	2.60
	1	133	3.00		1	27	2.96
2	0	81	2.75		2	31	3.06
	1	89	2.91		3	19	3.11
	2	64	3.11		4	9	3.22
3	0	38	2.60				
	1	60	2.65				
	2	49	2.90				
	3	21	3.38				

The wisdom of parents, in terms of their ability to correctly conceptualise costs and benefits associated with a male or a female child and assess current and future needs as well as the resources to finance the same, does play a significant role in the setting of the target family size. But this is all under the usual assumption, 'if everything goes well'. It is difficult to convince oneself that this target setting by parents is unrelated to the question of child composition they would want to have. When parents plan for a particular family size they have some broad idea of the composition for which they consider the target size 'optimal'. As the results of their successive 'trials' for realisation of the planned size start pouring in, their child preferences become manifest and play a major role in determining the *ex post* size. The more the results fail to come the expected way, the more prolonged usually the struggle becomes for achieving the minimum acceptable child composition. The planned size becomes a myth and in its place emerges a large unplanned family.

TABLE 4

Proportion of Parents in Each Parity Group giving Birth to a Male Child during each 'Trial'

Parity group (Family size completed)	Proportion of parents Trial					
	1	2	3	4	5	6
2	.58	.58				
3	.56	.50	.61			
4	.40	.48	.48	.67		
5	.30	.43	.47	.57	.61	
6	.45	.30	.33	.42	.51	.69

Why do Parents Want Children? Why Do They Have a Preference for a Male Child?

Ever since the birth of 'new home economics', economists have devoted considerable attention to analysis of parents' demand for children. Becker (1960, 1988) has suggested that demand for children can be treated analogous to the demand for producer or consumer durables, depending on whether parents expect net pecuniary returns from children or receive direct utility from them. He argues that utility of parents depends on the utility of each child (this is the sense in which he employs the term 'altruism' — parental altruism is purported to refer to their 'love' toward children). As more children are born, utility per child to parents is lowered. Griliches (1974) suggests that demand for children should be viewed in the mould of theory of demand for money. He distinguishes between three inter-dependent 'motives' for having children: (1) economic security (current labour and old-age provision); (2) the production of reciprocal caring; and (3) an attempt at immortality via one's offsprings.

When we view parents' demand for children in an average Indian family, we tend to believe that preference for a male child is deep-rooted into the socio-economic realities (one may argue that some of these realities are in fact myths) of their environment — low levels of women education and labour market participation, greater economic security associated with a male child, perception of male child as the only way to 'immortality' or salvation, widely prevalent social evils like dowry and atrocities on women — all these factors tend to strengthen the general belief that having a son is like really adding to one's net worth. For most parents the male children and not just children seem to have utility. In this regard observation of Ben-Porath and Welch (1976) appears to be quite appropriate: 'If boys and youngmen can be expected to contribute more than girls and young women to family income and if they are a more dependable source of old-age support this may be a reason for preferring boys to girls'' (p. 286).

SECTION II

Index of Male-Bias of Parents

For defining the concept of male-bias of parents two broad assumptions are made : (i) The number, composition and sequence of children existing at the time when parents want to decide whether or not they should restrict family size generally reflects, besides other things, their child-sex preference behaviour; and (ii) A decision by parents to restrict family size does not necessarily imply that they are most satisfied with the existing number and composition of children. Some parents may decide to restrict family size even when outcome of the last birth belies their expectation.

The situation existing before and after the last birth is of considerable significance. The fact that for a given number of existing children, so much so for the same child ratio and even sequence, some parents decide to restrict family after having a male in the last birth and some after having a female constitutes an instructing phenomenon for analysing and comparing the behaviour of parents. In this regard information presented in Table 5 is of considerable interest. For the same number and composition of existing children, the proportion of parents deciding to restrict family size is generally higher when they have a male rather than female child in the next birth or even thereafter. The birth of an additional female child lowers the child ratio. Accordingly parents feel less motivated to restrict family size.

In order to bring out the meaning of male-bias of parents in precise and measurable terms we consider two sets of complete families

TABLE 5

Proportion of Parents in Each Parity Group Deciding to Restrict Family Size after having Born a Given Number of Surviving Male/ Female Children in Succession

Parity group (Existing no. of children	No. of male children (Sex composition of children)	Number of male/female children born in succession 1 F	1 M	2 F	2 M	3 F	3 M
2	0	.07	.16	.03	.16	NIL	.06
	1	.18	.30	.07	.03	.02	.06
	2	.13	.16	.03	.10	.02	.02
3	0	.03	.13	NIL	.10	.06	NIL
	1	.13	.32	.08	.12	NIL	.06
	2	.12	.12	.02	.08	.03	NIL
	3	..04	.10	.04	.02	NIL	NIL
4	0	NIL	.08	.06	.15	.04	NIL
	1	.14	.20	NIL	.03	.04	.04
	2	.08	.22	.06	.15	.04	.04
	3	.12	.08	NIL	NIL	NIL	NIL
	4	.04	.02	NIL	NIL	.04	.04

of the same size, each with a male in the last birth in one set and a female, in the other. Let us call all families in the first set 'last-male' families and in the second set, 'last-female' families. The concept of male-bias can be explained in terms of three criteria. These criteria have been evolved so as to analyse and compare the behaviour of parents in a given situation with that of other parents placed in a similar or diametrically opposite situation. For instance, parents deciding to complete family with FMM composition (one female child followed by two male children) need to be compared with those who also, prior to the last birth, had one male and one female child but in the last birth who had a female rather than a male child (this is a case of identical situation). Further, the FMM category parents (having child ratio equal to 2) also need to be compared with MFF category parents who have children in a reciprocal of this ratio (this is a case of reverse sex situation). Finally, they need to be compared with MMF category as well, that is, with parents who have the same number of male and female children but in an opposite sequence (this is the case of reverse sequence).

(1) If the number of 'last-male' families having children (before the last birth) in a given sequence and ratio is, in general, greater than the number of 'last-female' families having children (before the last birth) in the same sequence and ratio, male-bias is said to be present. This concept of male-bias is based on 'identical situation' criterion.

(2) If, in general, it is found that the number of 'last-male' families having children (after the last birth) in a given ratio is greater than the number of 'last-female' families having children (after the last-birth) in a reciprocal of this ratio, male-bias is said to exist. This concept of male-bias is based on 'reverse sex' criterion. The application of this criterion requires exclusion of all 'last-male' families having a child ratio of one.

(3) If the number of 'last-male' families having children (after the last birth) in a given sequence and ratio is generally found to be larger than the number of 'last-female' families having children (after the last birth) in the same ratio but reverse sequence, male-bias is said to be operational. This concept of male-bias is based on 'reverse sequence' criterion. For application of this criterion only such cases should be considered in which both male and female births occur and in succession. For instance, the following cases should be excluded: FMFM, FFMF, MFFM, MMMM.

The pairs of families relevant to each of the above stated criteria are specified in Table 6 for only three parity groups. The corresponding frequencies (f) observed from empirical investigation have been indicated in parenthesis.

In order to construct Index of Male-Bias of Parents (IMBP) for a given parity group, we add up the corresponding frequencies of all 'last-male' families listed under the three criteria. The same is done in respect of 'last-female' families. The two sums are expressed as a ratio and this ratio gives us what may be called Index of Male-Bias of Parents. The index may be interpreted to measure the child ratio in which parents are believed to desire a given number of children so as to remain satisfied with it. The reduced forms of calculating the index are specified below for only three parity groups. The estimates of IMBP based on our study are specified in Table 6 (Col. 5).

Two-child parity group:

$$IMBP = \frac{f_{FM} + f_{MM}}{f_{MF} + f_{FF}}$$

Three-child parity group :

$$IMBP = \frac{3\,(f_{FMM} + f_{FFM}) + 2\,(f_{MMM} + f_{MFM})}{3\,(f_{FM} + f_{MFF}) + 2\,(f_{FFF} + f_{FMF})}$$

Four-child parity group:

$$IMBP = \frac{3\,(f_{FMMM} + f_{FFFM}) + 2\,(f_{MMM} + f_{MFMM} + f_{MMFM} + f_{FMFM} + f_{MFMM}) + f_{MFFM}}{3\,(f_{MMMF} + f_{MFFF}) + 2\,(f_{FFFF} + f_{FMFF} + f_{FFMF} + f_{MFMF} + f_{MMFF}) + f_{FMMF}}$$

The estimated values of IMBP imply that parents, in general, want to have male children in excess of what is permitted by the 'nature'. The only exception to this are the two-child parents. These parents are 'blessed', on average, with a child ratio, 1.4, that is, 1.17 male children each and they exhibit their intentions to remain content with this number. But the situation is different in respect of parents having larger families. The three-child parents desire to have a higher child ratio (1.52) as compared to the ratio granted by 'nature' (1.26), that is, they want to have, on average, 1.81 rather than 1.67 male children each — an increase of 8.38 per cent. By the same reasoning four-child parents desire to have, on average, 2.70 rather than 2.04 male children each — a an increase of 32.35 per cent.

What do the U-shaped and Inverted U-shaped Curves Really Imply?

We observe an inverted U-shaped relationship between proportion of families deciding to restrict their size and the proportion of male children in these families (Table 1). This means that amongst complete

TABLE 6

Criteria for Determination of Male-bias of Parents and Classification of Families under them

Parity Group (No. of children in a complete family)	Identical situation criterion		Reverse sex criterion		Reverse sequence criterion		IMBP (child ratio desired by parents)	Child ratio granted by 'nature'
1	2		3		4		5	6
2	MM (15)	MF (13)	MM (15)	FF (7)				
·	FM (13)	FF (7)			FM (13)	MF 13	1.4	1.4
	MMM (11)	MMF (9)	MMM (11)	FFF (5)				
3	FMM (8)	FMF (7)	FMM (8)	MFF (6)	FMM (8)	MMF (9)	1.52	1.26
	MFM (13)	MFF (6)	MFM (13)	FMF (7)				
	FFM (11)	FFF (5)	FFM (11)	MMF (9)	FFM (11)	MFF (6)		
	MMMM (7)	MMMF (3)	MMMM (7)	FFFF (2)				
	FMMM (2)	FMMF (2)	FMMM (2)	MFFF (2)	FMMM (2)	MMF (3)		
	MFMM (0)	MFMF (4)	MFMM (0)	FMFF (3)			2.08	1.04
4	MMFM (6)	MMFF (2)	MMFM (6)	FFMF (4)				
	MFFM (3)	MFFF (2)						
	FMFM (8)	FMFF (3)			FMFM (8)	MFMF (4)		
	FFMM (11)	FFMF (4)			FFMM (11)	MMFF (2)		
	FFFM (9)	FFFF (2)	FFFM (9)	MMMF (3)	FFFM (9)	MFFF (3)		

families of a given size, a relatively greater proportion consists of such families as do not want child composition to be tilted excessively either way. Likewise, the U-shaped relationship between proportion of families going in for another child and the proportion of male children (Table 7) indicates that when child composition is lopsided, a greater proportion of parents tend to go in for another child. Usually these relationships are interpreted "as an expression of a taste for balance in

TABLE 7

Proportion of Families in Each Parity Group going in for Another Child After Already Having a Given Number of Male Children

Parity group family	No. of male children	No. of families	Proportion	Parity group (Existing)	No. of male children	No. of families	Pro-portion
2	0	94	.92	4	0	19	89
	1	119	.78		1	45	.60
	2	80	.81		2	63	.52
3	0	45	.89		3	32	.65
	1	87	.72		4	16	.56
	2	80	.62				
	3	33	.67				

the sex composition of children" [Ben-Porath and Welch (1976, p. 297)]. This is not a correct interpretation. A relationship of this kind, in fact, implies that mostly parents have a taste for 'mixed' family. In order to determine whether these relationships also reflect parents' taste for a 'balanced' family, one needs to expose the data to various criteria and construct an index of Parents' Male-Bias. Our analysis reveals that parents, in general, have a taste for 'mixed' family. However, these are only two-child families in which parents' taste for a 'balanced' family is also visible. In the rest of the families we observe presence of male-bias. Parents' male-bias and their taste for a 'balance' cannot co-exist.

SECTION III

Conclusions and policy implications

The major findings of our investigation may be summarily stated as follows :

1. The phenomenon of parents' male-bias is widely prevalent in most families. Happily these are cnly the two-child families which are seen to be free from the male 'bug'.
2. The male-bias is largely responsible for failure of parents to restrict family size.
3. Another significant manifestation of male-bias relates to the birth interval. When parents have a greater proportion of female children they tend to go in for an additional child after relatively shorter intervals always hoping that next will be a male. This leads to deterioration in the health of expectant mothers and to a higher mortality rate among them.
4. The success of parents in accepting the small family norm is considerably due to benevolence of 'nature' than to anything else. The greater the male-female child ratio, the lower the family size – this is what one observes from the cross-section data (Table 2, Col. 1 and 4). Unless the child ratio in small families having 2-3 children is found to be close to one, it is very difficult to argue that the various family control programmes are having the desired impact. The real success of these programmes lies not in the number of parents submitting to family control but making them shed the male-bias. This is a long-term programme. But this is perhaps the only way to tackle the problem.

A small family is both the cause and effect of economic growth. Recently more and more economists are inclined to agree that economic growth leads to changes in fertility which, in turn, leads to a change in the growth rate. Nerlove (1974) in the context of attempts by economists to integrate 'new home economics' into a theory of growth and development observes, "The main link between household and economy is the value of human time, the increased value of human time (as a result of growth in labour productivity and wages) results in fewer children per household with each child embodying greater investment in human capital which in turn result in lower mortality and greater productivity" (p. 21) (the words in parenthesis are not a part of the quote). One of the pioneers in the the field of 'new home economics', Becker (1988) argues that since child rearing is time-intensive, the cost of rearing children is positively related to the opportunity cost of parents' time. In the course of economic growth when the capital-labour ratio, wage rates and per capita income increase, the value of parents' time, hence the cost of rearing children rises. The net effect of economic growth on fertility depends on income and substitution effects. Since child care requires considerable time and energy of parents, the negative substitution effect due to the rise in cost often dominates the positive effect of an increase in income. As a result demand for "child goods" decreases and for other goods and services increases; child-quality is substituted for child quantity. The increase in child-quality subsequently becomes the source of greater growth. Summarising his views on the interaction between growth and fertility or between family and economy, Becker remarks "Family behaviour is active, not passive, and endogenous, not exogenous. Families have large effects on the economy, and evolution of the economy greatly changes the structure and decisions of families" (p. 11).

Winegarden and Wheeler (1992) in their econometric model of fertility transition in Western Europe reach similar conclusions. Notwithstanding the role of "cultural and other non-economic factors" such as rising educational aspirations and improved status of women, they "strongly support economic growth gauged by real per capita incomes — as a cause of fertility changes in Western Europe" (p. 432).

Besides economic growth, there is another significant dimension of fertility or population growth, namely, income distribution. The relationship between population growth and distribution of income has been investigated by development economists and demographers for the last two decades. It is a widely held view that different income groups grow at different rates; the lower income groups generally grow at a faster rate. Given differential fertility rates across income groups, the interaction of population growth, differential fertility and inequality leads to confounding and accentuating the existing income disparities over time. [In this regard the interested reader may refer to Ahluwalia (1976), Repetto (1979), Rati Ram (1984) and Lam (1986)].

Obviously at the root of the problem of poverty and inequality in India lies the population or fertility problem. For accelerating the tempo of economic growth, an essential requirement is population control — small family as a general way of life. To achieve this efforts need to be directed to reshape parents' attitude towards desirability of male and female children. A greater emphasis on women education and their participation in labour market is expected to raise the socio-economic status of women and make them more desirable for parents. It will reduce the demand for children, in general, and reduce the obsession for a male child, in particular. [On mutual determination of family size, or fertility, and the labour force behaviour of married women see Becker (1960), Fleisher and Rhodes (1974), Winegarden (1984), Rosenzweig and Schultz (1985) and Vashist and Rana (1990)].

Given the existence of male-bias of parents and the urgent need for population control, there appears to be some justification for permitting pre-natal sex determination. However, in order to prevent the occurrence of imbalances in the sex composition of population, it is necessary that this facility is allowed only under well-defined circumstances (such as relating to existing number and composition of children, time interval since last birth) and is not open to commercialisation. Undoubtedly policy decision in this regard is extremely difficult as it involves questions of 'morality'. An important aspect of morality is respect for human life. If denial of birth to a human foetus is immoral, denial of right to a respectful life to the same after birth is both immoral and inhumane.

REFERENCES

1. Ahluwalia, M.S. (1976), "Inequality, Poverty and Development", *Journal of Development Economics*, Vol. No. 3.
2. Becker, G.S. (1960), "An Economic Analysis of Fertility" in *Demographic and Economic Change in Developed Countries*, Universities — National Bureau Conference Series No. 11, Princeton University Press, Princeton.
3. Becker, G.S. (1988), "Family Economics and Macro Behaviour", *The American Economic Review*, Vol. 78, No. 1.
4. Ben-Porath, Y. and Welch, F. (1976), "Do Sex Preferences Really Matter?" *The Quarterly Journal of Economics*, Vol. 90, No. 2.
5. Fleisher, B.M. and Rhodes, G.F. (1979), "Fertility, Women's Wage Rates and Labour Supply", *The American Economic Review*, Vol. 69, No. 1.
6. Griliches, Z. (1974), "Comment" on the paper of Nerlove (1974).
7. Lam, D. (1986), "The Dynamics of Population Growth, Differential Fertility and Inequality", *The American Economic Review*, Vol. 76, No. 5.
8. Nerlove, M. (1974), "Household and Economy : Towards a New Theory of Population and Economic Growth", *Journal of Political Economy*, Vol. 82, No. 2.

9. Ram, Rati (1984), ''Population Increase, Economic Growth, Educational Inequality and Income Distribution'', *Journal of Development Economics*, Ap., No. 14.

10. Repetto, R. (1972), ''Son Preference and Fertility Behaviour in Developing Countries'', *Studies in Family Planning*, Vol. 3, No. 4.

11. Repetto, R. (1979), *Economic Equality and Fertility in Developing Countries*, John Hopkins University Press, Baltimore.

12. Rosenzweig, M.R. and Schultz, T.P. (1985), ''The Demand for and Supply of Births : Fertility and Life Cycle Consequences'', *The American Economic Review*, Vol. 75, No. 5.

13. Vashist, B.K. and Rana, (1990), ''New Household Economics : Some Evidence in Support of It'', *The Indian Economic Journal*, Vol. 37, No. 4.

14. Winegarden, C.R. (1984), ''Women's Fertility, Market Work and Marital Status : A Test of the New Household Economics with International Data'', *Economica*, Vol. 51, No. 204.

15. Winegarden, C.R. and Wheeler, M. (1992), ''The Role of Economic Growth in the Fertility Transition, in Western Europe : Econometric evidence'', *Economica*, Vol. 59, No. 236.

13

PROCESS OF URBANISATION IN INDIA : A REGIONAL DIMENSION

P.G. MARVANIA

Introduction

In the late eighties the process of urbanisation and its related issues have received quite a predominant position among both policy makers as well as researchers. Though, the level of urbanisation in India, as compared to many other developing countries, is still low,[1] but the sheer largeness of total population makes the mass of urban population very large. The urban centres are pressed with problems of urban management with their declining standards of urban amenities and services. Despite, the obvious problems of the transitory phase, the process of urbanisation has several interesting components, when it is scrutinised at the state level. The whole process is meaningfully related to sectoral development and also it has positively contributed towards the economic transformation of the economy.

In this paper, an attempt has been made to present an outline of the process of urbanisation at all India level and state level. And also to highlight the prominent features of the same at both levels.

All India Scenario

In India, as seen from the data presented in Table 1, urban population has been rising steadily in each successive decade. From 62.44 million living in urban places in 1951, it rose to 217.61 million[2] in 1991. Within the last two decades of 1971—91, urban population has almost doubled from 109.11 million to 217.61 million.

The level of urbanisation too has been rising. It rose sharply during 1970s and 1980s. However, the tempo of urbanisation has decelerated during the last decade, *i.e.*, 1981—91. The decadal rate of growth of urban population declined from 46.23 per cent during 1971—81 to

36.09 per cent during 1981—91. This deceleration in the rate of growth of urban population is due to two reasons. First, for the first time, since independence the overall rate of growth of population declined from 24.60 per cent in 1971—81 to 23.50 per cent in 1981—91. Second, there has been a substantial reduction in the addition of new towns to the existing ones.

In India, urban population has tended to concentrate in Class I cities. Over the period, this tendency has accentuated. It is seen from the data presented in Table 2. The relative share of population in Class I cities to total urban population is very large. Not only that but it has increased from 57.24 per cent in 1971 to 65.20 per cent in 1991.

The concentration of urban population in million plus cities is even larger. The number of million plus cities have almost doubled from 12 in 1981 to 23 in 1991. Almost one-third of India's urban population lives in million plus cities. As shown by the data in Table 3, the rate of growth of population of million plus cities is very high, not only that but it is still rising.

These evidences indicate that India is rapidly getting urbanised. But the size-class distribution of urban population has remained highly skewed.

There are two views about India's urbanisation. According to one, India is over-urbanised[3], whereas a counter-view has rejected this position as valid.[4]

The proponents of over-urbanisation thesis have put forward following arguments for the justification :

(i) There is mis-match between the levels of industrialisation and urbanisation. Also the process of tertiarisation of the economy has out-paced its secondarisation. As a result, urban unemployment and underemployment are widespread and income levels are low.

(ii) Indian cities are growing at a faster rate than the capacity of economy to support them. This escalates the cost of urbanisation for the country. It is further argued that cities do not generate enough surpluses to invest in basic urban services and are dependent on transfers of resources from rural areas. This leads to less than optimal allocation of resources between the rural and urban sectors. Due to this, tempo of overall economic growth suffers in the process. Thus urbanisation is costly and impinges upon the rate of economic growth.

(iii) The existing urban infrastructure and services are inadequate to meet the large and fast expanding urban population. The problems relating to housing, environment, congestion and pollution are intensifying in Indian cities. As a result, the quality of life is fast moving towards a crisis situation.

Against this, a counter point of view is explained as follows. It is argued that India's experience of urbanisation is not different from that of many other developing countries from medium and low income groups in the world. In these countries also similar situations have developed along with rapid urbanisation and economic transformation. It is further argued that evidence have negated the issue of inoptimal allocation of resources between urban and rural sectors and slowing down of pace of economic growth thereby. On the other hand, urbanisation has positively aided the structural transformation of the economy. The present state of urbanisation in India is considered as a concomitant of the development path chosen by the country.

However, fact of scanty urban infrastructure services and over-crowiding of urban places with widespread poverty, unemployment and unhygienic health conditions remain quite visible at urban places. But one should not mistake these as outcomes of excessive urbanisation. To a large extent, these are the problems of management of urban places rather than that of the urban size *per se*.

Regional Scenario

The urbanisation in India has been marked by its regional variations. Urbanisation in one state has varied from the another, depending on structure, base and size of the state-economy. Hence, there emerges at state level a varied scenario of 'high-urban' states like Maharashtra, Tamil Nadu and West Bengal with their large industrial base and very large single cities and 'low urban' states like Uttar Pradesh, Andhra Pradesh and Madhya Pradesh with large agrarian sector, but nevertheless having an absolute large mass of urban population and a large number of cities and towns. This is evident by data presented in Table 4.

Uneven Spatial Distribution

The level of urbanisation has been rising quite steadily during the post-independence era in all states. However, there are clear differences in the magnitude and pace of gain in the level of urbanisation among different states. Traditionally, industrialised states like Maharashtra, Gujarat, Tamil Nadu and West Bengal have relatively high level of urbanisation. Others which joined with them include newly industrialised state like Karnataka and small-sized states with well-developed agriculture and agro-based industries like Punjab and Haryana. Whereas, despite low level of urbanisation, Uttar Pradesh, Madhya Pradesh and Bihar have large masses of urban population. In this way, at the state level the pattern of urbanisation is quite closely related to size of the state, base and structure of the state economy. The data presented in Table 4 gives a clear picture of regional concentration of urbanisation at the state level. A group of four states — Maharashtra, Gujarat, Tamil Nadu and West Bengal — accounts for 38% of India's total urban population with only 22% of India's geographic space. Whereas seven large most populous states — U.P., A.P., M.P., Orissa, Bihar, Rajasthan and Karnataka — accounts for 46% of India's total urban population with a share of 57% of India's geographic space. The data of state's relative share in India's urban population, given in Table 4 indicates that such shares have been stabilised over period. It implies that policies to reduce such inequality have not been very effective.[5]

Variations in the Growth Rate

The data relating to the rate of growth of urban population in different states given in Table 4 indicates that less urbanised states are growing at a faster rate than more urbanised states. The states with a higher decadal growth rate during 1971—81 had a very low proportion of urban population in 1981. A similar pattern has been observed for 1981—91 also. During this period, five states — Maharashtra, Gujarat, Tamilnadu, West Bengal, Karnataka — with the higher proportion of urban population registered lower decadal growth. Whereas eight states — U.P., Bihar, Orissa, Rajasthan, M.P., Haryana, Kerala, A.P. — registered higher growth. The small sized states with low level of urbanisation are continuing high urban growth whereas large-sized, high urban states are growing slowly. Only exception to this is Maharashtra.

Structure and Base of State Economy and Urbanisation

In India, the process of urbanisation is highly associated with level of industrialisation at the regional level. Beside, urbanisation is also related with a variety of positive features like, per capita SDP, sectoral composition of SDP, industrial locations, dispersal of socio-economic infrastructure and services, and relative proportion of Class I population in urban population. The data presented in Table 5 portrait broad relationship which is observed. That is the states having high per capita SDP experienced high level of urbanisation and *vice-versa*. Also level of urbanisation is associated, more particularly, with share of secondary sector in SDP. The regional per capita income variations and regional urbanisation seem positive correlate. This dispels the doubts such as urbanisation distorts the structural transformation of the economy.

Size-Class Distribution and Urban Morphology

The concentration of urban population in Class I cities have been found more in 'high urban' states and this concentration, over a period, has got accentuated. The states of Maharashtra, Gujarat, Tamil Nadu and West Bengal are such examples. The differences observed at regional level in the morphology of urbanisation tend to be in opposite directions between large and small states as also between the more and less industrialised ones. As seen from the data in Table 6, first, there are differences in regard to the concentration of urban population living in Class I cities. Relatively more urbanised states of Maharashtra, Gujarat, Tamil Nadu and West Bengal have more than 65 per cent of their urban population living in Class I cities. Similarly, newly industrialising states like Karnataka, A.P. and Kerala, too, have more than 65 per cent of their urban population in Class I cities. Second, states having industry-based urbanisation have relatively high concentration of urban population in million plus cities whereas less urbanised states are free from such distortions. Third, even among highly urbanised states, morphology of urbanisation differs. For example, in highly urbanised states of Maharashtra and Punjab, urbanisation morphology seems more balanced in Punjab than in

Maharashtra. Urbanisation in Maharashtra has been influenced more by industrialisation while in Punjab, it is under greater influence of agricultural development and associated industrialisation. Agricultural development seems to have ensured relatively more equitable distribution of urban population in different population size-classes. The million plus cities seem to be more a characteristic of industrialised states like Maharashtra, West Bengal, Gujarat, Tamil Nadu and Karnataka. Whereas, Urban population has tended to concentrate in cities of one to five lakh population in industrialising and agriculturally well-developed states like Punjab and Haryana.

Components of Urban Growth

In case of states like Maharashtra, Gujarat, West Bengal, Uttar Pradesh, Andhra Pradesh, Haryana, Rajasthan, Karnataka, Kerala, Orissa and Punjab, as indicated by the decadal growth rate of common urban agglomerations and towns being above that of SRS, implied that migration has played a substantial role in the growth of urban population of these states.

In case of Haryana, Maharashtra and U.P., the contribution by migration to urban growth, though substantial, appears to be less than the contribution of natural increase. Whereas in the cases cf Gujarat, Karnataka, M.P., Orissa, Punjab and Rajasthan, the contribution by natural increase seems to be a major factor, beside migration being also a significant factor. In case of Bihar and Tamilnadu the natural increase seem to be the sole factor to cause urban population in these states. The data is presented in Table 7.

Intra-Regional Concentration

Apart from the inter-state spatial variations in the distribution of urban population and pattern of urbanisation, there exists intra-state spatial variations in the pattern of distribution of urban population. Within a state, economically more dynamic regions have been found with clustering of urbanisation. They can broadly be categorised as follows :

(i) In and around metropolitan cities including Calcutta, Bombay, Delhi, Madras, Bangalore, Hyderabad, Ahmedabad, Kanpur, Pune, Lucknow, Jaipur and Nagpur.

(ii) Agriculturally advanced regions with significant agro-based industries. They are as follows :

Delta of Godavari-Krishna (A.P.), Southern part of Bihar Plain (Bihar), Eastern Haryana (Haryana); Tungbhadra Valley (Karnataka); Lower Godavari Valley (Orissa), Central Plain in Punjab; Ganganagar and Kota Region (Rajasthan); Ganga-Yamuna Doab, Terai Region (U.P.), Nilgiris (T.N.).

(iii) Industrial belts along transport routes including Ahmedabad-Vadodra-Bombay; Bombay-Nagpur; Bombay-Pune-Kolhapur; Madras-Salem-Coimbatore; Delhi-Amritsar; Delhi-Saharanpur; Dhanbad-Asansol-Calcutta, etc.

Urban Primacy at Regional Level

In case of India as a whole, there is no case of primacy. However, at regional level, some states do exhibit the tendency. Urban primacy is low in large and less developed states like Bihar, M.P., U.P., Rajasthan and Orissa. Whereas, urban primacy is high in large states which are relatively more industrialised and urbanised as seen in cases of West Bengal, Tamil Nadu, Maharashtra and Karnataka. Another pattern observed is that urban primacy is less conspicious in the states where agrarian and industrial development is giving rise to dispersed pattern of urbanisation as observed in cases of Punjab, Haryana, Gujarat and Kerala.

Conclusion

The Indian urbanisation is both, a function of expanding non-agriculture economic activity and also expanding population base. That, it reflects momentum of economic growth as well as population growth. Thus, Indian urbanisation has three facets, *viz.*, metropolitisation/industrialisation, commercialisation, trading and servicing and urbanisation of country side.

The overurbanisation rhetoric can be dispelled with as the process of urbanisation is found to be very much associated with the transformation of the economy. In India, it has been both, a cause as well as a result of the economic transformations. The sectoral development has a significant impact on both, level of urbanisation and morphology of urbanisation at regional level. The states having a more dispersed sectoral development have less of distortions in the process of urbanisation. Therefore, while evolving national urban policy, a due weightage must be given to sectoral linkages of the regional economy.

Notes

(1)

Type of Nation	Percentage of Urban Population 1992	Per Capita GDP in Dollar 1991
Low Income	39	350
Lower Middle Income	54	1590
Upper Middle Income	73	3530
High Income	77	21050
South Asian Countries	26	320
Sub-Saharan African	29	350
Middle East and North African	55	1940
Latin American	72	2390
Europe and Central Asia	64	2670

Source : *World Development Report 1993*, OUP, New York, 1993.

(2) *Population of India : 1991 Census*

Type	Urban	Total
Including Jammu & Kashmir	217611012	846302688
Excluding Jammu & Kashmir	215771612	838583988
Excluding J & K and Assam	213283817	816169666

(3) This view finds an expression in, Sovani 1969; Bose 1980; Becker 1986.

(4) This view finds an expression in *World Development Reports*, 1983; 1985; *Report of National Commission for Urbanisation*, 1987.

(5) India's Total Geographic space amounts to 3287000 sq. km.

States	Percentage Share of Geographic Area	Percentage Share of Urban Population
Maharashtra, Gujarat, Tamil Nadu, West-Bengal	22.1	37.89
U.P., A.P., M.P., Karnataka, Bihar, Rajasthan, Orissa	57.1	45.65
Kerala, Punjab, Haryana	4.0	8.91

REFERENCES

1. Bose, Ashish, (1980), *India's Urbanisation 1901-2001*, Tata McGraw Hill, New Delhi.
2. Sovani, N. (1964), "Analysis of Overurbanisation", *Economic Development and Cultural Change*, 12, 2 : 113-122.
3. Mills, E.S. and C.M. Becker (1986), *Studies in Indian Urban Development*, Oxford University Press, New York.
4. *State of India's Urbanisation*, (1988), National Institute of Urban Affairs, New Delhi.
5. *World Development Reports*; 1983, 1985, 1993; Oxford University Press, New York.
6. *Report of National Commission on Urbanisation (1988)*, Govt. of India, New Delhi.
7. Census Monogram No. 1; *Urban Growth in India 1951—1981*; (1986) Census of India 1981, Registrar General of India, New Delhi.
8. Census — 1991, Paper 2 of 1991; *Provisional Population Totals : Rural-Urban Distributions*, Registrar General of India, New Delhi.
9. Census — 1991, Paper 2 of 1992, *Final Population Totals*; Registrar General of India, New Delhi.

TABLE 1

Profile of India's Urbanization

Year	Nos. of Town and UAS	Total Population	Urban Population	Urban Population as % of Total Population	Decennial Growh Rate of Total Population	Decennial Growth Rate of Urban Population
1901	1827	238396237	25851873	10.84	—	—
1911	1815	252093390	25941633	10.29	5.75	0.35
1921	1949	251321213	28086167	11.18	— 0.31	8.27
1931	2072	278977238	33455989	11.99	11.00	19.12
1941	2250	318660580	44153297	13.86	14.22	31.97
1951	2843	361088090	62443709	17.29	13.31	41.42
1961	2365	439234771	78936603	17.97	21.51	26.41
1971	2590	548159652	109113977	19.91	24.80	38.23
1981	3378	683329097	159462547	23.34	24.66	46.14
1991	3768	846302688	217611012	25.71	23.50	36.19

Source : Paper 2 of 1992, *Census of India*, Registrar General, New Delhi, Final Population Totals.

TABLE 2

Percentage Share of Each Size Class in Urban Population

Class	Urban Population			Percentage Share		
	1971	1981	1991	1971	1981	1991
I	61225798	94503745	138801945	57.24	60.42	65.20
II	11697940	18189728	23309167	10.92	11.63	10.95
III	17125811	22409119	28079305	16.01	14.33	13.19
IV	11706334	14930267	16531064	10.94	9.54	7.77
V	4755659	5603015	5532033	4.45	3.58	2.60
VI	0472992	0783894	0613823	0.44	0.50	0.29
	106966532	156419768	212867337*	100	100	100

* (excluding Assam and J & K).

Source : Paper 2 of 1991, *Rural-Urban Distribution, Census of India*, Registrar General, New Delhi.

TABLE 3

Million Plus Urban Agglomeration/Cities 1901—1991

Year	No. of Million Plus UAS Cities	Population	Population as % of India's		Decadal Variation of Population (%)
			Total Population	Urban Population	
1901	1	1510088	0.63	5.84	—
1911	2	2763586	1.10	10.65	83.02
1921	2	3129518	1.25	11.14	13.24
1931	2	3406869	1.22	10.18	8.86
1941	2	5307540	1.67	12.02	55.79
1951	5	11746 616	3.25	18.81	121.32
1961	7	18101748	4.12	22.93	54.10
1971	9	27831065	5.08	25.51	53.75
1981	12	42121700	6.16	26.41	51.35
1991	23	70661259	8.37	32.54	67.76

Source: Paper 2 of 1991, *Rural-Urban Distribution*, Registrar General, Census of India 1991, New Delhi.

TABLE 4

Regional Profile of Urbanization 1991

State	Urban Population	% of Urban Population	% Share in Urban Population	Urban Population-Growth Rate	
				1971—81	1981—91
Maharashtra	30541586	38.73	14.04	39.99	38.66
Gujarat	14246061	34.40	6.52	41.42	33.60
Tamilnadu	19077592	34.20	8.76	27.98	19.28
West Bengal	18707601	27.39	8.57	31.73	28.90
Uttar Pradesh	27605915	19.89	12.73	60.62	39.17
Andhra Pradesh	17887126	26.84	8.20	48.62	42.64
Madhya Pradesh	15338837	23.21	7.07	56.03	44.98
Karnataka	13907788	30.91	6.38	50.65	29.09
Bihar	11353012	13.17	5.24	54.76	30.39
Rajasthan	10067113	22.88	4.62	58.69	39.24
Orissa	4234983	13.43	1.95	68.54	36.08
Kerala	7680294	26.44	3.75	37.64	60.89
Punjab	5993225	27.72	2.76	44.51	30.08
Haryana	4054744	24.79	1.86	59.47	43.07
All India	217611012*	25.72	100	46.24	36.19

*Refer Note 2.

Source : Paper 2 of 1992, *Final Population Totals, Census of India 1991*, Registrar General, New Delhi.

TABLE 5

Per Capita SDP Index, Sectoral Indicators and Urbanisation

State	Level of Urbani-sation (%) 1991	Relative Index of Per Capita Net SDP at F.C. at Curremt Prices 1990-91	Composition of SDP 1989-90		
			Agri. & Allied	Industry & Mining	Services
Maharashtra	38.73	147.73	22.74	35.73	41.52
Gujarat	34.40	120.83	26.54	34.79	38.67
Tamilnadu	34.20	88.29	17.17	33.28	49.46
West Bengal	27.39	94.71	35.47	27.80	36.73
Uttar Pradesh	19.89	70.84	41.15	20.88	37.96
Andhra Pradesh	26.84	94.15	40.75	17.72	41.53
Madhya Pradesh	23.21	72.06	41.46	28.58	29.96
Karnataka	30.31	94.45	33.76	29.15	37.10
Bihar	13.17	50.63	44.26	23.27	32.47
Rajasthan	22.88	79.42	50.26	17.96	31.78
Orissa	13.43	63.41	48.48	19.68	31.84
Kerala	26.44	76.63	34.44	24.48	41.08
Punjab	27.72	165.12	45.25	21.73	33.02
Haryana	24.79	138.30	43.90	23.08	33.01
All India	25.72	100.00	31.30	29.10	39.60

Compiled from *Basic Statistics*; States, September, 1992, CMIE, Bombay.

TABLE 6

Regional Size-Class Distribution of Percentage of Urban Population : 1991

State	CLASS					
	I	II	III	IV	V	VI
Maharashtra	77.85	6.94	10.39	4.13	1.03	0.11
Gujarat	66.43	12.73	10.52	7.69	2.42	0.21
Tamilnadu	65.96	15.21	11.19	6.11	1.38	0.15
West Bengal	81.71	6.58	7.66	2.59	1.35	0.11
Uttar Pradesh	55.99	11.46	13.94	12.25	5.86	0.50
Andhra Pradesh	66.88	12.60	16.53	3.30	0.64	0.05
Madhya Pradesh	50.38	13.94	12.82	16.15	6.58	0.13
Karnataka	64.60	7.35	17.68	7.73	2.09	0.55
Bihar	52.62	17.58	20.80	7.03	1.79	0.18
Rajasthan	50.09	13.67	21.31	13.08	1.82	0.03
Orissa	44.43	14.65	19.73	16.97	3.94	0.28
Kerala	66.34	7.22	19.08	6.78	0.58	--
Punjab	54.36	19.79	12.89	10.46	2.03	0.47
Haryana	58.54	15.11	11.95	10.43	3.74	0.23
All India	65.20	10.95	13.19	7.77	2.60	0.29

Source : Paper 2 of 1991, *Rural-Urban Distribution, Provisional Population Totals*, Registrar General of India, New Delhi.

TABLE 7

Components of Urban Growth 1971—81, Decadal Growth of Urban Population of Common UAS and Cities and Natural Increase of Population by SRS 1981—91

State	Components of Urban Growth 1971—81 (Percentage)			Growth of Common UAS/Cities 1981—91 (Percentage)		
	Natural	Migration	Reclassification	Decadal Growth	Natural Increase by SRS	Migration
(1)	(2)	(3)	(4)	(5)	(6)	(7)
Maharashtra	45.99	49.27	4.73	36.41	22.02	14.39
Gujarat	50.85	43.42	5.70	32.06	23.49	8.57
Tamilnadu	60.05	32.24	7.70	18.43	17.82	0.61
West Bengal	44.15	40.27	15.66	26.82	14.45	12.37
Uttar Pradesh	33.74	21.97	44.27	35.72	24.48	11.24
Andhra Pradesh	42.98	50.67	6.34	42.90	23.24	19.66
Madhya Pradesh	39.53	39.05	21.40	33.81	25.56	8.45
Karnataka	34.81	54.81	10.37	29.79	21.77	8.02
Bihar	20.98	47.63	31.39	25.53	25.99	— 0.46
Rajasthan	38.20	41.18	20.60	35.99	25.61	10.38
Orissa	29.02	44.93	26.03	30.91	21.90	9.01
Kerala	43.21	— 25.25	82.03	38.33	18.18	20.15
Punjab	45.24	29.03	25.71	31.36	23.74	7.62
Haryana	36.50	39.52	23.97	38.81	26.74	12.07
All India	41.25	40.13	18.60	32.80	21.65	11.15

Sources : (i) Paper 2 of 1991, *Rural-Urban Distribution*, Registrar General, New Delhi.

(ii) *Report of National Commission for Urbanisation*, 1988, Govt. of India, Delhi.

14

INDUSTRIAL DEVELOPMENT IN INDIA

The Industrial Policy Statement of July 22, 1991 has set out the broad outlines of the nation's industrial policy in the near-term future. In many respects, it signifies a return to the 1956 Industrial Policy Resolution with only one major exception, *viz.*, the reduction of the industrial activities exclusively reserved for the public sector from 17 to 8 industries. Indian industry has developed a highly diversified structure, considerable entrepreneurship and a vastly expanded capital market. All this makes it possible for the public sector to vacate many areas hitherto exclusively reserved for it and throw them open to private sector initiative. This will free scarce public resources for investment in priority sectors. Also, the new Policy emphasizes efficiency and surplus generating capability in the public sector, a larger entrepreneurial and managerial freedom for both domestic private sector and foreign investment, a more open access to technology and greater reliance on the capital market for raising resources.

India stands totally committed to a policy of mixed economy as propounded by Nehru and other founding fathers under which both the public sector and the private sector enterprises co-exist and function side by side. But both need to be efficient. It is this strong motive for inducting efficiency which has partially prompted the recent policy of partial disinvestment of the shareholding in the public sector enterprises. The other consequence will be to free part of the public resources locked up in these enterprises for deployment elsewhere where it is needed more.

The relatively open foreign investment policy has been dictated by the following considerations:

(i) A general awareness that foreign investment in India has been abysmally low and that the country has substantial absorptive capacity;

(ii) Realisation that foreign direct investment is less costly but more productive than international non- concessional credit at commercial rate;

(iii) Knowledge that to a limited extent foreign direct investment can provide both balance of payment support and ensure the inflow of latest technology.

There is, however, no intention to permit foreign investment in discriminately in all areas, but to welcome it selectively in desired or priority areas.

The Eighth Plan starts against a backdrop of impressive industrial growth during the eighties, a rate which was higher than that achieved by the great majority of other nations. The average annual growth rate of the industrial sector including mining, manufacturing and electricity generation during the Seventh Plan period was 8.5 % which though marginally lower than targetted 8.7% was much higher than the 3.5% achieved during the Sixth Plan.

The manufacturing sector which achieved an average annual growth rate of 8.9 per cent during the Seventh Plan period contributed significantly to this higher growth rate in the economy. Within the manufacturing sector, manufacture of electrical machinery and chemicals and chemical products achieved growth rates of 25.8 % and 1 1 .7 % respectively. These two groups contributed about 61% of the industrial growth in the manufacturing sector.

Compared to the Sixth Plan, the Seventh Plan achieved higher annual growth rates in the manufacturing and electricity sectors. The mining sector, however, witnessed a substantial slow down in growth from 12.7 per cent in the Sixth Plan to 5.6 per cent in the Seventh Plan. Among the major industry groups, the annual growth rates of textile products, basic metals and alloys, metal products and parts, electrical machinery and appliances, and other manufacturing products accelerated during the Seventh Plan period, whereas those of beverages, tobacco and tobacco products, wood and wood products decelerated.

The significant growth in industrial production during the Seventh Plan is attributable to a number of factors, the most important being improvement in the performance of the infrastructure *viz.*, power, coal, etc. The other contributory factors were : (a) changes in the area of licensing and procedures; (b) import of technology; (c) higher import of capital goods; (d) better utilisation of installed capacities; and (e) allowing broadbanding of products in a number of industries. The Seventh Plan also witnessed a higher dose of liberalisation measures such as (i) raising the assets limit for exemption to companies from the purview of MRTP Act; (ii) exempting 83 industries under the MRTP Act for entry of dominant industries; (iii) grant of exemption from licensing for industrial units with an investment of upto Rs. 50 crores in backward areas and Rs. 15 crores in other areas on the basis of a negative list; and (iv) delicensing non-MRTP, non-FERA companies for 31 industry groups and MRTP/FERA Companies in backward areas for 72 industry groups.

Performance of Central Public Sector Enterprises

As on 31.3.1991, there were 246 Central Public Sector Enterprises (PSEs) owned by the Government of India with a total investment of Rs. 113,234 crores. Out of these, 236 were operational enterprises with an employed capital of Rs. 101,702 crores and employee strength of 23.01 lakhs. Of these, 131 enterprises earned an overall net profit of Rs. 5731 crores during 1990-91 and 109 suffered a net loss of Rs. 3064 crores.

The performance of the Central Public Enterprises has been the subject of debate for some years now, and a number of Committees/ Working Groups have gone into the matter in detail. In the context of the role which the Public Sector is required to play in the prevailing environment, the Government has taken the following decisions :

(i) Portfolio of public sector investments will be reviewed with a view to focusing the public sector on strategic, high-tech and essential infrastructure. Whereas some reservation for the public sector is being retained, there would be no bar on areas of exclusivity being opened up to the private sector selectively. Similarly, the public sector may also be allowed entry in areas not reserved for it.

(ii) Public enterprises which are chronically sick and which are unlikely to be turned around will, for the formulation of revival/ rehabilitation schemes, be referred to the Board for Industrial and Financial Reconstruction (BIFR), or other similar high level institutions created for the purpose. 'A social security mechanism is being created to protect the interests of workers likely to be affected by such rehabilitation packages.

(iii) In order to raise resources and encourage wider public participation, a part of the Government's shareholding in the public sector would be offered to mutual funds, financial institutions, general public and workers. This is also expected to bring in greater public accountability and help create a new culture in the working of PSEs and improve their operational efficiency.

(iv) Boards of public sector companies would be made more professional and given greater powers.

(v) There will be a greater thrust on performance improvement through the Memoranda of Understanding (MOU) system through which managements will be granted greater autonomy and held accountable. Technical expertise on the part of the Government would be upgraded to make the MOU negotiations and implementation more effective.

(vi) To facilitate a fuller discussion on performance, the MOUs between the Government and the public enterprises will be placed in Parliament. While focusing on major management issues, this will also help place matters on day-to-day operations of public enterprises in their correct perspective.

The implementation of these decisions has already started. During 1991-92, it was possible to mop up Rs. 3038 crores through disinvestment of equity of PSEs. Similarly, the number of MOU signing companies is being gradually increased. The Government has also established a National Renewal Fund to provide a social safety net to protect the workers from the adverse consequences of the technological transformation.

State Level Public Enterprises

There are in all about 1100 State Level Public Enterprises (SLPEs) with an estimated investment of about Rs. 50,000 crores. Unfortunately, a large proportion of these State level public enterprises has not been working satisfactorily. As a first step towards making these PSEs more responsive, the Government has decided to disinvest from some of the SLPEs.

Subsidies by the State Governments

The State Governments have been offering various concessions to entrepreneurs for setting up new industrial units. It is anomalous that while the State Governments are raising power rates to meet the losses of State Electricity Boards (SEBs), they are also offering power subsidy to new units. Similarly, most State Governments have announced deferment/ exemption of sales tax for new units, capital subsidy and subsidy for purchase of generating sets . As most States are announcing similar incentives, it is a zero sum game, with the State Governments giving up revenue. It would only be appropriate that a detailed review of the various subsidies/concessions offered by the State Governments is undertaken so that a more rational policy frame is developed.

New Growth Centres Scheme

For promoting industrialisation of backward areas Government of India announced in June, 1988, a scheme to develop growth centres in all States/Union Territories. These growth centres will be endowed with adequate infrastructural facilities like power, water, communications, banking etc. so that they can act as magnets for attracting industries to these areas. It has been decided to develop about 70 growth centres during the Eighth Plan. The locations of 63 growth centres have so far been finalised in consultation with the concerned State Governments/Union Territory Administrations. However, the pace of implementation is slow.

With the abolition of licensing in most of the sectors, this is the only instrument available for facilitating regional dispersal. Considering the imperative need to minimise regional imbalances within the shortest time, intensive efforts would need to be made to ensure that these Centres are fully operational in the next 3-4 years.

Science and Technology in Industry and Minerals Sector

Research & Development (R&D) is the watch word for maintaining an edge in quality and cost in today's competitive world. Indian industry has made significant strides in building up a strong base for manufacture of various goods, largely through acquired technologies. There is an imperative need for assimilation, adaptation and improvement of imported technologies as well as development of indigenous technologies suited to local conditions.

A large number of industries in the public and private sectors have established corporate R&D facilities. Organisations like Steel Authority of India Ltd., Bharat Heavy Electricals Ltd., Project Development India Ltd., Hindustan Machine Tools, Instrumentation Ltd., Indian Petrochemicals Corporation Ltd., Petrofils Cooperative Ltd., Hindustan Organic Chemicals Ltd. and Hindustan Insecticides Ltd., have established in-house R&D facilities for product and process improvement and applied research. In addition, a large number of industry specific research institutes and Cooperative Research organisations are doing very useful work. Moreover, there are a large number of technical consultancy organisations having expertise in operational areas, a resource to be reckoned with for undertaking various developmental activities. Besides, in-house R&D efforts and foreign collaborations with reputed manufacturers abroad, UNIDO/UNDP assistance for frontier technologies is being sought for technological development in the country. However, there is need to improve the interaction between the industry and the academics.

Outlays and Expenditure

The Seventh Plan provided an outlay of Rs. 19,708 crores, out of which Rs. 17,268 crores were for Central sector (excluding coal and petroleum, which form part of the energy sector) and the balance Rs. 2,440 crores were in the Plans of States and Union Territories. The actual expenditure (at current prices) is estimated at Rs. 23,175 crores in the Central sector and Rs. 3,120 crores by States and Union Territories. Expenditure in the Central sector at constant prices has also been higher, being Rs. 18,564 crores.

The overall outlay envisaged in the Eighth Plan for Industrial and Mineral programmes in the public sector is Rs. 40,673.43 crores, out of which Rs. 35,150 crores are for the Central Sector and the balance of Rs. 5,523.43 crores is for the States sector.

Outlook for the Eighth Plan

With a view to consolidating the gains already achieved during the 1980s and providing greater competitive stimulus to the domestic industry, the Government has introduced a series of reforms in the industrial, fiscal, trade and foreign investment policies. These reforms are intended to de-regulate or unshackle the industry and enable it to take decisions on its own without the need for Government approvals for specific actions. With these, the industry will be able to take timely steps to adjust to the changes in internal as well as external environment and meet the needs of a dynamic market. These reforms will lead to increased globalisation of the economy and its greater integration with the world economy. The freedom and flexibility allowed to the industry will enable it to optimise its operations and improve its competitiveness. In this background, there will be less emphasis on quantitative targets and the planning will become more "indicative". The desired growth of different sectors will be achieved primarily through modifications in industrial, trade, fiscal policies and changes in duties and taxes rather than through quantitative restrictions on imports/exports or licensing mechanism.

Role of Public Sector

The public sector has played a pioneering role in the development of the Indian economy and has a number of achievements to its credit. It deserves a major share of the credit for the self-reliant growth of the economy so far. However, there are some notable weaknesses too the most important being the inability of the public sector to generate adequate resources for sustaining the growth process. Besides, the private sector has now come of age and has developed considerable entrepreneurial, managerial, technological, financial and marketing strengths. In this background, a review of the role of the public and private sectors is called for in order to enable them to jointly shoulder the responsibility for further development of the economy.

The new Industrial Policy of July 1991 has brought down the number of areas reserved for public sector from 29 — earlier 17 areas were reserved exclusively for public sector while twelve other areas were to be progressively State-owned with State generally taking the initiative in establishing new undertakings — to the following eight: arms and ammunition and allied items of defence equipment; defence aircraft and warships; atomic energy; coal and lignite; mineral oils; mining of iron ore, manganese ore, chrome ore, gypsum, sulphur, gold and diamond; mining of copper, lead, zinc, tin, molybdenum and wolform; minerals specified in the Schedule to the Atomic Energy (Control of Production and Use) Order, 1953; and railway transport.

The private sector is expected to play an increasing role in industrial activities, especially where security and strategic or social considerations are not very important. The public sector will concentrate increasingly on basic and core sectors. Even in these areas, emphasis will be on financing industrial and mineral projects primarily through internal and other extra-budgetary resources instead of depending on budgetary allocations. This is in line with the general philosophy of placing greater reliance on competitiveness of industries and efficiency of operations. The undertakings which are in a position to finance their development plans on their own will be allowed greater freedom for growth and diversification as a self-sustaining process. In the case of undertakings which are operating in core areas and are largely dependent on budgetary support, limited support will be provided in the initial years to enable them to stand on their own in the later years of the Plan.

As a result of the recent policy reforms, the industrial sector is expected to undergo considerable restructuring. First, in the past there has been considerable stress on import substitution at any cost. With the emphasis now being laid on competitiveness, future growth will be more in those sectors where the country has comparative advantage. Secondly, the size of individual companies, which is very small by international standards, not a single Indian company figures in the list of first 500 'Fortune' companies, is expected to grow through expansions, amalgamations, mergers, etc. Thirdly, there would be greater integration of indigenous production with outside. Those components/ sub-assemblies whose production is uneconomic, will be imported. On the other hand, some other components/sub-assemblies/finished products will be increasingly exported. Finally, there will be joint ventures abroad to exploit the complementarities of resource endowments in this country and the concerned foreign country.

Among the metallurgical industries, the country possesses a good resource base in the case of iron and steel and aluminium. These two industries have the potential to record a very good growth rate in the long-run. However, in the medium-term, the prospects are not so good because of inefficient production and constraints of infrastructure in the case of former and lack of bauxite linkages and inadequate availability of power in the case of latter. In the case of aluminium, it will be worthwhile to explore possibilities of large scale manufacture of alumina in the country, partly for exports and partly tor smelting abroad to meet the country's requirements of aluminium. Due to poor resource position, no major capacities are envisaged to be set up in the Eighth Plan in the case of copper, lead and zinc.

The capital goods industry has recorded impressive gains in the past in terms of quantitative increases in production. From a virtually non-existent base at the time of Independence, today the country is more or less self-sufficient in meeting the requirements of various user sectors. However, the qualitative performance of the industry leaves much to be desired. In most of the sectors, the performance of the indigenously manufactured capital goods is nowhere near the contemporary levels in terms of process technologies, quality of products, productivity and cost of production. This sector decides the efficiency of operations of the various user sectors. With increasing emphasis on competitiveness, the user sectors will be anxious to switch over to state-of-the-art technologies and processes. This will, therefore, be one sector which will be adversely affected by the opening up of the economy and allowing freedom to the entrepreneurs to select and import capital equipment and technologies. In due course, the leading capital goods manufacturers can be expected to go in for collaborations, foreign equity and import of technologies to update their products and emerge as suppliers of world class capital goods but in the medium-term, this sector will be adversely affected due to its inability to meet global competition.

In the areas of machine tools, transport equipment and accessories, electrical equipment and controls and instrumentation, the country has a good base. With upgradation of facilities through collaboration/foreign equity etc., it should be possible to build on this and achieve good growth in production as well as exports.

With low levels of capacity utilisation, poor productivity, inadequate ancillarisation, long delivery period and high cost of production, the ship building industry in the country is moribund. On the other hand, the ship repairing industry is reasonably competitive and has the potential to meet the growing demand and to save valuable foreign exchange. With greater attention to modernisation of ship repairing facilities, the industry is expected to achieve reasonable growth.

The growth of the electronics sector has been rather lopsided. The high growth rate recorded in the past has been largely due to the growth of the consumer electronics sector, especially the TV industry. The industry is characterised by a very weak components base and consequent high import intensity, grossly uneconomic scales of production and high cost of production. In the case of controls and instrumentation, there is considerable capacity in the country for manufacture of hardware but the capability to provide the requisite systems design and support is inadequate.

The exports of computer software have recorded reasonable increases in the recent past but it has hardly been possible to touch the fringe of the potential. The opening of the economy is expected to lead to restructuring of the entire electronics industry, including closure of a number of sub-economic units engaged primarily in screw driver technology consolidations and amalgamations of units and increased tie-ups with foreign firms to provide a sound base for sustained development of the industry. As this restructuring, process will take some time, the outlook in the medium-term does not look very promising.

The fertiliser industry will be virtually by-passed by the economic liberalisation in view of the controls on inputs and administered prices of inputs as well as outputs of' the industry. In the case of nitrogenous fertiliser, a decision on the pricing policy is imperative. On the one hand, the existing system of retention prices and subsidy is leading to increasing burden of subsidy on account of increases in production and costs of inputs, which are not matched by corresponding increases in the retail prices of fertilisers and on the other, adequate private sector initiative is not forthcoming because of lack of a clear cut policy and freedom to decide the feed stock as well as uncertainty about the returns from the investments. From time to time, *ad hoc* adjustments have been made in the norms for fixation of retention prices, creating considerable apprehensions among the potential investors about the viability of the projects. It is primarily on this account that there has been very slow progress in the three fertiliser plants which were to come up in the private sector along HBJ pipeline in the Seventh Plan. It is imperative to finalise the feed stock and fertiliser pricing at the earliest. The country may be heading for increased shortages and dependence on import of nitrogenous fertilisers.

In the case of phosphatic fertiliser, the country's resource base is very poor and purely on economic considerations, setting up of phosphatic fertiliser capacity is undesirable. In order to minimise dependence on large-scale imports of fertilisers, joint ventures abroad would need to be explored. For production within the country, a judicious mix of import of rock phosphate and sulphur, phosphoric acid and finished fertiliser would need to be adopted.

The prices of most of the petrochemical products in the country are well above the international levels, partly because of high administered prices of inputs and partly because of high rates of taxes. World over, the petrochemical products are finding increasing applications as substitutes for metals, alloys, etc. Large number of new applications are being found almost everyday. Similarly, in the textile sector, cotton is considered a luxury item and synthetic fibres are used for the common man's clothing abroad because of ease of convenience, durability etc. But in India, the reverse is the case. While the petrochemical industry has been delicensed, its growth will be guided to a considerable extent by the reductions in taxes and duties on its products.

India is a large producer of cement and cement machinery. In the last few years, the production of cement has risen substantially. The cement production in the country is internationally competitive. The cement industry is expected to record good growth in production as well as exports.

The sugar scenario has undergone a significant change during the past two years and the country has become a net exporter of the commodity from being a net importer for many years. The country is also a leading producer of sugar machinery and sugar production is quite competitive. With focus on increasing the per hectare yield of sugarcane, the sugar industry is likely to increase its production and exports substantially.

In spite of a phenomenal increase in exports of leather and leather goods in the recent past, India's share in world trade is minimal (0.7 per cent in the case of footwear, 9.5 per cent in footwear components and 4 per cent in leather garments). There is a growing market for leather products abroad and India can increase its exports substantially.

The textile sector has been undergoing a major restructuring. The mills in the organised sector are not able to meet competition from the powerlooms, though spinning continues to be profitable. Increasingly, the mills are modernising their plants and machinery and devoting greater attention to exports. A number of 100 per cent EOUs have also come up. This is a healthy development. This trend is expected to get accelerated and the textile exports are poised for a quantum jump. With improved availability of quality fabrics at competitive prices, the garments industry is also expected to record a healthy growth. The powerloom sector is likely to further increase its contribution and become the prime supplier of cloth for domestic market. The outlook for the handloom sector does not look promising. It will need to switch over to production of high value items and cater to the sophisticated exports market for specialised products.

A number of composite mills have closed down. In the context of the need to find resources for modernisation and growth of mills as well as paying legitimate dues of workers etc., it will he worthwhile to examine the possibilities of sale of land and buildings, which in many cases are surplus to the requirements of the concerned mills. While there are, no doubt, legal difficulties, the long term interest of the industry demands that all parties *i.e.*, Union Government, State Governments, managements and trade unions should sit together and evolve a workable strategy for realising the full commercial value of the property and utilising it for modernisation/diversification of the concerned mills as well as rehabilitation/re-deployment packages for surplus labour.

The jute industry is surviving virtually on oxygen being provided by the Government. Unless the industry takes up modernisation in a big way, concentrates on high value products and diversifies into new areas, it has a bleak future.

Of late, there has been considerable interest in the agro-food processing industry and a number of ventures are in the offing, some of them in collaboration with leading foreign companies and others as joint ventures with foreign companies. The marine export has also attracted a lot of attention. With the recent policy changes, these two sectors are poised for a rapid growth.

Public Enterprise Reform

Public Enterprises embody a major national capability in terms of physical, financial, institutional and human resources. Their effective utilisation can lead to significant economic growth. In the framework of the new Economic Policy, Public Sector industry has an important role as an autonomous competitive and efficient sector, to provide essential infrastructure goods and services, development of natural resources and areas of strategic concern. A positive and productive future awaits public sector industry. To reach that goal, considerable restructuring is involved. The Eighth Plan recognises this and proposes a major public sector reform initiative. This initiative will consist of the following integrated strategies:

i. Restructuring involving modernisation, rationalisation of capacity, product-mix changes, selective exit and privatisation is needed on a massive scale, to make public enterprises viable, efficient and competitive.

ii. Increase in autonomy and performance accountability of public enterprises is critical to make them a dynamic force. The system of Memoranda of understanding between administrative ministries and central public enterprises which has been launched in the Seventh Plan has these objectives in its design. However, its effectiveness needs to be improved.

iii. Changes in management practices at specific enterprise level to promote efficiency, dynamic leadership, resourcefulness and innovation are needed.

iv. State level public enterprises have serious problems. Interference, lack of professionalism and *ad hoc* investment and employment decisions have resulted in chronic sickness of many of them. A major effort is called for, in collaboration with the State Governments, to promote reforms in them.

v. In the changing economic environment, technology will be a major tool to improve competitiveness and efficiency of public enterprises. Their capability to develop, import and use technology effectively or, to integrate technology in their corporate strategies (expansion, diversification, marketing etc.) is weak now. The new reform initiative needs to address this through building active linkages among R & D laboratories, educational institutions and public enterprises. This is vital in the emerging inter-dependent and globalising economic environment.

vi. The organisation of Government (Ministries and agencies) for public sector has historically grown in a certain manner. Presently many regulations (price, distribution, investment and import controls) are being dismantled. This liberalisation not only calls for re-structuring of enterprises but also of the Government in the governance of industrial growth and management of inter-face with the enterprises. A new institutional capability is needed in Government that is responsive to environmental change, professional and can facilitate operation of market forces, through orchestrisation of the efforts of various (R&D, education, engineering, manufacturing, trade, etc.) organisations towards priority targets in select areas, by building a consensus and partnership among the different stakeholders.

The above call for a positive public sector reforms, by designed, selective and targeted interventions. The reform initiative needs to include : creating a knowledge base for reform, generating an institutional capability and developing a consensus among the stakeholders about policy goals and implementation strategies.

A network of institutions (academic, government, industry, consulting firms, financial institutions and international organisations) needs to be organised to design and implement the reforms. A coordinated strategy through a high powered task-force is needed to mobilize resources for achieving the objectives of reforms in the Eighth Plan period.

Targets for the Eighth Plan

The capacity and production targets for selected industries for the Eighth Plan are contained in Table 1. Brief highlights of industrial programmes and stratgies for major sectors are given in the subsequent paragraphs.

TABLE 1

Capacity and Production for Selected Industries — Indicative Targets for 1996-97

Sl. No.	Industry	Uuit	1989-90 Actuais		1990-91 Actuals		1991-92 Actuals/Ant		1996-97 Ind. Target	
			C	P	C	P	C	P	C	P
1	2	3	4	5	6	7	8	9	10	11
	Mining									
1.	Coal	MT		200.85		211.73		227.50		308.00
2.	Lignite	-do-		11.00		11.72		12.12		19.50
3.	Crude oil	-do-		43.09		32.99		31.00		50.00
4.	Iron ore	-do-		51.47		54.15		56.50		72.00
	Basic Metals									
5.	Hot Metal (Integrated Steel Plants)	-do-	15.46	11.95	17.26	12.69	17.36	14.26	20.46	20.09
6.	Pig Iron for sale (Integrated Steel Plants)	-do-		1.23		1.39		1.48		2.16
7.	Steel ingots (Integrated Steel Plants)	-do-	14.70	10.59	14.80	11.17	16.35	12.63	18.53	18.23
8.	Saleable Steel	-do-	15.07	12.61	16.67	13.12	20.12	14.26	25.43	23.22
9.	Saleable Steel (Integrated Steel Plants)	-do-	11.57	9.03	11.67	9.42	13.00	10.58	16.33	15.94
10.	Alloy and special steels	Th. T	1490.00	1040.00	1650.00	1150.00	1650.00	1120.00	2250.00	1800.00
11.	Sponge iron	-do-	570.00	300.00	1370.00	680.00	1400.00	1150.00	7000.00	5000.00
12.	Aluminium	-do-	610.00	427.12	610.00	449.38	610.00	514.17	772.00	656.00
13.	Copper (Blister)	-do-	47.50	41.70	47.50	40.40	47.50	46.75	62.50	55.00

14.	Copper refined	-do-	47.50	41.18	47.50	40.60	47.50	45.50	62.50	55.00
15.	Zinc ingots	-do-	99.00	75.22	99.00	73.00	169.00	102.00	179.00	154.00
16.	Lead ingots	-do-	30.00	23.01	54.50	41.73	89.50	48.39	104.00	96.00
	Non-Metallic Mineral Products									
17.	Cement	MT	60.00	45.30	63.00	49.00	65.00	53.00	90.00	76.00
18.	Petroleum products	-do-		48.30		51.77		50.21*		61.57*
	Basic Chemicals									
19.	Caustic soda	Th. T	1100.00	940.00	1138.00	999.10	1138.00	1022.70	1738.00	1600.00
20.	Soda ash	-do-	1460.00	1377.50	1557.00	1385.00	1557.00	1404.20	2200.00	2000.00
	Agricultural Chemicals									
21.	Nitrogenous fertilisers	-do-	8148.00	6747.00	8148.00	6993.00	8247.00	7350.00	10940.00	9800.00
22.	Phosphatic fertilisers	-do-	2750.00	1756.00	2750.00	2051.00	2750.00	2500.00	3100.00	3000.00
23.	B.H.C. (13 % isomers)	-do-	45.00	24.40	34.70	26.10	37.70	19.90	37.70	25.00
24.	D.D.T.	-do-	9.10	7.50	9.10	7.00	9.10	7.00	9.10	8.00
25.	Other pesticides	-do-	54.50	27.05	39.59	28.00	44.55	27.00	74.00	40.00
26.	Malathion	-do-	12.34	3.35	9.00	3.10	9.00	3.10	9.00	4.00
	Thermo Plastics and Synthetic Rubber									
27.	L.D. polyethylene	-do-	112.00	85.00	192.00	95.00	192.00	120.00	192.00	180.00
28.	H.D. polyethylene	-do-	50.00	34.40	185.00	40.00	395.00	44.00	680.00	400.00
29.	Polyvinyl chloride	-do-	159.00	136.90	158.00	140.00	258.00	170.00	542.00	450.00
30.	Polypropylene	-do-	55.00	44.60	115.00	45.00	115.00	64.00	215.00	155.00

TABLE 1 — *Contd.*

1	2	3	4	5	6	7	8	9	10	11
31.	Polystyrene	Th. T	28.00	23.53	28.00	25.00	34.00	20.00	160.00	110.00
32.	Styrene butadiene rubber	-do-	37.00	37.45	30.00	35.00	36.75	38.00	50.00	50.00
33.	Polybutadiene rubber	-do-	20.00	15.12	20.00	15.00	20.00	16.00	28.00	25.00
	Petrochemical Intermediates									
34.	Acrylonitrile	-do-	30.00	25.20	30.00	26.00	30.00	27.00	110.00	80.00
35.	DMT/PTA	-do-	235.00	249.00	235.00	290.00	335.00	310.00	575.00	450.00
36.	Caprolactam	-do-	20.00	20.64	70.00	30.00	70.00	50.00	220.00	150.00
37.	Detergent Alkylate	-do-	153.00	125.57	150.00	138.00	163.00	180.00	203.00	200.00
38.	Methanol	-do-	164.00	140.00	162.00	154.00	244.00	193.00	400.00	300.00
39.	Phenol	-do-	60.00	49.00	60.00	48.00	60.00	46.00	100.00	75.00
	Man-made fibres									
40.	Viscose filament yarn	-do-	53.20	49.20	60.40	50.90	69.00	53.00	80.00	60.00
41.	Viscose staple fibre	-do-	157.80	147.60	176.10	160.20	180.00	160.00	220.00	200.00
42.	Viscose tyre cord	-do-	21.20	7.54	21.20	7.10	21.20	8.00	22.00	10.00
	Drugs and Pharmaceuticals									
43.	Bulk Drugs	Rs. Crs		610.00		700.00		730.00		1500.00
44.	Formulations	-do-		3360.00		3600.00		3840.00		6000.00

	Food Products									
45.	Sugar	MT	9.34	10.99	9.85	11.90	12.00	12.00	16.00	15.50
46.	Vanaspati	Th. T	2000.00	851.00	2161.00	820.00	2400.00	850.00	2600.00	1050.00
	Textiles									
47.	Yarn (Cotton blended & mixed)	$	26.59	1639.00	26.67	1795.00	27.37	1780.00	30.00	2400.00
48.	Cloth (mill sector)	+	1.81	2649.00	1.78	2590.00	1.84	2400.00	2.10	3500.00
49.	Cloth (descent sector)	Mill. Mtrs.		13709.00		15228.00		15757.00		21200.00
50.	Jute manufacture	Th. T	1625.00	1304.00	1625.00	1430.00	1625.00	1450.00	1700.00	1600.00
	Leather and Rubber Goods									
51.	Leather footwear (Organised sector)	Mill. Pair	30.00	22.00	30.00	22.00	30.00	22.00	48.00	42.00
52.	Rubber footwear	-do-	60.00	40.00	60.00	40.00	60.00	40.00	80.00	60.00
53.	Bicycle tyres (Organised sector)	Mill. Nos	40.30	25.60	40.00	25.60	40.00	30.00	60.00	50.00
54.	Automobile tyres	-do-	28.80	17.20	29.80	18.40	30.00	26.00	36.00	32.00
	Paper and paper Products									
55.	Paper and paper board	Th. T	3049.00	1820.00	3284.00	1956.00	3284.00	2100.00	3500.00	2900.00
56.	Newsprint	-do-	300.00	277.00	313.00	280.00	313.00	295.00	350.00	300.00
	Soaps and Detergents									
57.	Soaps (Organised sector)	-do-	435.00	394.00	435.00	434.00	500.00	480.00	600.00	580.00
58.	Synthetic detergent (Organised Sector)	-do-	440.00	240.00	440.00	263.00	500.00	280.00	850.00	400.00

TABLE 1 — *Contd.*

1	2	3	4	5	6	7	8	9	10	11
	Industrial Machinery									
59.	Machine Tools	Rs. Crs.		728.10		867.00		875.00	1500.00	1150.00
60.	Mining Machinery	-do-		95.80		63.40		80.00	170.00	130.00
61.	Metallurgical Machinery	-do-		117.40		101.00		152.00	250.00	200.00
62.	Cement Machinery	-do-		31.50		31.00		42.00	120.00	75.00
63.	Chem. & Phar. Machinery	-do-		292.90		348.70		400.00	750.00	650.00
64.	Sugar Machinery	-do-		49.40		72.00		90.00	200.00	150.00
65.	Rubber Machinery	-do-		24.00		27.00		29.00	60.00	40.00
66.	Paper & Pulp Machinery	-do-		14.20		33.40		48.00	80.00	60.00
67.	Printing Machinery	-do-		30.00		31.00		32.00	60.00	40.00
68.	Textile Machinery	-do-		530.00		565.00		600.00	1100.00	800.00
69.	Boilers	-do-		884.10		887.80		800.00	1500.00	1050.00
	Electrical Power Equipments									
70.	Steam Turbines	Th. MW	4.50	4.17	4.50	2.33	4.50	2.50	4.69	3.96
71.	Hydro Turbines	-do-	1.50	0.52	1.50	0.45	1.50	0.75	1.80	1.00
72.	Transformers	MKVA	40.00	37.80	40.00	36.00	40.00	34.00	70.00	60.00
73.	Electric Motors	MHP	8.50	5.20	8.50	6.00	8.50	5.50	10.00	8.00

	Construction Machinery									
74.	Earthmoving Equipment	Nos.	6000.00	2631.00	6000.00	2690.00	6000.00	2600.00	6500.00	4200.00
	Agricultural Machinery									
75.	Tractors	Th. Nos.	130.00	125.10	150.00	143.50	160.00	155.00	270.00	240.00
	Rail & Water Transport Equipment									
76.	Elec. Locomotives	Nos.	140.00	130.00	140.00	140.00	140.00	140.00	200.00	200.00
77.	Diesel Locomotives	-do-	230.00	220.00	230.00	225.00	230.00	225.00	300.00	290.00
78.	Railway Coaches	-do-	2450.00	1554.00	2450.00	1800.00	2450.00	1800.00	3100.00	2500.00
79.	Railway Wagons	Th. Nos.	32.00	22.20	32.00	23.00	32.00	25.00	45.00	40.00
80.	Ship Buildings	Th. Dwt.	260.00	175.00	260.00	175.00	260.00	175.00	280.00	200.00
	Road Transport Equipment									
81.	Commercial Vehicles	Th. Nos.	264.00	126.70	264.00	145.80	264.00	135.00	290.00	200.00
82.	Passenger Cars.	-do-	190.00	181.60	190.00	179.60	190.00	165.00	280.00	250.00
83.	Jeeps	-do-	50.00	45.60	50.00	38.30	50.00	30.00	70.00	45.00
84.	Scooters, Motor Cycles and Mopeds	-do-	2200.00	1750.40	2200.00	1863.20	2200.00	1800.00	3000.00	2400.00
85.	Bicycle (Org. Sect.)	Mill. Nos.	8.00	6.79	8.00	6.76	8.00	7.40	10.00	9.00
	Mechanical Components & Consumer Goods									
86.	Ball and Roller Bearnings	Mill. Nos.	120.00	119.00	125.00	100.80	125.00	95.00	150.00	130.00
87.	Typewriters	Th. Nos.	180.00	115.10	180.00	115.90	180.00	120.00	180.00	130.00
88.	Sewing Machines (Org. Sect.)	-do-	568.00	146.60	568.00	92.80	568.00	130.00	568.00	160.00

TABLE 1 — *Concld.*

1	2	3	4	5	6	7	8	9	10	11
	Electrical Components									
	Consumer Durables									
89.	ACSR & A A Conductors	Th. T	150.00	46.80	150.00	59.70	150.00	70.00	150.00	100.00
90.	Dry Cells	Mill. Nos.	2200.00	1274.20	2200.00	1234.90	2200.00	1300.00	2500.00	2000.00
91.	Storage Batteries	-do-	4.00	2.84	4.50	3.65	4.50	3.50	6.00	5.00
92.	Domestic Refregerators	Th. Nos.	1200.00	1051.80	1300.00	1282.60	1500.00	1350.00	2500.00	2200.00
	Electronics									
93.	Consumer Electronics	Rs. Crs.		2850.00		3000.00		4900.00		8500.00
94.	Industrial Electronics	-do-		1360.00		1370.00		1800.00		5000.00
95.	Professional Equipments	-do-		2065.00		2345.00		3020.00		7000.00
96.	Computers including micro processor systems	-do-		835.00		820.00		1300.00		3300.00

Metallurgical and Mineral Industries

The metallurgical and mineral industries constitute the bed-rock of industrial sector as they provide basic raw materials for most of the industries. Their easy availability is an essential pre-requisite for growth of most of the other sectors.

India continues to be a net importer of minerals and metals. The gap between the projected demand and supply of most of the minerals is likely to increase in the coming years.

Considering the time lag between discovery and eventual production of minerals, a greater thrust on mineral exploration activities needs to be given during the Eighth Plan particularly towards exploration by adoption of improved technology, including remote sensing and geophysical techniques. The exploration strategy has to be reoriented and emphasis should be on those minerals in which the resources are poor *e.g.* gold, base metals, platinum group of metals, diamond, nickel, tungsten and rock phosphate, etc.

The State sector's contribution in mining of industrial/non-metallic minerals is quite significant. Reorganisation and strengthening of the concerned departments of the State Governments will be accorded priority in the Eighth Plan. Most of the non-metallic minerals are produced through small scale mining which will continue to co-exist with large scale mining.

Iron Ore

Iron ore constitutes one of the major exports of the country with foreign exchange earnings of about Rs. 1200-1300 crores in 1991-92. The major exporters are National Mineral Development Corporation (NMDC), Kudremukh Iron Ore Co. Ltd. (KIOCL) and private parties, particularly the Goan mine owners. The ore from Bailadilla mines of NMDC is by far the richest in the country. Until recently, the entire Bailadilla output was being exported, with the indigenous industry using inferior grades. It is imperative to reduce the level of exports of very high grade iron ore (+65% Fe) and utilise it increasingly in indigenous steel plants, particularly for direct reduction.

As a significant proportion of iron ore reserved is in the form of fines and blue dust, greater efforts will have to be made for their utilisation for which necessary R&D work will be taken up. In this context, the NMDC will undertake a project in collaboration with the Department of Electronics (DOE) on development of process technology for manufacture of various types of ferrite powders using indigenous raw materials/blue dust and their pilot plant production.

Iron and Steel

During the Seventh Plan and 1990-92, the expansions of Bokaro and Bhilai steel plants to four million tonnes each, the second phase modernisation/expansion of Tata Iron & Steel Company and the first phase facilities of Visakhapatnam Steel Plant (except light and medium merchant mill) were completed. In addition there has been impressive growth of production capacity in mini steel plants and induction furnace units in the secondary sector.

Indian steel industry has been suffering from a number of disabilities. Obsolescence of plant machinery and technology has been important factor for low capacity utilisation, low productivity, high energy consumption and high production cost. It is interesting to note that in the sixties the Indian Steel Industry was internationally competitive but it is no longer so. The programme of development of steel industry in the Eighth Plan is aimed at improving the technological health of the existing integrated steel plants and modernisation and upgradation of technology so as to achieve international competitiveness in respect of both cost and quality. Modernisation of existing integrated steel plants at Durgapur and Rourkela in public sector and Tata Iron & Steel Co. in the private sector is expected to he completed in the Eighth Plan. Upgradation of steel making in the secondary sector has been taken up/being contemplated in the Eighth Plan. All these measures intiated in the Seventh Plan will bring the Indian steel industry at par with global standards. The modernisation and rebuilding of the IISCO plant at Burnpur is also expected to be taken up in the Eighth Plan.

Under the recent policy changes no licence is required to set up iron and steel units. These policy changes are expected to give impetus to Indian steel industry to grow freely and also attract private investment. The initial response of the private sector to these changes appears to be encouraging.

Non-Ferrous Metals

During the Seventh Plan period, the non-ferrous metals sector made impressive progress with completion of the prestigious, integrated, multi-locational Aluminium complex of National Aluminium Company Ltd. (NALCO), setting up of a captive power plant for Bharat Aluminium Company Ltd. (BALCO), modernisation and debottlenecking of copper smelters and refineries of Hindustan Copper Ltd. and expansion of Vizag Zinc smelters of Hindustan Zinc Ltd. as well as Binani Zinc Plant in private sector, thereby raising capacities for aluminium, copper and zinc as targetted for the Plan. From a position of dependence on imports India has emerged as a net exporter of aluminium. As far as other major non-ferrous metals are concerned the share of imports in the consumption of lead and zinc registered some decline whereas in case of copper despite expansion of the existing capacity dependence on imports increased.

Aluminium

With the commissioning of Orissa Aluminium Complex of NALCO, the country has emerged as a net exporter of aluminium. However, this situation is expected to last only for a couple of years more and by 1994-95 the country may once again turn a net importer of aluminium.

Considering the advantageous position in the resource endowment and in view of the production being competitive, it would be desirable to maintain an exportable surplus. In this context the proposed expansion of Hindustan Aluminium Company Ltd.(HINDALCO) by 1.5 lakh tonnes would merit a high priority. NALCO's expansion by 1.15 lakh tonnes would also need to be considered as soon as they stabilise their production from the present capacity. BALCO would need to concentrate on energy conservation and setting up of downstream capacity. A number of 100% EOU proposals for manufacture of alumina in the private sector have been made but these have been pending for quite some time now for want of finalisation of bauxite linkages. This needs to be expedited. Such plants could serve as the first step for setting up of aluminium smelters at a later date or joint ventures abroad for aluminium smelting.

Copper

During the Seventh Plan, a marginal increase in the capacity was achieved by debottlenecking and modernisation of the existing smelters of Hindustan Copper Limited (HCL) with small investments. Production of copper is not internationally competitive because of the low grade of copper deposits and small scale of operations in comparison to world standards. Malanjkhand copper deposit appears promising. After an evaluation of the results of the exploration and feasibility study currently under way, a view will he taken on augmenting copper production. Since the deposits in India are very low in copper content, possibilities of bio-acid leaching need to he examined.

Lead and Zinc

With the commissioning of Rampura-Agucha-Chanderiya integrated project of Hindustan Zinc Ltd. (HZL) in 1991-92, the country has achieved near self-sufficiency in zinc. The integrated project will need to stabilise its operations before embarking on any large scale expansion in the Eighth Plan. No major new projects are envisaged in the Eighth Plan except for a replacement mine to feed Raipura Dariba concentrator.

Nickel

The entire requirement of nickel in the country is imported. Considerable efforts made in the past for commercial production from large low grade nickel resources of Sukinda (Orissa) based on indigenous technology have not been successful. It will, therefore, be necessary to carefully examine the plans for indigenous production. It would be desirable to look for imported technology for upgradation of ores before taking any investment decision on production of nickel.

Gold

The gold deposits have been steadily getting poorer and deeper with production costs becoming increasingly uneconomic. The future of gold mining in India will depend on the low grade small scale deposits in which mill recovery is a sensitive factor. Mining of scattered shallow gold deposits will have to be considered. A new approach to gold exploration and recovery of gold from low grade ore deposits and tailings deserves consideration.

With the liberalisation of gold import and consequential decrease in the gold prices, the operations of Bharat Gold Mines Ltd., have become still more uneconomic. The cost of production is two to three times the selling price of gold and the company is heavily dependent upon budgetary support even for its current operations. A hard look at the future of the company is overdue. The possibility of induction of private partners and 'state-of-the-art' technology and closure of' some uneconomic mines with re-settlement of surplus manpower in new ventures will need to be explored.

A National Materials Initiative

There are significant and rapid changes taking place in the world of materials. The emerging unity of many disciplines and areas in materials science and technology; the growing integration of activities in the materials cycle ranging from design to disposal; the intensive engineering efforts for superior performance; the targetted, high priority and integrated efforts on materials in many countries and the large potential for materials technology-based industrial development in India, call for a coordinated Indian strategy in technology development and innovation, industrial structure, human resources development, infrastructure development and international linkasges. Indian capability in Materials Science and Technology is large and diversified but is fragmented and has a poor impact on the production system. The National Materials Policy Project, under the auspices of the Technology Informations Forecasting and Assessment Council, Department of Science and Technology, has concluded that there is a priority need to promote a National Materials Initiative (NMI) to reach these objectives and has recommended the formation of a Materials Council with adequate resources to implement the strategy with and through other institutions, to make India a competitive world player in select materials. This will involve doubling our current national investment in materials technology development from about Rs. 125 crores per annum to Rs. 250 crores per annum by 1995.

Material Science and Technology will be the central instruments to achieve the goals of the National Material Initiative. Research and Technology Development in the following areas need to be promoted in collaboration with industry, R&D laboratories and Academic Institutions :

Raw material upgradation;

Performance improvement of conventional materials;

Value added production;

Development of advanced materials;

Applications/use technology;

Materials use efficiency;

Synthesis, Processing and Manufacturing;

Energy intensity;

Substitution and Conservation;

Environmental Sustainability; and

Materials Cycle linkages.

Material Technological Innovation in industry can he promoted by a competitive environment as envisaged in the New Economic Policy. A "Materials Council", when formed can, by strengthening the infrastructure and appropriate joint funding arrangements, stimulate this process. One of the Council's tasks is to identify specific areas of priority and promote alliances and partnerships of various institutions for materials technology development and use. The Council will seek to coordinate the diverse ongoing efforts for synergy among them.

The Material Council, when established, could be an autonomous body, and a collaborative venture of Industry, Government, S&T organisations and Financial Institutions. It could be set up through the initiative of the Department of Science and Technology and managed by an independent board. Initial funding by Government could be minimal in the Eighth Plan and larger resources can be raised with the help of financial institutions, international organisations, industrv etc. A Materials

Development Fund can be formed for this prupose. The main tasks of the Materials Council would be :

— Long term Industry/Technology forecasting and monitoring;
— Interagency coordination in materials technology;
— Promotion of partnerships and alliances among industry, S&T and academic institutions tor the development and commercialisation of technology;
— Integration of materials science and technology with corporate strategy at the industry level;
— International linkages development (import of technology, foreign investment, S&T cooperation agreement, etc.) and
— Information services and outreach efforts.

The Council's role will be to orchestrate, facilitate and catalyse various programmes rather than direct intervention. It will not seek to duplicate any efforts, but build on them. The experience of Japan, South Korea, European Community and United States of America suggest such an approach. The Council's performance in the long run is to be measured by the extent it has been able to promote a competitive and materials-technology-based industrial development.

Engineering Industry

The engineering industry provides the key to economic growth with its diversified forward and backward linkages with almost every sector of the national economy. The share of engineering in the total organised industrial activity is about 31.0% of the value of output, 33.2% of value added, 29.7% of employment and 28.4% of invested capital. During the Seventh Plan, output of the manufacturing sector as a whole grew at 8.8%, while the engineering industry grew at 10.5% per annum. This sector is mainly based on domestic resources and has good employment potential. The country has comparative advantage in this sector. However, the engineering industry has a number of weaknesses, the prominent being :

— Weak Design and Engineering base;
— Inadequate attention to modernisation and continued upgradation of technology;
— Inadequate R & D;
— Absence of companies of international standards which can take up turn-key and consultancy projects;
— Demand constraint leading to low capacity utilization;

— Paucity of domestic financial resources and availability of "tied aid" leading to avoidable imports;
— High cost of raw materials and other inputs;
— High cost of credit/finance and duty structure;
— Absence of sustained export initiative;
— Inadequate attention to training and manpower development; and
— Overmanning, which has often prevented modernization and also increased overheads.

The stress in the Eighth Plan will be on qualitative upgradation and elimination of the weaknesses mentioned above. Greater stress would need to be laid on import of drawings and designs, than on import of equipment. Establishment of closer linkages between academic institutions, manufacturers of equipment, users of equipment, national laboratories and the Government is also necessary.

Ship-building and Ship-repair Industry

At present there are about 40 shipyards in India. Out of these, seven are in the public sector, two in the State sector and the remaining in the private sector. The private sector shipyards are allowed to construct vessels of any size. However, at present, the private sector shipyards are not capable of building more than 10,000 DWT size crafts. In spite of so many shipyards in the country, ship-building industry is in doldrums partly because of very high cost of indigenous ships, unduly long delivery periods and poor viability of the shipyards and partly because of the ability of foreign shipyards to offer ships at marginal cost and shorter delivery period consequent on world-wide recession in ship-building industry. Hence, it is not proposed to set up any new ship-building yards in the Eighth Plan. Efforts would, however, be made to improve productivity and viability of the existing yards. Certain other measures under consideration are introduction of revised pricing formula as recommended by BICP, treating the ship-building industry as 100% export oriented industry with all related benefits, allowing duty free imports up to a limit of 60% of the realisable price of the vessel, providing working capital loans to shipyards on soft terms, etc.

Ship Repair Facilities

The ship repair activity is far more profitable than ship-building. At the same time, substantial outgo of foreign exchange (to the tune of Rs. 50 crores every year) on account of Indian vessels repairs at foreign shipyards can be avoided if domestic capabilities are strengthened.

Keeping this in view, most of the units in this sector are drawing up plans to increase their capacities. The Government has recognised the strength of this industry and given it the status of deemed export industry. A number of concessions, as available to 100% export-oriented units, have been provided.

Electronics

The electronics industry has the potential to be a powerful catalyst for improving productivity and efficiency in all sectors of the economy. It has achieved rapid growth, perhaps the fastest rate of growth among all industries over the past decade. The value of output of the electronics industry grew by about 25 per cent annually during the Sixth Plan and around 35 per cent per annum during the Seventh Plan. However, India's production of electronic goods is presently less than one per cent of the world production which is valued at over U.S. $ 750 billion per annum. The industry is employment-oriented and provides direct employment to around 2.60 lakh persons and indirect employment to approximately 5.20 lakh persons. The electronics exports, especially software exports, have recorded impressive increases but the import intensity of the sector is a cause for concern.

The focus of attention in the Eighth Plan, in electronics industry would be on production at internationally competitive scales, encouraging export-oriented production, technology development, manpower development, rural industrialisation and application of electronics in key socio-economic sectors. In the area of computer software exports, where the country has comparative advantage, Software Technology Parks are being set up. These would require certain facilities like quick and easy communications, already provided in a few centres. A project on Value Added High Speed Data Communication Network for Software Exports is being implemented.

Electronics has a very significant role to play in increasing productivity and reducing costs in virtually every sector of the economy. Over the last few years certain technologies have been developed for introduction of electronic systems and controls in a number of industries such as steel, cement, paper and pulp, sugar, tea and power and also in the areas of agriculture, social infrastructure and strategic electronics, which are appropriate for the needs of the country. In the Eighth Plan, efforts will be made for intensive application of these technologies in various sectors.

Another area needing attention is the training of manpower required for the electronics industry. In order to achieve the desired growth and to attract foreign investors, it has become necessary to ensure that adequately trained manpower is available. At present, training in electronics is being imparted both in Government and private institutions. Government has supported more than 450 institutions during the Seventh Plan. In the Eighth Plan, this aspect will be given special emphasis by introducing more and more job-oriented courses at ITI level and Post Diploma Degree level in the area of repair/maintenance of consumer electronics, industrial electronics, electro-medical equipment and computer systems. Some institutions like Centres for Electronics Design & Technology (CEDTs) etc. will generate special manpower in this field. Government is giving recognition to a number of private institutions engaged in various courses in computer education. Keeping in view the future requirement of manpower, there is an imperative need for augmenting and improving the training facilities available in ITIs, Polytechnics, Engineering Colleges and other institutions.

Fertilisers

During the Seventh Plan, four gas-based nitrogenous fertiliser plants at Aonla, Vijaipur, Jagdishpur (on HBJ line) and Namrup Expansion III and DAP project at Paradeep were commissioned. Four gas-based projects are under implementation at Babrala, Shahjahanpur and Kota along HBJ line and at Kakinada in Andhra Pradesh. Even after this, there will be a shortfall of about 3 million tonnes of nitrogen in 1996-97.

As the expansion of the existing units provides considerable savings in infrastructure and utilities, doubling of plants at Bijaipur, Aonla and Jagdishpur should be undertaken without further loss of time. Discovery of gas in Krishna-Godavari and Cauvery basins offers an opportunity to add small-sized gas-based plants in these regions. Subject to finding an effective transport route, surplus gas available in North Eastern region can be utilised for fertiliser production. There is also a need to promote use of low cost bio-fertilisers.

The raw material reserves for phosphatic fertilisers in the country are negligible. The choice is to import either rock phosphate and sulphur or intermediates like phos-acid or phosphatic fertiliser itself. The policy of a judicious mix of import of finished fertilisers and production of fertilisers through raw materials and intermediates would continue.

The prices of fertilisers are controlled. As retail prices are considerably lower than the fair cost of production plus freight, the manufacturers are compensated for the difference under the production-*cum*-transfer subsidy system. Calculation of fair prices is based on reasonable norms of production level, energy consumption, working capital margin etc. The pricing norms have been gradually tightened over successive pricing periods, each lasting 3 years. Despite this, the subsidy burden has been steadily increasing due to (i) escalations in the costs of inputs which are not compensated by corresponding increases in the retail prices of fertilisers; (ii) increase in the volume of production of fertilisers; and (iii) high capital costs of new fertiliser plants. On the other hand, the fertiliser industry has been complaining that though it is assured of a 12 per cent post-tax return on net worth, in actual practice, a number of items are excluded. Besides, there are inordinate delays in the release of the subsidy, adversely affecting the financial position of the fertiliser companies. There is a general feeling that the system of retention prices is not conducive to optimisation of the capital costs and operating efficiencies.

Complete de-control of prices can end the subsidy and pricing problem altogether. This will be in line with the philosophy of greater reliance on market forces and appears to be the most desirable option for solving the problem of mounting subsidies on the one hand and ensuring healthy growth of the fertiliser industry on the other. This will, of course, have to be accompanied by suitable increases in the procurement prices of agricultural products. However, this can have an adverse effect on the consumption of fertilisers especially by small and marginal farmers in the initial years. Phasing out subsidy will, therefore, have to be done gradually, giving time to farmers to adjust.

Group retention prices for newer plants based on gas can be introduced as an interim measure. This will be the second best option and it will give incentive to the new fertiliser plants to optimise the capital and operating costs.

There is a need to promote the use of slow release fertilisers through appropriate fiscal measures so as to optimise the nutrient usage. The use of bio-fertilisers also needs to be encouraged. These are environment-friendly, low cost inputs.

Petrochemicals

The petrochemicals industry, mainly based on a range of products derived from petroleum and natural gas, is highly capital and technology intensive. Being relatively new, the industry has the advantage of using state-of-the-art technologies, the production being internationally competitive. However, the industry suffers from the disadvantages of high input costs and high rates of taxes and duties. The result is that the prices of petrochemicals in the country are way above the international prices.

During the Seventh Plan, implementation of Maharashtra Gas Cracker Complex (MGCC) at Nagothane, with a capacity of 300,000 tpa of Ethylene, was taken up by IPCL. Because of an unfortunate accident, the project got delayed and was commissioned only in the last quarter of 1991-92. Besides, IPCL has implemented a number of schemes for rehabilitation/expansion of its Polypropylene (PP) plant, revamping of its naphtha cracker, additional Xylenes production, Bicomponent Acrylic Fibre, etc. at its Baroda Complex. The other major facilities commissioned are : Aromatics plants of Bharat Petroleum Corporation Ltd. (BPCL), Bombay and Cochin Refineries Ltd.(CRL), Cochin and a number of downstream units based on availability of propylene from refineries at Vizag, Madras and Bombay.

The petrochemicals industry has now been delicensed. Letters of Intent were earlier issued for setting up crackers at Hazira, Auraiya, Gandhar, Vizag, Haldia and Assam and for expansion of NOCIL cracker. The work on these crackers is in initial stages. It is expected that based on market considerations, these crackers would get phased suitably.

During the Eighth Plan, greater emphasis would be laid on performance plastics, (polyamides, polyacetals, polycarbonates, ABS) consumption of which is linked to the growth of automobile, electronics, telecommunication and other consumer items. The changing Indian scene with multi-fold growth of above industries would push the growth in consumption of these performance plastics. Application Development Centres are being set up to propagate use of performance plastics. Petrochemicals industry is technology intensive and linkages between research, manufacturing, design, engineering and academics are proposed to be strengthened.

Drugs and Pharmaceuticals

Indian drug industry manufactures a wide range of basic drugs and pharmaceuticals covering almost all therapeutic regimes. These include antibiotics, bacterials, steroids and hormones, vaccines, psychotropic preparations and a wide variety of synthetic drugs, including herbal preparations. The industry is quite widely distributed among FERA companies, public and private sector units and other medium scale units specialising in a few drugs. There were about 14,000 units producing drugs/formulations at the end of 1991-92. More than 30% of production of bulk drugs comes from units in the small scale sector, which, in turn, base their production on penultimate intermediates for a large number of items.

There are five public sector units namely, Indian Drugs and Pharmaceuticals Ltd.(IDPL), Hindustan Antibiotics Ltd.(HAL), Bengal Immunity Ltd.(BIL), Bengal Chemicals & Pharmaceuticals Ltd. (BCPL) and Smith Stanistreet Pharmaceuticals Ltd. (SSPL) . All of them, except

HAL, have been in the red mainly due to outmoded plants, inefficient technology, high labour costs, weak marketing efforts, concentration on bulk drugs manufacture and excessive reliance on institutional or traditional sales outlets etc.

Since introduction of the Drug Price Control Order (DPCO), 1986, the pharmaceuticals industry has witnessed a good growth and for the last three years, the country has been a net exporter of drugs. In line with the prevailing economic environment, there is a need to review the DPCO and allow greater freedom to the industry in the matter of price fixation. While price control may be continued tor a few life-saving drugs, the firms producing such drugs may be allowed to diversify into other areas where they can make enough profit to off-set these losses. Alternatively, the Government could consider subsidising the use of such essential life-saving drugs by poorer sections of the society while allowing the fixation of their prices by the market.

A strong technology base for the drug industry is necessary for its healthy development. This calls for vigorous and sustained R&D efforts. So far, the main thrust has been on process improvement and not much effort has been made to produce new drugs from the basic stage. During the last decade, processes for some of the important intermediates and raw materials have been developed within the country. A number of R&D Programmes have been identified to be taken up in a co-ordinated manner in the national laboratories, public sector undertakings and private sector units. Development of sophisticated formulations such as slow release forms, advanced drug delivery systems, etc., will also receive due attention. Research and development in the area of bio-technology by an understanding of DNA replication mechanism related to the country's needs will also receive due emphasis. Pollution control measures, industrial safety and energy conservation will be considered as integral parts of production activities.

Pesticides

As more and more farmers are adopting multi-cropping practices using hybrid seeds, pesticides have become an important input to minimise crop losses and also as part of public health programme. Pesticides are first manufactured as technical grade chemicals, which are subsequently formulated in ready-to-use form both in the organised sector and small industries. As many as 137 pesticides have been approved for use in India, out of which, two (*i.e.* DDT/BHC) are high volume pesticides. The others are largely used by farmers for fighting pests of a variety of crops such as fruits, vegetables, cotton, groundnut, sugarcane, rice, wheat, etc.

The country is largely self-sufficient in the manufacture of pesticides but some of the intermediates as also new varieties of insecticides are being imported. During the Seventh Plan, a number of new pesticides such as Butachlor, Isoproturon, Monocrotophos as well as Pyrethroids were taken up for manufacture to meet the specialised needs of the agricultural sector.

There is now greater awareness of environmental pollution and safety aspects and the new pesticides have to satisfy these criteria before being certified for use. DDT has been banned in Europe and U.S.A. as it was found to enter the human food chain ultimately. DDT production by Hindustan Insecticides Ltd. would also need to be gradually phased out. Existing centres in the country dealing with environmental and health monitoring of toxic substances under CSIR, ICMR and ICAR need to be upgraded to create facilities for regular monitoring of pesticides in the environment, with a view to minimising environmental and occupational health problems.

A UNDP aided Pesticides Development Programme has been taken up. The main objectives of this are :

(i) Development of new formulations of pesticides, suiting the requirement of crops and agro-climatic conditions of India;

(ii) To upgrade technical competence of personnel engaged in production, quality control and hazard management in the pesticide industry; and

(iii) Conducting training programmes on quality control for the industry personnel.

Cement

The gradual decontrol of cement has resulted in progressive increase in cement production as well as upgradation of technology. The country has now emerged as an exporter of cement. Besides, a good resource base, India has locational advantage in respect of cement trade as a number of neighbouring countries are importers of cement. The newer cement plants compare well with the plants in the world in terms of productivity and production cost and the country can easily export about 5 million tonnes per annum by 1996-97.

Sugar

India is the largest producer of sugarcane as well as sugar in the world. The sugar industry is the second largest agro-based industry in India. While the new generation of 2500 tpd mills produce better results, a number of old mills are in need of modernisation. Introduction of co-generation, electronic controls is being encouraged to optimise production parameters and improve productivity. Future sugar complexes should provide for down-stream industries using molasses and bagasse as raw-materials. To facilitate this molasses should be decontrolled so that the sugar complexes can be developed for optimal benefits. After many years, the country has resumed sugar export. Such exports should be on a continuous basis and should not be determined on a year to year basis.

Leather and leather goods

Leather and leather goods industry has emerged as one of the important foreign exchange earners in recent years. During the Seventh Plan, the value of exports rose from a level of Rs. 584 crores to Rs. 2030 crores. There is a constraint on the availability of hides and skins, especially for export production. To bridge the gap between the requirement and availability of hides and skins, a series of measures would be necessary. These include setting up of a network of mini-modern carcass recovery centres all over the country, use of improved flaying tools and techniques and viable modern slaughter houses.

Textiles

Textile industry is the single largest industry in India, accounting for about twenty per cent of the total industrial output and providing employment to around 15 million people. It is also an important contributor to India's exports, accounting for 26 per cent of the total value of exports in 1990-91. The textile industry passed through a severe crisis in the early part of the Seventh Plan mainly due to high cost of raw materials and labour, obsolete machinery, demand recession and competition from the powerloom sector. In order to promote modernisation of the industry, Textile Modernisation Fund (TMF) was introduced in 1986 with a corpus of Rs. 750 crores. The response of the industry has been quite encouraging and it is proposed to continue TMF during the Eighth Plan.

The progress and implementation of the Textile Policy,1985 were reviewed by a high powered committee set up in May, 1988 under the Chairmanship of Shri Abid Hussain, the then Member, Planning Commission. The committee has focused on the institutional arrangements needed for restructuring of textile industry for its integrated development. The major recommendations of the Committee include restructuring and modernisation of the organised mill sector and institutional arrangements like Textile Restructuring Asset Trusts (TRATs) for improving its efficiency; institutional arrangements for area-based development of handloom and powerloom sectors; upgradation of cotton processing facilities; pre-eminent role of cotton as the main raw material, realistic pricing of synthetic fibres/yarns; devising ways and means for increasing textile exports; and upgradation of technology in the readymade garments and textile machinery industries.

In the Eighth Plan, greater emphasis will be laid on production of value-added, diversified and quality goods for export and increasing capacity utilisation, sophisticated design and product-mix and appropriate technology. The organised mill sector would concentrate increasingly on exports with bulk of the indigenous demand being met by the powerloom sector. The handloom sector will concentrate on high value products for domestic as well as export markets. The textile exports are expected to be Rs. 28,000 crores in 1996-97 at a compound growth rate of 18% per annum. To achieve this, emphasis will be laid on exports of non-quota items, higher unit-value realisation and better marketing techniques.

Jute

The jute industry passed through a severe crisis in the early part of the Seventh Plan due to demand recession, imbalance in cost price structure and competition from synthetic packaging materials. The absence of desired thrust on modernisation/diversification and widespread sickness in the jute industry led to closure of a number of mills. In 1986, the Government announced a package of policy measures consisting of Jute Modernisation Fund Scheme (JMFS) of Rs. 150 crores, Special Jute Development Fund (SJDF) of Rs. 100 crores, duty free import of identified jute machinery items for modernisation and mandatory usage of jute packaging materials by specified end-user sectors. However, the pace of modernisation has been rather slow. As stated earlier, not only is this to be speeded up but jute industry will have to concentrate on diversification and production of high value products. The mandatory usage of jute for packaging should only be a temporary feature. Ultimately jute must compete on its inherent strengths.

Paper and Paper Board Industry

Paper Industry in India is more than a century old. The capacity is almost evenly divided between the large units (organised sector) and a number of small paper mills scattered throughout the country and mostly based on non-wood materials such as bagasse, fibrous crop residues, jute cuttings, cotton waste, cotton rags and waste paper, etc.

The main problems facing the large paper mills are inadequate availability of forest based raw materials, technological obsolescence, high energy consumption, high capital cost of modernisation, high cost of inputs, management deficiencies and scarcity of skilled labour. In the case of small paper mills, the problems are inefficient chemical recovery systems leading to high production cost as well as environmental pollution, obsolete equipment with low productivity and high energy consumption and shortage of raw materials. The National Forest Policy has ruled out captive industrial plantations and requires paper and other forest-based industries to procure their raw materials by establishing direct relationship with individual growers of trees. However, this arrangement has proved to be unworkable because growing trees takes 7-8 years. It is, therefore, imperative to review this aspect and consider making available degraded and waste lands to the industry for captive plantations. Privately owned lands should also be allowed to be used for plantations. The paper industry would also need to switch over as much of the existing capacity as possible to the use of bagasse and other agricultural wastes and modernise its equipment accordingly.

With steady increase in sugar production, there is a need for forward planning and integrating paper production with sugar production, using bagasse as the raw material. Such a plant has already been operating successfully in Tamil Nadu. Many more such plants need to be planned. This requires adequate supply of coal or some other alternative fuel, for feeding the boilers of sugar mills and co-generating power for paper production.

Newsprint

There are two major projects under implementation — Uttar Pradesh bagasse based newsprint project of NEPA with a capacity of 89,000 tonnes per annum and 200 tpd composite newsprint and printing and writing paper project of Punjab Agro Newsprints Ltd. Both these projects are scheduled to be completed by the end of the Eighth Plan. The newsprint manufacture is capital intensive and involves long gestation period. Even though the prices are not administered, profitability is comparatively low and the private sector is not coming forward to take up manufacture of newsprint. The country is spending about Rs. 300 crores of foreign exchange per annum on newsprint import. There is a need to encourage creation of bagasse based additional capacity in tandem with new sugar capacity. Such "Integrated sugar/newsprint Units" would have many external economies and would improve viability of both the industries.

Atomic Energy

The activities of the Department of Atomic Energy under Industry and Minerals sector pertains to requirement of heavy water, nuclear fuel, instruments and controls, spent fuel recovery and waste disposal for the nuclear power reactors.

During the Seventh Plan, the on-going heavy water project at Thal was completed and commissioned in 1986. The Manuguru project got inordinately delayed. It commenced production in March, 1991 alongwith the heavy water plant at Hazira taken up during the Seventh Plan.

The production of heavy water has been well below the capacity at most of the plants due to a variety of reasons such as feed limitation (Talcher, Nangal and Thal), steam and power limitations (Kota), reduced level of deuterium in the feed (Baroda, Tuticorin and Thal), etc. Efforts should be made to eliminate these limitations for a reasonable level of production.

The performance of Hazira and Manuguru Plants is expected to be quite good in view of the improvements made over the previous plants and provision of a captive power plant at Manuguru.

The following new units are proposed to be taken up during the Eighth Plan:

(i) A new Uranium Oxide Fuel Plant at Hyderabad;

(ii) A new Uranium Oxide Fuel Assembly Plant at Hyderabad;

(iii) Zirconium and Titanium Sponge Plants;

(iv) A Spent Fuel Reprocessing Plant at a greenfield site.

Titanium Sponge Plant and Zirconium Sponge Plant will be put up in same premises as a number of facilities are common. The possibility of setting up these units in the private sector is being explored.

15

RECENT DEVELOPMENTS IN INDIAN INDUSTRY

There was a modest recovery in the industrial growth to 4.1 per cent in 1993-94 and a more impressive surge to 8.0 per cent in April-October 1994. As per an advance index of industrial production (with a weight of 50 per cent in the Index of Industrial Production IIP), the industrial sector registered a growth of 9.3 per cent during April-December 1994. There are clear indications that a substantial and broad based industrial recovery is under way, following the economic policy reforms of the early 1990s. The capital goods sector, which had been in doldrums earlier, has emerged as a leading contributor to industrial buoyancy, turning in a growth of 21.7 per cent in April-October, 1994. This strong growth is partly attributable to the policy package in the 1994-95 Budget and partly reflects the normal lag in investment goods demand in response to recovery in other industrial sectors which was already detectable in the latter half of 1993-94. Consumer goods, both consumer durables and consumer non-durables, are also performing very well. Textile products other than cotton and jute, paper and paper products, metals and metal products, electrical machinery and transport equipment have continued to record substantial growth. Six major infrastructural industries, *viz.* electricity generation, coal, iron and steel, cement, crude oil and refinery products, constituting a 28.8 per cent weight in the IIP, maintained their general uptrend and registered a growth rate of 8.0 per cent during April-December 1994. The investment climate is strongly buoyant.

Major policy initiatives taken during the year 1994-95 included delicensing of almosts all bulk drugs and allowing automatic approval of foreign equity up to 51 per cent in most drugs and formulations. Basic telecommunication services, hitherto reserved for the public sector, were opened for private sector participation. Another healthy development is that many states are undertaking procedural and policy reforms to effect liberalisation at the grass root level. Of particular interest, is the bold new industrial policy of West Bengal, which aims to encourage private domestic and foreign investment in the state's economy.

The Indian industry is on a firm recovery course, with significant improvement in manufacturing production. The IIP registered a growth rate of 8.0 per cent in April-October 1994, compared to only 3.8 per cent in April-October 1993.

It is generally accepted that the existing data collection system does not fully capture the growth of some sectors, particularly small scale industries. This is due to non-availability of data for the unorganised sector and non-reporting, to some extent, by the organised sector. Considering the need for improvement in the methodology and data base for estimation of IIP, the base year of IIP is being shifted from 1980-81 to 1985-86, with a revised items basket and improved weighting diagram. The system of data collection for the industrial sector is also being strengthened and reviewed.

Industrial Policy Reforms

The process of industrial policy reforms initiated since July 1991 continued during the year. The policy changes during 1994-95 *inter-alia* included extension of MODVAT to more sectors, a thorough overhaul of the excise tax structure, further rationalisation and reduction of customs duties, deregulation of bank lending rates, delicensing of most drugs and pharmaceutical products and liberalisation of the telecommunications sector.

Reforms in Industrial Sector

Industrial licensing for almost all bulk drugs has been abolished.

Automatic approval of foreign investment upto 51 per cent and foreign technology agreements is permitted for all bulk drugs and formulations, barring only a few.

Basic telecommunication services have been opened to private participation, including foreign investments. Minimum lending rates for amounts over Rs. 2 lakh have been abolished. The rate for advances between Rs. 25000 and Rs. 2 lakh has been reduced to 13.5 per cent.

SLR is reduced to 31 .5 per cent to make more credit available for the commercial sector.

Import duties on capital goods have been reduced to 15 per cent on export related capital goods, 25 per cent for project imports and most capital goods, and concessional duties at 20 per cent for power projects, and nil for fertilizer projects have been continued.

MODVAT has been extended to capital goods and petroleum products.

Corporate tax has been reduced from 45 per cent for widely held companies and 50 per cent for closely held companies to 40 per cent for domestic companies, and from 65 per cent to 55 per cent for foreign companies.

The five year tax holiday to new industrial undertakings initially allowed for industrially backward states in the Budget for 1993 94, has been extended to all backward areas to be notified by the Department of Revenue.

Excise tax structure has undergone major overhaul, including rationalization of rates, elimination of most end-use exemptions and a general shift from specific to ad valorem duties.

Reforms in customs duties, including reduction of the peak tariff rate, elimination of most end-use exemptions and removal of exemptions from countervailing duties have continued.

In recent years, State Governments have also taken significant initiatives in the reform process and implementation of the new industrial policy.

Industrial Production 1993-94

The General Index of Industrial Production (IIP) recorded a growth of 4.1 per cent during 1993 -94, aided by a growth of 2.5 per cent in mining and quarrying, 7.4 per cent in electricity and 3.6 per cent in manufacturing. All the major sectors performed better during 1993-94, compared to 1992-93. Table 1 shows annual growth rates in major sectors of industry.

An analysis of IIP at the disaggregated level shows that only 4 groups, *viz.* food products, other textile products, electrical machinery and miscellaneous industries (with a combined weight of 12.8 per cent) of the 17 major industry groups in the manufacturing sector recorded negative growth rates during 1993-94. On the other hand, beverages and tobacco recorded the highest growth (21.3 per cent). Jute textiles, paper and paper products, leather and fur products, chemical and chemical products and basic metals registered growth rates exceeding 6.0 per cent. The slow progress of industrial growth in 1993-94 is attributable to a number of factors, such as inherent adjustment lags in the process of restructuring, slowdown in investments and imports, still high rates of interest and corporate taxes and better utilisation of inventories.

TABLE 1

Annual Growth Rates in Major Sectors of Industry

(Per cent)

Year	Mining	Manufacturing	Electricity	General
1	2	3	4	5
1981-82	17.7	7.9	10.2	9.3
1982-83	12.4	1.4	5.7	3.2
1983-84	11.8	5.7	7.6	6.7
1984-85	8.8	8.0	12.0	8.6
1985-86	4.1	9.7	8.5	8.7
1986-87	6.2	9.4	10.3	9.2
1987-88	3.8	7.9	7.6	7.3
1988-89	7.9	8.7	9.5	8.7
1989-90	6.3	8.6	10.8	8.6
1990-91	4.5	8.9	7.8	8.3
Average 1980-81 to 1990-91)	8.4	7.6	9.0	7.9
1991-92	0.6	– 0.8	8.5	0.6
1992-93	0.6	2.2	5.0	2.3
1993-94	2.5	3.6	7.4	4.1
April-Oct.				
1992-93	– 0.2	4.6	4.3	4.0
1993-94	3.1	3.1	7.7	3.8
1994-95	6.2	8.3	7.7	8.0

Industrial Production 1994-95

The overall industrial production during April-October 1994-95 registered an increase of 8.0 per cent, supported by a growth of 8.3 per cent in manufacturing, 7.7 per cent in electricity and 6.2 per cent in mining and quarrying. As per the advance index of industrial production provided by the Industry Ministry, 24 major industries having a weight of 50 per cent in the IIP, recorded a growth rate of 9.3 per cent in April-December 1994, compared with 5.0 per cent in April-December, 1993. Commercial vehicles registered an impressive growth of 52.5 per cent in April-December 1994, compared with a decline of 1.6 per cent during April-December, 1993.

An analysis of the growth rates of 17 broad groups within the manufacturing sector reveals that only four sectors, *viz.* cotton textiles, jute textiles, basic metals and miscellaneous manufacturing industries, with a combined weight of 25.0 per cent recorded negative growth rates during April-October 1994. However, the decline in cotton textiles was only marginal. All other groups, with a combined weight of 52.1 per cent, recorded positive growth rates. Other textile products, paper and paper products, electrical machinery, metal products and transport equipment recorded growth rates exceeding 12 per cent. This clearly indicates that the industrial turnaround during 1994-95 has been widespread.

The performance of the capital goods sector has been very impressive. It registered a growth rate of 21.7 per cent in April-October 1994, in contrast to a decline of 8.7 per cent in April-October 1993. Basic goods (4.2 per cent), intermediate goods (4.6 per cent), consumer durables (8.6 per cent) and consumer non-durables (7.0 per cent) also exhibited a good performance.

An analysis of the production data for April-October 1994 in respect of 172 selected industries, accounting for a weight of 88.1 per cent in the IIP, shows that generally the industrial recovery was widespread, except for a few products such as Sugar, Railway Wagons, Ship Building, Jute Manufactures, Jeeps, Graphite Electrodes & Anodes, Machine Tools and Diesel Engines. 121 industries with a weight of 74.2 per cent recorded positive growth rates and 51 industries with a weight of 13.9 per cent registered a negative growth. Some important industries which recorded growth rates of over 10 per cent include Radio Receivers (397.0 per cent), Road Rollers (369.2 per cent), Tetracycline (73.8 per cent), Apatite and Phosphorite (64.9 per cent), Commercial Vehicles (64.9 per cent), Polythylene L.D. (63.8 per cent), Phosphatic Fertilizers (47.4 per cent), Electric Generators (37.2 per cent), Earth Moving Equipment (28.9 per cent), Penicillin (20.7 per cent), Crude Petroleum (17.5 per cent), Cloth (decentralised sector) (16.9 per cent), Auto Ancillaries (15.5 per cent), Paper and Paper Board (14.5 per cent), Giant Tyres (14.1 per cent), Agricultural Tractors (12.5 per cent), Leather Cloth (10.5 per cent). However, their performance was partially offset by a decline in output in several sectors such as Railway Wagons (— 28.5 per cent), Jute Manufactures (— 12.9 per cent), Jeeps (— 10.1 per cent), Graphite Electrodes & Anodes (— 8.9 per cent), Sugar (— 6.9 per cent), Machine Tools (— 5.1 per cent), Ship Building (including repair) (— 5. I per cent), Caustic Soda (— 3.4 per cent), and Diesel Engines (— 3. I per cent).

Index of Industrial Production

The current IIP (Base 1980-81=100) covers 352 items. It is generally agreed that the SSI sector, which is a dynamic and fast growing sector of the Indian economy, remains under-represented in the weighting diagram due to non-availability of data; in particular, export-oriented segments like garments, leather, gems and jewellery remain under-represented. The 1980-81 weights do not also represent fully some organised sectors such as automobiles, leather goods and electronics, which showed substantial dynamism in the 1980s and 1990s. Further, there have been some slippages in data reporting after the delicensing of most industries since July 1991 and subsequent winding up of the DGTD. It is, therefore, felt that there is a need to shift the base to a more recent year and to have a more representative weighting diagram. After considered deliberations on the need for such a revision and difficulties that exist in data availability, the base year of IIP is being shifted from 1980-81 to 1985-86, and the number of items is being increased from 352 to 375. There are 28 new items, and 18 items as reported by DCSSI are included in the new index. The revised series has been tested for consistency with the earlier series at a 2 digit level and has been found to be largely satisfactory.

However, there is a need for continuous improvement to overcome a few problems that still persist. The small scale sector needs to be fully represented. The IIP needs to capture the dynamism and emerging scenario in the industrial sector as precisely as possible. The data collection and availability should be timely and accurate. It is, therefore, essential that an independent industrial reporting system be set up and the reporting be made compulsory for items covered in the index.

Investment Scenario

Economic reforms have had a positive impact on the investment climate in the country. They have also evoked a strong positive response from foreign investors and portfolio managers. The conventional indicators suggest that both the investment climate and the capital market remain buoyant. The buoyancy is reinforced by an increasing number of capital issues by Indian companies in both the domestic market and abroad, and the upgrading of Indian sovereign rating by international credit rating agencies such as the Japan Bond Research Institute (JBRI) and Moody's Investors Service.

There has been an encouraging trend in domestic investment, as is evident from sanctions and disbursements of term loans by All India Financial Institutions and capital market operations.

While the sanctions recorded an increase of 26.8 per cent in 1993-94, disbursements went up by 15.1 per cent. The financial assistance sanctioned by these institutions in April-December 1994 recorded an impressive growth of 59.2 per cent, but the disbursements showed a lower growth of 26.3 per cent mainly because of the availability of alternative cheap funds through Euro issues of convertible debentures and GDRs. The increase in financial assistance was supplemented by the buoyancy in the capital market.

The number of Industrial Entrepreneurs Memorandum (IEM) filed from 1991 to 1994 totalled 17,014, with an overall investment intention of Rs. 345000 crore.

The response by foreign investors was also encouraging. During the period from 1991 to 1994, the Government approved 5778 foreign collaboration proposals including 2806 foreign equity proposals amounting to Rs. 2223 8 crore. More than 80 per cent of these approvals are in priority sectors such as power generation, oil refinery, electrical equipment, chemicals and export related sectors. As a consequence of the amendments in FERA and the liberalization of foreign investment policy, many MNCs have increased their equity to over 51 per cent. Many companies like Coca Cola, IBM, which disinvested in the 1970s, have returned to India to avail of the new opportunities. Even in areas still reserved for the public sector (telecommunication, hydro carbons, coal, railways and postal services), the Government has adopted a more liberal approach towards private investments, including foreign investments.

In 1994-95, foreign investment was allowed for NRIs and persons of Indian origin in a wide range of construction and real estate related activities. Foreign investment was also allowed in constructing and operating highways, expressways and bridges on a toll tax system, generating electricity on Build-Operate Own (BOO) basis, basic telephone services and certain operations in railways on Build-Operate-Lease-Transfer (BOLT) basis. Without prior approvals, foreign investors can now own up to 24 per cent equity in any Indian firm and up to 20 per cent in new private banks.

Reforms in Public Sector Enterprises

The Industrial Policy Statement announced by Government in July 1991 envisaged disinvestment of a part of Government holdings in the share capital of selected Public Sector Enterprises (PSEs) in order to provide market discipline and to improve the performance of public enterprises. A total amount of Rs. 4950 crore has already been disinvested to the public sector financial institutions, mutual funds and general public till March 1994.

To protect the interests of public sector workers, a National Renewal Fund (NRF) was set up in February 1992 and schemes have been proposed to assist the employees in re-training, redeployment and counselling. Provision of funds through NRF also exists for cases where workers retire voluntarily or are declared surplus. To implement the NRF schemes an empowered authority has been created and a provision of Rs. 700 crore has been made in the current year's budget. An amount of Rs. 542.23 crore was released from NRF during 1993-94 and an estimated 75000 workers had opted for voluntary retirement under the scheme. A major portion of the amount has been utilised in the textiles sector.

In order to establish a system of rehabilitation and restructuring of PSUs without having Government to bear the whole financial burden, the provisions of the Sick Industrial Companies Act (SICA) have been amended to bring PSUs under its purview. Till the end of November '94, 52 central PSUs have already been registered with BIFR. BIFR have so far issued orders for revival of I.D.P.L. and Biecco Lawrie Ltd. They have also so far recommended the winding up of National Bicycle Corporation Ltd, Cawnpore Textiles Ltd. Elgin Mills Ltd and British India Corporation Ltd.

Performance of Selected Public Sector Undertakings

As on March 31, 1994 there were 240 Central Public Sector Undertakings (PSUs), excluding nine companies with Central Government investment but without direct responsibility for management, six insurance companies and three financial institutions. Of these, six were in the construction sector, 74 in services and 166 in manufacture.

Out of 240 operating PSUs, as many as 120 were profitable during 1993-94 as compared to 131 during the previous year. Profits of these profit-making enterprises went up from Rs. 7384 crore in 1992-93 to Rs. 9722 crore in 1993-94 an increase of 31.7 per cent (Table 2). But the losses of the remaining loss-making companies increased from Rs. 4113 crore to Rs. 5287 crore, an increase of over 28.5 per cent, during the same period. The overall rate of return over capital employed in the PSUs increased from 2.33 per cent during 1992-93 to 2.78 per cent during 1993-94. But the gross margin (*i.e.*, before depreciation, interest and taxes) of PSUs as per cent of capital employed declined from 18.01 in 1992-93 to 17.33 in 1993-94. The heavy capital investment in the past combined with a massive interest burden is reported to have reduced the gross margins of PSUs.

TABLE 2

Profitability Profile of Central PSEs

	1981-82	1990-91	1991-92	1992-93	1993-94
1	2	3	4	5	6
1. Operating enterprises	188	236	237	239	240
(i) Profitable enterprises	104	123	133	131	120
(ii) Loss-making enterprises	83	111	102	106	117
			(Rs. Crore)		
2. Capital employed	21935	102083	117991	140110	159307
3. Gross margin	4012	18312	22223	25227	27600
4. Gross profit	2654	11102	13675	15957	18438
5. Net profit	445	2272	2355	3271	4435
6. Profit of Profit-making enterprises	1293	5394	6079	7384	9722
7. Losses of loss-making enterprises	848	3122	3723	4113	5287
			(Per cent)		
8. Ratio of gross margin to capital employed	18.29	17.94	18.83	18.01	17.33
9. Percentage of gross profit to capital employed	12.10	10.88	11.59	11.39	11.59
10. Ratio of net profit to capital employed	2.03	2.23	2.00	2.33	2.78

The profitability of PSUs in terms of ratios of gross margins and gross profits to capital employed have not improved over the last ten years. However, the ratio of net profit to capital employed showed marginal improvement in 1993-94. Out of the 15 large enterprises, which are monopolies and operate in the core sector, the loss-making ones included Fertiliser Corporation of India, Indian Airlines Corporation, Delhi Transport Corporation, Vayudoot, Bharat Gold Mines and Rashtriya Ispat Nigam and Hindustan Shipyard.

The Memorandum of Understanding (MOU) system has been further strengthened. During 1993-94,101 PSEs signed MOUs as against 98 in the preceding year. Based on their audited accounts, performance of 100 PSEs was evaluated, out of which 46 were rated excellent (46 per cent), 29 as very good (29 per cent). 12 as good and 10 fair. In 1994-95, 106 PSEs have signed MOUs which is five per cent higher than last year.

TABLE 3

Year-wise/PSU-wise Details of Shares Disinvested Since 1991-92

S.No.	Name of the PSE	% of Central Govt. Holding				
		1.7.91	31.3.92	31.3.93	31.3.94	31.12.94
1	2	3	4	5	6	7
1.	Andrew Yule	71.30	62.80	62.80	62.80	62.80
2.	Bharat Earthmovers Ltd.	100.00	80.00	80.00	80.00	60.08
3.	Bharat Electronics Ltd.	100.00	80.00	80.00	80.00	75.86
4.	Bharat Heavy Electricals Ltd.	100.00	80.00	79.54	79.46	68.46
5.	Bharat Petroleum Corpn. Ltd.	100.00	80.00	70.00	69.62	69.62
6.	Bongaigaon Refineries and Petro. Ltd.	100.00	80.00	74.60	74.59	74.59
7.	CMC Ltd.	100.00	83.31	83.31	83.31	83.31
8.	Cochin Refineries Ltd.	61.16	55.04	55.04	55.04	55.04
9.	Dredging Corpn. Ltd.	100.00	98.56	98.56	98.56	98.56
10.	Fert. & Chem. (Travancore) Ltd.	98.99	97.46	97.35	97.35	97.35
11.	HMT Ltd.	100.00	95.14	90.32	90.32	90.32
12.	Hindustan Cables Ltd.	100.00	96.36	97.97	97.97	97.97
13.	Hindustan Copper. Ltd.	100.00	100.00	98.88	98.88	98.88
14.	Hindustan Organic Chemicals Ltd.[1]	100.00	80.00	80.00	80.00	80.00
15.	Hindustan Petroleum Corpn. Ltd.	100.00	80.00	70.00	69.72	62.72
16.	Hindustan Photofilms Mfg. Co. Ltd.	100.00	87.47	87.47	87.47	87.47
17.	Hindustan Zinc Ltd.	100.00	80.04	75.93	75.93	75.93
18.	Indian Petrochemicals Corpn. Ltd.[2]	100.00	80.00	80.97	62.40	62.40
19.	Indian Railway Const. Co. Ltd.	100.00	99.74	99.74	99.74	99.74
20.	Indian Telephone Industries Ltd.	99.65	79.72	77.79	77.67	77.67
21.	Madras Refineries Ltd.	84.62	67.70	67.70	51.80	51.80
22.	Mahanagar Telephone Nigam Ltd.	100.00	80.00	80.00	80.00	67.18
23.	Minerals & Metals Trading Corpn.	100.00	99.33	99.33	99.33	99.33
24.	National Aluminium Co. Ltd.	100.00	97.28	87.20	87.19	87.19
25.	National Fertilizers Ltd.	100.00	97.72	97.66	97.66	97.65
26.	National Mineral dev. Corpn. Ltd.	100.00	100.00	98.38	98.38	98.38
27.	Neyveli Lignite Corporation[2]	100.00	95.42	93.86	94.19	94.19
28.	Rashtriya Chemicals & Fertilizers	100.00	94.36	92.50	92.50	92.50
29.	Shipping Corpn. of India	100.00	81.49	81.49	81.49	80.12
30.	State Trading Corpn.	100.00	92.02	91.02	91.02	91.02
31.	Steel Authority of India Ltd.	100.00	95.01	89.49	89.45	89.36
32.	Videsh Sanchar Nigam Ltd.	100.00	85.00	85.00	85.00	85.00
33.	Container Corporation of India	100.00	100.00	100.00	100.00	80.00
34.	Indian Oil Corporation	99.88	99.88	99.88	99.88	88.17
35.	Oil & Natural Gas Corporation	100.00	100.00	100.00	100.00	98.00

[1] Recently the company had come out with public issue.
DPE don't have the latest details of Govt. holding after completation of public issue. The above information is based on approval given by the Govt.

[2] Due to further release of equity by Govt.

Since July 1991, the Government has also been disinvesting a part of its equity held in selected PSEs. Table 3 indicates changes in Central government equities in 35 selected public sector enterprises, where it has approved disinvestments, until the end of December 1994.

PERFORMANCE OF SELECTED INDUSTRIES

Steel

The production of various types of steel, after being sluggish in the last 2/3 years, has picked up significantly in 1994-95. The Budget for 1994-95 reduced the peak import duties on steel from 75-80 to 50 per cent and the duty on HR coils from 50 per cent to 40 per cent *ad valorem.*

The production of saleable steel by SAIL and VSP increased by 7.9 per cent in April-November 1994, compared with 6.7 per cent in 1993-94. Production of saleable pig iron by main producers registered growth rates above 15 per cent during 1993-94 and April-November 1994. While the production of finished steel by main producers recorded a reasonable growth, there was some slippage in production by secondary producers.

The exports of iron and steel increased by 144 per cent to 22.2 lakh tonnes in 1993-94. But exports of iron and steel so far have declined in 1994-95 due to various factors such as increase in domestic demand and reduced imports by major countries like China. Despite significant liberalisation, imports of steel remained almost stationary around an average annual level of 1.15 million tonnes in 1990—1994.

Liberalisation has brought about a qualitative change in the Indian iron and steel sector. With delicensing and decontrol of the steel industry and reduction of import duties on iron and steel items, producers have become more responsive to consumer needs. There is also increasing awareness of the need to improve quality and cut down costs.

Sugar

The sugar Industry is one of the few industries which consistently maintained a high growth in the three years ending 1991-92. The average annual growth of production of sugarcane in the past 3 years up to 1991-92 was 7.8 per cent. However, sugar production during the sugar year 1992-93 (October-September) at 106.09 lakh tonnes was 20.9 per cent less than the previous year's production. The recovery rate has shown an improving trend during the past 3 years. The production of sugar for the season 1993-94 was about 98 lakh tonnes. The decline in the 1993-94 season can be attributed to higher diversion of cane to gur and khandsari and fall in cane/sugar production in the major sugar producing state of

Maharashtra. However, since August 1994, sugar production has shown substantial buoyancy. It increased by 128.4 per cent during (Aug.—Oct.) 1994. The production of sugar is expected to go up by 20.0 per cent in 1994-95.

As reported in the last year's Economic Survey, sugar continues to be extremely controlled. The sugar industry continues to remain under a compulsory licensing regime. There is a Statutory Minimum Price (SMP) for sugarcane, fixed by the Central Government and State Advised Prices (SAP), over and above the SMP, fixed by the State Governments. SMP fixed for sugarcane for the sugar season (October-September) 1993-94 was Rs. 34.50 per quintal, linked to a sugar recovery of 8.5 per cent. The SAP varied from Rs. 36.00 per quintal to Rs. 62.00 per quintal. A certain portion (normally 40 per cent with lower rates for new units) of sugar production is allotted to the State/ UT Governments as levy. This is used for distribution through the Public Distribution System. Prices of levy sugar are fixed zone-wise, on the basis of SMP of sugarcane plus conversion costs as recommended by the Bureau of Industrial Costs and Prices. Though there is no price control on free-sale sugar, its market supplies are regulated by the Government by fixing monthly release quotas to maintain price stability. Export quotas are determined by the Government and a nominated agency handles sugar exports. Thus, almost all aspects of the industry from entry to exports are controlled by the Government. It is time to review if such extensive controls are still required and if greater efficiency cannot be achieved by relaxing some of these controls.

Automobiles

The automobile industry has seen a remarkable recovery during 1993 and is forging ahead in 1994. There has been an increase in sales in all the segments of the industry. During 1993-94, the sales of cars increased by about 20 per cent, jeeps by 30 per cent, commercial vehicles by 25 per cent, two wheelers by 18 per cent and three wheelers by 41 per cent. The buoyancy in the automobiles sector is continuing in 1994-95. Production during April-September 1994 has registered a growth of around 25 per cent over April-September 1993.

The automobile sector (including the auto components sector) is a net foreign exchange earner for the country. The exports of automotive vehicles have also been going up steadily. These have gone up to Rs. 1100 crore during 1993-94. as compared to Rs.737 crore during 1992-93.

There has been renewed interest in India amongst the world leaders in the automobiles industry. Several new joint venture agreements for the manufacture of cars have recently been signed between Indian companies and renowned car producers of' the world. The tie-ups include M/s. Hindustan Motors with General Motors of USA, PAL with M/s. Peugeot of France, TELCO with Mercedes Benz of Germany, DCM Toyota with Daewoo of South Korea and Sipani Automobiles with Rovers of' U.K. This is expected to provide a much more competitive environment to the industry and a wider choice to the consumer.

Fertilizers

Several measures have been undertaken by the Government to overcome the difficulties faced by the fertilizer sector. The measures include reintroduction of concessions for decontrolled fertilizer with some modifications, decanalization of Muriate of Potash (MOP), Mono Ammonium Phosphate (MAP) and Sulphate of Potash (SOP). At present only urea is covered under the statutory price and movement controls. The low analysis nitrogenous fertilizers, *viz.* CAN, Ammonium Sulphate, Ammonium Chloride were decontrolled with effect from June 10, 1994.

A production target of 78 lakh tonnes was fixed for Nitrogen for 1993-94. The actual production was 72.31 lakh tonnes. The shortfall in production was mainly due to reduced gas availability, equipment problems and poor performance of two sick public sector companies. The production of phosphate in 1993-94 was 18.16 lakh tonnes, against a target of 22 lakh tonnes. The shortfall in production was a consequence of several policy changes like decontrol of phosphatic fertilizers in August 1992. Despite several concessions announced in 1993-94, farmers still have to pay a substantially higher price than what they were paying prior to the decontrol. Furthermore, under the scheme of special concessions, some of the States have fixed unremunerative prices of indigenous DAP and complexes, forcing units, at times, to sell below their cost of production.

During the period April-November 1994, the rate of growth of fertilizer production was 7.7 per cent for Nitrogen and 49.9 per cent for Phosphate, over April-November 1993. However, the production of Nitrogen was 50.94 lakh tonnes and of Phosphate 14.44 lakh tonnes, against the target of 47.29 lakh tonnes and 10.30 lakh tonnes respectively, during the first seven months of 1994-95

The availability of Urea in Kharif 1994 was, by and large, in keeping with the demand. The sale of Urea during Kharif 1994, was 7 per cent higher over Kharif 1993. The availability of decontrolled phosphatic fertilizers in the country during Kharif 1994, was also, by and large satisfactory. During the Kharif, 1994 season, the sale of' DAP was 12 per cent higher than the corresponding period of 1993. Similarly, there was an increase of 36 per cent in the sale o f MOP during this period.

Electronics

The rate of growth of the electronics industry was 16.6 per cent during 1992-93 and 1993-94

Substantial excise duty concessions for the television industry announced in the 1993-94 Budget resulted in a turnaround of the television industry, which recorded significant growth rate of 22 per cent in 1993, compared to a negative growth in the last four years.

Exports of the electronics sector increased steadily from Rs.. 910 crore 1990-91 to Rs. 1,750 crore an 1993-94. One of the areas of extreme focus for exports is computer software. This sector continued to perform strongly, growing at a rate of above 25 per cent in dollar terms. Exports of computer software reached Rs. 750 crore in 1993-94, compared to Rs. 220 crore in 1990-91.

Under the Software Technology Park (STP) Scheme, software exporters are allowed a more flexible policy environment and are provided with certain key infrastructural amenities, such as core computers and high speed data links. All imports into STP units are completely duty free.

The Electronic Hardware Technology Park (EHTP) scheme is designed to attract investments for export oriented electronic production. EHTPs are duty free areas. Since the inception of EHTPs in April 1993, proposals involving an investment of Rs. 2,000 crore have been approved under this scheme and a number of units have commenced production.

Chemicals and Petrochemicals

The Chemicals, Pharmaceuticals and Petrochemical industries have performed well in the recent past. In the light of the experience gained over the years, the Government felt the need to modify the existing Drug Policy, 1991 and bring it in conformity with the Industrial Policy, 1991 and remove anomalies/aberrations observed in its working. The salient features of the modifications made in the policy announced on 15th September, 1994, are as follows :

(a) Industrial licensing for all bulk drugs and their formulations, and intermediates has been abolished, except for (i) five identified bulk drugs reserved for the public sector; (ii) drugs involving the use of recombinant DNA technology; and (iii) specific cell/ tissue targeted formulations.

(b) Automatic approval of foreign investments up to 51 per cent is allowed in all drugs, their intermediates and formulations. Automatic approval for foreign technology agreements is also allowed as per the industrial policy, for all products except those produced by the use of recombinant DNA technology.

(c) In the case of manufacture of drugs from the basic stage, a new price formula has been worked out.

(d) It has been decided to keep drugs with an annual turnover of Rs. 400 lakh or more, under price control. Consequently, the number of drugs under price control will be reduced to about 73 from the present 142, and the span of control to about 50 per cent from the present 70 per cent.

(e) A Uniform Maximum Allowable Post-Manufacturing Expenses (MAPE) of 100 per cent will be allowed in all cases of drugs under price control.

(f) In order to provide a more efficient mechanism for ensuring quality control and rational use of medicines, a National Drug Authority (NDA) will be set up.

(g) To provide better focus to the development and promotion of Ayurvedic, Unani, Sidha, Homeopathic and other traditional systems of medicines, a separate department, will be created under the Ministry of Health and Family Welfare.

The petrochemical industry had to withstand pressures of low priced imports during the year, considering the world recession and excess capacity, the bulk of which came in from the Asia Pacific region. The plans of expansion of existing projects and setting up of new plants continued to be deferred due to low margins, leading to poor internal resource generation.

Textiles

The textile industry continues to be the largest industry in our country. It accounts for 20 per cent of total industrial output, provides employment to 20 million people and contributes nearly 30 per cent to the total value of exports.

In line with the general policy of liberalization, several measures have been undertaken to eliminate/reduce controls and bring about greater transparency in the textile sector. The textile industry has been delicensed as per the Textiles (Development and Regulation) Order, 1993. The current Export Entitlement Distribution Policy (Known as Quota Policy), effective from January 1994 to December 1996, aims at making the system of quotas more transparent and simple and realising increased unit values from textile and garment quotas and encourages non-quota export of garments. The Agreement on Textiles and Clothing included as part of the Final Act of GATT, provides for a dismantling of the discriminatory quota regime practised under the Multi Fibre Arrangement (MFA), within a definite time span of 10 years.

The Indian textile industry continues to be predominantly cotton based, with about 70 per cent of raw materials consumed being cotton. The production of cotton during the 1993-94 cotton season was lower by 10 per cent than in 1992-93. The year started favourably, but because of a pest attack in the Northern States and crop damage in Pakistan and China, an unexpected shortage in availability of cotton was reported. The cotton year 1993-94 witnessed an abnormal increase in the prices of cotton from November 1993. However, several steps taken by the Government such as allowing imports of specified quantities (like permitting stipulated imports of viscose staple fibre cotton at zero or concessional rates of duty) and tightening of selective credit control measures for cotton, helped to contain the rise in cotton Prices.

Table 4 brings out the trend in fabric production and the share of mills, powerlooms and handlooms in total fabric production. There was a marginal decline in the share of the mill sector in fabric production.

Fabric production recorded an increasing trend over the years, except for a marginal setback in 1991-92. Total fabric production in 1993-94 was higher by 9.7 per cent than in 1992-93. Production of fabrics during April-November 1994 decreased by 0.4 per cent over April-November 1993. Production of spun yarn was almost entirely in the organised sector and showed a steadily increasing trend over the years, except for a marginal set back in 1991-92. Production of spun yarn increased by 9.1 per cent in 1993-94 but showed no change in April-November, 1994. The production of spun yarn by small scale units at 75 million kgs during 1993-94 now forms a significant part of total production.

The production of man-made fibres at 455.3 million kg. registered an increase of 19.2 per cent in 1993-94. Production during April-August, 1994 was 185.6 million kg., as against 177.1 million kg. in April-August 1993, recording an increase of 4.8 per cent. The production of man-made filament yarn also recorded an increasing trend over the years.

The export of textiles has been increasing at a fast rate during the last few years. During 1993-94, total exports of textiles (including coir, jute and handicrafts) was estimated at Rs.25,011 crore registering an increase

TABLE 4

Trends in Monthly Growth Rates of Industrial Production

(Per cent)

Period	General	Manufac-turing	Mining & Quarrying	Electricity
(weights)	(100)	(77.11)	(11.46)	(11.43)
1	2	3	4	5
1993				
January	– 3.2	– 5.4	– 1.4	7.6
February	– 3.1	– 4.4	– 3.1	4.6
March	– 1.2	– 3.7	8.5	5.3
April	– 0.5	– 2.1	1.4	6.4
May	2.3	1.2	0.4	9.5
June	2.8	1.1	– 4.9	9.9
July	6.7	6.8	5.5	7.3
August	9.2	8.8	6.6	13.3
September	3.7	3.5	2.8	5.5
October	2.6	2.8	1.1	2.3
November	2.2	1.5	1.8	6.7
December	6.4	7.2	1.5	6.2
1994				
January	6.5	7.2	4.0	5.0
February	6.0	6.7	1.1	6.9
March	1.1	– 0.6	1.4	10.7
April	6.9	8.4	– 0.9	5.7
May	8.0	8.4	5.6	8.3
June	7.0	8.1	0.8	6.8
July	6.8	7.2	3.4	7.4
August	8.9	9.8	7.8	4.7
September	7.9	7.1	11.3	9.2
October	10.3	9.2	15.6	11.8

of 30.9 per cent over 1992-93. Among the various items of textiles, ready-made garments achieved a growth rate of 31.7 per cent, cotton textiles

(mill-made, powerlooms and handlooms) 29.6 per cent, silk textiles 7.5 per cent, man-made fibre textiles 28.4 per cent, woollen textiles 43.1 per cent, handicrafts 39.8 per cent, jute goods 5.7 per cent and coir goods 32.2 per cent. Exports of cotton yarn had also increased by 37.9 per cent in 1993-94

Food Processing

The food processing industry encompasses industries like fruit and vegetable processing, milk, fish and meat. The industry has a tremendous potential for increasing agricultural productivity, providing significant and widespread employment and contributing substantially to exports. And all this, using relatively simpler technology.

To encourage private sector initiative in food processing, the Government has taken several steps. Union Excise duty on fruit and vegetable products was withdrawn in the 1991-92 Budget. Foreign equity participation up to 51 per cent and foreign technology agreements are provided automatically. There are no entry barriers in the food processing industry. Changes in Export-Import Policy and the liberalized exchange rate have also helped the sector.

Recent trends of production and exports of various segments of the industry show an impressive performance. This is largely the outcome of policy initiatives undertaken for the sector.

Incidence of duties on packaging material and various state levies are still considered to be impediments for further growth of the fruit and vegetables sector. Despite an impressive increase, in recent years, the commercial processing of fruits and vegetables has been barely 1.2 per cent of the total production.

Leather

A number of policy initiatives have been taken by the Government to encourage value added exports of leather products. Imports of raw materials and machinery have been liberalised. Manufacture of finished leather has been delicensed with effect from 28 April, 1993. The domestic manufacture of components for the shoe industry is being encouraged through measures like promoting joint ventures, and duty rationalisation on inputs required for the manufacture of such components.

A National Leather Development Programme (NLDP) with UNDP assistance is being implemented by the Government for integrated development of the leather industry, including a programme of technological upgradation, through selected institutions/agencies in the country. The Council for Leather Export has launched an image building programme (Leather Blitz) in the US market for boosting exports of value added leather products. This is one of the components of the National Leather Development Programme.

Small Scale units still dominate the production base of leather industry. The cottage sector, with its traditional rural artisans, dominates in leather tanning. The Indian leather industry is characterised by several inherent advantages. A large raw material base of about 166 million pieces of hides and skins available annually is the main strength of the industry. This, it is estimated, will go up to 185 million pieces in 1994-95 and 218 million pieces in 2000. Some Indian goat/calf/sheep skins are regarded as speciality products, commanding a good market. However, further skill and capacity upgradation is constrained to some extent by entry barriers against large scale units in major segments of the industry.

India's export of leather and leather products in the period April-September, 1994 was estimated at Rs.2089.6 crore, as against Rs.1945.5 crore during April-September 1993.

Small Scale and Village Industries

The number, employment, output and exports in the small scale sector as estimated by the office of the Development Commissioner, Small Scale Industries, are given in Table 5

TABLE 5

Small Scale Industries — Number, Outpput, Employment and Exports

Year	No. of units (in lakh) (As on 31st December)	Output at current prices (Rs. crore)	Employmnet (in lakh)	Exports (Rs crore)
1	2	3	4	5
1991-92	20.82	178699	129.80	13883
1992-93	22.35	209300	134.06	17785
	(7.3)	(17.1)	(3.3)	(28.1)
1993-94	23.84	241648	139.38	24000[1]
	(6.7)	(15.5)	(4.0)	(34.9)

[1] Rough estimate

Note: Figures in brackets give percentage increase over previous year.

In real terms, the Small Scale Sector recorded a growth rate of 7.1 per cent in 1993-94, as against 5.6 per cent in 1992-93, and 3.1 per cent in 1991-92. These rates were significantly higher than the growth rates achieved by the industrial sector as a whole.

The Small Scale Sector contributes 40 per cent to the gross turnover in the manufacturing sector and 35 per cent of total exports. Several policy initiatives have been undertaken to assist the small scale sector and enhance its competitive strength. The measures include :

— A new scheme of Integrated Infrastructural Development was launched recently to strengthen infrastructural facilities in 50 centres in rural and backward areas.

— The concessional rate of excise duty available for units with a turnover of Rs. 30 lakh to 75 lakh per annum was extended to the non-registered sector also.

— A Quality Certification Scheme was launched in 1994 to improve the quality standards of SSI products which are to be assisted by awareness programmes and financial support to acquire ISO 9000 or similar international quality standards.

Modifications were effected in the 'Single Window Scheme' operated by SIDBI. The project outlay under the scheme was raised from Rs. 30 lakh to Rs. 50 lakh as a whole, removing sub-limits for working capital and term loan components.

The Reserve Bank of India has accepted most of the recommendations of the Nayak Committee and has issued necessary guidelines. These include the following:

(a) To give preference to village industries, tiny industries and other small scale units in that order, while meeting the credit requirements of the sector.

(b) To prepare annual budgets on 'bottom up' basis to ensure that the legitimate requirements of the SSI sector are met in full.

(c) The 'Single Window Scheme' should be extended to all districts.

A new Entrepreneurship Development Institute has been set up in Guwahati, Assam, for improving the entrepreneurial base for the North Eastern Region.

Khadi andd Village Industries

Presently, KVIs produce output valued at Rs. 3,490 crore and provide employment of 55.50 lakh persons. The Government of India has been extending infrastructural and input support to the sector. The policy package consists of supply of raw materials at reasonable prices, upgradation of technology and productivity through research programmes, training for artisans, flow of concessional and adequate institutional credit. Recently, the Government of India had appointed a High-Powered Committee under the Chairmanship of the Prime Minister and the Committee has already submitted its report. An Action Plan incorporating its major recommendations has been formulated and launched on October 2, 1994. With the implementation of the Action Plan, the sector will get a boost with a quantum jump in production and employment.

Industrial Sickness

TABLE 6

Industrial Sickness

(Rs. crore)

	Number of Units			Amount Outstanding		
	End March 1991[1]	End March 1992[1]	End Sept. 1992	End March 1991[1]	End March 1991[1]	End Sept. 1992
1	2	3	4	5	6	7
1. SSI Sick Units	221472	245575	233441	2792	3101	3346
2. Non-SSI Sick Units	1461	1536	1599	5106	5787	6805
3. Non-SSI Weak Units	876	813	828	2870	2646	2436
Total	223809	247924	235868	10768	11533	12586
	Change over previous year/half year — per cent					
1. SSI Sick Units	1.2	10.9	— 4.9	15.0	11.1	7.9
2. Non-SSI Sick Units	0.4	5.1	4.1	12.5	13.3	17.6
3. Non-SSI Weak Units	7.6	— 7.2	1.9	20.3	— 7.8	— 7.9
Total	1.2	10.8	— 4.9	15.1	7.1	9.1

[1]Percentage change over December 1958.

Table 6 brings out the number of sick units (both in Small Scale and Non-Small Scale Sector) and the amount outstanding against them. At the end of September, 1992, there were 2.36 lakh sick or weak units. Of these, 2.33 lakh units were in the small scale sector. The amount outstanding has increased from Rs.11,533 crore at the end of March, 1992 to Rs.12,586 crore at the end of September, 1992, showing an increase of 9.1 per cent. Although small scale industries accounted for 98.7 per cent of total sick or weak units at the end of September 1992, their share in aggregate locked in bank credit was only 26.6 per cent.

Since inception, up to the end of September 1994, Bureau of Industrial and Financial Reconstruction BIFR received 2207 references under Section 15 of Sick Industrial Companies Act (SICA). Of these, 1602 references were registered for further action under the provisions of the Act. Of the 1602 references, 334 were dismissed as not maintainable, revival schemes were sanctioned or approved in respect of 463 cases and 343 cases were recommended to the concerned High Courts for winding up under the provisions of the Companies Act. 10 references were dropped as the net worth of the company became positive during the course of the inquiry. A recent study of the revival schemes under implementation, reveals that about 22 per cent of the cases are on the road to revival, in about 20 per cent cases it is too early to form an opinion and the progress is not satisfactory in the remaining 36 per cent.

As a result of the steps taken by BIFR to streamline internal procedures, it was possible to reduce the time taken between registration of a case and its first hearing. The average time taken during 1994 for the first hearing was 63 days, against an average of over 160 days in the first 5 years. The time taken for deciding cases was also considerably reduced from 700 days in the first 5 years of the functioning of the Board, to 187 days in 1993.

Barring cases held up due to stay by High Courts, all references registered in BIFR during 1987 stand disposed. The pending cases of 1988, 1989 and 1990 (barring those stayed by courts) number 4,5 and 9 respectively. These have either reached the penultimate stage, or are in an advanced stage of processing.

TABLE 7

Status of PSU cases referred to BIFR

	Central	State	Total
1	2	3	4
References registered	54	66	120
Dismissed as not maintainable	2	20	22
Revival scheme sanctioned	4	7	11
Winding up recommended to the concerned High Court	2	5	7
Stayed by Courts	5		5

Statistics relating to status on PSU cases are given in Table 7.

Delay in disposal of cases of PSUs has been due, *inter alia,* to inadequate information furnished by PSUs, non-availability of final views of the Central/State Governments, and the complexity of the cases.

Outlook

There has been a distinct improvement in the industrial sector during 1994-95, with significant improvement by capital goods and consumer durables. The capital goods sector, which had been performing poorly since 1992, has shown a complete turnaround, with a growth of 21.7 per cent in April-October 1994. The industrial recovery has also been broad-based and only a few sub-sectors such as Railway Wagons, Jute Manufactures, Jeeps, Graphite Electrodes and Anodes, Machine Tools, Ship-Building, Caustic Soda and Diesel Engines still show negative growth rates. The industrial recovery and the strong growth has been made possible by several policy initiatives taken by the Government, including extension of MODVAT to more sectors, further rationalisation and reduction of custom duties, reduction of corporate taxes and elimination of Government control over interest rates. The upsurge has also been facilitated by significant initiatives taken by State Governments in the reform process and implementation of the new industrial policy.

There are no major supply bottlenecks. The demand has picked up in a significant way. The dynamism and potential manifested by industry suggests with certainty that the high growth rates will be maintained and even go up in future. The year 1994-95 is expected to end with an industrial growth rate of above 8 per cent.

16

VILLAGE AND SMALL INDUSTRIES AND FOOD PROCESSING INDUSTRIES

VILLAGE AND SMALL INDUSTRIES

Overview

Village and small industries sector consists of two broad sub-sectors, *viz.*, modern small industries and traditional industries. The former covers small scale industries and powerlooms and the latter khadi, village industries, handlooms, sericulture, handicrafts and coir industry. With effect from 2nd April, 1991, an industrial unit in which investment in fixed assets in plant and machinery does not exceed Rs. 60 lakhs is regarded as a small scale undertaking. In the case of industrial units undertaking to export at least 30 per cent of the annual production by the end of the third year from the date of commencement of production, the ceiling of investment shall be Rs.75 lakhs. Further, in the case of ancillary industrial undertakings, the ceiling of investment in fixed assets has also been fixed at Rs. 75 lakhs. This measure is expected to result in greater technological input and export thrust in the small scale sector.

A policy package for small, tiny and village industries has been announced in August, 1991 with the primary objective of imparting more vitality and growth impetus to this sector. The ceiling of investment in the case of 'Tiny' enterprises has now been raised to Rs.5 lakhs, locational restrictions on setting of these enterprises have been removed and their scope has been enlarged to include all industry related service and business enterprises. Further, equity participation, not exceeding 24 per cent, by other industrial undertakings including that by foreign collaborators in the small scale sector has been permitted with a view to encouraging modernisation and technological upgradation. Other salient features of this policy pertain to the setting up of a monitoring agency to ensure that the genuine credit needs of this sector are fully met; review of all statutes, regulations and procedures and their modification to ensure that their operation does not militate against the interests of the small and village enterprises; encouraging industry associations to establish quality counselling and common testing facilities; sub-contracting exchanges and expansion of entrepreneurship development programme; further liberalisation of schemes of National Equity Fund and Single Window Loans,etc.

Review

The progress of village and small industries sector during the Seventh Plan (1985-90) and Annual Plans' (1990-91 and 1991-92) is indicated in Tables 1 and 2 respectively.

It will be observed from Table 1 that the value of output in this sector increased, at constant prices, at a compound rate of 12.06 per cent between 1984-85 and 1989-90. However, the production of khadi, village industries, handloom cloth and coir yarn and coir products fell short of their respective target. Exports from this sector have increased, at current prices, at a compound rate of 26.57 per cent. In the case of employment coverage (full time and part time employment), while the rate of compound growth is 4.43 per cent, it is short of the Seventh Plan target. The growth rate achieved during the Seventh Plan is not likely to be maintained during 1990-91 and 1991-92 on account of constraint of foreign exchange affecting the availability of imported raw materials, components and capital goods, credit squeeze, high rates of interest, recession in foreign markets, etc.

EIGHTH PLAN

Approach and Strategy

The Eighth Plan aims at a growth rate of 5.6 per cent. The growth rates for the manufacturing sector and exports have been kept at 7.3 per cent and 13.6 per cent respectively. While no growth rate has been indicated for the village and small industries sector, it has to be higher than that of the manufacturing sector.

In the new orientation to planning during the Eighth Plan, people's initiative and participation would be a key element in the process of development. Greater emphasis will be laid on private initiative in industrial development. The public sector will become very selective in the coverage of activities and in making investment. Small enterprises in the village and small industries sector are, more or less, based on private initiative and entrepreneurship.

TABLE 1

Village & Small Industries — Targets And Achievements In Seventh Plan (1985—90)

Industry Sl. No.	Unit	Estimated Production 1984-85	1989-90		Employment (Lakh Persons) 1984-85	1989-90		Export (Rs. Crores) 1984-85	1989-90	
		Achiev.	Target	Achiev.	Achiev.	Target	Achiev.	Achiev.	Target	Achiev.
Modern Small Scale Industry										
1. Small Scale Industries	Rs./Crores	50520.00	80220.00	92080.00	90.00	119.00	119.60	2350.00	4140.00	7626.00
2. Powerloom cloth	Mill.Mts.	4930.00	6400.00	7457.00	32.19	35.32	45.00			
	Rs./Crores	6423.00	8320.00*	9865.00						
Traditional Industries										
3. Khadi Cloth	Mill.Mts.	127.82	180.00	107.47	14.58	20.00	14.12			
	Rs./Crores	170.00	300.00	203.00						1.39
4. Village Industries	Rs./Crores	759.00	1700.00	1101.00	22.41	30.00	32.14	3.65	5.90	3.66
5. Handloom cloth	Mill.Mts.	3600.00	4600.00	4155.00	74.66	98.13	76.00	348.86	485.00	342.00
	Rs./Crores	2880.00	3680.00	3377.00						
6. Sericulture — Raw Silk	Tonnes	6754.00	10900.00	12016.00	43.20*	52.77*	50.00	129.05	190.00	400.61
	Rs./Crores	316.57	453.00*	493.00						
7. Handicrafts	Rs./Crores	3500.00	5400.00	7067.00	27.04	35.08	42.15	1700.00	2591.00	6400.00
8. Coir fibre	Lakh tonne	1.64	2.23	1.92	5.00*	7.50*	5.50	26.00	32.00	33.32
	Rs./Crores	100.00	170.00	128.00						
Total (VSI):	Rs./Crores	64668.57	100243.00	114314.00	309.44	398.52	384.51	4557.56	7443.90	14806.98

* Revised

TABLE 2

Village And Small Industries — Targets And Achievements In 1990-91 and 1991-92

S. No. & Industry	Unit	Estimated Production				Employment (Lakh Persons)				Export (Rs. Crores)			
		1990-91		1991-92		1990-91		1991-92		1990-91		1991-92	
		Target	Achieve.	Target	Ant. Achv.	Target	Achieve.	Target	Ant. Achv.	Target	Achiev.	Target	Ant. Achv.
Modern Small Scale Industry													
1. Small Scale Industries	Rs./Crores	159062	155340	160000	160000	125.50	124.30	133.30	126.00	7100.00	9100.00	7981.00	12658.00
2. Powerloom cloth	Mill.Mts.	10500	9469	11036	11036	63.36	63.36	53.00	53.00				
	Rs./Crores	13680	12337	14378	14378								
Traditional Industries													
3. Khadi cloth	Mill. Mts.	120	109	127	114	14.61	14.15	14.61		0.14			
	Rs./Crores	260	286	310	278								
4. Village Industries	Rs./Crores	1745	1994	2150	2150	31.28	34.42	35.40	35.40		6.29		
5. Handloom cloth	Mill.Mts.	4500	4541	5000	5000	100.27	100.27	106.00	106.00	360.00	360.00	450.00	450.00
	Rs./Crores	3600	3633	4064	4064								
6. Sericulture — Raw Silk	Tonnes	12633	12665	14060	13535	62.00	52.00	55.00	54.50	500.00	440.27	600.00	
	Rs./Crores	866	868	1038	996								
7. Handicrafts	Rs./Crores	11325	11325	13260	13260	43.84	43.84	48.25	48.25	8100.00	8100.00	9215.00	9215.00
8. Coir fibre	Lakh tonne	2.23	2.11	2.26	2.20	5.54	5.46	5.46	5.46	42.00	48.33	51.48	66.16
	Rs./Crores	170	161	172	168								
Total (VSI):	Rs./Crores	190708	185944	195372	195294	446.40	437.80	451.02	443.22	16102.00	18055.03	18297.48	22989.16

TABLE 3

Village And Small Industries — Eighth Five Year Plan (1992—97) : Indicative Targets

S.No. & Industry	Unit	Production 1991-92 Achiev.	Production 1996-97 Target	EMP.(Lakh Persons) 1991-92 Achiev.	EMP.(Lakh Persons) 1996-97 Target	Export (Rs. /Crs.) 1991-92 Achiev.	Export (Rs. /Crs.) 1996-97 Target
Modern Small scale Industry							
1. Small Scale Industries	Rs./Cr.	160000	233436.00	126.00	150.50	12658.00	20200.00
2. Powerloom cloth	Mill.Mts.	11036	15280.00	53.00	75.00		
	Rs./Crores	14378	19907.00				
Traditional Industries							
3. Khadi cloth	Mill.Mts.	114	160.00	14.61	16.50		
	Rs./Crores	278	560.00				
4. Village Industries	Rs./Crores	2150	3760.00	35.40	46.25		
5. Handloom cloth	Mill.Mts.	5000	7000.00	106.00	117.00	450.00	1000.00
	Rs./Crores	4064	5690.00				
6. Sericulture — Raw Silk	Tonnes	13535	21400.00	54.50	65.00	600.00	1000.00
7. Handicrafts	Rs./Crores	13260	29620.00	48.25	77.65	9215.00	27915.00
8. Coir fibre	Lakh tonne	2.2	2.77	5.46	5.84	66.16	100.00
	Rs./Crores	168	212.00				
Total (VSI)	Rs./Crores	195294	294775.00	443.22	553.74	22989.16	50215.00

One of the areas of priority of the Eighth Plan is generation of adequate employment to achieve near full employment level by the turn of this century. Several activities pertaining to this sector like processing of agricultural produce in rural areas, sericulture and allied activities have been identified as critical goals in priority sectors. It is possible to dovetail programmes of khadi, village industries, handlooms, sericulture and handicrafts to integrated local area development programmes for selected villages for poverty alleviation through increase in employment. It is also envisaged that entry into the services sector, which is expected to play a major role in generating employment during the Eighth Plan, and the informal sector will be made free of innumerable rules, regulation and bureaucratic controls. Further, research and innovation in the tools and techniques of traditional occupations, including those of rural artisans, will be encouraged and their extensive adaptation will be induced.

Physical Targets

Indicative targets in respect of production, employment coverage and exports for village and small industries for the Eighth Plan are given in Table 3.

Small Scale Industries

It will be observed from Table 3 that the growth rates in respect of production, employment and exports relating to small scale industries envisaged for the Eighth Plan are lower than those achieved during the Seventh Plan. These rates have been worked out taking into consideration the prevailing difficult resource position. Quick estimate of Index of Industrial Production for April-September, 1991, *vis-a-vis,* the corresponding period of 1990 indicates negative growth rate of 1.9 per cent in manufacturing sector. Similarly, export performance, net of devaluation and inflation, for the above period has not been encouraging.

Credit continues to be crucial for the establishment and expansion of small industries. Advances from commercial banks to the small scale sector as on 23rd March, 1990, was Rs. 15,543 crores as against Rs.6.766 crores at the end of June, 1985. This increased to Rs.17,151 crores as on 22nd March, 1991. In percentage terms, advances to the small scale sector were 15.7 per cent of the total bank advances in March, 1991. It would be necessary to increase the share of credit available to the SSI sector from commercial banks from the present 16-18 per cent. It is needless to reiterate that timely and adequate availability of credit is of greater importance than concessional credit. This would call tor strengthening of SIDBI and NABARD. With the establishment of SIDBI, certain new initiatives like sanction of composite loans under Single Window concept, concessional loans to State Corporations for infrastructure development and provision of factoring services have been introduced.

A development which is likely to increase the cost of credit to small scale industries is the deregulation of interest rates to be charged by banks on advances above Rs.2 lakhs. Its adverse effect would be felt by SSI units in general and tiny units in particular. Reserve Bank of India has appointed a Committee in December, 1991, to review the arrangements for meeting the working capital requirements of small scale industries and for the rehabilitation of sick small scale industries and to examine any other issues relating to small scale industries. The Commitee will also look into the above issues with a view to ensuring that the interests of SSI sector are not adversely affected.

Entrepreneurs have limited access to quality raw materials. In the case of critical raw materials, new enterprises face problem in obtaining these in the absence of a proper and equitable policy of raw material distribution. After the decontrol of steel prices, drying up of canalising agencies (like MMTC, etc) and the devaluation of Rupee, the availability of raw materials, particularly to the small producer, has been severely affected. Industry associations will be encouraged to come forward and evolve a suitable distribution mechanism so that the interest of this sector is protected.

In order to upgrade technology, greater emphasis has to be laid on the establishment of tool rooms and provision of training facilities. State intervention in improving the quality may be confined to establishment of tool rooms and assistance in the establishment of testing facilities. The operation of testing facilities should be the responsibility of the industry. During the Eighth Plan, a bigger programme of development of appropriate technology and technology upgradation has to be initiated.

Technological obsoloscence is high in small industries. To improve marketability, there is need to induct better and appropriate technology. Need is felt for an agency which can take up the functions of collection, documentation and storing information on technology, conducting studies and preparing technology guidelines, assessing the need for establishment of tool rooms, testing centres, PDTCs etc., provision of technology inputs, import of samples from abroad, assimilation of technology, assisting entrepreneurs in obtaining suitable know-how from indigenous sources, coordination with organisations engaged in technology development and its transfer. NSIC can handle these functions both for small industries as well as for others.

According to the ALL-India Census of Small Scale Industrial Units, with 1987-88 as the base year, registered working SSI units and closed units as on 31.3.1988 were 5,82,368 and 3,01,390 respectively. It is indicative of extensive sickness in the small scale sector. Though sickness is reported in all market economies, locking of resources in the form of bank loans, materials, equipment and loss of employment are serious matters of concern. The Centrally Sponsored Scheme for revival of sick SSI units has not proved effective. The causes of sickness are many, like selection of unviable projects, inadequate availability of raw materials, power shortage, marketing problems, obsolete technology, inadequate working capital, inefficient management, etc. In order to prevent sickness at the incipient stage, it is necessary that SFCs and commercial banks should properly monitor the project. The quality of consultancy, particularly in technology has to be improved. Rehabilitation of sick units is very difficult and it requires not only proper diagnosis but also effective coordination among the various organisations involved.

In the State sector, a number of programmes of subsidies on investments in fixed assets, purchase of diesel generating sets, electricity duty, etc., are under implementation leading to unhealthy competition among the States and Union Territories to attract private investment. Further, concessions on purchase of land and exemption from the payment of sales tax for a specified period/investment limit are also provided to entrepreneurs. These schemes, generally, lead to flight of investment from less developed States to developed ones. It is imperative to evolve a uniform policy on the above issues based upon consensus among the State Governments in the interest of growth of industry on healthy and equitable basis.

The cumbersome procedures and a large number of returns that entrepreneurs have to furnish, distract them from production and marketing activities. It is, therefore, necessary to undertake a comprehensive review of laws and procedures and to simplify them so that entrepreneurs are able to concentrate on efficient running of their units.

Marketing is one of the intractable problems of the SSI sector. Marketing assistance through Small Industries Corporations, NSIC, etc., has so far been able to cover only a very small fraction of turnover in this sector. The existing fiscal regime and the operation of labour laws are not conducive to vertical growth of SSI sector. There is need to modify them suitably. Industry associations will be encouraged to form marketing organisations which, besides marketing, will go into the quality aspect of products.

The Growth Centre approach has already been accepted as a suitable measure for industrial dispersal and is under implementation in large and medium industries sector. During the Eighth Plan, establishment of 70 Growth Centres has been envisaged. It is proposed to earmark a certain percentage of developed industrial area for small industries. There is also need to establish functional industrial estates at suitable locations in areas with substantial agricultural, vegetable and horticultural produce.

Besides the growth centres, integrated infrastructure development centres for tiny units in rural and backward areas would be set up involving the Centre, State Governments and industry associations.

The experience of economic growth the world over indicates that greater employment generation takes place in the tertiary sector. Hence, there is need for emphasis on the promotion of industrial units catering to services and maintenance of equipment. In rural areas and small towns such facilities do not exist. A programme of suitable training and provision of tool kits needs to be taken up.

Khadi and Village Industries

The production of khadi cloth in 1989-90, estimated at 107.47 million sq. metres, is less not only than the Seventh Plan target of 180 million sq. metres but also than the level of production of 127.82 million sq. metres achieved in 1984-85. Similarly, employment coverage of 14.12 lakh persons in khadi sub-sector in 1989-90 is less than the target as well as the employment of 14.58 lakh persons in 1984-85. This trend in production persisted in 1990-91 and 1991-92. In the case of village industries, the value of output in 1989-90 was Rs.1,101 crores at constant prices and Rs.1,705 crores at current prices against the Seventh Plan target of Rs.1,700 crores. However, the employment coverage in village industries in 1989-90 estimated at 32.14 lakh persons is marginally higher than the Seventh Plan target of 30 lakh persons. In 1990-91, there is a slight fall in employment coverage in village industries, *vis-a-vis*, the target. However, in 1991-92, the target of employment coverage of 35.40 lakh persons in village industries is expected to be achieved.

The decline in the growth ofkhadi sub-sector is attributable to several factors. Spinning on traditional charkhas in the northern belt could not be expanded due to low level of earnings and consequent decline in the number of traditional home spinners as well as preference of weavers for yarn produced by New Model Charkha (NMC). In some States adequate number of weavers are not willing to take up khadi weaving. The present structure as well as guidelines regarding lending to khadi institutions do not permit the Khadi and Village Industries Commission (KVIC) to advance loans to those institutions which have received over Rs.3 crores. These institutions have requisite infrastructure and expertise to increase the production of khadi, whereas new institutions which are eligible for funding take a lot of time to develop infrastructure and expertise. Further, as the production of khadi is bound by several restrictions such as certification, cost chart and its sale on no profit no loss basis, very few voluntary organisations come forward to take up this programme. It is, however, relevant to state in this context that the production of polyvastra which is a blend of polyester and cotton presently covered under village industries has been increasing during this period and in value terms it has increased from Rs.2.17 crores in 1984-85 to Rs.16.61 crores in 1989-90.

There are other areas in KVIC programmes in which performance is not satisfactory. A large number of artisans' cooperatives engaged in village industries have continued to remain dormant. Though the productivity and earnings of artisans have improved, they are lower than those obtaining in the farm sector. The linkages between KVI programmes and general programmes of area development like IRDP, are inadequate. The gaps in performance are partly attributable to the fact that since its inception, KVIC has continued the policy of assisting institutions/private individuals registered with it directly and consequently the State Governments have not been according priority to its programmes.

The main objectives of khadi and village industries (KVI) programmes during the Eighth Plan would be to create additional employment opportunities in the non-farm sector and to ensure increased wages/earnings to rural workers. For this purpose, it would be necessary to reorient khadi programme and identify thrust areas among village industries keeping in view the growth potential and the consumer demand, provide escort services to artisans and adopt aggressive marketing approach.

The KVIC depends on institutional finance, besides budgetary support for the implementation of its programmes. But the flow of funds to the KVI sector has not been commensurate with its requirements. Thus, the institutional finance flowing to the KVI sector under the interest subsidy scheme increased from Rs. 40.94 crores in 1984-85 to Rs. 120.61 crores in 1990-91. The KVIC issued interest subsidy eligibility certificates to State KVIBs and directly aided institutions for an amount of Rs. 234.27 crores in 1990-91, but KVI received only Rs. 120.61 crores of institutional finance during 1990-91. It is, therefore, essential to ensure adequate institutional finance for the stepped-up activities of KVIC. In this context, it is necessary to increase the active involvement of banks in funding of KVI programmes and in this process reduce their dependance on the budgetary support. It is also necessary to review the subsidies which are presently being provided for the development of Khadi and village industries. The present policy of KVIC to advance loans for the development of village industries to the beneficiary organisations at 4% rate of interest also needs to be reviewed in view of the hike in the lending rates of commercial banks.

Artisans engaged in khadi and village industries face problem in obtaining assured and timely supply of raw materials of requisite quality as well as quantity at reasonable rates to enable them to produce quality goods at competitive cost on account of their weak resource base. Though KVIC has arrangements for supply of some raw materials, like cotton, raw wool, polyster fibre, silk cocoons, edible and non-edible oilseeds and splints and veneers, requisite support in regard to supply of essential chemicals and raw materials for the remaining village industries, including the expanded village industries, needs to be provided.

It has been noted that the utilisation of S&T funds by KVI sector has not picked up during the past seven years. There is urgent need to develop new types of tools, equipment and machines. They should be tested on pilot basis before being recommended for adoption on a wide scale. It is, therefore, imperative that technical problems of this sector should be recognised by national laboratories and they should help this sector in a big way to produce marketable products. R&D should pay attention not only to production process but also to quality finishing, packaging etc. For agro and food processing industries in rural areas, the activities of CSIR and other research institutes functioning under its aegis, including CFTRI, should be reoriented and coordinated for development of appropriate technologies.

Due to their traditional character, the khadi products are unable to withstand the competition from the organised textile sector. It is, therefore, essential to adopt an aggressive marketing approach which takes into account the consumers taste, price and other related factors for increasing production of khadi. This would necessitate diversification of markets as also the product mix; introduction of modern marketing techniques; better inventory control; and better management practices etc. The question of rebate on the sales of khadi has been examined in depth by the Committees headed by Shri M. Ramakrishnayya and Shri Abid Hussain. These Committees have favoured its continuance in the khadi sector. However, restructuring in respect of silk khadi needs to be considered but any decision in this regard should cover both handloom and khadi sectors. In providing thrust to khadi sector, greater emphasis needs to be placed during the Eighth Plan on those activities which are economically viable without the support of subsidies. To achieve these objectives it would be necessary to popularise the New Model Charkha, diversify production of cloth so as to improve its blending with polyester, wool as well as silk and produce readymade garments in accordance with the customer's taste and latest trends in fashion.

Though the network of sales outlets set up by KVIC and State KVIBs would appear to be adequate, it is not so and the cost of rendering marketing assistance to artisans is high. While product diversification, design and fashion development and fashion shows in major cities would assist marketing of khadi, marketability of products of village industries could be enhanced by improving quality and packaging. Greater stress on R&D, besides ensuring improvement in quality, would help increase productivity and thereby reduce cost. Apart from sale of KVI products through Bhavans, Bhandars, mobile vans, and three wheelers in big cities, their marketing on commission basis at district and taluka market besides weekly *haats* needs to be encouraged.

For generating employment opportunities in rural areas, it is necessary to expand the coverage of villages and identify the thrust areas among the village industries for development. It is imperative to widen the base of village industries and increase productivity and thereby ensure higher earnings to artisans which would sustain them in the activity. Though 96 village industries are presently within the purview of KVIC, it would be desirable initially to concentrate on about 15 industries in respect of which requisite infrastructure and expertise is available. It would also be necessary to provide training to artisans in respect of improved tools as well as implements and methods of production. It would be necessary to upgrade their skills to enable them to produce quality products which would find ready acceptance in the market. The greatest weakness in the expansion of village industries programme is in the area of providing training facilities. The KVIC's departmental training centres and those assisted by it and run by voluntary organisations numbering about 100 can take care of the training of only trainers. Hence, skill transfer at the grassroot level to the artisans is the real problem in view of diversity of industries and the large number of people who are required to be trained. For this purpose, efforts should be made to link it up with the Plus Two vocational education system, to reorganise the syllabus and the training programmes devised by the Education Department and to include KVI trades in the vocational curriculum wherever they are not already included.

For effective promotion and development of khadi and village industries, it is necessary to ensure full participation of the State Governments in the implementation of KVI programmes by providing adequate outlays in the State Plans.

Coir Industry

Indian coir industry is an important cottage industry contributing significantly to the economy of the major coconut growing States and Union Territories, *i.e.*, Kerala, Tamil Nadu, Andhra Pradesh, Karnataka, Maharashtra, Goa, Orissa, Assam, Andaman & Nicobar, Lakshadweep, Pondicherry, etc. About 5.5 lakh persons get employment, mostly part time, in this industry. The exports from this industry are around Rs.70 crores. The coconut production in India is estimated at 9283 million numbers in 1989-90. Coconut husk is the basic raw material for coir products. Around 50 per cent of the available coir husk is used to produce coir products. Hence, there is scope for growth of coir industry.

During the Seventh Plan, while the production of 'white fibre' has remained stagnant, the production of 'brown fibre' has registered more than 15 per cent increase. The production of white fibre and brown fibre was 1,24,900 tonnes and 67,600 tonnes in 1989-90 against the respective level of' 1,24,800 tonnes and 39,600 tonnes in 1984-85. During this period, the export of coir yarn and other products has increased from Rs.26 crores to Rs.33.32 crores. The production of coir fibre in 1991-92 is anticipated to be 2.20 lakh tonnes against the target of 2.26 lakh tonnes. Exports are anticipated to be of the order of Rs.66.16 crores.

During the Seventh Plan period, encouragement was given for expansion of the home market through publicity and advertisement, product diversification, adoption of new technology, research and development, training for artisans, including women and social welfare measures for coir workers, most of whom are SC/ST and women.

The Eighth Plan programmes for coir industry aim at increased utilisation of coconut husk for production of coir fibre, growth of the domestic market, strengthening of research and development to find out new uses for coir fibre especially in the areas of geo-fibre, fire retardant, cement and gypsum polymer development, acquisition of new technology like PVC-tufted coir products, encouragement to cooperativisation and provision of social welfare, civic amenities and medical facilities to the coir workers. Emphasis would be laid on mechanisation in a phased manner without affecting employment to make Indian coir products competitive in the export market. The production of brown coir fibre would be encouraged by providing seed capital assistance. Modernisation of coir units has been envisaged by providing incentives for installation of modern equipments to make coir industry more competitive in the export market.

Special training programmes have been formulated for women artisans. Improved modern treadle ratts would he provided to trained women artisans to increase employment and earnings. Medical facilities, creche for children of coir workers, model coir villages for SC/ST coir workers and social welfare schemes would be implemented during the Eighth Plan period.

Emphasis has been laid on developing devices/equipment/ machinery through R&D to reduce drudgery and to improve productivity of coir workers. Development of improved variety of ratts and looms would help in improving the production of coir yarn spinning, coir mats, etc. In order to boost exports, the scheme of cooperative publicity programmes in the export markets which was started in the Seventh Plan would be continued.

The indicative target of production for coir fibre has been set at 2.77 lakh tonnes for the Eighth Plan. Export target is Rs.100 crores. The schemes to be implemented during the Eighth Plan would aim at increasing the share of full-time employment in this sector from the present level.

Handloom Industry

The handloom industry provides the largest employment among the traditional industries, next only to agriculture. By the end of the Seventh Plan, the estimated employment coverage in this industry was 76 lakh persons. The performance of the handloom industry in terms of production of handloom cloth, employment and exports during the Seventh Plan fell short of the respective targets. However, the anticipated achievements in the handloom industry in 1990-91 and 1991-92 are expected to equal the target.

The Textile Policy of 1985 envisaged preservation of the distinct and unique role of this sector. However, the permission for installation of new loomage given to the organised mill sector and the decentralised powerloom sector, fibre freedom and liberal imports had posed strong competition to the handloom industry and acted as deterrents to its growth.

During the Seventh Plan, the focus of developmental programmes for handloom industry was on cooperativisation, strengthening of Central and State level corporations, modernisation of handlooms, design development, training of weavers, assured minimum earnings through Janata Cloth scheme, etc. The inputs of technology, design and training were made available through Weavers' Service Centres (WSC) and Indian Institutes of Handloom Technology (IIHT); the latter functioning at Salem, Varanasi and Guwahati. Primary and apex societies of handloom weavers were given share capital assistance, managerial subsidy, assistance for opening new sales outlets, design collection and development, participation in exhibitions and Expos, organising publicity, etc. The National Handloom Development Corporation (NHDC) further enlarged its activity of supply ofbank yarn, dyes and chemicals. Hank yarn has been made available in yarn deficit States at mill gate prices to handloom weavers. The National Cooperative Development Corporation (NCDC), assisted handloom weavers' cooperatives to establish, modernise and expand yarn spinning mills to increase spindleage and availability of hank yarn to the weavers.

The Janata Cloth Scheme in the handloom sector was operational in 18 States and one Union Territory during the Seventh Plan. Production of Janata cloth increased from 397 million metres in 1985-86 to 548 million metres in 1989-90. Subsidy disbursement to all the States on Janata cloth was Rs.488 crores during the Seventh Plan. This scheme met partially its main objectives of providing consistent wages to weavers and making available cloth at reasonable prices to the weaker sections of society. However, the operation of this scheme has led to deskilling of weavers.

In spite of implementation of developmental schemes, the economic condition of handloom weavers did not improve as envisaged. Cooperative coverage is limited to only 30 per cent of the total weavers. Inadequate enforcement of, the challenging of the Handloom Act of 1985 in several High Courts and the stays granted to the powerloom operators by these Courts have rendered the law ineffective and encroachment on handloom products still continues. The inherent weaknesses of the handloom industry like weak organisation, officialisation of handloom cooperatives, inadequate credit from financial institutions, inadequate marketing infrastructure etc. have made it more vulnerable to competition from the organised mills and the decentralised powerloom sector. Steep increase in cotton yarn prices, build up of unsold stock and delayed payments to primary societies by apex societies, etc. further deteriorated weavers' condition.

The Institute of Rural Management, Anand had carried out an evaluation of the development programmes of handlooms in 1989. Based on this study, a change in the delivery system was effected and a new approach for the developmental and promotional schemes was adopted from Annual Plan 1990-91. The approach of 'project package' as indicated in the new Industrial Policy of August, 1991, has been adopted and it is proposed to do away with the limitation of routeing assistance only through cooperative/corporate organisations.

The programmes in the Eighth Plan for handloom industry seek to encourage employment generation, ensure reasonable wages for weavers, supply of hank yarn at reasonable prices, establish silk yarn bank, set up marketing infrastructure, help export development, etc. besides continuing the existing schemes for publicity and exhibitions, training and upgradation of technology through WSCs and IIHTs, research and development, enforcement of Handloom (Reservation of Products) Act, 1985 and welfare schemes. Production of Janata cloth is proposed to be phased out.

To retain employment in the handloom sector State intervention would be desirable for placing the Handloom Reservation Act, 1985 under the IX Schedule of the Constitution. The present list of reserved items would be revised. The revised list of reserved items would include selected products of handloom sector and only those items would be included which have higher design input, border and motif which are the strength and speciality of handloom sector.

During the Eighth Plan, the setting up of integrated handloom villages at places of concentration of weavers has been envisaged. These handloom villages would have worksheds and houses, pre- and post-loom facilities, depots for raw material, marketing infrastructure, banks, communication facilities and basic civic amenities for weavers.

With a view to providing marketing assistance, infrastructural facilities would be developed at the village, taluka, block and district levels besides metropolitan cities and important tourist places.

The apex societies along with NHDC would continue to be assisted to supply raw materials to the weavers throughout the country. Additional financial support would be required for their expanded activities to cover larger number of weavers. The apex societies would further augment assistance to the primary societies in the supply of raw materials and marketing.

To increase hank yarn availability to the handloom weavers, NCDC would provide financial support to weavers' cooperatives to instal new yarn spinning mills to improve the availability of hank yarn.

The State Governments would be encouraged to establish IIHTs and WSCs for upgradation of technology and increasing training and design inputs to the weavers. The workshed-*cum*-housing scheme would be taken up at enhanced level to provide more houses and worksheds to the weavers to improve their working condition and productivity.

The Indian handloom products have the potential to attract foreign buyers because of their natural fibre base, unique design, appearance and aesthetic appeal. Strict adherence to high quality standards from fabrics to made-ups and new design inputs to handloom sector would boost the exports. Funds would be provided to the apex societies and corporate organisations for export, arrangement of quality raw material for export orders, strict quality control and marketing expenses abroad, etc.

The Handloom Census (1987-88) data would be scientifically processed for planning for handloom sector. Information from the Census, 1991 about weavers would be integrated with the Handloom Census, 1987-88 data to provide a strong data base to the handloom industry.

Powerlooms

The Textile Policy, 1985 provided an opportunity for regularising unauthorised powerlooms and installation of new powerlooms. This sector has grown rapidly during the Seventh Plan period from a level of 8.36 lakh powerlooms as on 1.1.1985 to 11 lakh as on 31 3.1990.

During the Seventh Plan, production of powerloom cloth increased from 4,930 million metres to 7,457 million metres. This is anticipated to rise further to 11,036 million metres by the end of 1991-92. Further, the employment in this sub-sector increased from 32.19 lakh persons to 45 lakh persons during the Seventh plan. This is expected to go up to 53 lakh persons by the end of 1991-92.

To assist powerlooms in updating designs, training, testing facilities for yarn and fabrics and to give advice on technical matters, the Government has established 13 Powerloom Service Centres (PSCs) under the control of the Textile Commissioner. Encouragement of powerloom cooperative societies and provision of assistance for share capital has helped cooperative sector in Maharashtra, Tamil Nadu, etc.

The State Governments of Maharashtra, Gujarat, Tamil Nadu and Assam have adopted certain measures for the welfare of powerloom weavers during the Seventh Plan. However, these measures were not commensurate with the growth of this sector. Powerloom workers did not get statutory wages and facilities like provident fund, medical facilities, social welfare benefits, safe working environment, education for their children and training, etc., due to the extra legal status of powerlooms during the Sixth Plan period. The position in this regard did not improve during the Seventh Plan in spite of the legal status given to this sector by the Textile Policy of 1985.

The major problems in this sector relate to non-availability of yarn at stable prices, obsolete looms and outdated technology, inadequate pre-loom and post-loom facilities, inadequate financial assistance through financial institutions and dependence on middlemen for finance at high rates of interest.

In the Eighth Plan, efforts would be made to tackle the problems of weaver-owned powerlooms and powerloom cooperatives in the decentralised sector. There is need to extend working capital assistance to small powerloom weaver-owners by SFCs.

The Eighth Plan indicative target for cloth production in decentralised powerloom sector has been kept at 15,280 million metres, which implies a compound growth rate of 6.7 per cent. The employment target is set at the level of 75 lakh persons in 1996-97.

Sericulture

Sericulture, an agro-industrial activity based mainly on land and water, is carried on in 52,000 villages on 3.32 lakh hectares of irrigated and rainfed land under mulberry plants and on forest land and village grazing reserves in the case of non-mulberry sericulture employing about 55 lakh persons in planting, seed preparation, silkworm rearing, reeling, weaving and other operations. Non-mulberry sericulture, namely, tasar culture, sericulture and muga culture, is mainly practised by the tribals. Mulberry silk, accounting for more than 90 per cent of the total silk produced in the country, is concentrated in the States of Karnataka, Andhra Pradesh, Tamil Nadu and West Bengal. India, with a production of 12,450 tonnes of mulberry silk in 1991-92, holds the second position in the world, next to China whose production of mulberry silk was 35,800 tonnes in 1987. However, most of Chinese silk is of bivoltine variety whereas ours is multi x bivoltine. About 70 per cent of our silk is used by handlooms.

The Seventh Plan target of production of raw silk was exceeded. However, tasar and muga silks did not fare well. In the case of bivoltine silk, the performance was disappointing. As against the target of 500 tonnes, the production was estimated at 150 tonnes. The export of silk made-ups and goods was encouraging. However, imports of silk doubled from about 1181 tonnes in 1984-85 to about 2,500 tonnes in 1989-90. A National Sericulture Project costing Rs. 555 crores with assistance from IBRD/IDA and Swiss Development Cooperation was taken up in 1989-90. Production of silk during 1990-91 was slightly above the target but in 1991-92 a shortfall in achievement of the target is anticipated. Exports in quantitative terms have also not increased. The National Sericulture Project under implementation by Central Silk Board in 12 States and by the State Governments in Karnataka, Andhra Pradesh, Tamil Nadu, West Bengal and Jammu & Kashmir made poor progress except in terms of coverage of land under mulberry, particularly in the case of Andhra Pradesh.

During the Eighth Plan, the production of raw silk is envisaged to reach the level of 21,400 tonnes, including 2,000 tonnes of bivoltine variety. Whereas the productivity of mulberry silk in terms of kg/ha has risen from 32.09 in 1984-85 to 38.29 in 1989-90, the target set for the terminal year of the Eighth Plan is ambitious and would call for greater efforts in R&D. Sustained efforts are necessary to bridge the gap between productivity levels obtaining in India and those in countries like China and Japan. Production of bivoltine cocoons is essential for meeting the seed requirements, larger production of quality silk and lessening dependence on imports.

In Karnataka, a leading State in silk production, all the sericultural activities from plantation to weaving of fabrics have been promoted in an integrated manner. Similarly, in the States of Andhra Pradesh, Tamil Nadu and West Bengal, though reeling is not as extensive as in Karnataka, all other sericultural activities are integrated. Further, raw silk is also used in the production of silk khadi and weaving of silk carpets. Thus, sericulture has linkages with the sub-sectors of khadi, handlooms and handicrafts. The programmes for the development of sericulture during the Eighth Plan, therefore, will be dovetailed to achieve both the vertical and horizontal integration. This would result in harmonisation of the various sub-sectors and generation of employment in khadi, handlooms and handicrafts.

Another aspect which has caused considerable concern in the recent past is the outbreak of pebrine disease. In order to prevent its spread and contain it, emphasis will be laid on thorough moth examination and providing assistance to sericulturists and private graineurs.

So far, the emphasis has been on evolving improved varieties of food plants and silk worm races. However, reeling is an important activity. During the Eighth Plan, greater attention will be paid to improve reeling. Reelers will be trained and assisted in the establishment of cottage basins. Apart from the acquisition of skill in reeling, a reeler is handicapped on account of large requirement of working capital for the purchase of cocoons. There is provision of working capital loans through refinance from IDBI under NSP. Reeling under private sector would be promoted during the Eighth Plan.

There is hiatus in the availability of raw silk and weaving capacity in States like U.P., Bihar, Assam and Orissa. In these States, there is concentration of silk handlooms but production of mulberry silk is concentrated in Karnataka, Andhra Pradesh and Tamil Nadu. In order to remedy the regional imbalance and to improve the availability of raw silk to weavers, schemes for silk production would be taken up in new areas.

Finally, R&D activities have so far been directed towards mulberry sericulture. Since non-mulberry sericulture is practised by the tribals, there will be re-orientation of research activities so that production, employment and earnings of tribals engaged in these activities are improved and sustained.

Handicrafts

Handicrafts are not only a part of the country's rich cultural heritage but they have also been a unifying factor in the national life. Handicrafts items, which blend utility with beauty, cater to the needs of the elite as well as other classes of the population. They also occupy an important position in the economy of the country both from the point of view of employment and export potential. The value of output in handicrafts sub-sector increased from Rs.3,500 crores in 1984-85 to Rs.7,067 crores (1984-85 prices) in 1989-90 and exports from Rs.1,700 crores to Rs.6,400 crores during the same period. The production of handicrafts in 1991-92 is expected to reach a level of Rs.13,260 crores.

The implementation of various schemes for promotion and development of handicrafts upto the end of the Seventh Plan has not been able to provide assistance to large sections of craftsmen in so far as production-related inputs are concerned and the marketing of their products is still left largely to the private trade. Consequently, they have not made any discernible impact on their earnings and standard of living. Its potential in terms of employment and exports remains unexploited. The country's share in the global market for the handicrafts (1.5 %) is little more than the share of exports in general (0.5%) but it is insignificant compared to the enormous possibilities for growth. It is, therefore, necessary to reorient the schemes so that the basic needs of the artisans relating to raw material, credit and marketing are adequately met. In this context, the voluntary organisations can play an active and significant role. Further, the activities so far have been sponsored and implemented mainly by the Central Government and the role as well as involvement of State Governments have been inadequate. It is, therefore, imperative to remodel certain schemes in such a manner that would ensure the participation of these agencies also.

The main objectives of the Eighth Plan for the handicrafts sub-sector would be to enhance opportunities of employment and income from crafts as an economic activity and harness the export potential of crafts for increasing foreign exchange earnings of the country.

For promoting the growth of handicrafts, it is essential to service the production base of craftsmen. The services needed to support production include supply of raw material of requisite quality at reasonable prices, common facility, skill upgradation, design as well as technical guidance etc. and other related services. As handicrafts sector is decentralised and crafts are dispersed in the country, these services would be provided in a package in identified crafts pockets through the establishment of Crafts Development Centres (CDCs) by the States, cooperatives and voluntary organisations. It would be necessary to assess the impact of the 14 CDCs which have been set up recently before embarking on further expansion.

The importance of timely availability of raw materials in handicrafts cannot be over-emphasised. All materials have periodic spells of short supply. However, wool for carpets, silk for carpets, scrap metal and virgin metal for artmetalware, wood particularly sandalwood, seesum and teak, cane and shells are identified as critical to the sector. As the availability of the first three is dependent on import policy and the remaining two on forest policy, close liaison should be maintained with the concerned Ministries to make the forest policy and the import policy conducive to augmenting raw material supply for the handicraft sector. The Craft Development Centres should take up supply of raw material/processed raw material to the craftsmen according to their needs.

Though refinance to the handicrafts sub-sector is available from NABARD, the credit available to craftsmen and promotional organisations under these schemes is inadequate. It is, therefore, imperative that NABARD's response to the credit requirements of handicrafts should be both adequate and positive. It should also extend refinance for providing the working capital for corporations and promotional organisations so that they could get cash credit facilities at concessional rate of interest.

Training is presently being imparted to artisans through 515 departmentally run training centres, Master Craftsmen under the Apprenticeship Training Scheme and other organisations such as Corporations voluntary agencies, etc. Out of 515 departmental training centres, 436 are for carpet weaving, started in 1976 when the limited production base in carpet weaving could not cope with the heavy demand for Indian carpets in the international market. This activity should now he curtailed in the Central sector and carried on by the States and voluntary agencies. To begin with, instead of conducting basic and advanced training separately, each centre should conduct one course for basic and one course for advanced training with the ultimate objective of conducting only advanced training course because the aim of imparting training in handicrafts is to upgrade the skill of craftsmen rather than merely creating basic skills. During the Eighth Plan, the strategy would, therefore, be the promotion of other handicrafts like artmetal, wood carving, hand printed textiles, cane and bamboo, bidriware metal mirrors, brassware, embroidery, imitation jewellery, lacquerware, zari work, etc. Greater emphasis would be placed on training through master craftsmen under the Apprenticeship Training Scheme as well as training through voluntary agencies. Efforts would also be made for the revival of languishing crafts so as to protect employment and earnings of craftsmen. Training schemes relating to departmentally-run training centres need to be evaluated by an independent agency with a view to taking decisions regarding effecting modifications or their continuation in future.

The existing Regional Design and Technical Development Centres (RDTCs) and specialised craft Institutes such as Institute of Hand-printed Textiles at Jaipur, Institute of Carpet Technology at Bhadohi and Cane and Bamboo Development Institute at Agartala are unable to cater to the needs of handicrafts as they are too dispersed. Moreover, it is also necessary to attune the activities of these Centres to the marketing needs. It would, therefore, be necessary to reorient their activities during the Eighth Plan. Accordingly, the RDTCs, instead of merely evolving their own designs, would also solicit design orders from private trade and public sector organisations, establish linkages with the envisaged CDCs and collaborate with apex institutes such as NID, NIFT, etc. for design development, particularly in export-oriented crafts. Assistance would also be provided to other organisations like corporations, cooperatives and voluntary organisations to engage consulting designers.

As the impact of existing schemes on the marketing of handicrafts has not been significant on account of their implementation without any coordinated thrust and absence of innovative marketing, new marketing approaches would need to be adopted in the Eighth Plan so that the wages and income levels of artisans could be increased. As the rapidly expanding rural market offers great potential for consumer products including handicrafts, simple low-cost utility handicrafts should be evolved and their sale organised in local *haats* and market places. Though there is substantial demand for cane and bamboo products in various parts of the country and the raw material is available in abundance in the North Eastern Region, this potential is not being exploited fully on account of high transportation costs. To ensure cost effectiveness, it would be necessary to despatch processed raw materials to such centres where there is good demamd for cane and bamboo products and artisans could assemble and produce the finished products there. Apart from organisation of traditional melas, fairs and exhibitions, selected market places in rural areas, towns and cities would be identified and craft complexes would be developed at pilgrimage, tourist centres and metropolitan cities for marketing of crafts.

Out of the estimated total exports of handicrafts valued at Rs.8100 crores in 1990-91, the share of gems and jewellery is 85 per cent. The value addition in gems and jewellery is about 30 per cent. In view of the potential of gems and jewellery industry to earn foreign exchange, it would be necessary to set up functional estates with facilities of trading, training, establishment of units and other infrastructure. Further, the industry would need easy availability of foreign exchange for import of raw materials, machinery, tools and equipments, training facilities, market information about the latest trends in fashion and designs preference in importing countries for sustained growth.

In view of envisaged thrust on sericulture, there would be significant increase in the domestic silk production during the Eighth Plan which should be utilised for the production of silk carpets for boosting their exports as there is good demand for them in overseas markets. While India's exports of handicrafts are mainly handmade, the large part of the global trade belongs to articles and items which cater to the common man's needs and tastes which have to be produced in bulk. Although made by hand, they need mechanical support in processing and finishing. As the export market for 'cultural crafts' is limited, reliance will have to be placed on those crafts which cater to the common man's needs and tastes for boosting exports during the Eighth Plan. It would be necessary to ensure timely availability of both indigenous as well as imported raw materials and credit to boost exports. Further, mechanisation in certain areas which do not affect basic skill input but pertain mainly to processing and finishing should be encouraged. Both the designing and technical assistance should aim at adapting crafts to the utility based foreign market. Market research would also assist in the growth of exports and Export Promotion Councils should play an active role in the dissemination of requisite information to exporters. For encouraging the growth of exports, it would also be necessary to improve packaging and for this purpose the assistance as well as guidance of the Institute of Packaging should be solicited.

The absence of a comprehensive data base in handicrafts is a serious limitation in planning for and monitoring of the development in the sub-sector. Presently, the data base is mainly the Economic Census of 1977 and 1980 and figures maintained or extrapolated by the office of Development Commissioner (Handicrafts) on the basis of the aforesaid census. These censuses did not delineate handicrafts as such and figures are compiled from 47 industry groups which correspond to handicrafts. Consequently, the data are neither realistic nor reveal the actual status of the industry.

It is, therefore, essential to conduct a comprehensive survey of handicrafts in the country during the Eighth Plan.

Wool Development

India has the fifth largest population of sheep in the world. The sheep population is around 40 million and wool production was 43 million kgs. in 1989-90. However, productivity in wool production was 900 grammes per sheep which is quite low as compared to 5520 gms/sheep and 5320 gms/sheep in Australia and New Zealand respectively.

Sheep breeding and wool production are done mostly by tribals and the main problems faced by this sector are low productivity, poor quality of wool, non-existence of grading facilities, non-availability of good breeds, low level of education of the sheep breeder and migratory character etc. The wool industry also suffers from various problems like technological obsolescence and the fact that most of the units are in small scale and unorganised sector. Wool exports are negligible and there is vast scope to improve upon.

The Wool Development Board, set up in 1987, would promote the industry by way of assistance for wool marketing, establishment of wool testing and grading centres, industrial service centres, setting up of scouring and carbonising plants and collecting marketing intelligence. It will also implement other schemes like integrated sheep and wool development project, machine-shearing-*cum*-training centres, diversification of products and utilisation of coarse wool, etc. These development programmes will be supplemented by other schemes implemented in the handlooms and handicrafts sub-sector relating to promotion of exports of woollen carpets, Hill Area Wool Development Projects, Carpet Training Centres, encouragement to artisans, etc.

Science and Technology

With a view to reducing technological obsolescence, improving competitiveness and raising the level of earnings of artisans and craftsmen engaged in this sector, several programmes are being implemented. Ten tool rooms and training centres and specialised institutes, three PPDCs, five PDTCs with five sub-centres, one service and training centre for electronics, four regional testing centres, 20 field testing stations, two footwear training centres, 27 SISIs, 31 branch institutes and 37 extension centres are providing technological assistance and other common facilities to the small scale sector. Besides, modernisation programmes are run for 20 industries on all-India basis and for 38 industry groups on State concentration basis.

The KVIC implements several projects, both departmental and institutional, for technology development, transfer of technology, substitution of alternate raw materials, product diversification, quality control, standardisation and testing of tools, equipment and new machinery. These projects would continue during the Eighth Plan. The R&D programmes for coir industry relate to improved methods in coir extraction, reducing drudgery of workers, spinning of coir yarn, weaving of coir matting on improved looms with higher productivity, development of new products of coir, such as geo-textiles, coir polymer composites, coir gypsum composites, use of coir in improving soil stabilisation and erosion control, use of coir for cooling buildings by roof-surface-evaporation techniques, etc. For handloom weavers, assislance in design development, modernisation and cloth processing, ete, is being provided by the three IIHTs and 23 WSCs. Professional institutes are being engaged to carry out research and development and to study special problems of the handlooms sector. The Central Silk Board undertakes R&D activities relating to evolving of high yielding plant varieties, package of practices of cultivation of plants and silkworm rearing, control of pests, evolving of suitable silkworm races, etc. Under National Sericulture Project, breeding laboratories would be strengthened and additional laboratories for evolving region-specific improved silkworm races and disease-resistant races suited to different agro-climatic conditions of the country would be established. For craftsmen involved in different handicrafts, the programmes include strengthening the existing RDTCs and Craft Institutes like Institute of Hand-printed Textiles at Jaipur, Institute of Carpet Technology at Bhadohi and Cane Development Institute at Agartala.

During the Eighth Plan, two tool rooms with Danish assistanee and three tool rooms with German assistance are proposed to be established. It is envisaged that NSIC will be entrusted with the responsibility of collection and dissemination of technology and other relevant information to SSI units. Besides strengthening the existing R&D infrastructure for other industries, it is envisaged to modernise SISI workshops.

Food Processing Industries

The agricultural seetor contributes 31.3 per cent to our gross domestic product. The annual production of fruit is estimated at about 28 million tonnes, next only to Brazil. Similarly, India ranks second in the world after China in vegetables with an annual production of 69 million tonnes. The cattle population in the country is estimated at 15.4 per cent of the world cattle population. Our milk production is the highest among the developing countries. However, hardly 1.5 per cent of our food output and 0.5 per cent to 1.0 per cent of fruit and vegetables are processed. Post-harvest losses of cereals and legumes are currently placed around 15 to 20 per cent and those of perishable fruit and vegetables at 20 to 30 per cent. The development of the food processing industries in the country has, therefore, assumed importance and urgency taking into account the prevailing favourable conditions and the vast potential for export of its products.

The food processing industries in India are broadly classified into (a) unorganised and cottage scale industries; and (b) organised processed food industries, with further division into the following sub-sectors :

(i) Primary food processing;

(ii) Spice and Horticultural products;

(iii) Dairy and Livestock products;

(iv) Fish and fish products; and

(v) Consumer Goods Industry (other processed foods).

TABLE 4

Production Of Principal Raw Materials For Food Processing Industries

(Million Tonnes)

Commodity	1984-85	1989-90	1990-91	1991-92 Ant. Ach.
1. Foodgrains	145.54	171.04	176.23	172.60
2. Oilseeds	12.95	16.92	18.45	17.80
3. Milk	41.50	51.40	53.70	56.38
4. Fruit	23.76	26.80	28.20	30.00
5. Vegetables	35.84	40.00	42.45	45.68
6. Meat, Poultry Prod.	1.10	1.40	1.44	1.50
7. Eggs (billion Nos.)	14.25	20.20	21.25	22.00
9. Marine Fish	1.70	2.28	2.30	2.35

TABLE 5

Exports From Food Processing Industry

(Rs. in Crores)

Sub Sector	1991-92	1996-97 Target
Fish and Fish Products	1,373.96	3,000
Grain Milling (Rice and Wheat)	876.45	1,150
Fruit & Vegetable Products	332.37	650
Meat and Meat Products	230.52	500
Other Processed Products	—	700
Total	2,813.30	6,000

Primary Food Processing

The production of principal raw materials for food processing industries in the initial and the terminal year of the Seventh Plan and in the last two years is shown in the Table 4. Exports from food processing industries in 1991-92 amounting to Rs. 2813 crores are indicated sub-sector-wise in Table 5. India's share in world exports of food item has come down from 1.2 per cent in 1978 to 0.44 per cent in 1988. The use of processed food is becoming popular due to various socio-economic changes such as urbanisation, change in tastes, high cost of household labour, increase in the number of working women, improvement in the living standard of people in general etc. The demand for processed and fast foods by large urban population of the country is, therefore, likely to grow steadily in the near future.

Grain processing, which includes rice milling, flour milling and pulses processing, is the biggest component in the food sector constituting over 40 per cent of the total value. This notwithstanding, even the present capacity for processing paddy is not fully utilised. There are substantial grain losses due to obsolete machinery. Installation of modern rice hullers and rice mills is therefore being encouraged by the Government. There are 306 solvent extraction units in the country at present for extracting rice bran oil. While flour milling is done in the organised sector through licensed flour mills, in the unorganised sector it is through country flour chakies.

The pulse milling is mostly in the unorganised sector. The disconcerting feature, however, is that about 10 to 15 per cent of the pulses are lost due to obsolete technology used in the process.

The annual production of fruit in India, which is about 28 million tonnes, is targetted to increase to 40 million tonnes by the end of the Eighth Plan. Similarly, the annual production of vegetables in India, which is about 69 million tonnes, is also targetted to increase to 94 million tonnes by the end of the Eighth Plan. The total installed capacity of fruit and vegetables processing industry, which is around 9 lakh tonnes, is grossly under-utilised at the level of 30 per cent. In India, hardly one per cent of the annual production of fruit and vegetables is processed, while in Brazil and USA it is 70 per cent, in Phillipines 78 per cent, in Malaysia 83 per cent and in Thailand 30 per cent. High cost of packaging, non-availability of packaging machinery, non-availability of quality raw material at reasonable rates, lack of basic infrastructural facilities, etc., are some of the constraints faced by this sector.

Dairy and Livestock Products

The annual milk production is around 56 million tonnes, of which 30 per cent is being converted at present into milk products, ghee alone accounting for more than 85 per cent. While production of milk powder and infant milk increased from 22,000 tonnes in 1970 to 1,65,000 tonnes in 1989, it slid down to 1,55,000 tonnes in 1990. Production of malted milk food and cheese was 39,000 tonnes and 2,000 tonnes respectively in 1990. The Government has recently de-licensed production of dairy products subject to locational parametres, with ice cream continuing to be reserved for the small scale sector. Development of the milk product industry further is, however, dependent on the availability of liquid milk in adequate quantity and increase in milk output per cattle .

With huge cattle population, India has the potential to be one of the top producers of meat and meat products but the position is none too happy. Cattle and buffalos, when they outlive their productive life, are slaughtered. Sheep are reared mostly for raising wool and not for producing meat. While a few modern slaughter houses have come up in big cities like Bombay, Aurangabad, Hyderabad, Durgapur and Panjim, most of the slaughter houses in the country, numbering around 3,600, are suffering from poor water supply, insufficiency of electricity, processing/ storing facilities as also lack of adequate arrangements for moving carcasses. During the Fourth Plan, eight bacon units were set up for manufacture of value-added pork products to ensure remunerative prices to pig rearers. The capacity remained by and large under-utilised.

Nonetheless, buffalo meat constitutes the largest proportion of meat exports from India. There is good demand for buffalo meat in the Middle East countries but the export is inadequate due to lack of modern processing houses, prevalence of diseases like rinderpest and those of mouth in the animals. Unhygienic and filthy conditions in the slaughter houses also shy away prospective importers. The quality and quantity of nutrition provided to animals is very poor leading to low rate of growth. Apart from taking remedial measures, there is need to develop other meat sources like rabbit, etc. Loss of by-products like blood, offals, glands, bones, etc. also need to be avoided in the meat industry so as to afford additional profit to the meat Producers.

Fish and Fish Products

India has a coastline of 7,500 kms and an Exclusive Economic Zone (EEZ) extending to 2.02 million square metres with vast potential for marine fishery. There are 1.8 lakh country crafts (non-mechanised), 23,000 mechanised fishing vessels and 179 deep sea fishing vessels operating in the Indian Exclusive Economic Zone. The annual production of marine and inland fish and exports of marine products are indicated in Table 6. Shrimp alone remains so far the major component of the marine exports from India. The export of marine products was approximately 20,000 tonnes during 1990-91 and the reasons for the abysmal level of exports in this sector can be traced to the inadequate fish processing capacity. There are at present 216 freezing plants with a freezing capacity

TABLE 6

Production of Fish and Exports of Marine Products

Year	Fish Production (Lakh tonnes)			Exports of Marine Products	
	Marine	Inland	Total	Quantity (000 tonnes)	Value (in Rs. crores)
1986-87	17.13	12.29	29.42	85.80	460.67
1987-88	16.58	13.01	29.59	97.20	531.20
1988-89	18.17	13.35	31.52	99.80	597.85
1989-90	22.75	14.02	36.77	110.80	635.00
1990-91	23.00	15.36	38.36	138.40	890.40

of 2,200 tonnes per day and 25 canning units with a total capacity of 90 tonnes per day. On-board fish processing facilities are non-existent in the country. While Individual Quick Freezing Plants (IQFP) have recently been established, their capacity is inadequate as compared to that available in the advanced countries. As many as 5,000 cold storages, now available in the country, are also inadequate for handling the present volume of fish catches. In all, the deep sea fishing industry today stands on a very weak footing. Maritime Zone of India (Regulation of fishing by foreign vessels) Act, 1981 is implemented by the Coast Guards but they possess inadequate communication facilities. The Fishery Survey of India, Bombay is the nodal agency for conducting surveys and assessment of marine fisheries in the Indian waters.

To increase marine exports, there is need to use fish catches other than shrimps. New shrimp ground and non-shrimp resources also need to be identified by Fishery Survey of India since exploitation of the existing resources for shrimp catches have reached saturation level. Other aspects requiring greater attention are quality improvement, technology upgradation, value added products, development of infrastructure, improved methods of handling and preservation, etc.

Consumer Goods Industry

The consumer industry for eatable food processing items has a very wide spectrum and it is concentrated largely in the organised sector including public sector units and large corporations in private sector. There are more than 18,000 factories producing food products worth Rs.9,000 crores. There are large number of units in unorganised sector producing items like Pasta goods, traditional foods, Poha etc. This sector is also playing an important role. The Confederation of Indian Food and Trade Industry (CIFTI) is the apex body of food product manufacturing units while Agricultural and Processed Food Products Export Development Authority (APEDA) is promoting exports of a wide range of' Indian agricultural products and processed foods. Under the new industrial policy announced by the Government in July, 1991, licensing of food product industry has been dispensed with, except for non-potable alcohol, beer etc. Broad-banding has also been extended to all processed food items excluding the items reserved for the small-scale-sector.

Two Central Public Sector Undertakings, namely, Modern Food Industries (India) Ltd. (MFIL) and North Eastern Regional Agricultural Marketing Corporation (NERAMAC) are engaged in the production and marketing of food products. MFIL is manufacturing bread, soft drinks, ready-to-serve food/drink, edible oil, wheat products, nutritional diet, etc.

The NERAMAC is, on the other hand, engaged in the marketing and processing of fruit and vegetables grown in the North Eastern States. The unit also markets citronella oil, ginger, mustard oil cake, aromatic products of the regions, etc. It has a pineapple juice processing plant at Nalkata in Tripura having a capacity of producing 48 tonnes of pineapple juice per annum. This unit is incurring losses since its inception. Unless a major revamp is effected, it may not become viable.

Packaging Material for Food Industry

Several new trends have now emerged in new packaging materials like tatrapacks, multi-layered aseptic cartons, flexible plastic pouches, thermofarm cups and tray packing, shrink film transport packing, etc. Container transport mode introduced by the Indian Railways has improved transportation facilities, much needed for the food processing industries. The increased shelf-life of the products of food processing industries have made these products popular and also, to some extent, prevented post-harvest losses in fruit and vegetables.

The high cost and inadequate availability of quality packaging materials, coupled with their irregular supply where these are available and high excise duties, have resulted in serious constraints in the development of packaging industry. The main thrust in 'R&D' has to be on development of cost-efficient sophisticated packaging and consumer packs to meet international Standards.

Food Processing Machinery

The requirements of food processing machinery are being met by chemical processing machinery manufacturers, specialised machinery manufacturers and small-scale units. Most of them do not have the necessary design and infrastructure for developing new products and cost efficient machinery and equipment. There is need to upgrade technology available with the Indian manufacturers by enlisting foreign collaborations where required, for design know-how back-up. The Central Food Technology Research Institute, Mysore, would be actively involved in the research in food processing machinery. Encouragement to food processing industries would *ipso facto* increase demand of latest food processing machinery. Incentives and other facilities to Indian machinery manufacturer would, therefore, be required to enable them to enlist new foreign collaborations for food processing machinery as well as for high speed packaging machinery.

Eighth Plan

Government has recently liberalised the foreign investment norms as also equity participation up to 51 per cent. With liberalisations and other incentives, substantial investment is expected in food processing industries sector which may create additional 2.5 lakh jobs by the end of the Eighth Plan. From the present level of Rs.2,813 crores, export is expected to reach Rs. 6,000 crores. Further promotion of food processing industries would require establishment of large private sector units in rural areas for production of processed food items. When these come into being, they will serve as nucleus plants for small-scale units to be set up around these plants. Some large industrial houses have made investment and provided extensive services which has resulted in higher production and exports of food products.

Development of the food processing industries also helps in conserving energy which otherwise gets used by the households for cooking of foods. The R&D should focus on processed foods using enzymes so as to save energy. Adoption of low-cost preservation techniques like sun-drying of fruit and vegetables, storing of fermented vegetables, extension of shelf-life of fruit and vegetables in cool chambers, storage of fruit pulp/juices by addition of simple preservatives, etc. also need to be taken up.

Facilities would be created in conformity with the latest EEC or USDA standards to promote export of meat and meat products. A National Livestock Products Development Council is proposed to be set up to formulate policy measures for promotion and development of modern processing facilities for pork, sheep, goat, rabbit, poultry and egg, buffalo meat, development of infrastructure for storage and transport of meat export, etc. A National Marine Fisheries Development Board is proposed to be established to look after the promotion of deep sea fishing industries.

It is proposed to acquire deep sea fishing vessels by offering differential interest rate subsidy and provision of loans through Shipping Credit and Investment Corporation of India to Indian entrepreneurs. During the Eighth Plan period, three freezing storages (at – 40 to – 20 degree celsius) at major ports would be set up. Private sector entrepreneurs would be provided financial assistance for acquiring refrigerated vans.

Financial assistance is proposed to be given to food processing units for strengthening backward linkages between processors and growers and encouragement for contract farming. To encourage mushroom cultivators to set up spawn laboratories, compost-pasteurisation and other processing facilities along with supporting structures for mushroom growing, financial